THE U.S. MARINE CORPS

THE U.S. MARINE CORPS

An Illustrated History

Merrill L. Bartlett & Jack Sweetman

NAVAL INSTITUTE PRESS • ANNAPOLIS, MARYLAND

Naval Institute Press
291 Wood Road
Annapolis, MD 21402

Library of Congress Cataloging-in-Publication Data
Bartlett, Merrill L.
    The U.S. Marine Corps: an illustrated history / Merrill L.
        Bartlett and Jack Sweetman.
        p.   cm.
    Includes bibliographical references and index.
    ISBN 0-87021-768-2 (alk. paper)
    1. United States. Marine Corps—History.   I. Sweetman, Jack,
    1940–   II. Title.
VE23 .B37 2001
359.9′6′03973—dc21

                                                    00-51130

Printed in the United States of America on acid-free paper ⊗
08 07 06 05 04 03 02 01   9 8 7 6 5 4 3 2
First printing

Distributed internationally by Greenhill Books,
Park House, 1 Russell Gardens, London, NW11 9NN

Unless otherwise noted, photos are from the
National Archives and Records Administration,
Washington, D.C.

Marine Hymn

From the Halls of Montezuma
To the shores of Tripoli,
We fight our country's battles
In the air, on land, and sea.
First to fight for right and freedom,
And to keep our honor clean,
We are proud to claim the title
Of United States Marines.

Our flag's unfurl'd to every breeze
From dawn to setting sun;
We have fought in every clime and place
Where we could take a gun.
In the snow of far-off northern lands
And in sunny tropic scenes,
You will find us always on the job—
The United States Marines.

Here's health to you and to our Corps
Which we are proud to serve;
In many a strife we've fought for life
And never lost our nerve.
If the Army and the Navy
Ever gaze on Heaven's scenes,
They will find the streets are guarded
By United States Marines.

Contents

Preface   ix

Acknowledgments   xi

List of Abbreviations   xiii

1   Marines through the Ages   1

2   The Continental Marines, 1775–1783   10

3   The Early Years, 1798–1820   24

4   The Era of Archibald Henderson, 1820–1859   41

5   Marines in Blue and Gray, 1859–1865   65

6   At Sea in the Gilded Age, 1865–1898   87

7   Colonial Infantry, 1898–1917   105

8   Over There, 1917–1918   133

9   Between the Wars, 1919–1941   152

10   World War Two: The South Pacific Campaign, 1942–1943   172

11   World War Two: The Central Pacific Drive, 1943–1945   194

12   The Unification Struggle and Korea, 1945–1953   222

13   The Vietnam War, 1954–1975   245

14   The New Breed, 1976–2000   270

Notes   291

Selected Bibliography   297

Index   303

Preface

The history of the U.S. Marine Corps is among the greatest military success stories of all time. It is, in briefest summary, the story of how a service that throughout its first hundred years seldom exceeded the strength of an infantry regiment not only overcame repeated challenges to its existence but eventually attained a strength exceeding that of some armies, while at the same time consistently demonstrating an extraordinary level of combat effectiveness and acquiring what is arguably the world's most potent military mystique. Under such circumstances, it is scarcely surprising that the Corps has become the subject of an abundant literature. Nevertheless, it seemed to us that there was room for a new, illustrated history in which a concise narrative, balanced in terms of both chronological coverage and topical content, would be complemented by a generous selection of art. This book is the result.

Like that of all military organizations, the history of the Corps has two major motifs: the operational and the institutional. The operational investigates how the Corps has performed its assigned missions, especially in battle. The institutional examines the evolution of those missions, the changes in the Corps's structure, its internal politics, and its relations with its sister services and civilian authority. Within the limitations of space, we tried to develop both motifs, but since any armed service's fundamental reason for being is to fight, we were particularly attentive to the operational.

Of course, the history of any organization, military or otherwise, is the product of the actions of the individuals who compose it. For this reason we have profiled the services of some of the men who made exceptional contributions to the Corps's heritage—Presley O'Bannon, Archibald Henderson, Littleton Waller Tazewell Waller, John A. Lejeune, John H. Quick, Smedley Butler, Dan Daly, Christian F. Schilt, Manila John Basilone, Pappy Boyington, Howlin' Mad Smith, Chesty Puller, and Lew Walt, to name but a few. Other lesser known personages appear in these pages as well, including Anthony Gale, Archibald Gillespie, John Reynolds, Alfred C. Van Benthuysen, Oliver P. Smith, and Walter E. Boomer.

The illustrations are for the most part contemporary with the subjects they portray. A number have never previously been published, and others have not been reproduced since their original appearance in periodical literature a century or more ago. The later works on which we drew, usually in the absence of contemporary art, are taken mostly from the collection of carefully researched studies executed under the auspices of the Marine Corps's historical program.

Finally, we would like to emphasize that this is in no sense an official history. The views expressed are our own and do not necessarily represent those of the Navy Department or either of the naval services. The authors met and conceived the idea of this book while both taught history at the U.S. Naval Academy.

Acknowledgments

It is our pleasure to record our thanks to the many people who contributed to the completion of this book.

Research for the textual portions was facilitated by the expert and helpful staffs of the Marine Corps Research Center, Quantico, Virginia; National Archives and Records Administration, Washington, D.C.; Burton Collection, Detroit Public Library; New York Historical Center; Manuscripts Division, Library of Congress; Franklin D. Roosevelt Presidential Library, Hyde Park, New York; Nimitz Library, U.S. Naval Academy; Suzallo Library, University of Washington; Herbert Hoover Presidential Library, West Branch, Iowa; Vashon Island Branch, King County Library; Seattle Public Library; Naval Historical Center, Washington, D.C.; Library, U.S. Naval Institute; and Dwight D. Eisenhower Presidential Library, Abilene, Kansas.

Brig. Gen. Edwin H. Simmons, USMC (ret.), director (now director emeritus) Marine Corps History and Museums, assisted our research with the fullest range of resources at his disposal. Col. Michael F. Monigan, USMC (ret.), General Simmons's successor and now deputy director, continued to support our efforts. Benis M. Frank, chief historian, and his successor, Charles D. Melson, shared their knowledge on a variety of topics. Richard A. Long pointed the way through the invaluable collection of oral histories and to his special interest in that most mercurial of commandants, Anthony Gale. Evelyn A. Englander assisted in locating obscure and out-of-print materials. Danny J. Crawford's Reference Section

performed yeoman service. Besides Danny himself the authors are especially indebted to Robert V. Aquilina, Ann A. Ferante, and Sheila Gramblin. Jack Shulimson, formerly the chief Vietnam historian, Marine Corps Historical Center, shared his wealth of insight on Leatherneck participation in the conflict in Southeast Asia. Timothy K. Nenninger, Rebecca Livingston, and Trevor Plante assisted in locating elusive files at the National Archives and Records Administration on a variety of Marine Corps—related subjects. We are also indebted to Col. Joseph H. Alexander, USMC (ret.); Lt. Col. Jon T. Hoffman, USMCR; and Col. John G. Miller, USMC (ret.), themselves the authors of outstanding works on the Corps's history, whose corporate memory helped pin down arcane materials.

The selection and reproduction of the illustrations benefited from the generous cooperation of John T. Dyer Jr., art curator, Marine Corps Historical Center; Edwin C. Finney Jr., Photographic Section, Naval Historical Center; Rutha Beaom, Still Photographic Section, National Archives and Records Administration; Jo Ann Bromley, King-Visual Technology; David M. Sullivan, independent Civil War historian; Gene Jillson, Johnson Controls World Services, Department of Defense Still Medial Resources Center; M.Sgt. Alfred R. Biggs Jr., Fred Carr, and Sgt. Will Donaldson, Public Affairs, Headquarters Marine Corps; Karen White Doody, art director, Naval Institute Press; and Lena M. Kaljot, photographic reference specialist, Reference Section, Marine Corps Historical Center.

At the U.S. Naval Institute, Dave Hofeling, formerly photo editor for *Proceedings* and *Naval History,* located a number of wonderful photographs, and Jennifer Till, his successor in that post, cheerfully tied up some loose ends. Sigrid Trumpy, curator, and Leah Hubicsak helped select materials from the Beverley R. Robinson Collection, U.S. Naval Academy Museum. Patricia T. Roberson, Florida State Archives; Dawn Stitzel, manager, Library Services, and photo archivist, U.S. Naval Institute; Vernon L. Williams, Texas Christian University; Debora Wynne, archivist, Florida Historical Society; Rosanna Di Pinpo, Photographic Archives, Monumenti Musei a Gallerie Pontificie, Vatican City; and the staff of the Fitzwilliam Museum, Cambridge, England, all contributed to the search for new and unpublished materials to complement the text.

For their assistance in the ultimately unsuccessful search for a contemporary likeness of Capt. Archibald Gillespie we are grateful to Emily Wolff, curator of photographs, and Tanya Hollis, Reference Library, California Historical Society; Mary Haas, Fine Arts Museums of San Francisco; Peter Blodgett, curator of western art, Henry E. Huntington Library; Diane Curry, History Department, Oakland Museum of California; Jim Henley, manager, Sacramento Archive; Charles F. Fraccia, San Francisco Historical Society; Tom Carey, San Francisco History Center, San Francisco Public Library; Patrick Dowd, Santa Barbara Historic Trust; Simon Elliott, manuscript assistant, University of California, Los Angeles, University Library; Dace Taube, Regional History Center, University of Southern California; and the staffs of the Bancroft Library; California State Archives; California State Library; Los Angeles Museum of Natural History; Los Angeles Public Library; National Archives and Records Administration, Pacific Region; Society of California Pioneers; the University of California, Berkeley, Special Collections; and Vallejo Naval and Historical Museum.

Finally, our wives have endured more than a fair share of distractions as we researched and wrote *The U.S. Marine Corps: An Illustrated History.* Readers should recognize and appreciate, as the authors have, the forbearance and stoicism of Blythe Wright Bartlett and Gisela A. Tetzel Sweetman.

Abbreviations

More than one observer has suggested that any military person is capable of speaking at length without using words common to any civilized tongue. The abbreviations that punctuate everyday military and naval speech make it difficult if not impossible for the lay listener or reader to fathom the content of the discourse. We have attempted to keep the acronyms in the text to a minimum, but we consider the following common abbreviations and terms essential to the narrative.

Note on Unit Designations

Numbers separated by a virgule identify a battalion of a regiment; e.g., 1/2 would designate the 1st Battalion, 2nd Marines. A letter preceding the numbers identifies a company; e.g., A/1/2 would designate Company A, 1st Battalion, 2nd Marines.

AEF	American Expeditionary Forces
ARVN	Army of the Republic of Vietnam (South Vietnam)
BLT	Battalion Landing Team
CAP	Combined Action Platoon
CENTCOM	Central Command
CINCLANT	Commander in Chief, Atlantic
CINCPAC	Commander in Chief, Pacific
DMZ	Demilitarized Zone
FLEX	Fleet Exercise
FMF	Fleet Marine Force
FMFLANT	Fleet Marine Force, Atlantic
FMFPAC	Fleet Marine Force, Pacific
HMA	Marine Attack Helicopter Squadron
HMH	Marine Heavy Helicopter Squadron
HMM	Marine Medium Helicopter Squadron
HQMC	Headquarters Marine Corps
JCS	Joint Chiefs of Staff
LCI	Landing Craft, Infantry
LCM	Landing Craft, Mechanized
LCVP	Landing Craft, Vehicle and Personnel
LHA	Landing Ship, Helicopter
LPH	Amphibious Assault Ship
LSD	Landing Ship, Dock
LST	Landing Ship, Tank
LVT	Landing Vehicle, Tracked
MAAG	Military Assistance and Advisory Group
MAB	Marine Amphibious Brigade
MACV	Military Assistance Command, Vietnam
MAF	Marine Amphibious Force
MAG	Marine Air Group
MAU	Marine Amphibious Unit
MAW	Marine Air Wing
MEB	Marine Expeditionary Brigade
MEF	Marine Expeditionary Force
MEU	Marine Expeditionary Unit
MEU (SOC)	Marine Expeditionary Unit (Special Operations Capable)
NVA	North Vietnamese Army; also a soldier of that army

PLO	Palestine Liberation Organization	VMF	Marine Fighter Squadron
ROK	Republic of Korea	VMFA	Marine Fighter Attack Squadron
SOC	Special Operations Capable	VMF(N)	Marine Fighter Squadron (Night)
TF	Task Force	VMO	Marine Observation Squadron
VC	Viet Cong; Vietnamese Communist	VMSB	Marine Scout Bombing Squadron
VMA	Marine Attack Squadron		

THE U.S. MARINE CORPS

1

Marines through the Ages

The simplest definition of a marine is also the most traditional: a soldier of the sea. In the case of the U.S. Marine Corps, whose primary mission is amphibious assault and whose most famous battles have been fought on land, it might seem more accurate to say "soldier from the sea." The Corps's specialization is a relatively recent development, however. Marines of centuries past were neither expressly trained nor principally employed as amphibious forces. Although they participated in operations ashore, as a rule it was merely as the most proficient element of naval landing parties. For the first twenty-five hundred years of their existence, marines fought the majority of their battles at sea.

Until the mid-nineteenth century, when the introduction of explosive shells and long-range, rifled guns made it possible to sink a ship from a distance, every naval engagement was potentially a boarding action. The role of marines, who were often simply embarked soldiers, was to spearhead such actions. There were marine detachments aboard the Greek galleys that shattered the Persian fleet at the Battle of Salamis in 480 B.C., the climax of the first naval campaign in recorded history. Each of the Athenians' 180 vessels, for example, carried four archers and fourteen infantrymen protected with brass body armor and armed with a short sword and an eight-foot spear. The Greeks called their marines *epibatoe* (heavily armed sea soldiers). Their superiority in close combat over their Persian counterparts, mainly archers protected only by quilted tunics, was an important ingredient of the Greek victory.

Two centuries later, the Romans owed the transformation of the Mediterranean Sea into Mare Nostrum to the strong arm of their *milites classiarii* (soldiers of the fleet). Purely a land power at the commencement of her imperial career, Rome was compelled to become a sea power as well when the extension of her influence to the island of Sicily brought her into conflict with the maritime empire of Carthage. In the opening naval actions of the First Punic War (261–241 B.C.), the Romans quickly discovered that they lacked the skills necessary to counter the ram-and-run tactics of their seafaring antagonists. The only way to offset the Carthaginians' seamanship, they reasoned, was by finding a means to get Roman marines aboard the enemy vessels. Their solution was the invention of the *corvus* (raven), a heavy, fenced gangway about eighteen feet long and four wide that was secured in an upright position in the bow of each Roman galley. Attached to the underside of the upper end of this gangway was a great iron hook; the lower end was fastened into a swivel in the deck. When a Carthaginian galley approached to ram, the Romans released the tackle holding the *corvus;* the impact of the free-falling gangway embedded the hook in the enemy's deck; the marines charged across, two abreast; and that was that. Although the Carthaginians carried marines of sorts, they were no match for Rome's seagoing legionnaires. In time, the Romans learned to handle their ships expertly enough to do without the *corvus,* but they continued to rely on boarding actions to win battles.

The fragmentation of political authority in Western

Milites classiarii—Roman marines—line the deck of their galley in a relief originally in the Temple of Fortuna at Palestrina (ancient Praeneste), Italy. The work dates from the latter half of the first century B.C. The Vatican Museum

Europe following the collapse of the Roman Empire in the fifth century A.D. spelled an end to regular naval and marine forces but did nothing to affect the tactics of war at sea. Throughout the Middle Ages, boarding by soldiers embarked for that purpose remained the decisive element of Mediterranean galley warfare. Often, ships of a squadron were actually lashed together to create a floating battlefield. If enemy boarders gained a foothold on any one vessel, reinforcements from neighboring ships were fed into the fray to repulse them. At the Battle of Lepanto in 1571, in which the Christian League's fleet defeated that of the Ottoman Empire in the last great galley action, twenty-five to thirty vessels crowded into a space of approximately 250 by 150 yards to support the engagement between their respective flagships, each of which carried several hundred men-at-arms.

The boarding action also retained its primacy in northern European waters, where high-sided sailing ships called cogs began to be used in combat early in the thirteenth century. Elevated "castles" were built fore and aft as fighting platforms for men-at-arms, while archers, crossbowmen, and stone throwers took position in the crow's nest. Sometimes the ship's boat was slung halfway up the mast to accommodate additional missile men. Normally, the side that established fire superiority would seek to postpone boarding until its projectiles had cut down most of the opposing fighting men. Grappling hooks were used to prevent an enemy from disengaging, and, as in the Mediterranean, friendly ships often roped or even chained themselves together.

In the sixteenth century, the age-old format of war at sea was broken by a revolutionary weapon system cre-

Medieval marines clash in a miniature from an English manuscript of 1271 A.D. The Fitzwilliam Museum, Cambridge, England

ated by the integration of two technological innovations that had appeared approximately one hundred years earlier. They were the three-masted, square-rigged ship, an ocean-sailing vessel of unprecedented efficiency; and the single-piece, cast-bronze cannon, the first reasonably reliable gun. When such guns were positioned to fire broadside along the length of such ships, it became readily possible to disable an opposing vessel without coming into physical contact with her. This potential gave birth to a new age of naval tactics, destined to last into the twentieth century, in which the gunnery duel supplanted the boarding action as the principal mode of combat. The change was signaled by the defeat of the Spanish Armada in 1588. Both the English and the Spanish fleets consisted almost entirely of broadside-firing ships; but the towering Spanish galleons were much less maneuverable and their cannon were mostly short-range, heavy-caliber ship smashers intended to soften up the enemy for boarding, to which the Spanish remained committed. Finding that their agile vessels could easily evade the Spaniards' attempts to close, the English kept out of their grasp while maintaining a galling fire that reduced the Invincible Armada to a mob of fugitive ships.

But the advent of the gunnery duel did not end the usefulness of marines. Battles were still fought at very close quarters. As late as the War of 1812, the maximum effective range of naval guns was no more than four hun-

dred yards. Serious engagements usually opened at two hundred yards, and a captain with strong nerves might hold fire until half that. In these actions, marines positioned on their ship's deck or aloft in her fighting tops would rake the enemy with musketry. Their fire began to become effective at two hundred yards and increased in accuracy as the range fell until, at one hundred yards or less, an average marksman could hit a man-sized target more often than he would miss. The distance between Lord Nelson, the most illustrious victim of ships' small arms fire, and the unknown Frenchman who put a musket ball through his spine from the mizzen-top of the *Redoubtable* at the Battle of Trafalgar was approximately fifteen yards.

Marines also joined in the boarding actions that, despite the ascendancy of the gun, often formed the last act of such close combat. In contests between ships of comparable sizes, the side that found itself getting the worst of the gunnery duel would frequently attempt to reverse the tide of battle by boarding. Conversely, the side that dominated the gunnery action might try to board and capture a beaten ship rather than batter her to pieces.

In addition, marines stiffened the parties their ships sent ashore in landings and raids. This had always been one of their functions, of course, but its importance increased as the expansion of Europe made possible by the ship and the gun extended the interests of the Atlantic powers to the four corners of the earth. The colonial and maritime conflicts that ensued did more than give marines active employment, however. In the sixteenth and seventeenth centuries the spoils of these struggles contributed to the rise of governments that could afford to maintain their own full-time, professional armed forces, institutions that had been absent from the Western world since the fall of Rome.

The first regularly constituted marine formation in modern times, the French regiment la Marine, was founded by Cardinal Richelieu in 1627 to guard the country's ports and "form the garrison" of ships.[1] Richelieu embodied a second marine regiment, the Royal Vaisseaux, in 1635, and later in the century his successors organized two others. Meanwhile, Great Britain had established the Duke of York and Albany's Maritime Regiment of Foot—commonly called the Admiral's Reg-

AN OFFICER
OF THE
DUKE OF YORK AND ALBANY'S MARITIME REGIMENT OF FOOT
(THE LORD HIGH ADMIRAL'S REGIMENT.)

A SOLDIER
OF THE
DUKE OF YORK AND ALBANY'S MARITIME REGIMENT OF FOOT
(THE LORD HIGH ADMIRAL'S REGIMENT.)

An English officer and an enlisted man of the Admiral's Regiment, 1664–1685. Their coats were yellow with red cuffs and lining, and their breeches, stockings, and the officer's sash were red. From L. Edye, *The Historical Records of the Royal Marines* (London: Harrison, 1893)

iment, for the duke was Lord High Admiral of England— by an Order in Council of 28 October 1664 directing that "twelve hundred Land Souldjers be forthwith raysed . . . to be distributed into his Ma^{ts} Fleets prepared for Sea Service."[2] The United Provinces of Holland followed suit by the creation of their Korps Mariners on 10 December 1665.

The evolution of British marine forces was naturally the most relevant to the military experience of the American colonists. The Maritime Regiment of Foot was dis-

banded in 1690 after active service afloat and ashore in the Anglo-Dutch Wars, the Low Countries, and North Africa; one company had also done two years' peace-keeping duty in Virginia. The reason for the regiment's dissolution was probably its presumed sympathy for its first colonel, the Duke of York, who, having ascended the throne as King James II in 1685, had been driven off it by the Glorious Revolution of 1688. That the value of marines was not an issue is indicated by the fact that two new units, the 1st and 2nd Regiments of Marines, were organized later in 1690. Detachments of both entered combat almost immediately. In 1698 the two regiments, apparently much reduced in numbers, were consolidated and three infantry regiments were converted into marines. But by then the country was at peace, and all four regiments were disbanded in 1701.

The peace was short-lived. In May 1702 Britain intervened in the War of Spanish Succession, and in June Queen Anne called for the formation of six regiments of marines. These units served with distinction throughout the conflict, taking part in the destruction of a Spanish fleet at the Battle of Vigo Bay, the capture and subsequent defense of Gibraltar, the capture of Barcelona, and numerous other campaigns along the coasts of Spain and France and in the Mediterranean.

All six regiments were also represented in the assault on the French base at Port Royal (afterward renamed Annapolis Royal), Nova Scotia, in 1710, an undertaking in which they were joined by colonial American forces. Although this was not the colonists' first amphibious operation—they had already mounted several expeditions against the French in Canada and the Spanish in Florida —it was the first in which they fought beside British troops. The landing force consisted of fourteen hundred regular infantry, six hundred marines (one hundred from each regiment), fifteen hundred American militia (two battalions from Massachusetts, one from Connecticut, and a composite battalion from New Hampshire and Rhode Island), a detachment of Indians, and some guns. Arriving off Port Royal on 23 September, the expedition suffered its only reverse the next day, when thirty men were drowned in the wreck of a transport. Otherwise, everything went smoothly. The troops landed on 25 September, laid siege to the fort on the twenty-sixth, and received its surrender on 2 October. An American company formed a cordon on either side of the gate through which the French marched out of the fort, and afterward the British officers gave a farewell breakfast to the ladies of the garrison.

In the military cutbacks following the peace of 1713 the British marines were again disbanded, three regiments being transferred to the Army and three paid off. The same fate befell ten regiments raised at the outbreak of the War of Jenkins's Ear in 1739 and retained through the War of Austrian Succession but disestablished with the restoration of peace in 1748. Seven years later, the onset of war with France prompted another—the century's third—revival of marines, of which the Admiralty organized fifty independent companies. The uninterrupted existence of the Royal Marines (a title granted in 1802) begins with this force, which, unlike its forerunners, was not dissolved after the shooting stopped.

Among the amphibious campaigns of the preceding conflicts were several undertaken wholly or in part by American forces. The War of Jenkins's Ear, so called because its proximate cause was the unremitting indignation of Capt. Robert Jenkins, a merchant mariner who claimed that a Spanish customs official had cut off his ear, consisted mainly of seaborne assaults on Spanish possessions in the New World. In 1740 militia units from Georgia and South Carolina and five hundred Indians under the command of Gen. James Oglethorpe invaded Florida, capturing two Spanish posts on the St. Johns River and laying siege to the Castillo de San Marcos at St. Augustine. The old fortress proved superior to the colonials' siegecraft, and after two months outside its coquina walls they withdrew. A second attempt on the fortress in 1743, also led by Oglethorpe, was equally unsuccessful.

In the meanwhile, the first authentic American Marines had shared in a debacle that might stand as a model of everything an amphibious operation ought not to be. After reestablishing its own marines in 1739, the British government decided to raise four additional battalions in North America, whose inhabitants were presumed to be better suited than Britons for campaigning in the Tropics, where the deadliest foe was always disease. Some thirty-six hundred men were enlisted and organized in one very large regiment. As was customary in British forces, the unit took the name of its commander, Col. William Gooch, the lieutenant governor of Virginia, and was called Gooch's Marines. With the exception of about thirty British younger sons, the officers came from the upper levels of colonial society; the rank and file came from the nethermost, the majority of the colonies having filled their quotas with criminals, debtors, and derelicts.

Sailing from New York in October 1740, Gooch's Marines joined eight thousand British troops—six regi-

A contemporary French map depicts the operations against Cartagena. Fort St. Lazare stood to the east of the city, below the six English ships in the inner harbor at left center. Beverley R. Robinson Collection, U.S. Naval Academy Museum

ments of marines and two of infantry—being assembled at an advanced base in Jamaica. Early in March 1741 the combined force set out in a fleet of 138 sail to attack Cartagena, on the coast of present-day Colombia, at the northern end of a harbor that could be entered only through a narrow channel commanded by forts on both sides. A beachhead was secured on 9 March. The forts covering the channel were captured on 25 March, and on 5 April fifteen hundred troops were landed in the inner harbor to attack Fort St. Lazar, the last fortification outside Cartagena.

Unfortunately, by then British leadership had become its own worst enemy. The naval commander, Adm. Edward Vernon, was a most impatient man; the land force commander, Brig. Gen. Thomas Wentworth, an ex-

tremely deliberate one. The stately pace of the preceding operations ashore had convinced Vernon that Wentworth was a dolt, and of the interservice cooperation vital to amphibious warfare there was no trace. When the general asked the admiral to land additional troops for the assault on Fort St. Lazar, Vernon declined. Wentworth's remonstrances finally caused him to relent, but he refused to provide naval gunfire support for the attack, insisting that the harbor in that area was too shallow, an opinion shared by few others. For his part, Wentworth made no attempt to emplace his own artillery, the only officer believed capable of constructing a battery having been killed. The result was summarized by one of the century's great novelists, Tobias Smollett, who served in the campaign as a naval assistant surgeon: "A resolution was taken . . . to attack the place with musketry only. This was put into execution, and succeeded accordingly; the enemy giving them such a hearty reception, that the greatest part of the detachment took up their everlasting residence on the spot."[3]

The plan called for simultaneous predawn assaults to be made on the fort's northern and southern faces by columns that were to move inland from the beach at 4:00. The northern column consisted of five hundred grenadiers; the southern of a thousand British marines. Behind both came parties of American Marines carrying extra hand grenades, scaling ladders, and wool packs to fill the ditches surrounding the fort. The columns lost their way in the darkness and suffered heavy casualties storming the fort's outworks, some of which they had been told to expect and some of which they had not. Eventually the Spanish were driven into the fort, but daybreak found the British at the foot of its walls. The commander of the northern column, Colonel Grant of the 5th Marines, was mortally wounded there. He is reputed to have expired with the words, "The general ought to hang the guides and the king ought to hang the general."[4]

The conduct of Gooch's Marines may charitably be characterized as prudent. To quote a contemporary account:

> The Americans finding that they were knocked down without any arms to defend themselves, threw down their ladders, etc., and retired to their camp. Three only were brought up to the trenches, upon which about ten of our Grenadiers and a Sergeant mounted the walls of the fort, but being unsupported, were immediately cut to pieces except for the Sergeant who saved himself by jumping down again.[5]

Recognizing the futility of further sacrifice, Wentworth ordered a retreat. Together the two columns had lost forty-three officers and six hundred men killed and wounded. Shortly thereafter Vernon conceded defeat, and in May the expedition withdrew. In the course of the siege, battle casualties and disease, especially the latter, had reduced its strength to four thousand men. Only twenty-seven hundred remained alive to make an abortive landing in Cuba in August, and three months ashore there finished most of them. The arrival of three thousand British reinforcements in February 1742 simply swelled the expedition's cemetery. By midsummer,

the great offensive against the Spanish colonies had literally died away.

One thing that had been accomplished was to reveal the error of the assumption that North Americans would flourish in the Tropics, for only 10 percent of Gooch's Marines survived them. However else it might be esteemed, there is no gainsaying Allan Millett's conclusion that "as an experiment in social purification, the regiment was a success."[6] Among the handful who came home was Capt. Lawrence Washington. A company commander in the Virginia contingent, he had a great respect for Admiral Vernon—so great, in fact, that he named his estate after him. When Captain Washington succumbed to a disease contracted at Cartagena, Mount Vernon was inherited by his young half-brother, George.

The last expedition of the decade in which Americans took part ended, quite unlike Cartagena, in victory. Moreover, it was basically an American affair. In 1744 France officially entered the War of Austrian Succession, in which Britain had intervened several years earlier. The colonial extension of the conflict was called King George's War. The French had just completed the construction of a great fortress at Louisbourg, on Cape Breton Island, to guard the mouth of the St. Lawrence River, the umbilical cord of New France. The hostilities opened when a detachment from Louisbourg seized a New England fishing base at Canso, Nova Scotia. Governor William Shirley of Massachusetts thereupon proposed launching an assault on Louisbourg. It was an audacious initiative. The British government promised to furnish naval support, and a force of four thousand Massachusetts, Connecticut, and New Hampshire men was organized under the command of Col. William Pepperell, a fish merchant by trade. Sailing from Boston in its own transports, the expedition reoccupied Canso on 1 April 1745. Three weeks later a Royal Navy squadron appeared to cover the landing on Cape Breton, and the New Englanders invested Louisbourg. Amateur soldiers though they were, their conduct of the siege was highly creditable. On 17 June the largest coastal fortification on the continent hauled down its flag. Acclaimed as "the severest blow that could have been given the Enemy, and in the tenderest part," the capture of Louisbourg was the major event of the war in North America.[7]

The capture of Louisbourg by New England forces in 1745 was celebrated by a print published soon afterward in London. Beverley R. Robinson Collection

To its conquerors' dismay, the fortress was returned to France by the peace of 1748, so Canada was as well defended as ever when the French and Indian War broke out six years later. In the long struggle that followed, the New England colonies again mounted an amphibious operation of their own, sending two thousand militia bolstered by 250 British regulars to seize two French Canadian outposts in 1755. They also contributed troops to several British expeditions. The army that retook Louisbourg in the summer of 1758 included a battalion of five hundred New England rangers, and a slightly larger contingent of Americans was present at the capture of Quebec in 1759.

By then, the contest for Canada had become merely one of the theaters of the Seven Years' War (1756–63), in which Spain imprudently allied itself with France in 1761. Already having made close to a clean sweep of the

French overseas empire, the British promptly laid plans for an attack on Havana, the supposedly impregnable capital of Spanish Cuba. Some four thousand men were recruited in Connecticut, New Jersey, New York, and Rhode Island to take part in the campaign. Mindful that Americans would not have forgotten the fate of Gooch's Marines, the British disingenuously declined to specify the expedition's objective, promising only the prospect of "very agreeable" service. The first fourteen hundred colonials joined the army besieging Havana on 28 July 1762. The British, ashore since early June, had almost overcome the city's defenses, but yellow fever, malaria, and dysentery had so depleted their ranks—the mortality rate approached 50 percent—that the newcomers were a welcome reinforcement. Havana surrendered on 11 August. Only seven of the Americans were killed or wounded in action, but nearly half of the others died of disease before they were withdrawn in October. This was the last amphibious operation in which Americans served as subjects of the British Crown.

Thus, by the close of the Seven Years' War, the employment of marine forces and the practice of amphibious warfare had become part of the American as well as the British military experience. Furthermore, Britain's marines had begun to assume an important new responsibility that would later become, and long remain, one of the principal functions of the U.S. Marines as well: the maintenance of order—or, more bluntly, the prevention of mutiny—aboard ship.

The Royal Navy's need for an internal security force arose from its recruiting methods. At least in wartime, about half the seamen in an average crew had been kidnapped by naval press gangs; and the nature of life within Britain's wooden walls was not calculated to reconcile men to their lot. As early as 1690, an English writer had observed that "the whole body of seamen on board the Fleet, being a loose collection of undisciplined people and (as experience shews) sufficiently inclined to mutiny, the Marine Regim[ts] will be a powerfull check to their disorders, and will be able to prevent the dangerous consequences that may thence result."[8]

After being put on a permanent footing in 1755, British marines began to serve precisely that purpose, to the great satisfaction of generations of sea officers and the disgust of generations of seamen, who viewed their red-coated shipmates as seagoing police. It was, in fact, to honor its members' steadfast support of authority during the unrest in the Mediterranean Fleet between 1798 and 1800 that the Corps was granted its "Royal" title. But all this lay in the future in the victory year of 1763, when Britain, having extinguished the French threat in North America, seemed to have secured an empire that would soon be lost.

2

The Continental Marines, 1775–1783

Late in May 1780, Capt. James Nicholson's Continental frigate *Trumbull* stood to sea from New London, Connecticut, on her first cruise in the War of Independence. No record exists of the ship's exact dimensions, but she must have measured approximately 125 feet from stem to stern and displaced seven hundred tons. She carried thirty guns, most of them along the single gun deck characteristic of frigates, and two hundred men. The latter included a detachment of thirty Marines commanded by Capt. Gilbert Saltonstall and Lts. Jabez Smith Jr. and David Starr. Also aboard were two unattached Marine officers serving as volunteers, Capt. John Trevett and Lt. David Bill.

The *Trumbull* was some three hundred miles north of Bermuda around 10:30 on the morning of 1 June when lookouts spotted a sail on the horizon. As the ships closed to within hailing distance, the other vessel revealed herself to be the thirty-two-gun British privateer *Watt*. Captain Saltonstall described the engagement that followed in a letter to his father on 14 June:

> We saw a sail from mast-head directly to windward; as soon as she discovered us she bore down for us; we got ready for action, at one o'clock began to engage, and continued, without the least intermission, for five glasses [two and a half hours], within pistol shot. It is beyond my power to give an adequate idea of the carnage, slaughter, havock, and destruction that ensued. Let your imagination do its best, it will fall short. We were literally cut all to pieces; not a shroud, stay, brace, bowling, or any other of our rigging, standing. Our main top-mast shot away; our fore, main, mizzen and jigger

masts gone by the board; two of our quarter deck guns disabled; thro' our ensign 62 shot, our mizzen 157, mainsail 560, forsail 180, our other sails in proportion; not a yard in the ship but received one or more shot; six shot through her quarter above the quarterdeck, four in the waste; our quarter, stern and nettings full of langrage [a type of scattershot made up of bits of scrap iron, nails, bolts, and flints], grape and musket ball. . . . After two and a half hour action, we hauled her wind. Her pumps going, we edged away; so that it may fairly be called a drawn battle.[1]

Both ships had fought well. Of the *Trumbull*'s people, thirteen had been killed or mortally wounded and eighteen others were hit. Among the dead were four Continental Marines, three officers, and Sgt. Ezekial Hyatt. Lieutenant Bill was killed early in the action when a piece of langrage took off the top of his head.

Lieutenant Starr, wrote Saltonstall, "was wounded in the later part of the engagement with a grape shot, which went in just above the right hip bone and was cut out behind. He lived until four o'clock Monday morning following, when he died without a groan or struggle. I was with him most of the time."[2] Lieutenant Smith lingered on until 28 June.

The surviving officers also contributed to the *Trumbull*'s casualties. Trevett received two wounds, one of which cost him an eye. Saltonstall had "eleven different wounds from my shoulder to my hip, some with buckshot, others with the splinters of the after quarter-deck gun. I had some shot through the brim of my hat; but was not so disabled as to quit the quarter-deck until after the engagement."[3] The *Watt* suffered even more than the *Trumbull,* losing thirteen men killed and seventy-nine wounded. At one time the inrush of water through hits the *Trumbull* scored below the British ship's waterline threatened to overwhelm the one pump that had not been disabled. As Saltonstall told his father in a follow-up letter of 19 June:

> Though we were cut to pieces [the *Watt*] has nothing to boast of should she get in—her sides were damaged as much as our sails and rigging—her maintop mast was hanging over the side just ready to go as well as her mainmast—her sails and rigging were not damaged as much as ours—as we fired principally at her hull, whence we concluded we did more execution than they, though they did well enough. Had we a sufficiency of langrage, I think we should have carried her—our wads [bundles of rope yarn that were tamped down the bores of muzzle-loading cannon to keep the powder charges in place; their flaming remnants were expelled with enough force to travel a short distance] set her netting on fire on her larboard quarter, which they cleared themselves of by cutting part of their nettings away.[4]

The range at which the *Trumbull* and the *Watt* engaged, never more than eighty yards and usually fifty yards or less, was so close that the hammocks stowed between the rope screens—netting—that ran along a wooden warship's gunwales were ignited. In battle the rope screens served to reduce the sprays of splinters that were among the deadliest features of sea fights in the age of sail. Saltonstall continued:

> We saw them heave sundry of their men overboard during the action. Their wads set our nettings afire on our starboard bow—our main and quarter-deck guns expended 388 rounds, 86 of which were fired on the quarterdeck; the Marines fired pistols during the engagement exclusive of which they fired near 1200 rounds. Upon the whole there had not been a more close, obstinate, and Bloody engagement since the war.[5]

Limping home their separate ways, the *Watt* reached New York on 11 June, and the *Trumbull* anchored off Nantasket, Connecticut, on the fifteenth. Their encounter was unique in that in Saltonstall's letters it produced the most detailed account of a sea battle known to have been written by a Continental Marine. Otherwise, it was a representative if exceptionally ferocious example of the type of action American Marines fought during the War of Independence.

The corps to which Gilbert Saltonstall belonged had been founded in November 1775. The revolution was then six months old. Congress had taken the first steps toward creating a Navy in October by authorizing four vessels to be outfitted to attack British supply ships. The foundation of the Continental Marines did not follow from this legislation, however. The impetus was provided by the good citizens of Passamaquoddy, Nova Scotia, who petitioned Congress "to be admitted into the association of North Americans, for the preservation of their rights and liberties."[6] In the deliberations of the five-man committee appointed to report on this request, the pleasing prospect of carrying liberty to Passamaquoddy was overshadowed by the still more appealing idea of capturing the big British naval base at Halifax. The report on Passamaquoddy's petition was therefore a recommendation to raise two 550-man Marine battalions from Washington's army outside Boston in preparation for a landing on the coast of Nova Scotia in December. Even should Congress deem that operation impractical, the committee urged it to approve the organization of the Marines, who would be of "utmost service, being capable of serving either by land or sea."[7] Agreeable to both ideas, on Friday, 10 November 1775, Congress voted to propose the Nova Scotia project to Washington and further resolved "that two battalions of Marines be raised, consisting of one Colonel, two Lieutenant Colonels, two Majors & Officers as usual in other regiments, and that they consist of an equal number of privates with other battalions. . . . That they be distinguished by the names of the first & second battalions of American Marines."[8]

These battalions were never raised. When he was informed of the resolutions, Washington replied with remarkable restraint that he doubted the wisdom of weakening the army besieging Boston in order to invade Nova Scotia. Further, he thought that the stipulation that Marines were to enlist for the duration of the war would make them difficult if not impossible to recruit. Congress deferred to his judgment and on 30 November notified him that the Marines would be raised separately from the Army. Congress had already begun appointing Marine officers.

Maj. Samuel Nicholas, as portrayed by a contemporary miniature.

The earliest commission, a captaincy dated 28 November, went to Samuel Nicholas, a thirty-one-year-old Philadelphia Quaker whom the U.S. Marine Corps honors as its first commandant. Nicholas himself never used that title and apparently gave only a single order to a unit outside the Philadelphia area, but he remained the senior officer of the Continental Marines and as such served as the "muster master" to whom the Corps's strength reports were forwarded. Relatively little is known of his private life. The son of a prosperous blacksmith, Nicholas attended the Academy of Philadelphia, a precursor of the University of Pennsylvania, and then emerged into the elite of Philadelphia society, a status attested by his membership in two prestigious clubs, the Schuylkill Fishing Company and the Gloucester Fox Hunting Club. After the revolution he was a tavern keeper at the Sign of the Conestoga Wagon, which may have been his prewar occupation as well, although according to one report he was a shipowner's agent in the merchant marine.

Another nine officers were commissioned within days, and they began raising five companies to serve in the little fleet of converted merchantmen being equipped by Congress. Following the custom of the day, gaily caparisoned drummers were sent parading through the streets to attract recruits. They ended their rounds at a "rendezvous," usually a tavern, where an officer waited to enlist the men who followed them. Legend has it that the Marines' principal rendezvous was Tun Tavern, at the corner of Tun Alley and King (now South Water) Street. Unfortunately for legend, proof is lacking. Robert Mullan, commissioned a captain of Marines in June 1776, was probably the proprietor of Tun Tavern; if so, its association with the Corps may have begun the previous year, but existing records allow a variety of interpretations. In any case, five companies had been recruited by the end of December.

The men who enlisted that month were not actually the first Marines of the revolution. On two occasions earlier in the year soldiers had been detailed to act as Marines in vessels operated by the Army. Continental troops served in two ships that patrolled Lake Champlain from the capture of Fort Ticonderoga in May until the invasion of Canada in October, and in the schooner Washington sent to raid British shipping in September, a month before the foundation of the Continental Navy. These men remained soldiers, however, and as such are not considered forerunners of the U.S. Marine Corps. In addition, many of the two thousand or more American privateers that put to sea during the war carried their own private marines, and most of the eleven known state navies included marine forces.

The fleet to which the Philadelphia Marines were assigned put to sea on 17 February 1776. Commanded by Commo. Esek Hopkins, a Rhode Island merchant skipper, it numbered eight vessels: Hopkins's flagship, the *Alfred;* the ship *Columbus;* the brigs *Andrew Doria* and *Cabot;* the sloops *Hornet* and *Providence;* and the schooners *Fly* and *Wasp.* All except the *Fly* carried Marines. The largest detachment, and the only one in uniform, was the sixty-two-man company under Captain Nicholas in the *Alfred.* On the fleet's second day at sea a serious collision occurred between the *Hornet* and the *Fly;* the *Hornet* was forced to return to port, and the *Fly*

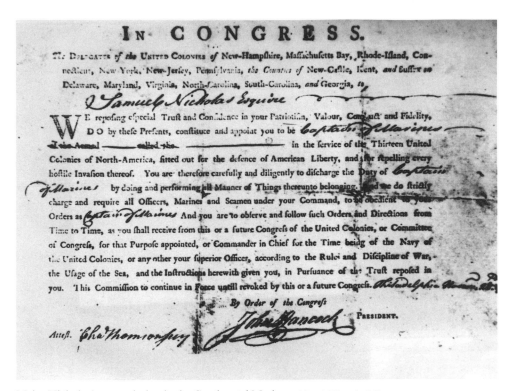

Major Nicholas's commission in the Continental Marines. Naval Historical Center

In 1775 Tun Tavern would have looked much the way it does in this drawing A. T. Manookian made more than half a century ago.

The First Recruits, December 1775, by Col. Charles Waterhouse, USMCR, shows Capt. Samuel Nicholas, 1st Lt. Mathew Parke, and a scowling sergeant with prospective Leathernecks on the Philadelphia waterfront. The vessel behind them is the *Alfred,* flagship of the Continental Navy.
Art Collection, Marine Corps Historical Center

dropped behind the rest of the fleet. This accident reduced the force with which Hopkins had resolved to seize Nassau, capital of the Bahamas, to six ships carrying 580 seamen and 234 Marines.

There was no mention of Nassau in Hopkins's instructions from Congress, which specified that he was to clear the Chesapeake Bay and central seaboard of British naval forces. But they contained the usual loophole, through which he shaped course for the Caribbean. His decision probably stemmed from his knowledge of a secret report to Congress that the military stores at Nassau included a large quantity of gunpowder, a commodity of which Washington's army was in dire need. Whatever the commodore's reasons, they led to the first landing of Continental Marines.

Nassau stands on the northern side of New Providence Island along the shore of an elongated harbor between New Providence and Hog Island (now Paradise Island). The eastern and western entrances to the harbor were guarded by two small masonry works, Forts Montagu and Nassau, respectively. A small British garrison had been withdrawn months earlier, leaving the island's defense to its militia.

Arriving off Nassau at dawn on 3 March, the fleet anchored six miles east of the settlement and began off-loading Captain Nicholas's Marines around noon. The addition of fifty seamen to his command raised its strength to 284 officers and men. The governor of the Bahamas, Montfort Browne, had known of the Americans' approach since 1 March, when a whaler reported sighting the fleet off Great Abaco Island, but he had not acted on the information, and the landing was unopposed. The ships' appearance finally started his adrenalin flowing, and by 2:00 P.M., the hour at which Nicholas's troops began moving down the coast toward Nassau, 140 militiamen had been sent to garrison Fort Montagu. When scouting parties scurried back with the news that the Americans were indeed coming, Browne became apprehensive that they would swing inland around the fort to occupy the town and ordered his men to fall back to Fort Nassau. For the sake of appearances, before leaving he had three cannons fired in the direction of the Marines.

These harmless shots proved to be the only ones fired in the defense of Nassau. Finding Fort Montagu deserted Nicholas decided to rest his men there overnight and sent a message informing Hopkins of its uncontested occu-

The landing on New Providence Island, 3 March 1776, re-created in a modern painting by V. Zveg. Naval Historical Center

pation. This report apparently encouraged Hopkins to believe that the operation could be completed without bloodshed, for he immediately issued a proclamation to the citizens of New Providence announcing that his objective was "to take Possession of the Powder and Warlike Stores belonging to the Crown and am I not Opposed . . . the Persons and Property of the Inhabitants Shall be Safe."[9] Nicholas's men put this manifesto into circulation among the residents of eastern Nassau.

Hopkins's assurances, coupled with the self-evident impossibility of defending the town from its far side, undermined Governor Browne's hope of making a fight. At a council of war he held in Fort Nassau that evening, the majority of the militia officers and local notables voted for surrender. They did agree to transfer 162 barrels of powder stored in the fort to two merchant ships, which then slipped out the western end of the harbor, Commodore Hopkins having contented himself with blockading the eastern end. All of the powder might have been saved, but Browne felt that it would be politic to let the

Americans capture a little. Thereafter the militia melted away. At dawn Nicholas's advance from Fort Montague was met by an emissary bearing word that Fort Nassau would not be defended.

Despite Browne's success in spiriting away most of the powder, the New Providence raid reaped a rich haul: fifty-eight cannon, fifteen mortars, more than sixteen thousand shot and shell, and assorted other hardware. It took Hopkins's men almost two weeks to load the booty aboard their ships. The governor spent this period under guard of a Marine detachment, whose members, he afterward complained, helped themselves to his liquor. On 17 March the fleet sailed for home.

Most of the return voyage was uneventful, but off the coast of Rhode Island the sea suddenly filled with enemy shipping. Two small naval vessels and several merchantmen were gobbled up on 4 and 5 April, and at 1:00 on the morning of the sixth the fleet encountered HMS *Glasgow,* a twenty-gun frigate admirably commanded by Captain Tryingham Howe. The three-and-a-half-hour running battle that ensued revealed that whatever Hopkins's merits, he was not up to controlling a fleet in action. Engaged in awkward succession by the *Cabot,* fourteen guns; the *Alfred,* thirty; and the *Columbus,* twenty-eight, the *Glasgow* beat off their attacks and, although heavily damaged, made good her escape. American casualties were nine men dead and sixteen wounded. They included two Marine lieutenants, John Fitzpatrick of the *Alfred,* the first Marine officer killed in action, and John Hood Wilson of the *Cabot,* who was mortally wounded. The *Glasgow*'s losses—one man killed and three wounded—were inflicted by Marine musket fire. After this disappointing encounter the fleet continued on course for New London, where it dropped anchor on 8 April 1776.

The New Providence expedition appeared to augur well for the institutional integrity of the Continental Marines. Even though the landing force consisted of independent companies, it had functioned as a battalion of the sort envisioned by the Corps's founding legislation and in the type of amphibious operation that legislation anticipated. The expedition's two failures—missing the gunpowder and allowing the *Glasgow* to escape—could hardly be blamed on the Marines. Congress indicated its satisfaction with their performance by promoting Nicholas to major, a rank he was the only Continental Marine to attain.

But the auguries were illusionary. New Providence was the last as well as the first operation in which Continental Marines participated as an integral corps. In the seven years of war that followed there were fewer than seven occasions when as many as three companies saw action together, and only one, the Penobscot expedition, was an amphibious assault. Otherwise, the history of the Continental Marines is an episodic account of independent companies whose fortunes followed those of the ships in which they served.

The decentralization of Marine operations after the New Providence expedition reflected the practice of the British marines, who were organized in independent companies. Even had Americans been inspired to ignore precedent, however, the conditions of the conflict would have made the maintenance of a unified corps impractical. The key factors in the naval war were, first, the overwhelming preponderance of the Royal Navy, and, second, the extreme difficulty experienced in manning the Continental Navy, small as it was. The New Providence raid was the only time the Continental fleet operated as such. Never again could enough seamen be collected for the fleet to put to sea as a unit. Only in rare instances did as many as three ships sail together, and single-ship cruises were the rule. The problem was not a shortage of seafarers. America had plenty of sailors, but they preferred to serve in privateers, which offered the prospect of far greater financial reward than the Navy.

Considering the odds, the dispersion of the American naval effort was, on the whole, a good thing. For the Continental Navy to have operated as a fleet would have been to court disaster. At the onset of the conflict the Royal Navy had 268 vessels in commission; thereafter its numbers increased. Granted that its full strength was never committed to the American theater, there was still no possibility that the Continental Navy could win even local command of the sea. From necessity its operations took the form of commerce raiding, a weaker navy's usual resort, and attempting to punch an occasional hole in the British blockade of the American coast, either by driving blockaders away from a particular port or by shepherding a convoy home from the West Indies. These activities, plus chance encounters with enemy warships, set the stage for Continental Marines' battles at sea.

In December 1775 Congress had appropriated funds to build thirteen frigates. None got to sea in 1776, but two merchant brigs whose conversion was approved that March, the *Lexington* and the *Reprisal,* were soon ready for action. The *Lexington* sailed that very month; the *Reprisal* the following July. The latter's Marine detachment included the first black Marine, John "Keto" Martin, who went down with her on the Newfoundland Banks in September 1777. Six of Commodore Hopkins's vessels also made successful single-ship cruises in 1776, capturing several small British warships and numbers of merchantmen. At year's end there were approximately six hundred Marines in service.

Meanwhile, the Army had raised another force of freshwater Marines. The American conquest of Canada had come to grief outside Quebec in December 1775. British reinforcements sailed up the St. Lawrence the following spring, and in June an eight-thousand-man army pushed down the Richelieu River into New York. Realizing that the enemy's advance through the wilderness depended on water transport, General Benedict Arnold—prior to his treason among the ablest of the Continental commanders—began building ships to contest the control of Lake Champlain. The British were compelled to halt and do likewise. Eventually Arnold's fleet counted seventeen vessels manned by nine hundred soldiers, seamen, and Marines. The American fleet was obliterated by a more powerful British force at the Battle of Valcour Island in mid-October 1776, but Arnold's defeat turned out to be a victory, for the British concluded that winter was too close to continue the campaign and withdrew to Canada. "Gentleman Johnny" Burgoyne's renewal of the advance the next spring ended in his army's surrender at Saratoga, which persuaded France to come into the war on the American side. Her intervention would prove decisive.

Yet France would not officially enter the war until June 1778. In the meantime, the revolution was to pass through its darkest days. Those days began in August 1776, when the British launched a campaign to pacify the central colonies by capturing New York City. By the onset of winter they had advanced as far as the Delaware. Conscious of the need to revive his countrymen's flagging morale, Washington conceived plans for a bold attack on the British outpost line in New Jersey. Among his troops were three Marine companies that had been recruited to serve in the frigates being built near Philadelphia. Organized into a small battalion under Major Nicholas and sent to reinforce Washington's troops early in December, they were subsequently incorporated into a Philadelphia militia brigade commanded by Brig. Gen. John Cadwalader.

Cadwalader's troops were unable to get over the icy Delaware to share in Washington's victory at Trenton on 26 December, but they managed to cross a day later. On 2 January 1777 the brigade fought in the delaying action at Assunpink Bridge, where it helped hold off a superior enemy force moving to support the threatened garrisons, and on 3 January it was roughly handled in the opening minutes of the battle in which Washington scattered three British regiments outside Princeton. The role Major Nicholas's 130 Marines played in these engagements is unknown, but only 80 were left to enter the Army's win-

ter quarters at Morristown, Pennsylvania. One company was detached to escort British prisoners to Philadelphia in February; another returned to the city in April; and the remnant of the third was dissolved.

The British capture of Philadelphia in September 1777 again involved Marines in the war inside America. To deny the enemy the advantage of access to the sea, American forces sought to hold Forts Mercer and Mifflin, which commanded the Delaware a few miles below the city. Six Continental ships, including the *Andrew Doria* and the new frigate *Delaware,* both of which carried Marines, and the entire Pennsylvania State Navy were committed to the defense. The *Delaware* ran aground and was captured while engaging a British battery at Philadelphia on 27 September. Four days later a British squadron working its way upstream reached the American positions, and seven weeks of heavy fighting took place on the Delaware and along its banks.

Finally, the pressure on the forts became overwhelming. Mifflin was evacuated on 15 November, Mercer fell on the twenty-first, and the ships that had helped defend the river were burned to keep them out of British hands. The British Army would winter in the comforts of Philadelphia; Washington's men, in the misery of Valley Forge.

These operations notwithstanding, Marine activities continued to center on the war at sea. The scale of the Continental naval effort increased in 1777. Four new frigates—*Boston, Hancock, Raleigh,* and *Randolph*—made their first cruises, as did the sloop-of-war *Ranger,* and three smaller vessels were outfitted in France. All carried Marines. Shortly after the *Randolph* sailed, Capt. Samuel Shaw's company quashed a mutiny by a group of English sailors in her crew. That was the first of several instances in which Continental Marines suppressed attempted mutinies.

In the course of the year Continental vessels captured more than fifty merchantmen and privateers and one frigate (which was soon recaptured), at the price of four ships and three Marine detachments. The *Cabot*'s men escaped when she beached herself on being overhauled by an enemy vessel twice her strength; the *Reprisal* was lost with all hands except her cook in a storm; and the *Hancock* and the *Lexington* were forced to strike in actions with British ships.

American losses were heavier in 1778. The first occurred on 7 March when the thirty-two-gun frigate *Randolph* blew up while audaciously engaging—and apparently getting the better of—the sixty-four-gun ship-of-the-line *Yarmouth* until an unlucky shot touched off her magazine. Capt. Samuel Shaw and his Marines perished with their ship, from which there were only four survivors. Three other vessels—the *Alfred,* the *Columbus* (all of whose people escaped ashore), and the new frigate *Virginia*—were captured or destroyed that same month, and the *Raleigh* was driven aground while engaging two British warships in September. However, these losses were more than offset by the additions to the Continental Navy: five new frigates, the *Alliance, Confederacy, Deane, Providence,* and *Warren;* the *Queen of France,* an old frigate purchased in that country; and the prize brigantine *General Gates.* Each carried Marines, as did the frigates *Boston* and *Trumbull* and the sloops *Providence* and *Ranger.* Thus, at year's end eleven detachments remained afloat.

In addition to their services on the high seas in 1778, Marines conducted a daring amphibious landing and an unsavory riverine operation. The latter was the brainchild of James Willing, a well-connected young Philadelphian who had drunk his way through his patrimony after setting himself up in business in Natchez, Mississippi. Returning home in 1777, Willing persuaded the Commerce Committee of Congress to entrust him with command of an expedition whose objective was to seize control of the Mississippi from the confluence of the Ohio to the Spanish colonial frontier at Manchac (near present-day Plaquemine), Louisiana. He was also authorized to seize British property encountered along the river, an instruction in whose fulfillment he showed exemplary zeal.

Commissioned a captain in the Navy, Willing proceeded to Fort Pitt, Ohio, where he raised a Marine company of two officers and thirty-four men from the garrison. On 10 January 1778 the expedition set off down the Ohio in the ten-oared barge *Rattletrap.* On the way south Willing augmented his force by recruiting ten river ruffians, including George Girty, one of the notorious renegade brothers. (Willing made him a lieutenant, but he deserted anyway.) By the time the expedition reached New Orleans in March, it had well and truly pillaged the loyalist plantations along the Mississippi, burning houses and crops, slaughtering livestock, and making a haul of movable property ranging from silverware to shirts.

At New Orleans, Willing quickly antagonized the city's capable Continental agent, Oliver Pollock, and Spanish governor Bernardo de Gálvez. Forces from British West Florida captured the garrison Willing had left at Manchac, substituting one of their own, and by mid-April his dubious achievements had been undone. He lingered in New Orleans until August, having in Pollock's opinion "only thrown the whol river into confusion and created a Number of Enemies and a heavy Expense which would not have happened had [the expedition] been otherwise Governed."[10]

The year's amphibious assault was made on New Providence Island. In contrast to Commodore Hopkins's large-scale landing, it was carried out by a solitary frigate, Capt. John Peck Rathbun's *Providence,* and a twenty-eight-man Marine detachment commanded by Capt. John Trevett. The idea originated with Rathbun, who seems to have been motivated mainly by the desire to capture the British privateer *Mary,* which he had learned was being overhauled at Nassau. His sailing master had been killed in a brush with the *Mary* in 1777, and he intended to settle the score. Trevett, a veteran of the first New Providence expedition, realized the risks of attempting to duplicate it with so diminutive a force, but agreed to try. In his diary he wrote: "I have had A long time to think of What I am A Going to undertake but I am Very well satisfied that we Are in a Good Cause & we are a fiting the Lords Battel."[11]

The plan called for the Marines to land under cover of darkness and seize Fort Nassau by surprise. Once in possession of the fort, they could hold the town hostage to its guns. Around midnight on 27 January 1778, the *Providence* anchored off Hog Island, and Trevett, Lt. Michael Molton, and their twenty-six Marines rowed into the night. From his previous visit Trevett remembered that one of the stakes had been missing from the fort's palisade. It was missing still, and he led his men through the gap and up their scaling ladder into the fort. Greatly to his relief, he found that the garrison consisted of a pair of night watchmen, who were overpowered before they could give the alarm. At dawn Trevett hoisted the American flag and informed Nassau's startled residents that he had occupied the fort with thirty officers and two hundred men from a fleet anchored off Abaco Island. His orders, he continued, were to seize the *Mary* and other "warlike stores"; the persons and property of the inhabitants would be respected.

Trevett's bluff worked to perfection. Concluding that resistance might entail "the disagreeable consequence of the destruction of the Town," the town council elected not to oppose the occupation.[12] Although a few tense moments intervened, Trevett held Fort Nassau for the four days Rathbun needed to ready the *Mary* and four captured American vessels found in the harbor for sea. On the morning of 1 February, Trevett and his men returned to the *Providence,* having accomplished one of the war's most audacious undertakings.

By this time Continental naval forces had expanded their activities to European waters. Extended operations there were made possible by the cooperation of France, which even before her official entry into the war allowed American warships to use French ports as bases. The first cruise from France was made by the *Reprisal* in January 1777. Of the many others that followed, the most famous were those of John Paul Jones in the *Ranger* (April–May 1778) and the *Bonhomme Richard* (August–October 1779).

The *Ranger* carried a small Marine detachment commanded by twenty-three-year-old Lt. Samuel Wallingford, a judge's son from New Hampshire. When Jones took two boat parties to set fire to the shipping in the British port of Whitehaven on the night of 22–23 April, he gave Wallingford command of the second boat. It was the first time since 1667 that a foreign foe had set foot on English soil. Although the townsfolk extinguished the fires before much damage had been done, the moral effect of the raid was tremendous.

On 23 April Jones included Wallingford in the party he landed at St. Mary's Isle to kidnap the Earl of Selkirk, whom he intended to hold hostage for the good treatment of American prisoners in British hands. To Jones's chagrin the earl was absent, although his spirited, very pregnant young wife was at home. Worse yet, Sailing Master David Cullam and Lieutenant Wallingford proposed looting the Selkirk mansion; after all, the British were looting New England homes. Jones reluctantly consented to the liberation of the Selkirks' silverware (which he later restored to them at his own expense) and returned to the boat landing. Cullam and Wallingford told Lady Selkirk to have her servants collect the silver, which was soon done. Afterward she gave the officers a glass of wine. Informing her husband of these events, she wrote that Cullam "seemed by nature a very disagreeable & one may say a bad man" with "a vile blackguard look," but the junior officer, "a civil young man . . . seemed naturally well bred and not to like his employment."[13]

The next day the *Ranger* captured the British sloop *Drake* after an hour's action. Among the dead were the *Drake*'s commanding officer, Cdr. George Burden, and Lieutenant Wallingford, both shot through the head by enemy marines. In reply to Jones's letter promising that his silver would be returned, the Earl of Selkirk noted that "we were all sorry afterwards to hear that the younger officer . . . had been killed, for he in particular showed so much civility."[14]

There were 137 marines aboard the *Bonhomme Richard* during her epic engagement with HMS *Serapis* on 23 September 1779, but they were red-coated acting marines of the French Army's Infanterie Irlandaise, Regiment de Welsh-Serrant. Their musketry made an important contribution to Jones's victory by preventing the British from cutting the lines to the grappling hooks that pinned the *Serapis* to the *Richard* and by driving the enemy seamen and marines out of her fighting tops. The absence of opposing marines made it possible for William Hamilton, a Scots seaman, to shinny out on a yardarm and begin dropping grenades on the deck of the *Serapis.* One of them fell through an open hatch and exploded amid a pile of powder sacks on the gun deck below, killing twenty men and injuring many others. Still later the French marines helped discourage an enemy attempt to board. When the *Serapis* surrendered after almost four hours of fighting, 150 men had been killed and wounded out of the *Richard*'s complement of 325. The number of Infanterie Irlandaise in the former figure is not known, but it must have been substantial. American Marines served in another ship of Jones's little squadron, the *Alliance,* commanded by the psychotic Frenchman Pierre Landais; but, aside from pouring three broadsides

Penobscot River

American lines

Fort George

Bagaduce Peninsula

Bagaduce Harbor

3rd position

2nd position

British
sloops
1st position

Banks Island

American batteries:

△ Finished

∧ Unfinished

The Penobscot Expedition, July–August 1779

into the *Richard,* the *Alliance* took no part in the action.

In 1779 Marines assisted in the capture of more British vessels than in any previous year. During this same year, however, Continental naval forces suffered the first of two blows from which they would never recover. On 15 June, 640 British regulars under Brig. Gen. Francis McLean landed on the Bagaduce Peninsula on Penobscot Bay, Maine, then part of Massachusetts and now the site of the town of Castine. The objects of the occupation were to establish an advanced naval base for operations against American privateers and to provide support for local loyalists. Informed of the enemy's pres-

ence, the government of Massachusetts—accustomed since colonial days to mounting amphibious operations—resolved to expel the British before they could become entrenched, and an expedition was quickly assembled. Massachusetts committed the three brigs comprising its navy and chartered a dozen privateers and twenty-three merchantmen for use as transports; the Continental Navy contributed the *Warren,* the sloop *Providence,* and the brig *Diligent,* with their Marine detachments; and New Hampshire furnished a chartered privateer. Only 873 of the 1,500 militiamen summoned actually appeared; this number, added to the 227 Marines of the Continental and Massachusetts Navies, gave the landing force a strength of 1,100 men. Command was divided between Capt. Dudley Saltonstall of the Continental Navy and Brig. Gen. Solomon Lovell of the Massachusetts militia.

The wooded Bagaduce Peninsula lay on the northern side of a harbor of the same name. Approximately two miles long and one wide, it was connected to the mainland by a narrow isthmus midway along its northern face. To the south the peninsula was roughly paralleled by several islands along the southern side of the harbor. Arriving on the scene on 25 July, the Americans discovered that the British were constructing a log fort (Fort George) in the center of the peninsula and had established a battery on Banks Island. Fire from the fort and the battery overlapped to cover the entrance to the harbor, which was also defended by three British sloops. Taken together, these were the elements of an amphibious equation the Penobscot expedition failed to solve.

Operations began on 26 July 1779 when Marines led by Capt. John Welsh, the expedition's senior Marine officer, seized lightly defended Banks Island and opened fire on the British sloops, which withdrew up the harbor to an anchorage off Fort George. Having accomplished this much, the expedition's commanders disagreed on what to do next. Lovell wanted to land on the southern side of the peninsula, where there was a good beach. First, however, Saltonstall would have to enter the harbor and dispose of the sloops; but he balked at sending his ships into "that damned hole" before Lovell had captured the fort.[15] After a day's debate, they settled on a less suitable landing site on the precipitous western end of the peninsula.

The assault, supported by fire from four ships, was made at dawn on 28 July. Captain Welsh's Marines, who formed the right wing of the landing force, met the toughest resistance. Taken under musket fire while still in their boats by British troops on the headland, once ashore they found that their beach lay at the foot of a slope so steep that they had to grasp shrubs to pull themselves up. Welsh was killed almost immediately. Lt. William Hamilton fell mortally wounded, and thirty-two other men were hit. But their comrades pressed ahead and drove the British back to Fort George. Following in their footsteps, a company of Massachusetts Marines reached the edge of the clearing around the fort. As yet the walls were barely a yard high. Inside them General McLean stood by the flagstaff, ready to haul down his colors as soon as a few shots were fired for honor's sake against the attack he was sure would come.

None did. Fearful of exposing his men to the fire of the sloops, Lovell called a halt. "Our general," a Marine veteran recalled, "was said to be *a very good sort of man,* but these good sort of men seldom make good Generals. . . . Mr. Lovell would have done more good . . . in the deacon's seat of a country church, than at the head of an American Army."[16] In succeeding days Lovell undertook the methodical procedures of eighteenth-century siegecraft, building earthworks, blockhouses, and batteries, all the while entreating Saltonstall to go after the sloops. Fearful of exposing his ships to the fire of the fort, Saltonstall with equal persistence refused.

By 13 August the American lines had inched to within half a mile of Fort George. That afternoon a British fleet hurrying to the rescue was sighted entering Penobscot Bay. During the night the American troops ashore were reembarked. The next morning, after essaying to form a line of battle across the entrance to the harbor, the American ships suddenly and simultaneously fled up the Penobscot River. The British pursued, and by the afternoon of 15 August every vessel afloat at Penobscot two days earlier had been captured or destroyed. Although many of its members escaped through the wilderness, the Penobscot expedition had ceased to exist. Estimates of personnel casualties range as high as five hundred.

The offensive fiasco in Maine was followed by a defensive disaster in South Carolina. Having failed to pacify the central colonies, late in 1779 the British adopted a "southern strategy" intended to extinguish rebellion in the region where loyalist sentiment was believed strongest. The campaign opened with an assault on Charleston. In anticipation of the attack, Congress dispatched four ships—the frigates *Boston, Providence,* and *Queen of France* and the sloop *Ranger,* with their Marines—to bolster the defense. This proved a mistake. In February 1780 a vastly superior British amphibious force trapped the ships in Charleston harbor and landed troops whose fire drove the American fleet up the Cooper

Charles Waterhouse's *Fighting Tops, 29 May 1781* specifically relates to the engagement between the frigate *Alliance* and the British sloops *Atalanta* and *Trepassey,* but it typifies the activities of the Leathernecks who fought aloft in all the Continental Navy's actions.
Art Collection, Marine Corps Historical Center

River and effectively out of the battle. The *Queen of France* was scuttled to obstruct the river channel, and all four ships' complements were plugged into the American lines ashore. The Marines joined Army artillerymen manning five waterfront batteries. They had been committed to a losing fight. Outnumbered almost three to one, Charleston's 5,400 defenders surrendered on 12 May. It was the greatest American defeat of the war.

That defeat was also nearly the swan song of the Continental naval forces. After Charleston, only five Continental ships—*Alliance, Confederacy, Deane, Saratoga,* and *Trumbull*—and their Marine detachments remained afloat. Moreover, they were a wasting asset. Congress was finished building ships, which were expensive and all too clearly subject to loss; besides, the French fleet posed a greater challenge to the Royal Navy than the

Americans could aspire to mount. The Continental war at sea was winding down.

Nevertheless, a few hard battles remained to be fought. The *Trumbull* took the *Watt* in June 1780; and the *Alliance,* thirty-six guns, captured the British sloops-of-war *Atalanta,* sixteen, and *Trepassey,* fourteen, in an equally grueling encounter on 29 May 1781. At the beginning of the latter action the air was too still for the *Alliance* to maneuver. By using long oars called sweeps the lighter British vessels reached positions athwart the *Alliance*'s bow and stern, where few of her guns could return their fire, and pounded the hapless frigate at their pleasure for nearly three hours. American casualties suffered during this period included Marine Lt. Samuel Pritchard, mortally wounded by a 6-pound shot; Lt. James Warren Jr., a Harvard graduate who received a wound that cost him a leg; and Sgt. David Brewster, drilled through the head by a British marine. Finally a breeze sprang up, allowing the *Alliance* to bring her broadsides to bear, and her tormentors were quickly battered into submission.

The *Alliance*'s victory was more than balanced by the loss of three frigates and their Marines in 1781. The *Saratoga* went down with all hands in a Caribbean gale in March; the *Confederacy* surrendered to two Royal Navy vessels in April; and in August the *Trumbull* was taken in an action with two enemy ships. These reverses reduced the effective strength of the Continental Marines to the detachments in the *Alliance* and the *Deane*.

By the end of 1781, however, the condition of Continental naval forces had ceased to matter. In September Britain's southern strategy reached a catastrophic climax when American and French forces commanded by Washington and Rochambeau closed around Cornwallis's army at Yorktown, Virginia. A French fleet fended off the Royal Navy's rescue attempt, and on 19 October Cornwallis surrendered. The War of Independence had been won. But it was not over. A year and a half would pass before the peace was settled; in the meanwhile, the war at sea continued. Checkered as its career had been, the Continental Navy went out in style. Both the *Alliance* and the *Deane* (later renamed *Hague*) made successful cruises in 1782 and 1783. Continental Marines fired their last shots in an engagement between the *Alliance* and the British frigate *Sybil* on 10 March 1783. With the conclusion of peace the two ships were laid up, later to be sold, and their complements discharged. Lt. Thomas Elwood of the *Alliance* was the last Marine to be retained on active duty. His release in September 1783 brought the history of the Continental Marine Corps to a close.

From first to last, 131 officers and approximately two thousand noncommissioned officers and men had served in the Continental Marines. Although surviving documentation is too scanty to permit an exact reckoning, they had suffered heavy losses. Of the officers, for whom records are fairly complete, 15 had been killed in action, died of wounds, or gone down with their ships; 1 had fallen overboard and drowned; 3 are known to have been wounded; and 22 were captured: a casualty rate of 33 percent. Enlisted casualties must have been in the neighborhood of five hundred (25 percent). Clearly, Continental Marines had done their share to win America's independence. The little navy in which they served had been unable to do much more than nip at the heels of its mighty adversary, but they had contributed to its successes and helped maintain its discipline. Even more important, perhaps, they had made Marines part of their new country's military heritage.

3
The Early Years, 1798–1820

For nine years following the sale of the last Continental warship, the new nation did without a navy. The weak government provided by the Articles of Confederation simply could not support one. Authority to "provide and maintain" a navy financed by taxation was among the powers vested in Congress by the Constitution adopted in 1789, but a stalemate between the Federalist and Republican parties prevented this power from being put to use. The Federalists argued that a navy was needed to protect maritime trade and uphold national interests. The Republicans insisted that a navy would ruin the country's finances and stir up needless wars.

The impasse was broken by Algiers. For centuries the four Barbary powers on the coast of North Africa—from west to east: Morocco, Algiers, Tunis, and Tripoli—had derived most of their income by charging seafaring nations an annual fee to abstain from attacking their shipping. Although the United States had been dutifully paying this "tribute," in 1793 it bridled at the amount Algiers demanded. The U.S. Navy was created in consequence.

The Navy Act of 27 March 1794 called for the acquisition of six frigates, cruising vessels able to outsail any enemy they could not outfight. To satisfy the Republicans' scruples, the act included a proviso that the program would be canceled if a diplomatic settlement with Algiers was reached before the ships entered commission. Algiers did in fact come to terms while the ships remained under construction, but the Federalists negotiated a compromise that saved the infant U.S. Navy from being stillborn. Three vessels would be completed; the

others would be placed "in ordinary," the equivalent of today's "mothballs."

A new source of maritime friction arose shortly thereafter. Britain and France had gone back to war in 1793. Each claimed the right to suppress neutral trade with its enemy, a potentially serious threat to the American merchant marine. At first it seemed that the threat might not materialize. The Jay Treaty of 1794 brought about an understanding with Britain, and for several years France forbore from molesting American commerce. In July 1796, however, the French government announced that henceforth any vessel found to have been trading with Britain or carrying any article of British manufacture in her cargo would be subject to seizure. By the end of 1797 approximately three hundred American merchantmen had fallen prey to French ships—a few naval vessels and scores of privateers—based on their country's West Indian colonies.

These losses spurred the newly elected Federalist administration of President John Adams to take action. On 27 March 1798 Congress resolved that the three finished frigates should be readied for service. Authorizations for the acquisition of additional vessels and the completion of the other frigates followed in succeeding months. The Navy Department was founded on 30 April. On 24 May the *Ganges,* a converted merchant ship carrying twenty-six guns, became the first U.S. naval vessel to put to sea. The government initiated the purely naval Quasi-War with France on 28 May, instructing American men-of-war to attack French armed ships. On 7 July the twenty-gun sloop-of-war *Delaware* became the first of the Navy's ships to enter action, capturing the fourteen-gun French privateer schooner *Croyable* off the coast of New Jersey. Four days later Congress formally established the U.S. Marine Corps.

There had never been any question that the naval service would include Marines. The Navy Act of 1794 had specified that each of the six frigates would carry a Marine guard: an officer and 54 men on the four 44-gun ships and an officer and 44 men on the two 36s. Eight officers had received Marine commissions before there was a Marine Corps, and one of them, 1st Lt. Daniel Carmick, had taken a detachment of two dozen men to sea in the *Ganges* in May. The Corps created in July was to number thirty-three officers (a major, four captains, and twenty-eight lieutenants) and 848 noncommissioned officers and men, including thirty-two "drums and fifes." Not quite eight months later, the Act of 2 March 1799 increased the authorized strength of the Corps to forty-one officers and 1,044 other ranks. The effect of the change was slight. Unlike the Army and Navy, the Marine Corps was not allowed to offer enlistment bounties, and during the opening decade of its existence its actual strength probably never exceeded 600 men.

To command the new Corps, President Adams personally selected forty-year-old William Ward Burrows, a wealthy Philadelphia lawyer and businessman with strong Federalist ties. A South Carolinian by birth, Burrows had studied and practiced law in London before the Revolution. He returned home in 1775 and may have served an inconspicuous stint in the state militia during the war. In any event, prior military experience was clearly not the reason why Adams chose Burrows for the post. Burrows became the commandant because of his managerial and social skills and his political connections. Described by Washington Irving as "a gentleman of accomplished mind and polished manner," he would prove the president's confidence well justified.[1]

Major Burrows opened Marine Corps headquarters at Philadelphia, then the national capital, on 23 August 1798. A Marine camp was set up outside the city a few days later. From the start, Burrows sought to establish the Corps as a separate sea service and to define a distinctive role for its guard detachments at sea, where many naval

Maj. Daniel Carmick, one of the Corps's original officers, served with distinction in the Quasi-War with France and the War of 1812.

officers were inclined to treat Marines as supernumerary seamen. He understood that the achievement of these aims would require the Corps to establish a glowing image with Congress and the public at large.

Burrows's program was an ambitious one for an embryonic organization, but under his leadership much of it was accomplished. Officers were assured of their commandant's support in resisting attempts by naval officers to misuse Marines to perform seamen's duties. This support was amply demonstrated in November 1799 in the aftermath of an altercation onboard the *Ganges*. Navy Lt. Allen McKenzie had put a Marine in irons without consulting the guard detachment's commander, 1st Lt. Anthony Gale. When Gale demanded an explanation, McKenzie called him a rascal and struck him. The ship's captain brushed off the incident, but as soon as the cruise ended, Gale challenged McKenzie to a duel. McKenzie chose pistols, and Gale shot him dead. Burrows heartily approved. "It is to be hoped," he wrote in a letter to Gale, "that this may be a lesson to the Navy officers to treat Marines as well as their officers with some more Respect."[2] A year later, Burrows virtually ordered 2nd Lt. Henry Caldwell to challenge a Navy officer who had struck him: "[W]ithout you wipe away this insult offer'd to the Marine Corps, you cannot expect to join our officers."[3] Bloodshed was averted by the offender's apology. Finally, in August 1801, Burrows persuaded Secretary of the Navy Robert Smith to issue a circular setting forth the duties to which Marines were and were not subject aboard ship.

To promote the Corps's public relations, Burrows took advantage of its allowance of thirty-two "drums and fifes" to form a regular band. Late in 1798 each of his officers was assessed ten dollars—almost half a second lieutenant's monthly pay—to purchase its instruments. Their money proved to be well spent. Beginning with its public debut at a Fourth of July celebration in Philadelphia in 1800, the Marine Band was an immediate success.

Of course, Burrows's main responsibility was to provide guard detachments for the ships that sailed to fight the Quasi-War. One of the units formed prior to the foundation of the Corps had been in the *Delaware* under the command of 1st Lt. James McKnight when she took the *Croyable* in July. The captured privateer was commissioned in the U.S. Navy as the *Retaliation* and given a Marine guard under 1st Lt. Simon W. Geddis. In November the tables were turned. The *Retaliation*, mounting fourteen guns, fell in with two French frigates mounting a total of seventy-six. Her captain surrendered without offering resistance, and Geddis and his men became the first U.S. Marines to be taken prisoners of war.

All of the Navy's other meetings with French ships ended in the enemy's capture or flight. Marine guards were present at most of these encounters. Detachments commanded by 1st Lt. Bartholomew Clinch fought onboard Capt. Thomas Truxtun's frigate *Constellation* in the two major actions of the war: the capture of the frigate *Insurgente* on 9 February 1799 and the defeat of the *Vengeance* on 1 February 1800. The close combat both engagements included gave the *Constellation*'s Leathernecks the opportunity to perform the traditional Marine function of directing small arms fire at enemy personnel. Clinch's men made an especially valuable contribution to the second victory, a brutal night battle in which their musketry and lobbed grenades helped beat off an attempt by the *Vengeance*, a larger ship with a big-

ger crew, to board the *Constellation*. Other detachments' musketry played a role in the capture of the frigate *Berceau* by the *Boston* on 12 October 1800 and in the sometimes sharp actions smaller U.S. vessels fought with French privateers.

Marine guards also demonstrated their worth in several clashes with the barge pirates who were preying on American shipping in the Bight of Léogâne, off the west coast of Haiti. The biggest fight occurred on New Year's Day 1800, when twelve barges, some mounting light cannon, manned by more than five hundred Haitians attacked a becalmed convoy of four merchant vessels escorted by a twelve-gun schooner, the *Experiment,* carrying a crew of seventy and a fourteen-man Marine guard. The Leathernecks were commanded by 2nd Lt. Nathan Sheredine. Between 7:00 A.M. and 4:00 P.M., the pirates made three distinct assaults on the convoy, returning to their base after the first and second to unload their dead and wounded and take on replacements. At the end of the day they succeeded in taking two merchantmen that had drifted away from the convoy; but two barges had been sunk, and the *Experiment*'s grapeshot and musketry had smashed every effort to grapple with her. Edward Stevens, an American diplomat who happened to be onboard, attributed this outcome in part to the "great steadiness and activity" of Sheredine's Marines.[4]

The Quasi-War also engendered the U.S. Marines' first two landings on foreign soil. The earliest took place at Puerto Plata, on the northern coast of Santo Domingo, on 12 May 1800. A French privateer, the eight-gun schooner *Sandwich* (a captured British vessel whose name had been retained), lay at anchor under the guns of the little Spanish fort there. Informed of her presence, Commo. Silas Talbot, commanding the USS *Constitution,* conceived a plan for cutting her out of the harbor. An innocuous American trader, the *Sally,* would be sent into the harbor with a few men visible above deck and eighty-five other seamen and Marines packed into her hold. Once the *Sandwich* had been seized, the Leathernecks would go ashore and spike the fort's guns to preclude any interference from the Spanish during the hours it would take to get the ship rigged and ready to catch the evening breeze off the island. In overall command of the expedition Talbot placed the *Constitution*'s first lieutenant,

R. A. Salmon showed Captain Carmick's Marines in the cutter *(right),* on their way to spike the Spanish fort's guns, in his contemporary painting of the capture of the *Sandwich.* Boston Athenaeum

Isaac Hull. Capt. Daniel Carmick and 2nd Lt. William Amory led the Marines.

Talbot's plan worked smoothly. The Americans boarded the *Sandwich* unopposed, and within moments her twenty-three startled crewmen were confined below deck. The next day Captain Carmick wrote a friend that

> the only disagreeable part of the business was being cooped up in a small vessel for 12 hours. . . . [I]t put me in mind of the wooden horse at Troy. . . . The men went on board like devils and it was as much as the first lieutenant and myself could do to prevent blood being spilt. I believe it was not half an hour after the ship was taken that I had possession of the fort and all the cannon spiked and returned again on board. . . . I presume [the Spanish] were rather surprised. . . . By six o'clock [P.M.] the lieutenant had everything in order and the men stationed at the cannon, ready with my Marines to oppose all their force, which we understood was about 500 men. They sent several flags of truce making different requests, to which we answered that we had only executed the orders of our commander. . . . [The Spanish commandant] concluded we must have been pretty determined before we undertook the business, as we had no other alternative but to die or succeed. He however remained very quiet, and we came out in the morning and joined our commodore.[5]

For his part, their commodore was pleased as punch. "Perhaps no enterprise of the same moment was ever better executed," Talbot declared, "and I find myself under great obligations to Lieutenant Hull, Captain Carmick, and Lieutenant Amory . . . for the handsome manner and great address with which they performed this daring adventure."[6]

The second Marine landing occurred at Willemstad on Curaçao, a Dutch possession that was invaded by a force of fifteen hundred French troops from nearby Guadeloupe early in September 1800. On the twenty-second of that month two U.S. sloops of war, the *Merrimack* and the *Patapsco,* appeared off the island in response to an appeal for help from the American consul. By then the four hundred Dutch defenders—and a number of American volunteers from the merchant ships trapped at Willemstad—had retired into Fort Amsterdam, which overlooked the entrance to the harbor. The next day the twenty-four-gun *Patapsco* silenced the batteries the French had erected to cover an assault on the fort, and on the twenty-fourth landed seventy seamen and Marines to reinforce the defenders. Their intervention proved unnecessary. Convinced by the *Patapsco's* bombardment that it would be impossible to storm the fort in the face of the ships' fire, the French withdrew from the island that afternoon.

Less than a week later, on 30 September 1800, the Convention of Mortefontaine brought the Quasi-War with France to an end. Neither side had ever really wanted the war, and both were glad to be out of it, even if the terms of peace did not represent a triumph for either. At sea, the conflict was clearly a triumph for the U.S. Navy, which had captured eighty-five French privateers and two French Navy frigates at the cost of a single vessel, the little *Retaliation.* Marine guards had rendered valuable services in a number of engagements—most important, perhaps, the *Constellation*'s action with the *Vengeance* and the *Experiment*'s convoy battle. The cost to the Corps was 6 men dead and 11 wounded. No Marine officer was killed or wounded in battle, but 2nd Lt. Dyre S. Wynkoop became the first to lose his life in the line of duty. He and his detachment were among the 340 men who perished when the ex-French frigate *Insurgent* went down with all hands some time after sailing for the West Indies from Norfolk in August 1800.

Meanwhile, the seat of government had moved to the new "federal capital" at Washington, D.C. Lieutenant Colonel Commandant Burrows—a rank and title he acquired in April 1800—and Marine Corps headquarters followed that summer. The Marine Band also came along, of course. In March 1801 it played at the inauguration of President Thomas Jefferson—as it has at every subsequent presidential inauguration—and thereafter was heard at the White House so often that it soon became known as the "President's Own." That same month the commandant and the president, who were personal friends, rode out together to select a site for the Washington Marine barracks. They selected the block between Eighth and Ninth and G and I (Eye) Streets, Southeast, not far from the Washington Navy Yard. Among the buildings put under construction at the site was the commandant's house, of which Burrows's successor became the first occupant. A small Federalist mansion, it has been the home of every succeeding commandant and is today the oldest public building in use in Washington except for the White House.

In March 1804 ill health and financial problems forced Burrows to resign from the Corps he had served so well. His departure occurred toward the close of a war in the climax of which a tiny Marine detachment would play a vital role. In May 1801 Yusef Karamanli, the pasha of Tripoli, declared war on the United States, which he had decided was paying him insufficient tribute. The United States responded by sending an annual succession of squadrons to blockade the port city of Tripoli. The first squadron, dispatched when reports of the pasha's discontent were received in Washington, reached the Mediterranean in July.

Combat operations began on 1 August, when the twelve-gun schooner *Enterprise* fell in with the enemy's fourteen-gun *Tripoli*. Battles between wooden ships were usually over within an hour; theirs lasted for three. The Barbary corsairs favored boarding tactics, but the *Tripoli*'s repeated attempts to close were repulsed by broadsides from the *Enterprise*'s well-served battery and the musketry of 2nd Lt. Enoch S. Lane's Leathernecks. Of the *Tripoli*'s eighty crewmen, fifty were killed or wounded. The *Enterprise*'s ninety-four seamen and Marines did not suffer a single casualty.

This spirited affair proved to be the last of its kind off the shores of Tripoli. American squadrons lacked sufficient shallow-draft vessels and adequate charts to conduct a very effective blockade of Tripoli's dangerous coast, and it had never been Tripolitan policy to seek engagements with enemy warships. There was not another ship-to-ship action in the entire war, and not another action of any sort until boat parties totaling fifty sailors and Marines, the latter under Lieutenant Lane, landed near Tripoli on 22 May 1803 to destroy some coasting vessels that had been forced to beach themselves. The Americans succeeded in setting fire to the ships at a cost of fifteen killed and wounded, but following their withdrawal the Tripolitans extinguished the flames.

The tempo of operations increased after Commo. Edward Preble assumed command in the Mediterranean in September 1803 with the firm intention of winning the war. His prospects of doing so suffered a severe setback the following month when the frigate *Philadelphia,* one of his two big ships, ran hard aground while chasing a blockade runner and was surrounded by a covey of Tripolitan gunboats. Concluding that resistance would be futile, her captain surrendered without a fight. First Lt. William S. Osborne and his forty-two Marine guards were among the 307 Americans made prisoner. Two days later abnormally high tides enabled the Tripolitans to re-float the *Philadelphia* and tow her into port.

The naval part of the enormous problem this created was solved on the night of 16 February 1804. Reprising the ruse employed to cut out the *Sandwich,* seventy-four volunteers under Lt. Stephen Decatur entered Tripoli harbor onboard an innocent-looking coastal trader, over-powered the *Philadelphia*'s caretaker crew, set the frigate ablaze, and escaped without the loss of a man. Seven Marines led by Sgt. Solomon Wren took part in the exploit, which renowned British Adm. Horatio Nelson praised as "the most bold and daring act of the age."[7] The diplomatic difficulties stemming from the fact that Yusef Karamanli retained 307 American bargaining chips persisted throughout the conflict.

That spring, Preble decided that the best way to compel the pasha to come to terms would be by bombarding his capital. The American squadron lacked the types of vessels needed for a close inshore attack, but the King-dom of the Two Sicilies, which was also at war with Tripoli, agreed to supply six gunboats and two bomb vessels. These craft would be supported by the fire of Preble's flagship, the frigate *Constitution,* and six smaller American vessels.

The first bombardment of Tripoli took place on 3 August. The Tripolitan flotilla—nineteen gunboats and two galleys—came out to drive off the small craft, and a di-vision of three gunboats commanded by Stephen Decatur soon became engaged in a fierce melee. Decatur person-ally led boarding parties that captured two gunboats. Sergeant Wren, who had been with him in the destruc-tion of the *Philadelphia,* was among the wounded.

Lt. John Trippe, commanding *Gunboat No. 6,* also called away boarders and leaped from his vessel to the deck of an enemy gunboat. A moment later the two craft drifted apart, leaving Trippe, Midn. John D. Henley, Sgt. Jonathan Meredith, and eight seamen and Marines to contend with thirty-six Tripolitans. Trippe engaged their

captain, from whom he quickly received eleven saber wounds about the head and shoulders. Another Tripoli-tan circled around to strike him from behind. Sergeant Meredith bayoneted the man while Trippe succeeded in plunging his boarding pike into his opponent's chest. Within moments more than half of the Tripolitans had been killed or wounded; the others laid down their arms. Besides Trippe, three members of the boarding party, two of them Marines, were wounded.

Four days later Preble renewed the attack on the city. This time the Tripolitan vessels made no move to close. Ships as well as shore fortifications returned the Ameri-can fire, however, and either an enemy shot or an acci-dent touched off the magazine of *Gunboat No. 9.* Sixteen of the twenty-eight men onboard became casualties; the dead included gallant Sergeant Meredith.

Unfortunately, neither of these bombardments, nor three others conducted in following weeks, nor an at-tempt to blow up the vessels in Tripoli harbor with a powder ship that exploded prematurely, induced the pasha to reduce his demands. Late in September Preble rotated home thinking himself a failure, only to discover that his aggressiveness had made him a national hero.

In the meanwhile, another American had been think-ing of a way to win the war: William Eaton, a forty-year-old (in 1804) Revolutionary War veteran, sometime schoolteacher, and former U.S. Army captain who had become familiar with Barbary politics while serving as U.S. consul at Tunis. Yusef Karamanli had become pasha of Tripoli by shooting his oldest brother, Hassan, and driving his older brother Hamet into exile. Eaton be-lieved that the ideal solution to the Tripolitan imbroglio would be to restore Hamet to the throne. Returning to the United States in the summer of 1803, Eaton eventually lobbied a dubious Jefferson administration into approv-ing the project. In July 1804 he sailed for the Mediter-ranean to carry it out.

Finding Hamet, who had taken refuge in Egypt, and making preparations for the campaign turned out to be a lengthy process, but on 8 March 1805 "General" Eaton (as he styled himself in a treaty with Hamet) was ready to set out from Alexandria on a six-hundred-mile desert march to the Tripolitan frontier. All told, his little army

Lt. Presley O'Bannon carried the American flag to the shores of Tripoli.

numbered approximately four hundred men: 325 Arabs; a mercenary company of thirty-five Greeks; another mercenary company, also Christian, of twenty-two cannoneers; and nine Americans—a midshipman and seven Marines under 1st Lt. Presley N. O'Bannon.

A twenty-nine-year-old Virginian, O'Bannon had entered the Marine Corps in 1801 and had already served a tour in the Mediterranean. In a letter written to the commandant during that deployment, his ship's captain described O'Bannon as "one of the Happiest fellows Living," adding, "he has just returned from spending the evening with a Brilliant Circle of Spanish Ladies, & by way of Consolation for the loss of their company, Philosiphy & the fiddle is called to his aid, on the latter he is now playing, Hogs in the Cornfield—."[8] Ashore in North Africa the carefree fiddler would show himself to be, as Eaton recorded, an "intrepid, judicious, and enterprising Officer."[9]

The long march across the desert was grueling. Provi-

sions ran short, and on several occasions O'Bannon's l Leathernecks, supported by the Christian mercenaries, had to face down threatened mutinies by Hamet's Arab followers. Finally, on 25 April, the army reached the heights overlooking the Tripolitan frontier city of Derna. The next day Eaton sent the governor a polite request to allow him free passage. "My head or yours," came the reply.[10]

Eaton attacked Derna on 27 April. A number of Arab horsemen had joined the expedition since it left Egypt, giving him upward of six hundred combatants more or less under command. He deployed them for a two-pronged attack. Hamet's cavalry would swing inland to threaten the city from the south while the Marines, the Christian mercenaries with the army's solitary cannon, and a few Arab foot soldiers stormed the barricade screening its eastern face. Three of the Mediterranean Squadron's smaller warships were on hand to furnish fire support.

At first progress was slow. The naval bombardment silenced the city's battery, but the gunners reinforced the infantrymen behind the barricade. Seeing the mercenaries beginning to waver, Eaton decided that "our dernier and only resort" was to charge.[11] In his words:

> We rushed forward against a host of Savages, more than ten to one. They fled from their Coverts, irregularly, firing in retreat from every Palm tree and partition wall in their way. . . . Mr. O'Bannon accompanied by Midshipman [George] Mann of Annapolis, urged forward his Marines, Greeks, and such of the Cannoneers as were not necessary to the management of the field piece, passed through a shower of Musketry from the walls of houses, took possession of the Battery, planted the American Flag upon its ramparts, and turned its guns upon the Enemy.[12]

In half an hour Eaton's forces were in undisputed control of Derna. One Marine private was killed and two were wounded, one mortally, in its capture. Eaton himself was shot through the left wrist, and the mercenaries suffered ten casualties. The general made no record of Arab or hostile Tripolitan casualties, but the governor escaped with his head.

Eaton's scheme did indeed bring the Tripolitan War to an end, though not in the way he had imagined. Hamet's presence in Derna prompted Yusef Karamanli to rethink his position. On 3 June he concluded a treaty with U.S. negotiator Tobias Lear agreeing to free the *Philadelphia*'s

This somewhat fanciful period engraving shows Lieutenant O'Bannon's Leathernecks marching behind "General" Eaton in the advance on Tripoli. The mounted man at left is Hamet Karamanli.

company and waive all claims to future tribute in exchange for a one-time payment of sixty thousand dollars—by Barbary standards, a bargain-basement price. Eaton protested angrily that he and Hamet had been betrayed, but there was nothing he could do. The Americans, Hamet and his retinue, and the Christian mercenaries were evacuated from Derna onboard the *Constellation* on 12 June.

In the United States, Eaton and O'Bannon were hailed as heroes. Congress honored them and the other Americans who fought at Derna with a joint resolution of thanks; Eaton's native Massachusetts awarded him a huge land grant; and Virginia presented O'Bannon with a costly Mameluke sword (on which it misspelled his name "Priestly"), traditionally believed to have been modeled after one given him by Hamet Karamanli. Sadly, there was not much a Marine Corps with only four captain's slots could do to reward heroic first lieutenants, and in 1807 O'Bannon resigned his commission. In civilian life he made a good marriage, settled in Kentucky, became a large landowner, and served several terms in the state legislature, dying at the age of seventy-four. But

although he spent only six years in the Marine Corps, Presley O'Bannon has been one of its icons ever since. The exploits of his tiny detachment would often be cited to refute the arguments of those who questioned the Corps's usefulness, and its officers still carry the elegant Mameluke sword (officially adopted in 1826) that came into fashion because of him.

The Marine Corps had fought the last year of the War with Tripoli under a new commandant. On 7 March 1804, a day after Lieutenant Colonel Burrows resigned, thirty-six-year-old Capt. Franklin Wharton, the Corps's senior officer, was appointed to replace him. A member of one of Philadelphia's most prominent families, Wharton had obtained one of the Corps's original captaincies in 1798 and served afloat during the Quasi-War with France. Since then he had commanded the Marine barracks at the Philadelphia Navy Yard.

In many respects Wharton proved to be an excellent commandant. Like Burrows, he understood the relationship between esprit de corps, public relations, and political capital, and the role spit and polish could play in fostering all three. Significantly, the Corps's first uniform

Lt. Col. Commandant Franklin Wharton.

regulations were issued within a month of his appointment. Wharton also introduced the hand salute and made Marine Barracks, Washington, "the school where young officers and recruits are to be instructed in the various duties which they may be called upon to perform."[13] He continued Burrows's support of the Marine Band, which had become a fixture in Washington. The urbane commandant himself became one of the capital's civic leaders. Yet at the critical moment of his career Wharton acted in a manner that many of his fellow Marines deemed disgraceful.

The first few of Wharton's years as commandant were mostly quiet. In 1809 the threat of war with Spain prompted Congress to raise the Corps's authorized strength to forty-six officers and 1,823 men, but it was unable to recruit more than 1,100 men of all ranks. By that date the Corps was supplying guards for the Navy yards at Norfolk, Boston, Brooklyn, Charleston, and New Orleans as well as Washington and Philadelphia. In January 1811 the New Orleans detachment, commanded by Maj. Daniel Carmick since 1809, participated in an expedition against "Negro insurgents"—presumably bands of escaped slaves—in the wilderness north of the city. To Carmick's disgust, the insurgents fled after a brief exchange of fire; "they gave us but little opportunity to put ourselves in danger," he grumbled.[14]

A year later, another Marine unit became involved in a deadlier struggle resulting from a covert attempt to annex Spanish East Florida: the so-called Patriots' War. The scenario called for a group of American "Patriots"—civilians promised land grants in reward for their services—to seize the town of Fernandina and proclaim the Republic of Florida, which they would immediately cede to the United States. Then, with the support of U.S. forces pre-positioned on nearby Cumberland Island, Georgia, they would push south to capture the Spanish provincial capital of St. Augustine. The town of Baton Rouge had been filched from Spanish West Florida by a similar scheme in 1811.

At first, all went well. The Patriots occupied Fernandina on 17 March 1812, and within a month the U.S. Regiment of Riflemen joined them on the outskirts of St. Augustine. There the operation began to go sour. The Americans lacked the artillery needed to assault the city's formidable Castillo de San Marcos, and in June they made a disastrous error by rebuffing the Seminole Indians' offer to take their side. The Seminoles then turned to the Spanish, who did not repeat the invaders' mistake. Soon the American lines of communication were being raided by Seminole war parties. In July a company of Marines under forty-six-year-old Capt. John Williams was ordered forward from Fernandina to convoy supplies to the front.

Bound by the kind of rules of engagement that would madden Marines in future "twilight wars," Williams found his assignment frustrating. In a letter written to the Corps's adjutant on 6 September he complained, "I wish you . . . would find out the reason of the U.S. Troops being kept in this province without the liberty of firing a gun unless we are fired upon. Our situation is an unpleasant one."[15]

Six days later, the foreboding that underlay the captain's letter was realized. Twenty Leathernecks and Patriots under his command were ambushed by fifty to sixty Seminoles and Spanish troops while escorting a wagon train through a swamp. The attackers were beaten off, but one Marine was killed and scalped, and eight other men

Swamp Ambush, by Charles Waterhouse, depicts the Spanish attack on Captain Williams's supply train on 12 September 1812.
Art Collection, Marine Corps Historical Center

were wounded, including Captain Williams, who was shot eight times. Game to the end, he dictated a report of the action for the commandant, adding, "You may expect I am in a dreadful situation, though I yet hope I shall recover in a few months."[16] On 29 September he died.

By then the difficulty in bringing up supplies had caused the Americans to pull back from their position outside St. Augustine. Yet Williams's death did not go unavenged. In February 1813 Marines commanded by his replacement, Lt. Alexander Sevier, took part in a punitive expedition that burned the villages of the Seminoles who had ambushed him. But the little war in East Florida was a sideshow the United States could ill afford in view of the big war it had begun with Great Britain. In April U.S. forces were ordered to evacuate Spanish territory.

Anglo-American relations had deteriorated steadily since 1803, the year Britain and France resumed their long struggle after the short-lived Peace of Amiens.

Charged with conducting a blockade that eventually embraced the continent of Europe, the Royal Navy not only seized American ships but also impressed thousands of American seamen to fill its crews. The ill will these practices created was aggravated in 1811 by the discovery that British forces in Canada were supplying the Indian tribes resisting American settlement of the Ohio Valley. The obvious solution to that problem was congenial to the spirit of expansionism current in American society and politics, and on 18 June 1812 the United States declared war with the aim of expunging British power from North America.

The war's supporters assumed that the conquest of Canada would be, as Jefferson once prophesied, nothing more than "a matter of marching." Senile generals, unreliable troops, poor planning, and an energetic enemy combined to confound that expectation. All three of the U.S. invasions of Canada in 1812 ended in failure. Dur-

First Lt. William S. Bush, a contemporary painting by Jacob Eichholz. Art Collection, Marine Corps Historical Center

The *Constitution*'s victory over the *Guerrière* is commemorated by this French engraving. Beverley R. Robinson Collection

ing that same year, however, the U.S. Navy covered itself with glory (and salved the national psyche) in startling victories in three consecutive frigate actions. In each case, the U.S. ship had the advantage of the heavier broadside—as would be true of the winner in all but two of the twenty-five single-ship engagements with Royal Navy vessels on the high seas. But that was beside the point. In the wars with France and France's allies, British ships routinely beat opponents with heavier broadsides. In this war, they did not. Ship for ship and man for man, the U.S. naval service had shown that it was second to none.

Marine musketry contributed to two of the Navy's three opening victories. In the first, the *Constitution*'s battle with the *Guerrière* (19 August 1812), the British captain and both his first and second lieutenants were hit by small arms fire. But the carnage was not wholly one-sided. The commander of the *Constitution*'s Leathernecks, 1st Lt. William S. Bush, had promised a friend, "Should an opportunity be afforded for boarding the enemy, I will be the first man on his deck."[17] As the two ships crashed together, he climbed to the *Constitution*'s rail and shouted to the captain, "Shall I board her, sir?"[18] An instant later, one of the *Guerrière*'s Royal Marines drilled him through the head.

The war's second frigate action, between the *United States* and the *Macedonian* (25 October 1812), was won outside musket range. In the next, the *Constitution* against the *Java* (29 November), the antagonists again came to close quarters, and the *Java*'s captain was mortally wounded by a musket shot. The fourth action broke the string of American victories, but there was none in which Marines displayed more valor.

The defeat occurred on 1 June 1813, when Capt. James Lawrence, only ten days in command, took the *Chesapeake* out of Boston harbor with an untried crew to engage HMS *Shannon* under Capt. Philip Vere Broke, probably the most formidable frigate in the Royal Navy. The battle lasted barely a quarter of an hour. By the time Broke led his boarders over the *Chesapeake*'s bulwarks, British fire had made a bloody shambles of her deck. Every exposed officer had been shot at least once, and many seamen had fled below. The commander of the ship's Marine detachment, 1st Lt. James Broome, was down with a mortal wound, but the NCOs and men still on their feet put up the only organized resistance the British encountered. Fourteen of the *Chesapeake*'s forty-four Leathernecks were killed outright or died of wounds, and twenty (including both sergeants) were wounded—a casualty rate of 77 percent, more than twice that of the ship's crew.

A British officer who served in the *Shannon* supervised the composition of this print depicting the action between his ship and the USS *Chesapeake*. Beverley R. Robinson Collection

Subsequently, Marine guards played a conspicuous role in three of the U.S. Navy's ten remaining victories at sea. At the climax of the engagement between the sloop-of-war *Wasp* and the British brig *Reindeer* (28 June 1814), the *Reindeer*'s captain, William Manners, already twice wounded, called away boarders and climbed into his ship's rigging, sword in hand, to lead them. As he did so, two Marines in the *Wasp*'s maintop put bullets through the top of his skull. The Americans then boarded and captured the *Reindeer.* Neither side tried to board during the *Constitution*'s double victory over the smaller frigate *Cyane* and sloop-of-war *Levant* (20 February 1815), but the battle opened at so close a range that the *Constitution*'s Marines were engaged almost from the beginning. Afterward, the ship's captain commended them for their "lively and well-directed fire."[19] In the action between the sloops-of-war USS *Hornet* and HMS *Penguin* (23 March 1815), the latter's captain was picked off as he closed with the intention of boarding. His first lieutenant succeeded in laying the *Penguin* alongside the *Hornet,* but the British seamen, apparently impressed by American musketry, ignored the call for boarders. The *Penguin* surrendered minutes later.

The War of 1812 also included the first—and to date the last—naval battle in which a Marine commanded the American ship engaged. In February 1813 Capt. David Porter took the frigate *Essex* around Cape Horn to attack the British whaling fleet in the South Pacific. Over the next few months the *Essex* took so many British vessels that Porter ran short of naval officers to use as prize captains, and in May he assigned his Marine officer, 1st Lt. James Marshall Gamble, to command the *Greenwich,* a whaler armed with ten guns. "[T]o make up for his want of nautical knowledge," Porter explained, "I put two expert seamen with him as mates."[20] On 14 July the *Greenwich* defeated the fourteen-gun British whaler *Seringapatam* while within sight of the *Essex*—and a very nervous David Porter. In a letter written to Gamble a few days later, a friend in the frigate told him that

Capt. Porter chewed as much tobacco and kept his poor spyglass as constantly employed as ever I knew him to. At one time, when the *Seringapatam* tacked, Capt. Porter became more anxious than ever; fearful you would tack at the same time and receive a raking shot, he exclaimed, "Now, Mr. Gamble, if you'll only stand on five minutes and then tack, I'll make you a prince." You stood on a while, when he again

The part the *Wasp*'s Marines played in her engagement with HMS *Reindeer* is illustrated in a modern painting by Sgt. John Clymer, USMC. Art Collection, Marine Corps Historical Center

exclaimed: "Now is your time"; just when we observed your ship in stays [in the process of tacking], which gave you the raking shot that did the enemy so much injury. So now, my dear fellow, you stand a chance of being princed, knighted, or something else. The Captain was much pleased.[21]

Not all naval actions took place on the high seas. The two of greatest strategic significance, both American victories, were fought on inland waters: the Battles of Lake Erie (10 September 1813) and Lake Champlain (11 September 1814). By winning control of Lake Erie, Commo. Oliver Hazard Perry frustrated British plans to block American expansion into the Ohio Valley; by defeating Britain's attempt to win control of Lake Champlain, Commo. Thomas Macdonough repulsed the major enemy offensive of the war, an invasion from Canada by ten thousand veteran troops. Thirty-four Leathernecks served in Perry's ships at Lake Erie. Four

were killed in action or died of wounds, and another fourteen were wounded. Among the dead was their commander, 2nd Lt. John Brooks. Mangled by a British cannonball, he begged for someone to put him out of his misery before succumbing to shock or loss of blood. There were no Marines in Macdonough's squadron at Lake Champlain, but the army detailed soldiers to perform their duties.

The invasion from Canada was only one element of the offensive that the wind-down of the war with France enabled Britain to mount against the United States in 1814. The other was the dispatch of an amphibious striking force—fifty-four hundred men under Maj. Gen. Robert Ross—to raid American cities with the aim of diverting troops from the invasion front and undermining support for the war. Convoyed by a squadron stronger than the entire U.S. Navy, Ross's army landed at the

John Marshall Gamble, circa 1815, in a contemporary painting by Samuel Lovett Waldo. Art Collection, Marine Corps Historical Center

Patuxent River town of Benedict, Maryland, on 19 August and marched north toward Washington.

The forces available to Brig. Gen. William H. Winder to defend the capital consisted of approximately fifty-five hundred militia, a single regiment of regular infantry, and a naval brigade led by Commo. Joshua Barney. As commander of the Chesapeake gunboat flotilla, Barney had vainly contested the British advance up the Patuxent. Once the action passed him by, he struck out overland for Washington with the flotilla's 420 seamen and Marines and five guns, plus a detachment of 103 Marines that Wharton had sent from the Washington barracks under the Corps's adjutant and inspector, Capt. Samuel Miller, to support the flotilla's operations.

The armies made contact on the west bank of the Eastern Branch of the Potomac (today's Anacostia River) opposite the village of Bladensburg on 24 August. There were, in effect, two battles of Bladensburg. The first, and the only one the Americans had any possibility of winning, had already been lost by poor generalship and panicky militia before the naval brigade, which Winder had neglected to order forward, reached the field.

Barney formed a front along a ridge that crossed the Washington Turnpike approximately a mile behind the original American line. Two 18-pounders under Barney's personal command were sited to fire directly down the pike; the three 12-pounders, assigned to Captain Miller, were wheeled into a field to the right. The seamen and Marines not detailed to serve the guns deployed into a firing line. Other late-coming units aligned on the brigade's flanks: militia on the right, the regular infantry regiment and more militia, including a battery of five guns, on the left.

Flushed with their easy victory in the battle's opening round, the British attacked straight down the pike. The artillery and musket fire that slammed into their ranks from the ridgeline drove them back in surprise. Quickly re-forming, they came on again, only to suffer another repulse. A third assault, bravely mounted minutes later, met the same fate. Barney seized the moment to counterattack, and the bloodied British regiments to his front gave ground to the brigade's seamen (shouting, "Board 'em! Board 'em!") and Marines.[22]

Hurrying to the scene with reinforcements, General Ross ordered his troops to work around the American flanks. He need not have bothered. Almost simultaneously General Winder, intent on saving whatever he could of his army, directed the units there to retire. Inexcusably, he omitted to notify Commodore Barney. Soon the naval brigade found itself under fire from three directions. Barney took a bad wound in the thigh. Captain Miller, himself handling a musket, was hit in the arm by a British soldier with whom he was exchanging shots. Seeing that the situation had become hopeless, Barney gave the order to spike the guns and retreat. Both he and Miller were captured.

On meeting Barney, General Ross complimented him on his command's gallant stand. The compliment was well deserved. Of the 249 British casualties at Bladensburg, nearly all occurred during the second phase of the action. The same was true of the approximately 150 American casualties, the Marines' share of which was eight dead and fourteen wounded. And in a sense, it had been for nothing. There was never any realistic chance that the naval brigade and the neighboring units could hold off Ross's army. Yet in a larger sense, the fight they put up achieved a great deal. It did not save the national capital, but it saved the national honor.

Lieutenant Colonel Wharton remained at the Marine barracks during the battle. When it became known that the redcoats were coming, he collected his headquarters detachment, the Marine Band, and the Corps's records and pay chest and marched to the Washington Navy Yard. Despite an order from the secretary of the Navy to withdraw to Frederick, Maryland, the fleeing government's designated refuge, Wharton volunteered to assist Commo. Thomas Tingey in the yard's defense or destruction. Tingey declined the offer, and Wharton proceeded to Frederick. He was, of course, only following orders; but a number of the Corps's fire-eating young officers found his failure to do something more inexcusable.

After burning Washington's public buildings (but not, for unknown reasons, the Marine barracks and the commandant's house), the British army returned to its ships. Its next objective was Baltimore. Among the ten thousand defenders—again, mostly militia—hurriedly concentrated in anticipation of the attack was a thousand-man naval brigade including the Marines who had fought at Bladensburg and detachments from several nearby ships and stations. The British landed southeast of the city on 12 September, but no new Bladensburg ensued. The militia they encountered stood firm; an American sniper killed General Ross; and the British ships' fire failed to subdue Fort McHenry at the entrance of the harbor. On 14 September the invaders withdrew.

Following this check, the British assembled an even more powerful amphibious force for their next operation. This time the target was New Orleans. The expedition anchored off the Louisiana coast on 8 December. Rather than sail upstream against the strong Mississippi River current, the British chose to approach the city via Lake Borgne, an arm of the Gulf of Mexico. Their passage was contested by five U.S. gunboats embarking 147 seamen and thirty-five Marines. On 14 December these vessels were carried in hand-to-hand fighting by British boat parties numbering nearly a thousand men, but Maj. Gen. Andrew Jackson used the time they had bought him to strengthen the defense of New Orleans.

Ashore, Major Carmick's Marines took part in each of

This engraving of a Marine officer in full rig, published in 1823 after an 1819 painting by 2nd Lt. C. R. Floyd, USMC, is among the earliest images of a member of the Corps. Note the Mameluke sword.

the ensuing actions: Jackson's night attack on the British advance guard on 23 December; British exploratory attacks on 28 December and 1 January 1815; and the British grand assault, which was shot to pieces on 8 January. But after 28 December the Marines were no longer led by Daniel Carmick. Before the battle he had been placed at the head of a battalion of New Orleans volunteers. There, an observer recorded, "he was struck by a rocket, which tore his horse to pieces, and wounded the Major in the arm and head."[23] The Leathernecks completed the campaign under the command of 1st Lt. F. B. De Bellevue. Carmick died in 1816, perhaps as a result of his wounds. At the time, he was the senior Marine officer after Wharton. Had he lived, he would no doubt have succeeded him as commandant, and thereby spared the Corps the embarrassment of Anthony Gale. Tragically, all the deaths resulting from the Battle of New Orleans were unnecessary. U.S. and British negotiators meeting in Belgium had signed a peace treaty restoring the prewar status quo on 24 December.

In the War of 1812, U.S. Marines cemented the reputation to which they had laid claim in earlier conflicts as first-class fighting men. If their overall casualties were not heavy—forty-six dead and thirty-three wounded—they were proportionate to those suffered by the seamen and soldiers with whom Marine detachments served. Congressional approval of the Corps's performance was evident in two acts passed in 1814. One raised its authorized strength to ninety-three officers and 2,622 men, an increase of more than 60 percent; the other made Marine officers eligible for brevet promotions for "gallant actions or meritorious conduct" or after having spent ten years in grade. The six officers who received brevets during or for the war included Capt. Samuel Miller, the hero of Bladensburg, and the commander of the *Constitution*'s Marines during her action with the *Cyane* and *Levant,* Capt. Archibald Henderson.

Operationally, the years following the War of 1812 were relatively quiet for the Corps. Marine guards sailed in the two squadrons sent to the Mediterranean in 1815 to chastise the Barbary powers, which (Morocco excepted) had taken advantage of the Navy's wartime absence to begin misbehaving, but after four U.S. ships gobbled up an Algerine frigate, the offenders peaceably acceded to American demands. Nearer home, in Spanish East Florida, Marine detachments took part in expeditions that destroyed pirate lairs on the Apalachicola River in 1816 and Amelia Island in 1817. In March of the latter year Congress imposed the first of what would become routine postwar cutbacks on the Corps, passing a Peace Establishment Act that reduced its authorized strength to fifty officers and 865 NCOs and men.

Institutionally, the same years were anything but quiet. A number of Marine officers considered Lieu-tenant Colonel Commandant Wharton's failure to take the field against the British an act of rankest cowardice. None was more disgusted than Bvt. Maj. Archibald Henderson, who in 1817 preferred charges that brought Wharton before a court-martial. There were two specifications: neglect of duty and conduct unbecoming an officer and a gentleman, in that he had declined to take steps to silence criticism of his actions in 1814 "so highly injurious to his own character and of great disadvantage to the Corps." The court acquitted Wharton on both charges. But the commandant did not have long to savor his vindication. The following year he sickened, and on 1 September he died.

With Wharton's demise, thirty-six-year-old Bvt. Maj. Anthony Gale, the duelist Burrows had commended for shooting Lieutenant McKenzie, became the Corps's senior officer. Irish by birth, Gale joined the Marine Corps in September 1798, served afloat in the Quasi-War and the War with Tripoli, commanded the Philadelphia barracks, and took part in the defense of Baltimore. His brevet rank had been awarded in 1814 in virtue of ten years in grade.

As seniority alone generally governed promotions and appointments in the U.S. armed forces, it might have been expected that Gale would be named to succeed Wharton as promptly as Wharton had been picked to succeed Burrows. Instead, six months passed, during which Archibald Henderson served as acting commandant. The delay was clearly caused by doubts raised by Henderson and Bvt. Maj. Samuel Miller regarding Gale's fitness to occupy the Corps's premier post, for which they considered themselves eminently qualified. Henderson stood second on the seniority list; if Gale was passed over, he would have the strongest claim to the appointment. Miller, whose efforts to promote his own candidacy permanently alienated Henderson, was sixth on the seniority list, but he had Bladensburg and at least one highly impressed congressman in his favor. The uncertainty culminated in a court of inquiry convened in February 1819 to investigate updates of two charges of which Gale had been cleared by a court of inquiry in 1816: misuse of government funds and "conduct unbecoming" by being drunk on duty. At the close of its hearings the court ruled that neither charge had been upheld, and on 3 March

Anthony Gale was appointed commandant of the Marine Corps.

Lamentably, the accusation of intemperance was justified. In the summer of 1820 Gale came to cross-purposes with Secretary of the Navy Smith Thompson, who granted some Marines furloughs without consulting him. Gale thereupon wrote to the secretary seeking to clarify their command relationship. Thompson responded by countermanding two of the commandant's officer personnel assignments. This frustrating situation set Gale off on a colossal jag, during which he was arrested by the police. Another court-martial ensued, and on 18 October Gale was dismissed from the Corps. He died in obscurity in 1843. Today unhappy Anthony Gale is the only deceased commandant of the Marine Corps whose gravesite is unknown.[24]

4

The Era of Archibald Henderson, 1820–1859

Fortunately, as it turned out, the Gale affair did not shake official faith in appointment by seniority, and effective 17 October 1820 Archibald Henderson became commandant of the Marine Corps. Samuel Miller cannot have been surprised by his new commander's ready acceptance of his resignation of the post of adjutant and inspector.

Born at the village of Colchester, Virginia, a few miles from present-day Quantico, in January 1783, Henderson had begun his career as a second lieutenant at the age of twenty-three. He was then a slender, red-haired, soldierly, and extremely ambitious young man. Both before and after the War of 1812, dissatisfaction with his prospects of advancement had caused him to seriously consider leaving the Corps. His efforts to oust Wharton from the commandancy and to prevent Gale from ascending to it have been recounted. Now Henderson had attained his goal, and in the nick of time. Although the Corps retained a reservoir of goodwill from its performance in the War of 1812, the problems that had surrounded the office of commandant ever since the Battle of Bladensburg had undermined the authority of its headquarters. Strong leadership was urgently needed. Archibald Henderson provided it for the next thirty-eight years.

Henderson acted swiftly to restore the authority of Marine Corps headquarters, insisting on the sanctity of the chain of command. When in 1822 Samuel Miller moved President Monroe to countermand an order from Henderson sending him to sea, Henderson responded to the president's intervention by offering to resign. Soon Washington officialdom as well as the Corps's officers came to realize that this was a commandant who could not be ignored.

Henderson took an abiding interest in the Corps's personnel. He was especially concerned with increasing the quality and professionalism of its officers, many of whom owed their commissions to political patronage rather than martial aptitude. This goal could be accomplished, he believed, by recruiting graduates of the U.S. Military Academy; but his repeated requests for permission to do so were denied. Refused that remedy, Henderson carefully monitored the accession of applicants from civil life and continued the practice of ordering all newly commissioned officers to the Washington barracks for orientation and training. He was also prepared to eliminate the unfit. Under his predecessors, a Marine officer had been cashiered or dismissed on the average of once every four and a half years; under Henderson, the frequency of such actions nearly doubled.

Stern as he was with the Corps's officers, Henderson showed much sympathy for the Spartan lot of its NCOs and men. To make enlisted service less onerous—and thereby, he hoped, to reduce the chronically high desertion rate and facilitate recruiting—he made Sunday a day of rest; abolished flogging ashore two decades before the Navy abolished it afloat; provided better barracks; and secured at least modest increases in pay and allowances for fuel, clothing, and rations. Although these measures must have been appreciated by long-service Leathernecks, they failed to produce the anticipated institutional

Archibald Henderson, circa 1811–1820, in a contemporary painting by Gilbert Stuart. Art Collection, Marine Corps Historical Center

at the time he entered the Corps: providing security for the Navy's yards and furnishing ships' guards to discourage mutiny, scour enemy decks with musket fire, and contribute a contingent of trained light infantry to naval landing parties. Yet, in another respect, Henderson was an innovator. Throughout his years as commandant he maintained a battalion—because of the constant manpower crunch, a very small battalion—at Eighth and Eye as a force in readiness capable of deploying at a moment's notice. This practice was to pay rich dividends in terms of both service to the country and the renown of the Corps.

The Corps's renown was of great concern to Henderson, not merely as a matter of institutional pride but also of existence. While Americans no longer questioned their nation's need for an Army and Navy, some regarded its Marine Corps as an extravagance that should be absorbed by one of the larger services. Henderson understood that his Leathernecks' survival would depend on the esteem in which they were held by members of the public—at least those with political influence—and in the halls of Congress. He overlooked no opportunity to enhance that esteem.

Like his predecessors, Henderson encouraged the activities of the Marine Band, which became even more popular following the appointment of Francis Marie Scala, a Neapolitan clarinetist, as bandmaster in 1845. But Henderson never forgot that in the final analysis, the Corps's reputation rested on Marines' performance in battle. The United States engaged in two major conflicts —the Seminole War and the Mexican War—while he was commandant. He saw to it that Marines had the chance to enter battle in both.

Aside from their operations in the course of those conflicts, Leathernecks made more than forty landings during Henderson's decades at their head. The earliest occurred in the Caribbean, where in the 1820s the U.S. Navy and the Royal Navy collaborated to suppress the piracy that still flourished off the coasts of Cuba, Puerto Rico, and Central America. At the peak of the American effort, in 1823–24, three hundred Marines were serving with the West India Squadron. A number of minor actions occurred afloat and ashore, but the pirates were no match for regular naval forces, and the Corps's

benefits. Desertion remained rampant, and even by bending regulations the Corps was never able to enlist the number of men it was authorized. In addition to the steps Henderson took to retain men already onboard, he ceaselessly campaigned for authority to recruit more. At first Congress turned a deaf ear, but eventually his persistence began to be rewarded. By the time Henderson died in harness, the Corps's establishment stood at sixty-three officers and 2,010 NCOs and men, more than double its strength at the date he had become commandant.

What Henderson viewed as Marines' bread-and-butter missions were the same ones they had been performing participation in the campaign, virtually concluded by 1826, passed almost unnoticed.

In contrast, the suppression of the Massachusetts State Prison revolt of 1824 by Marines from the Boston Navy Yard brought the Corps a public relations bonanza. An account of the incident caught the eye of William Holmes McGuffey, who found in it an illustration of the virtues promoted by his ubiquitous *Readers*. As a result, a Marine officer became an exemplar of courage, coolness, and compassion to three-quarters of a century of American schoolchildren.

The trouble began when prison officials announced that three inmates were to be flogged for violating regulations. In protest, 283 prisoners armed with hammers, chisels, and other tools from the prison workshops seized control of the dining hall and declared that they would not disperse until the sentence had been remitted. After the guards' attempts to persuade the convicts to return to work had been rebuffed, they sent a message to the commander of the Marine barracks, Bvt. Maj. Robert D. Wainwright, requesting his assistance in restoring order. A veteran of seventeen years in the Corps, Wainwright soon arrived at the head of a detachment of Marines. The prison authorities suggested that he have his men open fire on the convicts through the dining hall's high windows, at first with powder only, and then, should that prove unavailing, with ball cartridge. Wainwright demurred. Instead, he led the Leathernecks into the dining hall and informed the prisoners that he had been instructed to quell the insurrection. They replied that they were ready to die where they stood. *McGuffey's Reader* continued:

> Major Wainwright now ordered his Marines to load their pieces, and that they might not be suspected of trifling, each man was told to hold up to view the bullet which he afterwards put into his gun. This only caused a growl of determination, and no one blanched. . . . They knew that their numbers would enable them to bear down and destroy the handful of Marines, after the first discharge.
>
> The Marines were ordered to take aim; their guns were presented; but not a prisoner stirred, except to grasp more firmly his weapon. Still desirous, if possible, to avoid such a slaughter as must follow the discharge of the guns, the major advanced a step or two, and spoke even more firmly than before, urging them to depart. Again . . . they declared their in-

tention of fighting it out. The intrepid officer then took out his watch and told his men to hold their pieces aimed at the prisoners, but not to fire till they had orders. Then, turning to the convicts, he said, "You must leave this hall. I give you three minutes to decide. If at the end of that time a man remains, he shall be shot dead. I speak no more."

> No more tragic situation than this can be conceived: at one end of the hall a fearless multitude of desperate and powerful men waiting for the assault; at the other a little band of well-disciplined Marines, waiting with leveled muskets . . . and their tall commander holding up his watch to count the lapse of the three allotted minutes. For two minutes not a person or a muscle moved; not a sound was heard except the labored breathing of the infuriated wretches. . . . At the expiration of the two minutes, . . . two or three of those in the rear, and nearest to the further entrance, went slowly out; a few more followed their example, dropping out quietly and deliberately; and before half the last minute was gone, every man was struck by panic, and crowded for the exit, and the hall cleared as if by magic. Thus the steady firmness of moral force, and the strong effect of deliberate determination, cowed the most daring men, and prevented a scene of carnage which would have instantly followed the least precipitancy or exertion of physical force.[1]

The potential value of such publicity became fully apparent in December 1829 when President Andrew Jackson sent Congress a message recommending that the Marine Corps should be merged into the Army. The president's action was provoked by a treasury audit which found that although the Corps was about the same size as an infantry regiment, it cost at least two and a half times as much a year to maintain—between $185,000 and $220,00 versus $75,000. The difference was to a considerable extent due to officer pay and allowances. By 1829, for example, the Corps included no fewer than five brevet lieutenant colonels, "who," the president acidly noted, "receive the full pay and emoluments of their brevet rank, without rendering proportionate service."[2]

Jackson's proposal became the subject of hearings in both houses of Congress the following year. Testifying in its favor before the Senate Naval Affairs Committee, Secretary of the Navy John Branch candidly presented the results of an informal survey of senior naval officers showing that some believed Marines were no longer needed onboard American warships, but others considered them invaluable. The president's recommendation died in committee. That was not the end of the matter, however. Late in 1831 a new secretary of the Navy, Levi Woodbury, renewed the contest by proposing that the Corps should be either abolished or absorbed by the Army or the Navy. Congress again declined to act, but the Corps's future was still clouded when, a few months later, a landing party of bluejackets and Leathernecks became engaged in the most spirited action fought by U.S. naval forces since 1815.

On 7 February 1831 Malays from the settlement at Quallah Battoo (Kuala Batu) on the northwestern coast of Sumatra plundered the trader *Friendship* out of Salem and murdered three of her crewmen. Immediately on receipt of the news, the forty-four-gun frigate *Potomac,* then in New York harbor under the command of Commo. John Downes, was ordered to proceed to the scene and exact retribution. She sailed on 27 August.

The *Potomac* dropped anchor off Quallah Battoo on 5 February 1832. That afternoon a group of officers made a close inshore reconnaissance in one of the ship's boats. The landing party, 286 seamen and Marines under the ship's executive officer, Lt. Irvine Shubrick, disembarked early the next morning. Organized and drilled on the long voyage out, the party consisted of three divisions of seamen, each headed by a Navy lieutenant, and the *Potomac*'s Marine guard, led by 1st Lt. Alvin Edson and 2nd Lt. George H. Terrett—a young man destined to see as much combat as any Leatherneck of his generation—plus an artillery detachment of sailors hauling a 6-pounder affectionately known as Betsy Baker.

Landing shortly before dawn, the party fanned out to attack the three forts that had been identified by the previous afternoon's reconnaissance. These were substantial works, with citadels built on elevated platforms mounting small cannons. Shubrick took the first and third seaman divisions to assault the largest fort. The second division and the Marine detachment were each assigned to storm one of the others. The Malays proved to be formidable adversaries, "fighting with . . . undaunted firmness," wrote a member of the landing party, "and displaying such an utter carelessness of life as would have been honored in a better cause."[3]

The two lesser forts were soon captured. The principal work continued to hold out even after the Leathernecks and the second seaman division joined Shubrick's force outside its walls. Eventually their combined fire, augmented by Betsy Baker's grapeshot, cut down most of the defenders, and the citadel was carried by a rush. A fourth, previously unobserved, fort at the edge of the jungle then opened fire, but was promptly overrun by seamen and Marines. After torching the forts and the village, the landing party withdrew. Two of its members had been killed and eleven wounded, including four Marines. The Malays were estimated to have lost 150 dead, among them Rajah Po Mahomet, whom American traders considered the area's chief malefactor. Later that day the *Potomac* bombarded the ruins of Quallah Battoo, and in the afternoon a Malay delegation paddled to the frigate and professed the desire to establish amicable relations with the United States.

The extent to which Congress was influenced by reports of Marines' prowess at Quallah Battoo can only be conjectured, but in June 1834 the Jackson administration's ongoing challenge to the Corps was quashed by the passage of an act that enjoyed Archibald Henderson's blessing "for the better organization of the Marine Corps." Until that date Marines had been subject to the Army's Articles of War while ashore and Navy Regulations while afloat. The act's most important feature eliminated this anomaly by defining the Corps as an individual sea service, distinct from the Navy but within the Navy Department and governed by Navy Regulations—a status it retains today. Other provisions raised the rank attached to the office of commandant to full colonel and increased the Corps's authorized strength to sixty-three officers and 1,224 NCOs and men. Inevitably, there were trade-offs. Marine officers were made subordinate to Navy officers of equivalent rank, even if the latter were junior in date of rank, and the practice of granting officers brevet promotions after ten years in grade was discontinued; henceforth, brevets would be awarded solely for distinguished conduct. Finally, the act expressly confirmed the power previously vested in the president to attach the Marine Corps to the Army in time of need.

The attack on Quallah Battoo has been tidied up in this contemporary woodcut.

Two years later, Henderson took advantage of the latter provision to commit the Corps to a land campaign. In 1830 Congress passed the Indian Removal Act, which directed the government to encourage and assist tribes residing in the eastern United States to move west of the Mississippi. Seven chiefs representing the Florida Seminoles subsequently consented to the removal. Afterward several of them claimed to have signed the treaty under duress, and by the time the exodus was scheduled to begin, the majority of the Seminoles were strongly opposed to leaving Florida. War broke out on 28 December 1835 when two companies of troops under Maj. Francis L. Dade were attacked and destroyed while on the march from Fort Brooke (the site of present-day Tampa) to Fort King, one hundred miles to the northeast. Although Seminole warriors numbered at the most fourteen hundred, their canny tactics and superb field craft, coupled with the support of numerous escaped slaves and the difficulty of the terrain, made the conflict the longest and most costly Indian war the United States ever waged.

The following spring, three bands of Creek Indians staged an uprising in southern Georgia and eastern Al-

abama. Marines were already serving in the Seminole War at that time: ships' guards had gone ashore to reinforce Fort Brooke following the Dade massacre, and others continued to take part in the Navy's patrol of the Florida coast; but with the spread of hostilities Henderson concluded that the Corps could do more. In May 1836 he volunteered to muster a regiment of Marines to serve with the Army in the Creek campaign. On the twenty-third of the month, President Jackson accepted the offer.

Using the force he maintained at Eighth and Eye as a nucleus, Henderson was able to assemble a four-hundred-man battalion ready to take to the field in just ten days. Washington's *National Intelligencer* must have been almost embarrassing in its praise of the deployment, which it called "another striking evidence of the great value of this arm of the national defense; it has shown itself as prompt to defend its country on the land as on the water."[4] On 1 June the battalion began its movement to the theater of war with Henderson at its head. As second in command he took his old bête noire, Bvt. Lt. Col. Samuel Miller. Legend holds that Henderson posted a note on his office door: "Gone to fight the

City of Washington from beyond the Navy Yard, a painting by G. Cooke, circa 1834, copied as an aquatint by W. J. Bennett. The flag flies over Marine Barracks, Washington. The original painting hangs in the Blair-Lee House, Washington, D.C. Library of Congress

Indians. Will be back when the war is over."[5] A second battalion of 160 men drawn from northeastern Navy yards followed within days.

Henderson's battalion spent the summer in a camp named for its commander fifteen miles south of Columbus, Georgia. Despite aggressive patrolling, the Marines failed to make a firm hostile contact before the recalcitrant Creeks were subdued. The second battalion proceeded to Fort Mitchell, Alabama, but was soon transferred to northern Florida. Henderson's battalion joined it there in late August, and the two were consolidated into a six-company regiment that sailed from Apalachicola to Fort Brooke in October. Of the regular troops in Bvt. Maj. Gen. Thomas S. Jesup's Army of the South at the end of November, Leathernecks accounted for 18 of 76 officers and 303 of 1,681 NCOs and men.

On 22 January 1837, the Army advanced eastward into central Florida from a position near the Dade battleground. Jesup had placed Henderson in command of one of its brigades, a force consisting of a mounted battalion of Alabama volunteers, a battalion of friendly Creeks, and a company of mounted Marines (the original "horse Marines") under Capt. John Harris. On the morning of the twenty-seventh, scouts found numerous Indian signs on the prairies west of Hatcheelustee Creek, not far from today's Disney World. Jesup ordered Henderson's brigade forward to reconnoiter. The result was the only battle in which a serving commandant of the Marine Corps has exercised tactical command.

Henderson's advanced guard soon struck a Seminole camp, capturing five Indian women and children, nineteen runaway black slaves, and more than one hundred ponies. The remainder of the Indians had fled into the nearby Big Cypress Swamp. The troops plunged in after them. As was invariably the case when Seminole camps were taken by surprise, the warriors' only interest was in delaying their pursuers long enough to allow their families to escape. A quarter of a mile inside the swamp they made a stand behind the Hatcheelustee, a deep creek twenty to twenty-five yards wide bridged by two fallen trees. Henderson deployed his men to the right and left to establish a crossfire on the enemy bank, and Captain Harris and three other officers scrambled across the trunks, followed by their men. Seeing another officer swim the creek, Henderson set out to do the same, but quickly concluded that he had better use a tree trunk.

Deeper inside the Big Cypress the Seminoles made another brief stand. From that point their trail led out of the swamp and through a pine woods before doubling back to reenter the swamp three quarters of a mile away. Henderson and his men followed. Twice more the warriors paused to exchange fire with their pursuers, breaking contact when the troops came too close. A black family of three was captured shortly after the last of these encounters. By then it was four o'clock in the afternoon, and Henderson decided to regroup his scattered command.

During the day's fighting, the troops passed the bodies of one Seminole and two blacks. Otherwise, hostile casualties were unknown. All of Henderson's losses were Leathernecks: two dead and four wounded, and all of the wounded soon died. In his after-action report Henderson praised the conduct of his entire command, but he could not resist paying special tribute to the Marines. "The killed and wounded show where they were," he wrote.[6]

Few Seminoles lost their lives or freedom at the Hatcheelustee, but the battle gave them a considerable shock. Within a week their chiefs entered negotiations that, though ultimately unsuccessful, caused many persons, Jesup and Henderson included, to believe that the war was as good as over. Furthermore, Henderson felt that it was time to be getting back to Eighth and Eye. Jesup granted his request with a gracious commendation, and late in May Henderson set out for Washington with four of his six companies. The other two, organized as a little battalion under Samuel Miller, remained at Fort Brooke. In July, Miller was relieved by Capt. William Dulany, whose detachment served in Florida until April 1838.

Marine operations on the Florida mainland were not over, however. In April 1839 the Navy detached the assortment of small craft and open boats being used to patrol the lower peninsula from the West India Squadron and established an autonomous Florida Expedition ("for the Suppression of Indian Hostilities"), promptly dubbed the Mosquito Fleet, based on Tea Table Key. By that date most of the Seminoles who had not been killed or captured had retired into the watery fastness of the Everglades. Lt. John T. McLaughlin assumed command of the Mosquito Fleet in January 1840 with a fierce determination to penetrate that refuge. The 622 officers and men that his force numbered at peak strength included two companies of Marines, successively commanded by 1st Lts. George H. Terrett (who had also served in Henderson's regiment) and Thomas T. Sloan.

Beginning in April 1840, the men of the Mosquito Fleet made numerous expeditions into the Everglades and waterways to the north, frequently in concert with Army units. On 31 December 1840, a party of 150 seamen and Marines under McLaughlin's personal com-

In 1840 *U.S. Military Magazine* published this lithograph of a Marine sentry on duty on the Capitol grounds. The monument behind him, in memory of the naval officers killed in the War with Tripoli, was later moved to the U.S. Naval Academy.

mand left Fort Dallas (where downtown Miami now stands) to become the first white men to cross the Everglades, emerging on the Gulf coast on 19 January 1841. McLaughlin crossed the swamp again in November 1841, and detachments were constantly on patrol between December 1841 and March 1842. Although the troops encountered few Indians on those forays, they destroyed many cultivated fields, dwellings, and canoes. Losses to hostile action were next to nil, but disease and extreme exertion often incapacitated as many as a quarter of the members of an expedition.

The Seminoles never surrendered, but by May 1842 fewer than four hundred were believed to remain at large, and U.S. forces simply suspended operations. Three Marine officers were awarded brevets for their services in the struggle: Henderson to brigadier general and Capt. John Harris to major, both for gallant and meritorious conduct, and Capt. William Dulany to major for meritorious conduct.

The Seminole War was Samuel Miller's last campaign. At age seventy he volunteered for active service on the outbreak of the Mexican War. By then he had become the Corps's lieutenant colonel, but Henderson decided that he was a little old for field soldiering. The hero of Bladensburg died in 1855, still in uniform at age eighty.

By the start of the Seminole War the U.S. Navy had established six overseas squadrons: the Mediterranean Squadron (reestablished in 1815), the Africa Squadron (1820), the West India Squadron (1821), the Pacific Squadron (1821), the Brazil Squadron (1826), and the East India Squadron (1835). None was very sizable; at times a squadron might consist of no more than a pair of ships. Nevertheless, they enabled the Navy to act in what contemporaries considered an expeditious manner to protect American commerce, lives, and property—and to retaliate for attacks on them—in potentially difficult or dangerous parts of the world.

The Navy's nearly global presence was reflected in the geographical range of the landings in which Leathernecks participated from 1835 to 1846. Of these operations, one took place in South America (1835), one in the East Indies (1839), four in the South Pacific (two each in 1840 and 1841), one in the Mexican province of Upper California (1842), five on the west coast of Africa (1843), one in China (1844), and one in Vietnam (1845). Six landings—in the East Indies, the South Pacific, and one in Africa—were punitive in nature, usually involving an action with native warriors and invariably climaxing in the burning of one or more villages; the others passed off peacefully. All but three were undertaken directly or indirectly in support of American trade. The exceptions were the short-lived seizure of Monterey, California, by the commodore of the Pacific Squadron, Thomas ap Catesby Jones, under the erroneous impression that war had broken out with Mexico (a miscue that cost him his command); a landing in West Africa, where a local tribe was menacing the American black settlement of Liberia; and a confused attempt to rescue a French missionary from his Vietnamese captors.

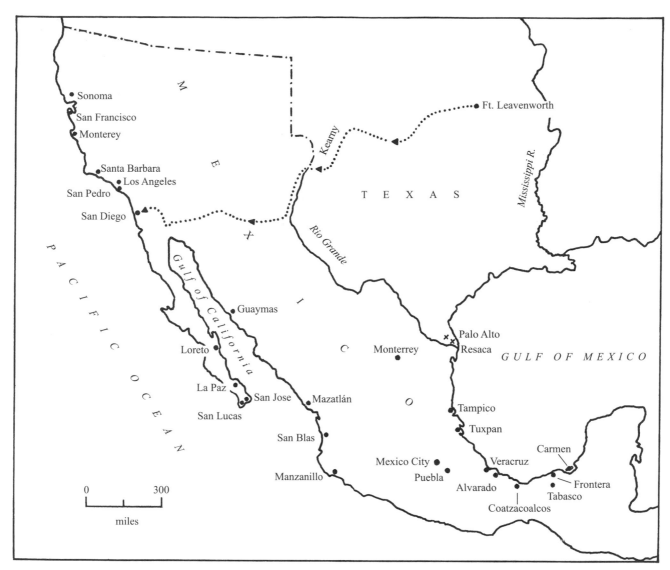

The Mexican War, 1846–1848

Commodore Jones had jumped the gun, but three years to the month after he relinquished Monterey the Marine Corps was represented, in the redoubtable person of 1st Lt. Archibald H. Gillespie, in the onset of the real war with Mexico. In March 1845 Congress voted to annex the Republic of Texas, which Mexico regarded as a wayward province. Whether or not the outrage this action engendered in Mexico City would result in war was uncertain. Yet the expansionist administration of incoming President James K. Polk was not content with Texas. Polk also harbored designs on California and a lively apprehension that Britain did the same.

In the fall of 1845 Polk decided on a policy calculated to lead to the acquisition of California without overtly in-

volving his administration in an act of aggression. Americans in the province should secretly be encouraged to revolt against Mexico and discouraged from accepting the protection of any power other than the United States. The next step was to communicate this policy to the man who would presumably be responsible for carrying it out, Thomas O. Larkin, the U.S. consul at Monterey. Of course, instructions could be and were sent by ship, but the long voyage around Cape Horn might take nine months. The fastest way to get a message to California would be for its bearer to make two much shorter voyages by proceeding overland across Mexico from the Gulf port of Veracruz to the Pacific port of Mazatlán. In view of the contents of this particular message, that was not an itinerary for the faint of heart. Lieutenant Gillespie set out on the journey early in November.

Gillespie had received his instructions at a secret meeting with Polk in the White House on 30 October. He was also charged with delivering a packet of personal letters to Army Capt. John C. Frémont, the son-in-law of powerful Senator Thomas Hart Benton, then leading an exploring expedition to the Pacific. An energetic, red-bearded thirty-three-year-old, Gillespie had served briefly as an enlisted Marine before being commissioned. Nine of his thirteen years' service since then had been spent afloat. He had yet to see combat. How Polk came to select him for this mission is unknown. Gillespie was fluent in Spanish, obviously an important qualification, but other Spanish-speaking officers and officials were available.

Whatever his reasons, the president had made an excellent choice. Traveling in the guise of a salesman for MacDougal Distilleries, Ltd., of Edinburgh, Gillespie crossed Mexico without undue incident—he had prudently burned his instructions after committing them to memory en route to Veracruz—and reached Monterey on 17 April 1846. The ship carrying the duplicate dispatches did not arrive for another three months.

After conferring with Larkin, Gillespie rode north in search of Frémont. They met at Klamath Lake, Oregon, on 9 May. Neither man ever recorded exactly what passed between them, but the course of ensuing events makes clear that Gillespie gave Frémont a briefing on Polk's policy along with his letters. That night the Marine officer received his baptism of fire when he helped to beat off an Indian attack that left three of Frémont's sixty men dead. The next day the party headed south.

American settlers in California were already restive under Mexican rule. The return of Frémont's expedition, which the Mexican authorities had ordered out of the province earlier in the year, spurred them to take action. On 4 July, a gathering at Sonoma proclaimed the independence of the Bear Flag Republic. Frémont responded by organizing the California Battalion, 230 men strong. Gillespie accepted the appointment of captain and second in command.

The critical moment was clearly at hand. As early as 31 May the commander of the Pacific Squadron, ailing old Commo. John D. Sloat, had received unofficial reports that fighting had broken out between U.S. and Mexican forces in Texas, but, mindful of his predecessor's gaffe, he had waited to receive official notification before committing himself. The news that Frémont had thrown in with the Bear Flaggers convinced him he could wait no longer. Between 7 July and 6 August, ships of the Pacific Squadron landed parties that peacefully occupied Monterey, San Francisco, Santa Barbara, and San Pedro, peeling off a few Marines to garrison each, and deposited the California Battalion at San Diego. On 8 August Frémont advanced on the provincial capital of Los Angeles with 120 men, leaving Gillespie with 50 others to hold San Diego. Three days later vigorous Commo. Robert F. Stockton, who had replaced Sloat on 29 July, marched out of San Pedro at the head of 360 seamen and Marines bound for the same place. Both forces entered Los Angeles unopposed on 13 August. The handful of Mexican troops nearby surrendered the next day. California had been conquered in less than six weeks.

The conquest came undone just as quickly. Stockton divided California into three military districts. To command the southern district, with headquarters in Los Angeles, he installed Archibald Gillespie. That was a mistake. Gillespie's robust administration so antagonized Los Angeles's citizens that they rose in revolt. On 23 September Gillespie, with sixty Bear Flaggers, found himself besieged by several hundred irate Californians. Six days later he negotiated a capitulation that allowed his command to evacuate the town and march under arms to board a ship at San Pedro. The American garrisons also withdrew from Santa Barbara and San Diego.

The first attempt to recapture Los Angeles followed almost at once. During the siege one of Gillespie's men had slipped through Mexican lines carrying an appeal for help to Monterey. In response, Capt. William Mervine arrived at San Pedro in the frigate *Savannah* on 6 October. Gillespie's garrison was still onboard an American merchant ship in the harbor. Mervine decided to launch an immediate counteroffensive. Gillespie urged him not to act rashly. Most native Californians, feeling little love for the Mexican government, had sat out the original occupation, but now they were up in arms. Mervine ignored his advice. The next day 225 seamen and Marines from the *Savannah* marched on Los Angeles. The Leathernecks formed the column's advance guard; Gillespie's riflemen covered its flanks. On 8 October the Americans encountered some 130 mounted Californians. The Californians had one fieldpiece; the Americans had none. After three charges failed to capture the gun, which the Californians withdrew each time their adversaries approached, Mervine concluded that it was no go. Gillespie's detachment covered the retreat. It was then transported to San Diego.

In succeeding weeks Commodore Stockton made plans for a convergent advance on Los Angeles by a naval force under his command and Frémont's California Battalion. The former would set out from San Diego; the latter, from Santa Barbara. Before the commodore's preparations had been completed, a courier reached San Diego with startling news. Brig. Gen. Stephen W. Kearny, whose Army of the West had recently occupied New Mexico, had entered California with an escort of only one hundred dragoons with four guns, having heard that the territory was at peace. In less than two hours, Gillespie was riding east with thirty-nine men to guide Kearny to San Diego.

Gillespie joined Kearny on 5 December. Late that afternoon they learned that a troop of Californian cavalry was camped outside the nearby village of San Pasqual. The next morning the Americans attacked. Unfortunately, the attack was disjointed, and although the Californians were outnumbered two to one, the lances they carried proved far superior to the Americans' swords in the hand-to-hand combat that followed. Gillespie was unhorsed by a thrust that struck him in the back while he was parrying one in the front. Before he could get to his feet, he received another, deeper, thrust in the back and a glancing blow to the mouth. He finally escaped from the melee and fired one of the cannons; as a result (Gillespie insisted), the Californians retired. Nineteen Americans had been killed and fifteen wounded. One Californian was captured and about a dozen wounded. That night another messenger slipped away to San Diego, and on 10 December a relief column reached the battered command.

Meanwhile, another, apparently unconnected, revolt had broken out in the north. To put it down Capt. Ward Marston, twenty-seven years a Marine, marched out of San Francisco with thirty-four Leathernecks, sixty-seven volunteers, and one gun. On 2 January 1847 he defeated a slightly stronger Californian force near Mission Santa Clara. The next morning the Californians' leader appeared under a flag of truce and accepted an armistice that restored peace to the region.

A few days later, Stockton and Kearny fought the decisive battle in the war for California. They had advanced from San Diego with a heterogeneous collection of 607 men—Leathernecks, sailors, dismounted dragoons, elements of the California Battalion, and volunteers—on 28 December. The convalescent Gillespie commanded one of the four divisions into which these groups were organized. On 8 January the column encountered the Californian Army, a mounted force of approximately equal strength, posted on high ground beyond the San Gabriel River. The Americans formed square—the standard formation for infantry confronting cavalry—and forded the stream under fire from two guns. Just beyond the bank they unlimbered their own more powerful battery, which soon forced the enemy artillery to withdraw. Its shot also checked a body of 100–150 lancers that started toward the left face of the square. Stockton then ordered the advance to resume. While most of the Californians slowly gave ground, the band of lancers who had earlier been repulsed made a wide circuit of the square and charged its rear face, where Gillespie commanded, only to be repulsed by his men's musketry. Still, the Californians were not ready to concede defeat. Half a mile from their original position they rallied and brought their guns back into action. The fire superiority Stockton's artillery again established finally convinced them to call it a day. Both sides had suffered about a dozen casualties.

One more battle remained to be fought. Several hours after breaking camp the next morning, the Americans found the Californian Army, reduced by desertion to some three hundred men, deployed to oppose their advance across La Mesa, the broad plain south of the Los Angeles River. The action was essentially a repetition of its predecessor, on a smaller scale. The American guns overpowered the Californian artillery, and the lancers who charged the square were stopped eighty yards from its face. The following day Archibald Gillespie was given the honor of hoisting the same flag he had hauled down in September over Los Angeles's Government House. Frémont reached the town on 14 January, having stopped

Sword in hand, Commodore Stockton urges the Pacific Squadron's Leathernecks forward in *Bayonets at San Gabriel,* by Charles Waterhouse. Art Collection, Marine Corps Historical Center

en route to negotiate the surrender of the remnant of the Californian Army.

Following the reconquest of Upper California, the Navy turned its attention to Baja California and the Pacific coast of Mexico. Beginning in March 1847, parties of seamen and Marines were landed long enough to raise the flag, conclude conventions acknowledging American authority, and/or spike the guns at San José del Cabo, San Lucas, La Paz, and Loreto in Baja; and Guaymas, San Blas, and Manzanillo, Mexico. In July two companies of New York volunteers went ashore from the Pacific Squadron's storeship to occupy La Paz, the capital of Baja California, and in November the Navy seized Mazatlán, Mexico's second-largest port.

None of these operations was opposed, but Baja did not remain quiet. In early November rumors of an impending revolt led to the landing of two dozen Marines under 1st Lt. Charles Heywood at San José. The rumors proved to be true. The New Yorkers beat off three attacks on La Paz that

month, and at San José Heywood withstood two sieges, the first from 19 to 21 November 1847 and the second from 22 January to 14 February 1848. An offensive by the reinforced garrison of La Paz crushed the revolt in March. Leathernecks also took part in four clashes between naval landing parties and Mexican units in and around Guaymas between November 1847 and March 1848.

Despite the vast territory at stake, from a military standpoint the operations in the Californias and on the Pacific coast of Mexico were strictly a sideshow. President Polk expected the war to end not far from where it began, just inside the Rio Grande, with Maj. Gen. Zachary Taylor's victories at Palo Alto and Resaca de la Palma in May 1846. After receiving additional transport and reinforcements, Taylor advanced into Mexico and captured Monterrey, the capital of Nuevo León, in September. Successes such as these, together with the blockade the Navy's Home Squadron clamped on the Mexican coast, were supposed to convince the enemy that the sensible thing to do was

Lancers at La Mesa, by Charles Waterhouse, shows the repulse of the Californian cavalry by Archibald Gillespie's men. Art Collection, Marine Corps Historical Center

make peace. The Mexicans' refusal to accept that conclusion obliged the Americans to revise their strategy. Apparently it would be necessary to carry the war to Mexico City. For Taylor's army to cross the four hundred miles of difficult, barren terrain separating it from that objective was deemed impractical even by Taylor. His view clenched Polk's decision to adopt a plan proposed by Maj. Gen. Winfield Scott to execute an amphibious end-run to Veracruz, only two hundred miles east of the Mexican capital, and advance on it from there. In November, Scott was entrusted with conducting the campaign.

In the meantime, the Home Squadron had launched the first in a series of smaller amphibious operations in which its Leathernecks would see action along the Gulf coast. Attempts to take Alvarado in August and October failed when the steamers towing the landing party's boats were unable to cross the bar at the mouth of the Alvarado River. Later in October a force under the squadron's second in command, Vice Commo. Matthew C. Perry, cap-

tured Frontera and Tabasco (Villahermosa) on the Tabasco (Grijalva) River, though it did not occupy either. Prior to the expedition, Perry had arranged to have the squadron's guard detachments concentrated in a two-hundred-man landing battalion under Capt. Alvin Edson, the Leatherneck commander at Quallah Battoo. On 14 November the battalion took part in the unopposed occupation of Tampico, the port selected to serve as a base for the assault on Veracruz.

The Home Squadron put Scott's army of eighty-six hundred men ashore in an uncontested landing a few miles south of Veracruz on 9 March 1847. Edson's Leathernecks were attached to the Third Artillery during the siege of the city, which surrendered on the twenty-seventh. Three days later, Congress, somewhat belatedly anticipating the expiration of the one-year enlistments of the many volunteer units serving with Scott, authorized the raising of ten new regiments and a wartime increase of twelve officers and a thousand men in the strength of the Marine Corps.

This lithograph of Commodore Perry's landing at Seven Palms, below Tabasco, appeared in 1849. Based on an eyewitness painting by Lt. Henry Walke, USN, it is the first contemporary view of Marines (and seamen) making an amphibious assault. Perry is the figure at the top of the hill just to the right of the flag bearer. U.S. Naval Academy Museum

Archibald Henderson took this as his cue. Once again, as at the time of the Creek uprising, he volunteered to furnish a Marine regiment to serve with the Army. The president and the secretary of war welcomed his overture, and on 21 May the secretary of the Navy authorized the deployment.

A battalion of twenty-two officers and 324 NCOs and men sailed within a month. In Mexico it was to be joined by the Home Squadron's Marine battalion to form a six-company regiment. Henderson, now sixty-four, stayed home this time. As regimental commander he selected Bvt Lt. Col. Samuel E. Watson, a veteran of thirty-five years in the Corps. The Leathernecks reached Veracruz on 1 July.

During the intervening months, the Home Squadron had been busy buttoning up the Mexican coast. Alvarado was rather embarrassingly captured by a single small gunboat sent ahead of a major expedition at the end of March. Immediately afterward Commodore Perry, who had assumed command of the squadron that month, or-

ganized a naval brigade of two thousand men, including Captain Edson's Marines, to be employed in amphibious operations. The Leathernecks and several of the blue-jacket battalions in this force made their first hot landing on 18 April to capture the defended port of Tuxpan.

No resistance was offered to the seizure of Coatza-coalcos and Carmen the following month, but members of the brigade saw action again in June, when Perry decided to make a second expedition up the Tabasco River to occupy the town of that name. The Mexicans had strengthened Tabasco's defenses since his last visit by throwing up several additional earthworks along the river below it. At a bluff called Seven Palms, about four miles south of the town, Perry landed at the head of 1,173 men with seven guns. The successive Mexican works were either outflanked, stormed, or overcome by ships' fire, and by mid-afternoon, at the cost of five wounded, the American flag was floating over Tabasco.

Maj. Levi Twiggs sat for this portrait by an unknown artist in July 1840. *Art Collection, Marine Corps Historical Center*

Perry's amphibious interests frustrated Archibald Henderson's designs. On the arrival of Watson's battalion at Veracruz, the commodore refused to surrender more than a handful of his squadron's Leathernecks. On 16 July the battalion that would not become a regiment set off in company of other troops for Puebla, seventy-five miles from Mexico City. Scott had been awaiting replacements for his time-expired men there since mid-May. Joining his army on 6 August, the Marines were assigned to the 4th Division, commanded by Brig. Gen. John A. Quitman, and linked with the 2nd Pennsylvania Volunteers to form a brigade of which Watson was given command. Maj. Levi Twiggs, a burly Georgian who had fought the British, the Creeks, and the Seminoles, took over the Marine battalion. Scott marched on Mexico City the next day.

The American Army entered the Valley of Mexico only eight miles southwest of the capital on 17 August. Detailed to guard the baggage train, Quitman's division played no part in the first three battles that followed—Contreras, Churubsco, and Molino del Rey. In the next,

it would see all the action its most ardent member could have craved.

On 10 September, two days after Molino del Rey, Scott decided to make a full-scale assault on Chapultepec Castle, which screened Mexico City's western face. Formerly the residence of the Spanish viceroys, now the site of the Mexican military academy, the castle crowned a volcanic outcropping two hundred feet high and eighteen hundred feet long. High stone walls enclosed both the castle and the ridge. No intelligence was available as to the strength of the garrison; in fact, it numbered approximately a thousand, including the military academy cadets.

The operation opened with a day-long bombardment on 12 September. Three of the Army's four divisions were to attack the next morning: Brig. Gen. Gideon J. Pillow's 3rd Division from the west, and Quitman's division from the south, along the road extending from the village of Tacubaya. Brig. Gen. William J. Worth's 1st Division would support Pillow. The 2nd Division, commanded by Brig. Gen. David E. Twiggs (a relative of the Marine major), was split in two. One of its brigades was sent to support Quitman while the other staged a demonstration against the southern face of the city. The stakes were high. Wastage and casualties had reduced Scott's army to seventy-two hundred effectives. His opposite number, General Antonio López de Santa Anna, had at least three times as many men at his disposal. The Americans could not afford a defeat.

Each of the attack divisions was to be preceded by a storming party. On Scott's orders, Brigadier General Twiggs supplied Quitman with a detachment of 250 men to serve in that capacity. Loathe to have his assault spearheaded by strangers, Quitman also organized a second, volunteer, storming party from his division, 120 men whom he placed under the command of Major Twiggs. A 40-man pioneer storming party equipped with scaling ladders, pickaxes, and crowbars was entrusted to another Marine, Capt. John G. Reynolds. The Marine battalion, Quitman's only regular unit, was to follow at the head of Watson's brigade and give the storming parties covering fire.

At dawn on 13 September the American batteries resumed their bombardment. The infantry started forward at 8:00. Quitman's storming parties had reached a point

The Battle of Chapultepec, 13 September 1847

about 250 yards from Chapultepec's outer walls when fire from a battery directly ahead forced them and the Marine battalion to take cover in a ditch that had been dug across the road to impede an enemy advance. As soon as he was apprised of the situation, Quitman directed the Pennsylvania regiment and his other brigade to turn off the road before reaching the point where the storming party had been checked and sent the brigade on loan from Twiggs to swing wide to the right to protect his flank. Watson was ordered to hold his position.

A lively firefight between the Marines and soldiers in the ditch and the Mexicans in the battery to their front and the castle grounds to their left continued for some time. Presently Major Twiggs, favorite shotgun in hand, climbed out of the ditch onto the roadway, apparently intent on getting things moving. Captain Reynolds joined him. They exchanged a few words and Twiggs was shot through the heart. Reynolds carried his body behind a

stone wall. There he found Watson and Bvt. Maj. William Dulany, who were worried about the expenditure of ammunition. Reynolds urged Watson to renew the advance, but the colonel was unwilling to move without orders.

Meanwhile, Pillow's and Worth's divisions had broken through the Mexican defenses on their front and were storming Chapultepec Castle; the units Quitman had sent to the left had begun entering breaches in the outer wall; and Twiggs's brigade, having completed its swing to the right, was about to envelop the batteries at the end of the Tacubaya road. Quitman now sent the storming party orders to charge. Capt. George H. Terrett had been aching for just such a command. That it did not pertain to the Marines was a detail he dismissed. Without a moment's hesitation he led his sixty-some officers and men up the road and overran one of the Mexican batteries. The rest of the battalion remained behind, performing its assigned mission of providing the attackers

The Storming of Chapultepec was painted by an American eyewitness, James Walker, an artist present with Scott's army.

with covering fire. After the charge, it joined Quitman's other units inside the walls of Chapultepec, where it captured some dispirited Mexicans. Captain Terrett took his little company in search of new adventures.

From the northeastern face of Chapultepec two divergent causeways ran toward Mexico City: the Calzada de Belén to the Garita de Belén, a fortified stone police and customs station, and the Calzada de la Verónica to the Garita de San Cosmé, farther north. The Americans called the *garitas* "gates," although neither actually included any such structure. Strangely, Scott's plans did not extend beyond the capture of Chapultepec, and some time passed before the Army was ready to exploit its victory and move on to Mexico City. Pillow having been wounded, Quitman enterprisingly attached two of his colleague's regiments to his own division. The combined force, including the Marine battalion, then advanced to attack the Belén Gate, which was occupied after heavy fighting at

1:20 P.M. Six Leathernecks were killed and two wounded in the capture and subsequent defense of the work.

At the same time that Quitman's division started down the causeway toward the Belén Gate, Worth's division, reinforced by one of Pillow's brigades, began moving up the Calzada de la Verónica—along which Terrett's company and a number of small Army detachments led by junior officers with the bit in their teeth were already fighting their way. Terrett would later defend his arguably excessive initiative by stating, "What Colonel Watson's orders were, whether to enter the gate of the Castle or not, I am ignorant, as I did not receive from him any order or direction, and in going forward, deemed I could not be wrong, so long as the Enemy in large numbers were ahead."[7]

In their advance along the causeway Terrett's men supported three pieces of horse artillery in breaking up a counterattack by Mexican infantry and cavalry. The guns then retired to replenish ammunition, but the

Capt. George Terrett fought at Quallah Battoo, in the Seminole War, in the Mexican War, and in the Civil War, in the last as a Confederate Marine.

Leathernecks pushed ahead, forcing another body of enemy troops to abandon a barricade by turning its flank. Two miles north of Chapultepec, at the point where the causeway met the San Cosmé road, they were halted by an entrenched gun and infantry firing from housetops. Soon they were joined by about two dozen members of the 4th Infantry, among them 1st Lt. Ulysses S. Grant. Making a reconnaissance to the west of the causeway, Grant discovered that the Americans could outflank the entrenchment by moving behind two sides of a walled garden. A company of infantry that had just come up reinforced the movement, while the Leathernecks and soldiers who remained in front charged. The Mexicans retreated, and the Americans, in hot pursuit, overran a second barricade halfway between the intersection and the San Cosmé Gate. What happened next is debatable.

According to almost every history of the Corps, the Marines pressed forward from the barricade and seized the San Cosmé Gate, making them the first American troops to set foot in the Mexican capital. Fifteen minutes later, hearing bugles sound the recall, they withdrew. Most accounts add that Grant's detachment accompanied the Leathernecks on their lunge into the city. The problem with this account is that it contradicts the one contained in Grant's *Memoirs.* According to Grant, the advance did not proceed beyond the second barricade. The detailed histories of the war written by Roswell S. Ripley and Cadmus M. Wilcox, officers in Scott's army, agree. The undisputed fact that this barricade was abandoned soon after being overrun suggests that somehow it became confused with the San Cosmé Gate. Yet, however far Terrett's company advanced, it was far enough for glory.

Worth's division captured (or recaptured) the gate about six o'clock that afternoon. The Mexican Army evacuated the city during the night, and the Americans occupied it the next morning. General Quitman, appointed military governor, sent the Marine battalion to evict a mob of looters that had invaded the Palacio Nacional, and Leatherneck 2d Lt. A. S. Nicholson became the first man to raise the American flag over the Halls of the Montezumas. Prolonged peace negotiations resulted in the signing of the Treaty of Guadalupe Hidalgo on 2 February 1848. The war it officially ended had cost the Corps eleven dead and forty-seven wounded. More than half of these casualties had been suffered at Chapultepec; but there is no truth to the legend that the red stripe Leathernecks began to wear on their trouser legs not long afterward is a "blood stripe" to commemorate the losses there.

Shortly after the Marines returned to Washington, the capital's citizens presented the Corps with a handsome new flag featuring an eagle and anchor, with a motto that would, with a little editing, become famous: "From Tripoli to the Halls of the Montezumas." No fewer than twenty-seven Marine officers were awarded brevets for the Mexican War, fourteen of them for Chapultepec. Archibald Gillespie received not one but two brevets, captain for the defense of Los Angeles and major for San Gabriel. He left the Corps as a captain in 1854, settled in (where else?) California, and died in San Francisco in 1873.

In the following decade Marines took part in more than twenty landings abroad and one at home. The latter

Commodore Perry's Marines parade on the temple grounds at Shimoda, Japan, 8 June 1854. Shimoda was one of the two Japanese ports opened to American ships by the treaty Perry had negotiated. This lithograph by Eliphalet Brown and William Heine was published in 1856.

occurred in January 1856 when the sloop-of-war *Decatur* sent her Marine guard and some seamen ashore to drive off a band of Indians that was threatening the little settlement at Seattle, Washington. This action turned out to be the Leathernecks' last experience of Indian fighting.

Seven of the foreign landings occurred in Central and South America. Six were made to protect American lives and property during revolutions or riots—at Buenos Aires, Argentina (twice in 1852); Greytown (now San Juan del Sur), Nicaragua (1853); Montevideo, Uruguay (1855 and 1858); and Panama City, in what was then New Granada (1856). Aside from a skirmish with a mob of looters in Buenos Aires in February 1852, the only deployment that involved the use of force was the bombardment and destruction of Greytown by the sloop-of-war *Cyane* on 13 July 1854 in retaliation for the municipal authorities' refusal to make amends for having forcibly detained the U.S. ambassador overnight.

All the other landings occurred in or across the Pacific. Six officers and two hundred men served in the East India Squadron during Commo. Matthew C. Perry's momentous expedition to establish relations with Japan. Aware that his reception would depend in part on the show he put on, Perry used his Marines to help create a scene of martial pageantry in his meetings with Japanese officials at Uraga in July 1853 and Yokohama Bay in March 1854. At the latter the entire squadron's guard detachments were organized into a battalion under Perry's senior Marine officer, Bvt. Maj. Jacob Zeilin. The Japanese were highly impressed by the Leathernecks' precision drill.

The following year, reports of the mistreatment of American traders in the Fiji Islands prompted Cdr. E. B. Boutwell to proceed there in the sloop-of-war *John Adams*. Lt. John L. Broome's Marine guard took part in each of the four landings Boutwell ordered in September and October 1855. The first three eventuated in peaceful palavers or demonstrations intended to induce the

Ballou's Pictorial Drawing-Room Companion for 16 August 1856 included this illustration titled
Mess Room of the Marines at the Charleston Navy Yard in Boston. Beverley R. Robinson Collection

The same issue of *Ballou's* also pictured the *Sleeping Apartments of the Marines at the Charleston Navy Yard.* Beverley R. Robinson
Collection

The Attack on the Barrier Forts near Canton China, a lithograph by J. H. Buffords. Franklin D. Roosevelt Collection, Hyde Park, N.Y.

islanders to mend their ways. The fourth was a return visit to Vita Levu, where King Tui Viti had reneged on the engagements into which he had been dragooned. It eventuated in a brisk little battle and the burning of three villages.

Marines made four landings in China, then in the throes of the great Taiping Rebellion. When in April 1854 government troops began to encroach on the International Settlements at Shanghai, the sloop-of-war *Plymouth* landed sixty seamen and Marines, who together with 150 of their British counterparts and thirty-seven American and British volunteers dispersed the interlopers at the cost of a dozen casualties. A recurrence of the threat to the Settlements led to the landing of the frigate *Powhatan*'s Leathernecks in May 1855, but on that occasion there was no fighting. That August, the *Powhatan* collaborated with HMS *Rattler* in a boat attack on a Chinese pirate fleet in Ty-Ho Bay, near Hong Kong. Seventeen junks were captured in a day's combat. By a grim coincidence, the allied forces each lost two Marines and two seamen killed in action. They were jointly commemorated by a granite monument in Hong Kong's Happy Valley.

The final action in Chinese waters involved the heaviest fighting in which Marines had engaged since the Mexican War. On 15 November 1856 the Barrier Forts

on the Pearl River below Canton—four modern, granite-faced works designed by European engineers—began firing on ships and boats of the East India Squadron, apparently in an outburst of xenophobia inspired by difficulties with the British. The next day, the twenty-gun *Plymouth* returned the compliment. Neither shot nor an attempt to open negotiations produced any effect, and on 19 November the *Plymouth*'s captain, Cdr. Andrew Hull Foote, the senior officer present, resolved to storm the forts. A landing party had already been organized from the seamen and Marines of the *Plymouth,* the twenty-two-gun sloop-of-war *Levant,* and the frigate *San Jacinto,* which remained downstream at Whampoa. Early the following morning, while the *Plymouth* and *Levant* laid down covering fire, Foote led 287 men ashore. The Marine contingent numbered two officers and 50 men under Bvt. Capt. John D. Simms.

By the afternoon of 22 November, the landing party had captured the four Barrier Forts and their 176 guns, plus a 6-gun battery, and repulsed three counterattacks by three thousand Chinese troops from Canton. American casualties were seven dead and twenty-two wounded, six of the latter being Marines. Foote estimated Chinese losses to be about 250. Simms's men played a conspicuous role in all three days' fighting, spearheading the advance on the forts—in two of which the

An artist for the *Illustrated London News* sketched these officers and Marines aboard the U.S. steam frigate *Susquehanna* in 1857.

Leathernecks' standard-bearer, Cpl. William McDougal, was the first man to plant the American flag—capturing the battery, and beating off two of the Chinese counterattacks. "It may be seen," Foote wrote in his after-action report, " . . . how efficient our marines are in service of this kind; and the inference is inevitable that an increase of . . . the number of officers and men attached to our ships, would tend to insure success in like expeditions."[8]

Despite the passing of the years, Archibald Henderson's warrior spirit remained as keen as ever. He displayed it once again during the election-day riots in Washington, D.C., on 1 June 1857. The Know-Nothing Party, a violence-prone populist group, had imported a gang of Baltimore hoodlums called the Plug-Uglies to take control of the city's polling places. With them the Plug-Uglies brought a brass cannon. When the police were unable to preserve order, Mayor William Magruder asked President James Buchanan to call in the Marines from Eighth and Eye. A two-company battalion under Capt. Henry B. Tyler, the Corps's adjutant and inspector, marched to the city hall. Henderson accompanied the detachment in civilian clothes.

On their way through the city the Marines encoun-tered a mob of Plug-Uglies. The rioters followed them, dragging along the cannon and shouting threats. From the city hall the mayor accompanied the battalion to one of the polls that had been forced to close. On reaching the scene, the Leathernecks halted and ordered arms. The Plug-Uglies responded by trundling their cannon forward and sending a party to tell Captain Tyler that they would open fire unless his force withdrew at once. At that moment, seventy-four-year-old Archibald Henderson stepped forward to block the cannon's mouth with his body. "Men," he said, "you had better think twice before you fire this piece at the Marines."[9]

To take up the account in the next day's *Washington Star:*

[Henderson] informed the crowd that the [Marines'] pieces were loaded with ball cartridge, and warned them repeatedly; warned the citizens to leave the spot. The general, finding that the piece would be fired unless captured immediately, crossed over to Captain Tyler, and gave the order for ten or fifteen Marines to take it. During this time a number of pistol-shots were fired at General Henderson, some of the parties standing within a few feet of him. One platoon charged the piece on the run. Those in charge of the piece

Archibald Henderson and the Plug-Uglies, a woodcut from *Frank Leslie's Illustrated Newspaper* for 20 June 1857.

instantly retreated, and a dozen or more revolvers were discharged at the platoon, which had laid hold of the gun and were taking it away. . . .

A man ran up to the general within two feet of his person, and was about to discharge his pistol, when a private with his musket struck his arm causing the weapon to fall; at the same time the general seized the villain and marched him off to the mayor, into whose hands he placed him. The pistol-shots now rattled around like hailstones, and the officers had great difficulty in restraining their men from returning the fire. General Henderson and all the officers were constantly admonishing the men not to fire until the order was given.[10]

Nevertheless, the Marines—sixty of them green recruits—finally did fire before the order was given. The *Star* reported that the men reached the breaking point after several had been struck by stones and a private received "a dreadful wound" from a shot in the face. On the other hand, a Marine officer present insisted that discipline had held firm and the firing had resulted from a misunderstanding; seeing the private shot, Mayor Magruder cried out, "Why don't you fire?" and the men had taken the last word as a command.[11]

Although the volley sent the Plug-Uglies scuttling down the street, they soon stopped to regroup. Scattered shots continued to ring out, and presently a Marine was hit in the shoulder. Tyler then ordered the battalion to prepare to fire. That was sufficient. The Plug-Uglies took to their heels.

The remainder of the era of Archibald Henderson passed quietly. Following the election-day riot, no Leatherneck fired another shot in anger until October 1858, when forty seamen and Marines from the sloop-of-war *Vandalia* landed on Waya in the Fiji Islands to avenge the murder of two American traders. Exactly three months later, on 6 January 1859, Archibald Henderson returned home from headquarters and lay down on the sofa for his afternoon nap. He never awakened. President Buchanan and the members of his cabinet were among those who attended Henderson's funeral. Almost forty years ago Col. Robert Debs Heinl Jr., one of the Corps's foremost historians, wrote: "The debt the Marine Corps owes its fifth Commandant is incalculable. . . . No Commandant served longer than Henderson, and none has left a better legacy."[12] Those words still ring true.

This time there was no struggle for the succession. Only two days after Henderson's death, sixty-eight-year-old Lt. Col. John Harris was appointed commandant. The Corps's senior officer, Harris had been commissioned in 1814, led the horse Marines at Hatcheelustee, commanded a Marine battalion sent to Mexico too late to engage in hostilities, and spent twenty years at sea. Unfortunately, by 1859 the fire had gone out of his belly. Indeed, it had ebbed as early as 1847, when the prospect of being ordered to Mexico had led him to advise Henderson that "I have no desire to go," although "if you think the good of the service demands it I shall not hesitate to do so."[13]

Harris's devotion to the good of the service remained strong. In less troubled times he might have made an unexceptionable if unenterprising commandant, but he was hardly the man to lead the Corps through the national convulsion that broke out two years later. Symbolic of the change at Eighth and Eye, the uniform regulations of 1859 replaced the Mameluke saber Henderson had authorized for wear by Marine officers and NCOs in 1826 with the straight sword carried by their counterparts in the U.S. infantry.

5
Marines in Blue and Gray, 1859–1865

While Archibald Henderson was creating a professional Marine Corps, the nation it served was drifting toward civil war. The Corps played a key role in a harbinger of the bloodbath to come when the abolitionist John Brown and twenty-one of his followers seized the federal arsenal and armory at Harpers Ferry, Virginia, before dawn on 16 October 1859. Brown believed that his action would spark a slave uprising. Events revealed his error. There was no uprising; the townsmen and the militia sprang somewhat gingerly to arms, and after a few fusillades in which men died on both sides the raiders withdrew into the arsenal's sturdy brick firehouse. With them they took eleven hostages, including Col. Lewis Washington, a great-grandnephew of the first president.

Virginia's governor, John Letcher, requested federal assistance the next morning. The nearest regular troops were the Marines at Eighth and Eye, and that afternoon the officer of the day, thirty-five-year-old 1st Lt. Israel C. Greene, set out with eighty-six NCOs and men and two 12-pounder howitzers on the train to Harpers Ferry. Hand-picked by Archibald Henderson to add an artillery course to the instruction given at Marine Barracks, Washington, Greene was one of the Corps's best and brightest. Accompanying him in an advisory capacity was Maj. William W. Russell, the Corps's paymaster, who had fought in the Mexican War but, as a staff officer, lacked command authority.

Reaching Harpers Ferry around midnight, the Marines met the Army officer who had been put in command of the operation, Col. Robert E. Lee, and his aide,

1st Lt. J. E. B. Stuart. At sunrise, Lee moved to bring the incident to a close. Stuart approached the firehouse under a white flag with a note from Lee calling on Brown to surrender. When Brown refused, Lieutenant Greene led a storming party of twelve Marines forward to break down the building's sturdy double doors. After failing to make an impression with sledgehammers, they used a ladder as a battering ram to punch a hole through which a stooping man could scramble. To reduce the danger to the hostages, Lee had ruled out the use of firearms; the Leathernecks would rely on cold steel. Greene, sword in hand, was the first man inside. Close behind him came Major Russell, unarmed except for his rattan cane. The third man to enter the building, Pvt. Luke Quinn, was mortally wounded by a bullet through the stomach. The next, Pvt. Matthew Ruppert, was shot in the face.

Meanwhile, Greene had reached the rear of the firehouse and encountered Colonel Washington, who pointed out a kneeling figure in the act of reloading a carbine as John Brown. Greene slashed at the man's head. Brown tried to dodge the blow and was sent sprawling when Greene's sword sliced into the back of his neck. Greene followed with a thrust at Brown's heart, but the point of his dress sword failed to penetrate and the blade bent double. Only then did he see that Brown was unconscious. Two other raiders were impaled on the fixed bayonets of the Marines who had continued to plunge through the shattered door, and the survivors surrendered. None of the hostages had been harmed. Greene noted that the entire action had taken not quite three minutes.

Marines storm the engine house held by John Brown's raiders at Harpers Ferry in this contemporary woodcut from *Harper's Weekly*.

Tried and convicted of treason, John Brown was hanged at Charleston, Virginia, on 2 December 1859. But as the "Battle Hymn of the Republic" put it, his spirit went marching on. The raid on Harpers Ferry did nothing to improve relations between North and South, and in November 1860 the election of Abraham Lincoln, whom many southerners regarded as a closet abolitionist, brought the sectional crisis to a head. On 20 December 1860 South Carolina became the first state to secede from the Union. Six others had joined it to form the Confederate States of America by 12 April 1861, the day the bombardment of Fort Sumter signified the commencement of the Civil War. Four more states, including Virginia, seceded between that date and June in reaction to President Lincoln's call for seventy-five thousand volunteers to suppress the rebellion.

On 2 November 1860 the Marine Corps had numbered sixty-three officers, 252 noncommissioned officers, 113 musicians, and 1,347 privates, for an aggregate of 1,775 men, slightly more than 10 percent of the strength of the regular Army. Almost a third of the officers cast their lot with the Confederacy, but hardly any of the Corps's other ranks imitated their example. Nevertheless, there were few old hands available for the battalion Colonel Harris consigned with "feelings of great anxiety" to the Union Army that marched south from Washington to win the war on 16 July 1861.[1] The battalion commander, Maj. John G. Reynolds, was, at age sixty, a seasoned campaigner with service dating back to the Seminole War, but of his twelve officers and 353 men, only 17 had been in uniform for any length of time. Among the exceptions was Bvt. Maj. Jacob Zeilin, who

First Lt. Israel Greene commanded the Marines at Harpers Ferry and later served as adjutant of the Confederate States Marine Corps. *Art Collection, Marine Corps Historical Center*

volunteered to take command of one of Reynolds's four companies.

Five days later, fate placed the Marine battalion at the very fulcrum of the Battle of Bull Run, on the rolling terrain of Henry House Hill, where the Union advance was halted by a brigade commanded by a certain Thomas J. Jackson, ever afterward known as "Stonewall." The guns of Griffin's battery, which the Leathernecks had been directed to support, changed hands three times in the seesaw struggle that ensued. Finally, around 4:00 P.M., two fresh Confederate brigades broke the deadlock and the Union Army went streaming back toward Washington. Like its neighbors in the firing line, the Marine battalion dissolved. Late that night, Major Reynolds led seventy men he had waited to collect at the Long Bridge over the Potomac back to Eighth and Eye.

In his report to Secretary of the Navy Gideon Welles, Colonel Harris declared that Bull Run was "the first instance recorded in [the Corps's] history where any portion of its members turned their backs to the enemy."[2] Al-though Harris was clearly chagrined, Reynolds felt that for a force composed largely of raw recruits his battalion had fought well, a contention its casualties—forty-four killed, wounded, or missing—would tend to support. Major Zeilin was among the wounded.

Bull Run was the only overland campaign in which the U.S. Marine Corps fought during the Civil War. All its other field service occurred within the naval and amphibious framework of the strategy known as the Anaconda Plan. This scheme called on the Navy to isolate the agrarian South from the industries of the outside world by blockading its coasts and closing its ports, and, in conjunction with the Army, to cut it in two by seizing control of the Mississippi River. For its part, the Army was to maintain relentless pressure on the Confederate land frontiers.

A month after Bull Run, Marines participated in the landing at Hatteras Inlet, North Carolina, the first of the advanced bases established to support the blockade. This detachment consisted of ships' guards, but in September, Flag Officer Samuel F. Du Pont, who had learned the value of Leatherneck landing parties during the Mexican War, requested the assignment of an integral battalion to an expedition being organized under his command to seize another advanced base at Port Royal Sound, South Carolina. Colonel Harris accordingly furnished a battalion of three hundred men under Major Reynolds. The expedition sailed from Hampton Roads, Virginia, on 29 October 1861. Five days later the transport carrying the Marines sank in a storm. Though all but seven of them survived, none reached Port Royal in time to aid in its capture. Anticlimax continued to dog the battalion in succeeding months. Sent to attack Fernandina, Florida, in March 1862, the Marines arrived to find that the city had already surrendered. The same thing happened two weeks later at St. Augustine, and at the end of the month the battalion was disbanded.

Its misadventures notwithstanding, the battalion's mere existence appeared to augur a significant role for the U.S. Marine Corps in the amphibious operations instrumental to the Anaconda Plan. That appearance was deceptive. Of the five Marine battalions that saw amphibious service after the Port Royal expedition, all except one were improvised by combining a squadron's

Leathernecks parade outside Marine Barracks, Washington, early in the Civil War. This woodcut appeared in *Harper's Weekly* for 14 September 1861.

guard detachments for a specific undertaking, at the conclusion of which they returned to their ships.

Four other battalions were assembled for miscellaneous duties ashore. One took over the security of the recently recaptured Norfolk Navy Yard in May 1862. Seven months later, another was sent to establish a Marine barracks at Mare Island Navy Yard near San Francisco, California. Small battalions were also included in the naval brigades deployed by the Brooklyn Navy Yard to help maintain order during the draft riots of July 1863, and by the Philadelphia Navy Yard to guard the railroad bridge at Havre de Grace, Maryland, at the time of Gen. Jubal Early's raid in July 1864.

The battalion ordered to California, 112 officers and men under Maj. Addison Garland, suffered the Corps's most embarrassing Civil War experience. On 7 December 1862 Capt. Raphael Semmes's Confederate cruiser *Alabama* captured the entire unit aboard an unarmed passenger steamer off the eastern end of Cuba. Semmes had the Marines sign paroles—promises not to bear arms against the Confederacy until properly exchanged—and sent them on their way. (The insult did not go un-

avenged. In June 1864 a sergeant's guard participated in the engagement in which the *Alabama* was sunk by the USS *Kearsarge*.)

The limited role the Corps played in the war was to an extent dictated by its numbers, despite the fact that these were doubled soon after the outbreak of hostilities. On 25 July 1861 Congress raised the Corps's manning level to ninety-three officers and 3,074 men, and later President Lincoln took advantage of an existing law allowing the chief executive to substitute Marines for landsmen aboard naval vessels to increase its authorized strength by another 1,000 men. At the height of the Union naval effort in 1864, however, Marine guards were serving in a hundred ships and providing security at nine Navy yards. Such commitments would have made it difficult to maintain a sizable amphibious force.

At the same time, Colonel Harris and his senior officers continued to view the Corps's primary mission as the performance of the same shipboard duties it had fulfilled in the War of 1812. If the lengthening range of rifled cannon threatened to eliminate the opportunity to deliver small arms fire during naval engagements, the growing

The Marine guard in the *Kearsarge* during the Civil War.

interest in ramming tactics promised to preserve it. Furthermore, the Corps had already established a fallback position, a Navy general order of June 1859 having authorized guard detachments to man some of their ships' big guns. The institutional weakness of this expedient was that it merely duplicated an activity performed mainly by seamen. For Marines, to serve as gunners was a task; it was not a reason for being.

In contrast, the Confederate States Marine Corps soon formed a battalion that served as both a key component of the defenses of Richmond and a source of immediately deployable detachments for operations elsewhere. Although this unit's inception owed to accident rather than design, its retention led Ralph W. Donnelly, the pioneer historian of the CSMC, to conclude that "in many ways, the Confederate States Marine Corps was the true connecting link between the Marine philosophy of Commandant Archibald Henderson and the U.S. Marine Corps of today."[3]

The grayback Corps was established by the Confederate Congress at Montgomery, Alabama, by an act of 16 March 1861. This legislation provided for a Corps of six companies, each to consist of a captain, a first and second lieutenant, eight noncommissioned officers, two musicians, and one hundred men. On 20 May 1861, following the capital's removal to Richmond, another act increased the Corps's strength to 46 officers and 944 NCOs and privates—the equivalent of a ten-company regiment—including a headquarters composed of a colonel commandant, a lieutenant colonel, a major, an adjutant, a paymaster, and a quartermaster (all holding staff rank as major); a sergeant major; a quartermaster sergeant; and two principal musicians. Finally, an act of 24 September 1862 authorized another 40 NCOs and forty more musicians. Probably as a result of recruiting laws that favored the Confederate Army, the Corps never attained its prescribed strength, and peaked in 1864 at about six hundred officers and men.

A nucleus of trained officers was available in former members of the U.S. Marine Corps. Of the sixty-three

A young Marine (with crossbelt) drills in a pivot-gun crew on the gunboat *Miami* on blockade duty off Roanoke Sound, South Carolina, in 1864.

officers on active duty in early 1861, twenty "went South" in the course of the year. Nineteen took commissions in the Confederate Corps; the twentieth entered the Army. Their loss was even more damaging to the USMC than their numbers would suggest, for they included a disproportionate share of its ablest officers. Among them were its adjutant and inspector, Maj. Henry B. Tyler, a veteran of thirty-eight years' service, the commander of Marine Barracks, Washington; Capt. George H. Terrett, the warrior who had stolen the show at Chapultepec; three officers who, like him, had won brevets for gallantry in the Mexican War—Capts. Algernon A. Taylor and Robert Tansill, and Bvt. Capt. John D. Simms Jr., who had commanded the Marines in the assault on the Barrier Forts in China; and 1st Lt. Israel Greene of Harpers Ferry fame.

Tyler became the Confederate Corps's lieutenant colonel. Terrett was appointed its major of the line, and as such held its principal operational command throughout the conflict. Taylor became its quartermaster, Simms its senior company commander, and Greene its adjutant. Only Tansill jumped ship, resigning from the Corps in February 1862 to enter the Army, in which he attained the rank of colonel. Tyler and Terrett served stints of detached duty as acting brigadier generals in the Army, as did another former U.S. Marine, Capt. John R. F. Tatnall. Tatnall seems to have spoken for all three when he declared that he would rather command a company of Marines than a brigade of volunteers.

From the first to the last, a total of fifty-eight officers were commissioned in the C.S. Marine Corps. Ironically, the thirty-nine with no prior Marine experience included its colonel commandant, Lloyd J. Beall. A West Point graduate (class of 1830), he probably owed his position to an old acquaintance with President Jefferson Davis, another West Pointer (class of 1828) and onetime regimental comrade in the 1st Infantry. Beall had subsequently transferred to the 2nd Dragoons, but in 1844 he accepted a staff appointment as paymaster major, the rank he resigned in 1861. The management of the Confederate Marine Corps indicates that he was a capable administrator. In operational matters it seems probable that he relied on the advice of Lieutenant Colonel Tyler and Majors Terrett and Greene.

Other than its commandant, only three men who had not belonged to the U.S. Marine Corps were commissioned above the rank of lieutenant in the C.S. Marine Corps. They were Richard T. Allison, a former U.S. Navy paymaster appointed its paymaster major, and two of its original captains: Reuben T. Thom, who had served as an infantry officer in the Mexican War, and Alfred C. Van Benthuysen, the Confederate Marine Corps's most colorful character. Just twenty-four when he raised one of its first three companies, Van Benthuysen had already fought in the Taiping Rebellion in China in 1857–58 and served as a staff officer with Garibaldi's Red Shirts in the Italian campaign of 1860. Amiability was not among his virtues. Twice in 1862 courts-martial sentenced him to be dismissed from the Corps in consequence of altercations with brother officers, once while in his cups. On both occasions his punishment was commuted to suspension from duty and pay. That he was a nephew-in-law of President Davis cannot have hurt him. But he was a fighter, and in 1864 he commanded the Confederate Leathernecks in one of their finest hours.

The remaining thirty-five officers were commissioned as first or second lieutenants. Among them was Archibald Henderson's son Richard, who had been practicing law in Washington at the approach of war. All except eight had served as enlisted men in the Confederate Army, but none came from the ranks of the Confederate Marine Corps. Not a single Confederate Marine officer was killed in action, but up to the fall of Richmond, twelve company-grade officers had been wounded or captured—in four cases, both—for a casualty rate slightly in excess of 20 percent. Eight other officers were dis-

Lloyd J. Beall, colonel commandant of the Confederate States Marine Corps.

missed, four as a result of what was politely termed intemperance, and one deserted.

The Confederate Marine Corps enlisted its first men at Montgomery in late March 1861. Recruiting then moved to New Orleans, and by late July three companies (A, B, and C) had been raised and concentrated at Pensacola, where Confederate forces ashore and Union troops on Santa Rosa Island were exchanging occasional artillery bombardments and raiding one another's shipping. In addition, the Corps had furnished guard detachments for the commerce raider *Sumter,* which ran the blockade of the Mississippi on 30 June, and the river defense gunboat *McRae.* Confederate Marines had also seen their first action, fifty-five men under Captain Thom having taken part in an expedition (5–9 July) that occupied Ship Island, in the Gulf below Biloxi, Mississippi, and drove away a Union blockader.

The concentration at Pensacola was short-lived. In September, Company A was ordered to Savannah; in

Marine detachments were serving in both vessels when the CSS *Virginia* (formerly the USS *Merrimack*) rammed and sank the USS *Cumberland* on the first day of the Battle of Hampton Roads.

November, Company C was sent to Norfolk; and in February 1862, Company B went to Mobile. Captain Thom's Company C drew the most eventful assignment: to provide guards for the principal vessels of the James River Squadron, the wooden gunboats *Patrick Henry* and *Jamestown* and the ironclad ram *Virginia,* which was being built on the hull of the U.S. frigate *Merrimack.*

All three ships carried Marine guards into the two-day Battle of Hampton Roads on 8–9 March 1862. There were fifty-four Marines under Captain Thom in the *Virginia;* twenty-four under 1st Lt. Richard Henderson (the commandant's son) in the *Patrick Henry;* and twenty under 1st Lt. James R. Y. Fendall in the *Jamestown.* In the first day's action, an attack on the wooden ships of the blockading squadron anchored in the roads, the *Virginia* rammed and sank the sloop-of-war *Cumberland* and destroyed the frigate *Congress* with shellfire. Returning the next morning intent on adding the grounded frigate *Minnesota* to her score, she encountered the

USS *Monitor,* which had arrived on the scene around midnight. The two ironclads then fought to a draw in the first battle between ships of their kind.

Captain Thom commanded two of the *Virginia's* eight broadside guns on both days. What part his men played is unclear. One of Thom's guns was manned by a militia unit, so it seems reasonable to assume that the other was served by some of his Marines. In any case, Thom's conduct earned the approbation of the *Virginia's* commander, Flag Officer Franklin Buchanan, a hard man to please. In his report of the first day's battle, Buchanan wrote: "The Marine Corps was well represented by Captain Thom, whose tranquil mien gave evidence that the hottest fire was no novelty to him."[4]

Thom was not the only Marine officer commended for his conduct at Hampton Roads. Both of the Union ships destroyed the first day carried guard detachments, and twenty-two-year-old Capt. Charles Heywood, whose father had defended San José del Cabo, fired the sinking

Drewry's Bluff in Relation to Richmond and Petersburg

Cumberland's last shot. Her captain's report that Heywood's "bravery . . . won my highest applause" prompted the U.S. Marine Corps to award the young officer the brevet rank of major.[5] Fourteen of his forty-four Leathernecks went down with the ship. The *Congress*'s guard, sixty-two strong, suffered nine casualties.

The *Virginia* and her consorts returned to Hampton Roads to offer battle on several occasions in April and May. The *Monitor* had orders to stand on the defensive, however, and the ironclads did not meet again before the approach of Union troops compelled the Confederates to evacuate Norfolk on 9 May. Efforts to lighten the *Virginia* enough to allow her to withdraw up the James River with the wooden gunboats were unavailing, and early the next morning, her officers blew her up lest she fall into Union hands.

By that date Capt. Julius E. Meiere, a prewar U.S. Marine at whose November 1860 wedding President-elect Lincoln cut the cake, had succeeded Captain Thom in command of Company C and a second company of Confederate Leathernecks had reached Norfolk, Captain Van Benthuysen's Company B having been transferred from Mobile in March. These units' retreat upstream ended at

a steep promontory on the south bank of the James seven miles below Richmond, where an artillery captain named Augustus Drewry had just emplaced three guns to oppose a Union advance up the river. Situated at the end of one of the many bends through which the James twists toward the city, Drewry's Bluff offered its defenders a picture-perfect field of fire for a mile straight downstream. The Confederates quickly set about enhancing the position's natural strength. Army engineers threw up earthworks on its crest while members of the James River Squadron manhandled five of their ships' guns up the slope to reinforce Drewry's battery, and sank the *Jamestown* and several smaller vessels to obstruct the river channel.

A Union squadron consisting of the ironclads *Galena* and *Monitor* and three gunboats appeared below the bluff at about 7:30 on the morning of 15 May. The gunboats halted at a respectful distance, but the *Galena,* followed by the *Monitor,* closed to approximately six hundred yards, anchored to present her broadside to the battery, and began returning fire. At the same time, Confederate riflemen in pits on both sides of the river started sniping at anyone who showed himself above her bulwarks. The Marines, organized as a little battalion under Captain Simms, occupied a line of bluffs only two hundred yards from the nearest Union vessels. "We immediately opened a sharp fire on them," Simms reported, "killing three of the crew of the Galena certainly, and no doubt many more. The fire of the enemy was materially silenced at intervals by the fire of our troops."[6]

It soon became evident that their elevation gave the gunners on the bluff an advantage over their opponents on the river below. The Union ironclads nevertheless maintained the contest for almost four hours. In its course, Cpl. James Mackie, commanding the *Galena*'s guard detachment, became the first Marine to win the Medal of Honor, established in December 1861 to reward enlisted members of the sea services for extraordinary heroism in the line of duty. "As enemy shell fire raked the deck of his ship," his citation read, "Corporal Mackie fearlessly maintained his musket fire against the rifle pits along the shore and, when ordered to fill vacancies at guns by men wounded and killed in action, manned the weapon with skill and courage."[7] But brav-

Capt. John D. Simms Jr., who led the U.S. Marines at the Barrier Forts, became the senior company commander in the Confederate Marine Corps battalion at Drewry's Bluff. This photograph was taken in 1860. Courtesy David M. Sullivan

Cpl. Mackie, by Charles Waterhouse. Mackie won the Medal of Honor while serving in the *Galena* at Drewry's Bluff, Virginia, on 15 May 1862. Art Collection, Marine Corps Historical Center

ery does not cancel ballistics. By 1:00 P.M. the thin-skinned *Galena* had taken more than forty hits, thirteen of which pierced her armor. Thirty-three of her crewmen had been killed or wounded, and she was almost out of ammunition. The Union ships retired.

Without at first realizing it, the Confederate Marine Corps had found a home at Drewry's Bluff, which now became a naval link in the chain of defenses around Richmond. Company A was ordered there from Savannah a few months after the battle, joining B and C to form a three-company battalion under Major Terrett. This force remained in being throughout the war. The Marines at Camp Beall, as their bivouac came to be called, spent the summer of 1862 under canvas, but at the approach of

winter the colonel commandant obtained funds enabling them to build cabins. The Confederate States Naval Academy opened aboard the *Patrick Henry* on the James in October 1863, and Drewry's Bluff quickly acquired the amenities of an established naval station, with married quarters, flowered walks, kitchen gardens, a post office, a chapel, and a cemetery.

For the Confederate Corps, Camp Beall served much of the purpose Archibald Henderson had envisioned for Marine Barracks, Washington, maintaining a force in readiness for instant deployment and providing training and orientation (including spit and polish) to newly joined officers. "Everything is so different from the Vol. Army to which I have been accustomed," wrote one such officer, 2nd Lt. Ruffin Thomson, in a letter to his Dear Pa. "Here all the formalities & etiquette of the Regular Service are rigidly enforced."[8]

The Confederate Marine Corps camp at Drewry's Bluff, Virginia, in the summer of 1862. This woodcut of a sketch by British war artist Frank Vizetelly was published in the *Illustrated London News* for 15 November 1862. Library of Congress

Meanwhile, the implementation of the Anaconda Plan had brought about the war's greatest naval action—the Battle of New Orleans. Marines of both navies took part. All told, there were 333 U.S. Marines in guard detachments in the ships of Flag Officer David Glasgow Farragut's fleet when, on the night of 24–25 April 1862, it fought its way up the Mississippi past Forts Jackson and St. Philip and smashed the southern naval forces beyond them, breaching the defenses of the Confederacy's most populous city and principal port. Twenty-six Marines were killed or wounded in the engagement, and three of their officers received brevet promotions. The Confederate Marine Corps was represented by a sergeant's guard of about twenty men aboard the gunboat *McRae*. The detachment appears to have been taken prisoner after she sank of battle damage a few days later.

Anchoring off New Orleans on 26 April, Farragut sent officers ashore to demand the city's surrender. When three days of meetings with local authorities produced no result, he directed his fleet Marine officer, Capt. John L. Broome, to form a landing battalion. Together with a detachment of seamen, Broome's battalion formally took possession of the city on the twenty-ninth. An army of occupation began to arrive on 1 May. The Battle of New

Orleans marked the end of Confederate Marines' participation in the Mississippi campaigns. In contrast, U.S. Marine guards continued to see action along the river until the fall of Vicksburg in July 1863 cut the Confederacy in half. Later still, guard detachments served in the unsuccessful Red River expedition.

The measures put under way to strengthen the defenses of other southern ports soon led to an expansion of the Confederate Corps's sphere of activity. Guards were assigned to the ships of the Mobile Squadron in August 1862; the Charleston Squadron probably received its first Marines around the same time; and early in the winter of 1862–63 a detachment was sent from Mobile to form a guard for the newly commissioned ironclad *Atlanta* at Savannah. In October 1862 Captain Meiere was ordered to take command of the Marines at Mobile. This unit was subsequently designated Company D. Capt. John R. F. Tatnall commenced recruiting Company E at Savannah in January 1863, and beginning in April, Meiere raised another company, F, at Mobile. A little more than a year later, Company F was dissolved and its members transferred to Camp Beall.

Altogether, the Confederate Marine Corps supplied guards for twenty-five warships and two floating batteries in home waters, plus the three commerce raiders—*Sumter, Tallahassee/Olustee,* and *Chickamauga*—that put to sea from southern ports. No detachments were furnished for the raiders outfitted in Europe, but the *Shenandoah*'s commander, Lt. James I. Waddell, organized one at sea from the members of his crew. Individual Leathernecks also served in at least six other combatants at home or abroad.

In the spring of 1863, persistent rumors that Union forces were planning to move against Charleston prompted the dispatch of a battalion of two hundred Marines from Camp Beall under Captain Simms to aid in the defense of the city. On 7 April an attack on the harbor fortifications by eight Union ironclads was repulsed. Weeks of quiet followed, and at the end of the month the battalion returned to Drewry's Bluff.

Yet the capture of Charleston, the cradle of secession, remained high on the Union wish list. Operations to take the city by siege began on 10 July with the landing of three thousand troops on Morris Island, on the south side of the main ship channel into Charleston harbor. The next morning the Union advance was checked by Battery Wagner, a Confederate earthwork at the north end of the island. A week later, the work's defenders beat off another major assault. Rear Adm. John A. Dahlgren, who had been placed in command of the South Atlantic Blockading Squadron expressly to prosecute the naval side of the siege, put his ships' guards ashore as an ad hoc battalion to support the struggle for Battery Wagner and requested additional Marines.

Thus, for the second and last time in the war, the U.S. Marine Corps assembled an integral battalion for amphibious service. The new unit, three hundred men under Major Zeilin, reached Morris Island on 10 August. On Dahlgren's orders it was combined with the battalion already ashore to form a Marine regiment with Zeilin at its head. Unfortunately, illness quickly invaded the unit's ranks. An ailing Zeilin could be replaced by that apparently indestructible old campaigner Lt. Col. John Reynolds, but there were not enough indestructible old campaigners to go around. By the time the Confederates evacuated Battery Wagner on 7 September, Marine strength on Morris Island had dwindled to a small battalion.

Dahlgren decided to follow up the occupation of the battery with an assault on Fort Sumter, in the mouth of the harbor, the very next night. Although Union bombardments had silenced Sumter's guns and savaged its brick walls, the fort was still held by a Confederate garrison of unknown strength. The admiral's plan called for the formation of five assault divisions, four from the seamen and Marines of his squadron and one composed of Marines from Morris Island, each numbering approximately ninety men. A tug would tow the force's boats as close as possible to the fort. The naval divisions would then row forward to carry the work under covering fire from the Marines. Neither the officer named to lead the expedition, Cdr. Thomas H. Stevens, nor the commander of the Marine division, Capt. Charles G. McCawley, thought much of the plan. When Stevens expressed his misgivings to Dahlgren, the admiral dismissed them with the promise: "You have only to go and take possession. You will find nothing but a corporal's guard to oppose you."[9]

That night, the junior officers' forebodings proved well founded. The corporal's guard at Fort Sumter numbered 320 men; the crowd of small boats seen calling on the flagship and the Confederates' unsuspected ability to read the fleet's signal code had put the defenders on the alert. Furthermore, probably owing in part to the haste with which the operation had been mounted, most of Stevens's subordinates misunderstood his instructions. He intended to send one division forward to make a feint that would trick the defenders into revealing their strength. As soon as that division had started to pull for the fort, however, most of the others, assuming that the order to advance had been given, raced after it. Stevens tried to recall them, but they kept going, and he unhappily ordered the boats that had remained under control to follow.

Chaos ensued. A rocket soared into the sky above Sumter, and a moment later the batteries on nearby James and Sullivan Islands and the ironclad *Chicora* (which carried an officer's guard of Confederate Marines) began to sweep the area with shrapnel and canister. Simultaneously, Sumter's parapets filled with riflemen who took the expedition's boats under a brisk fire. The parties that pushed ahead to land beneath the fort found themselves unable to scale its walls. They also found themselves exposed to a rain of hand grenades, bricks, and debris from above. Soon the men whose boats remained intact with-

The boat attack on Fort Sumter on the night of 8 September 1863. From R. U. Johnson and C. C. Buel, eds., *Battles and Leaders of the Civil War* (New York: 1887).

drew; those whose boats had been smashed or swamped had no alternative to surrender. In the confusion Captain McCawley tried to rally several boats that retreated past his before the futility of prolonging the agony became evident. In twenty minutes it was all over.

This little disaster cost the attackers 124 casualties, most of whom were captured. The latter group included two Marine officers (one mortally wounded) and thirty-nine NCOs and men. McCawley and five other officers present received brevet promotions for gallantry. Shortly afterward the Marine battalion was moved to Folly Island, south of Charleston. In 1864, it was dissolved.

Confederate Leathernecks also took part in a number of special operations. Early in 1864, plans were made for a combined assault on the enemy enclave on the Neuse River at New Bern, North Carolina. While Army units attacked the Union lines, boat parties would deal with any gunboats—three of which were active in the area— that might come to the garrison's aid. The naval contin-

gent was commanded by the redoubtable John Taylor Wood, a kind of freelance aide to President Davis, at once colonel, CSA, and commander, CSN, who had conducted several similar expeditions in Virginia waters. His party consisted of 115 officers and men from the James River Squadron, ten midshipmen from the Naval Academy, and twenty-five Company C Marines under Capt. Thomas S. Wilson from Camp Beall.

The Confederate ground attack miscarried on 1 February. Wood resolved to carry on with the naval part of the program, and shortly after 2:30 the following morning he and his men captured the gunboat *Underwriter* in hand-to-hand combat off New Bern. A Union lookout spotted the raiders three hundred yards from the ship, so the last part of their approach had to be made in the face of a stinging small arms fire from her deck. The Union fire was returned by Wilson's Leathernecks, who had been distributed among the expedition's boats for just that purpose. Afterward a southern midshipman recalled

Marine Barracks, Washington, and the commandant's house *(left)* during the Civil War.

the "conspicuous . . . conduct of the Marines . . . [who] rose and delivered their fire, taking accurate aim, [and] reloading still under the heavy fire from the enemy."[10] They then joined the fighting aboard the gunboat. One Marine lay among the five Confederate dead, and four were in the eleven wounded. Of the *Underwriter*'s crew, nine were killed and nineteen wounded; twenty-three escaped. When the force ashore began shelling the gunboat, her captors set her afire and withdrew.

All the expedition's members were honored by a joint resolution of thanks from the Confederate Congress. In a letter to Colonel Beall, Wood recorded his satisfaction with "the fine bearing and soldierly conduct of Captain Wilson and his men. . . . As a body they would be a credit to any organization, and I will be glad to be associated with them . . . at any time."[11]

Confederate Marines were also assigned a major role in what would have been an even more audacious undertaking: the liberation of the fourteen thousand Confederate prisoners of war confined at Point Lookout, Maryland, where the Potomac flows into the Chesapeake Bay. The operation was proposed by Gen. Robert E. Lee on 26 June and approved by President Davis, who en-

trusted its execution to John Taylor Wood. The latter quickly assembled a party of approximately 150 seamen from the James River Squadron and 130 Marines from Camp Beall and the two Richmond navy yards under Capt. George Holmes, the commander of Company A. With this force Wood planned to sail from Wilmington, land at Point Lookout, overwhelm the camp guards, and lead the ex-prisoners north around Washington into Virginia. Rifles enough were collected to arm two thousand of them, and Gen. Jubal Early, whose army crossed the Potomac into Maryland on 5 July, was told to be ready to detach a cavalry brigade to screen their march. Security leaks caused Davis to telegraph Wilmington canceling the expedition as it was putting to sea on the evening of 10 July.

By then, war had returned to Drewry's Bluff. On 5 May, Union Maj. Gen. Benjamin F. Butler, one of the war's outstandingly incompetent political generals, landed thirty thousand men at Bermuda Hundred on the James River roughly ten miles southeast of the bluff and twelve miles northeast of Petersburg. At that moment, the back door to Richmond was guarded by fewer than four thousand men. These included at most 350 artillerymen and Marines at Drewry's Bluff, whose defense had been entirely the Confederate Marine Corps's responsibility since March, when a manpower shortage had necessitated the withdrawal of the seamen stationed there. (In light of this development, Major Terrett was granted the additional commission of temporary colonel, CSA.)

To Richmond's relief, Butler failed to exploit his opportunity. Not until 12 May, after several timid probes toward Petersburg, did he advance on Drewry's Bluff. In the intervening week the Confederates had concentrated twenty thousand men around it. During a day's skirmishing on which Camp Beall's adjutant recorded that Major Terrett was "in the trenches" with his Leathernecks, the Union advance ground to a halt.[12] Four days later the Confederates counterattacked, drove Butler back to Bermuda Hundred, and proceeded to pen up his army behind a line of entrenchments, where it remained for the rest of the war.

The U.S. Marine Corps's commandant, Col. John Harris, died at age seventy-three on the day Butler attacked Drewry's Bluff. Not long before, he had performed what was perhaps his greatest service to the Corps as its commandant. Anticipating yet another congressional resolution to transfer it to the Army, he had shrewdly solicited testimonials from a galaxy of admirals extolling the Corps's value as a branch of the naval service. These statements helped squash the measure that was put forth soon after his death.

Harris's demise left Secretary of the Navy Welles embarrassed for a successor. The most likely candidate might have seemed to be John Reynolds, whose record of service was second to none, but he had ruined his chances in 1862. That spring Reynolds had become convinced that, despite the tradition barring staff officers from command, Paymaster Major Russell was conniving to position himself to become the Corps's next commandant, and that his scheme enjoyed Colonel Harris's blessing. Reynolds thereupon favored the commandant with a sharp open letter upholding the prerogatives of the line. While this may have cooked Russell's goose, it scorched Reynolds's gander. An outraged Colonel Harris court-martialed him on charges of drunkenness and disrespect. There was probably something to the first of these specifications. In his diary Welles recorded that pri-

Jacob Zeilin and his family posed for these postwar miniatures (hand-painted on cloth) following his promotion to brigadier general. On the left is Zeilin; above is his son, 2d Lt. William Freeman Zeilin; to the right is General Zeilin's wife, Virginia Freeman Zeilin; his elder daughter, Margaret Freeman Zeilin, is below. General Zeilin's younger daughter, Annie Valery Zeilin, is not pictured.

vately Reynolds himself acknowledged the failing, and a young officer who admired him wrote, "Colonel Reynolds always has everything about him in order, and, drunk or sober, duty must be carried on right."[13] Nevertheless, the court found him innocent on both counts. Reynolds celebrated his acquittal by filing charges against Harris, at which point the exasperated Secretary Welles brought the matter to a close by sending both men letters of reproof.

So it seems no wonder that following Harris's death Welles wrote grimly, "The higher class of Marine officers are not the men who can elevate or give efficiency

In 1863, 1st Lt. David G. Raney Jr. posed for a portrait that includes perhaps the clearest contemporary image of the black-trimmed gray coat of a Confederate Marine Corps officer. A year later, he commanded the ironclad *Tennessee*'s guard at the Battle of Mobile Bay. Florida State Archives, Tallahassee

to the Corps. To supersede them will cause much dissatisfaction. . . . But there is a duty to perform."[14] On 10 June he retired all four officers in the Corps above the age of sixty—as a consolation, they were allowed to remain on duty for the duration of the war—and fifty-seven-year-old Maj. Jacob Zeilin became the seventh commandant.

Although Welles's diary suggests that he was less impressed by Zeilin than unimpressed by his seniors, the new commandant possessed good credentials. A non-graduate of the West Point class of 1826, he had been commissioned into the Marine Corps in 1831, won a brevet for gallantry during the Mexican War, and served as Commodore Perry's senior Marine officer in the expedition to Japan. So far in the Civil War, he was the only

Marine besides Reynolds to command a battalion at the front. Neither Welles nor anyone else appears to have expected Zeilin to promote any major changes in the Corps, and he did not surprise them.

In contrast to their Union counterparts, most Confederate Marine officers would have been delighted to have the Army adopt their Corps. Apparently convinced that the Navy Department lacked sufficient influence to advance the Corps's interests—and no doubt frustrated by the limitations its size imposed on promotions—nearly all of them signed a petition to President Davis late in 1864 proposing that the Marine Corps be transferred to the Army and enlarged to a brigade of three regiments. One regiment was to be designated "Marine Infantry" and furnish ships' guards; the other two presumably would have consisted of Marine artillerists employed to garrison coastal fortifications. A resolution calling for the Committee on Naval Affairs to investigate the expediency of transferring (though not enlarging) the Corps was, in fact, introduced in the Confederate Senate on 6 February 1865, only to be tabled two days later.

The battered Confederacy of February 1865 would have had little use for Marine artillerists in any event. Most of the ports they would have defended had already been lost. At the beginning of June 1864, Mobile, Savannah, Charleston, and Wilmington remained in Confederate hands, and the first and last were havens for the swift gray steamers that still ran the blockade. Eight months later, all four ports had been captured or closed.

The process began at the Battle of Mobile Bay, an action in which both Marine Corps participated, on 5 August 1864. As at New Orleans, only this time in broad daylight, a Union fleet under Admiral Farragut had to fight its way through a narrow channel under fire from two masonry forts (Gaines and Morgan) with Confederate warships waiting to engage its leaders as they emerged. Farragut's force included four monitors and fourteen wooden sloops and gunboats. Adm. Franklin Buchanan's Mobile Squadron consisted of the ironclad ram *Tennessee* and three gunboats. The U.S. Navy did not assign Marines to monitors, but there were guard detachments on the other Union ships. All the Confederate vessels except the *Selma* carried officer's guards, and Captain Meiere collected two officers and twenty-five

A U.S. Marine Corps officer and men in the uniform worn during the Civil War. This photograph was probably taken in 1865.

NCOs and men from the Marines serving ashore to join a provisional battalion rushed to reinforce Fort Gaines.

The battle lasted barely three hours. Only a single Union vessel, the monitor *Tecumseh,* which strayed into a minefield, was lost during the passage of the forts. Inside the bay the others quickly disposed of the Confederate gunboats. The *Selma* struck her colors, the *Gaines* ran aground, and the *Morgan* retreated to Mobile. Left to carry on alone, the *Tennessee* was hammered into submission by Union gunfire after a wild melee. Her guard of thirty-three Marines was captured with her. Meiere's detachment followed them into captivity when Fort Gaines surrendered three days later. Union casualties totaled 315 killed and wounded, 8 of whom were Marines. Farragut's senior Marine officer, twenty-four-year-old Bvt. Maj. Charles Heywood, who had been in the *Cumberland,* won the brevet of lieutenant colonel and the sobriquet "the boy colonel." Sent to post a guard in the *Ten-*

nessee, he could not resist remarking to Admiral Buchanan that they had met before. The other two Marine officers present also received brevet promotions, and eight enlisted Marines were awarded the Medal of Honor. Mobile remained a Confederate city, but with Union ships in Mobile Bay it ceased to be a Confederate port.

Savannah's turn came next. On 15 November 1864 Gen. William T. Sherman set out from Atlanta on his March to the Sea. To facilitate his advance by complicating enemy troop movements, the South Atlantic Blockading Squadron organized an expedition of seamen, Marines, and assorted Army units to push up the Broad River from Port Royal, South Carolina, with the objective of cutting the Savannah-to-Charleston railroad. The Marine contingent, formed from ships' guards, consisted of 182 men under 1st Lt. George G. Stoddard, the squadron's sole Marine officer. Although the Leathernecks distinguished themselves in a series of sharp little

The Second Attack on Fort Fisher, 15 January 1865

actions and Stoddard earned a brevet captaincy, the defenders stopped the expedition short of the tracks.

The southerners' success was ephemeral. On 10 December Sherman's army of sixty thousand appeared outside Savannah, where the Confederates had been able to assemble only a quarter of that number to face them. Marines of Captain Tattnall's Company E served in the trenches during the skirmishing that preceded the evacuation of the city on 21 December. That night, most of the company boarded the railroad to Charleston while a sergeant's guard in the ironclad *Macon* started up the Savannah River to Augusta.

Wilmington was now the eastern Confederacy's only open port, and the Union had already initiated measures to close it. The city stood ten miles from the sea on the east bank of the Cape Fear River, whose entrance was defended by an enormous earthwork named Fort Fisher. Located near the tip of a peninsula curling down from the

north, the fort was built in the shape of a capital T, minus the right half of the crossbar. The left half bisected the peninsula above the high-water mark, a distance of approximately half a mile, and was called the land face. It mounted twenty heavy guns positioned one or two each in individual chambers connected by heavy traverses. The upstroke of the T, called the sea face, extended for more than a mile along the shore and mounted twenty-four guns in similar chambers. About fifty feet in front of the land face the peninsula was again bisected by a palisade of sharp-pointed logs, some five hundred feet in advance of which the defenders had laid a field of electrically detonated mines. To the left of the upstroke, at a landing on the river side of the peninsula, was Battery Buchanan, a detached work armed with four guns manned by naval personnel. Its purpose was to prevent enemy vessels from entering the river to attack the fort from the rear, and, should the fort fall, to serve as a strong point to which the garrison could retreat and from which it might be evacuated.

The first Confederate Marines had come to Wilmington from Camp Beall in January 1864 to furnish guards for the ironclads *North Carolina* and *Raleigh.* Capt. Alfred Van Benthuysen assumed command of these detachments in June, shortly after the expiration of the sentence imposed by his second court-martial enabled him to return to active duty. In November an officer's guard was assigned to Battery Buchanan, and when an enemy armada anchored off the coast on 23 December, Van Benthuysen took his Wilmington Marines to join Fort Fisher's garrison.

As it turned out, there was no need for them. For a day and a half a powerful Union fleet commanded by Rear Adm. David Dixon Porter subjected the fort to heavy but not especially accurate fire. Two thousand men, almost a third of Maj. Gen. Benjamin Butler's expeditionary force, landed the second afternoon. A close look at the fort led their commanders to conclude—probably with good reason—that it had not been damaged enough for an assault to be feasible. On 26 December the troops reembarked and the fleet withdrew.

Undeterred by this setback, Union leaders promptly organized a second Fort Fisher expedition. Porter retained his command, but Butler was replaced by capable Maj. Gen. Alfred H. Terry and the Army contingent was increased to eight thousand men. The new armada appeared off Fort Fisher late on 12 January 1865. Captain Van Benthuysen's seventy-some Marines were among the seven hundred reinforcements that reached the fort via Battery Buchanan over the next thirty-six hours, raising the strength of the garrison to fifteen hundred men. They were in for the fight of their lives.

This time the Union fleet's fire proved extremely accurate. Starting on the fourteenth it was seconded by batteries emplaced by the troops who had begun landing the day before. By 3:00 P.M. on the fifteenth, the hour chosen for the assault, all except one of the guns in Fort Fisher's land face had been silenced, the underground wires to the minefields had been severed, and gaps had been opened in the palisade.

The Union plan called for simultaneous assaults to be made against both ends of the fort's land face. The west-

ern attack, along the riverbank, would be delivered by Terry's infantry; the eastern attack, along the seashore, by a naval brigade from Porter's fleet. The latter consisted of sixteen hundred seamen grouped in three divisions led by their ships' officers and an improvised battalion of four hundred Marines under Capt. Lucian L. Dawson. In overall command Porter placed his fleet captain (chief of staff), Lt. Cdr. K. R. Breese.

According to the instructions Dawson received from Breese, the Marines were to advance by stages to occupy three successive lines of rifle pits being dug by naval working parties, the last only two hundred yards from the fort. In this position they would provide covering fire for the naval divisions, which had been armed with pistols and cutlasses. On the order to attack, the sailors would charge through them and, as Porter quaintly put it, "board the fort on the run in a seamanlike way."[15] Once the sailors had passed, the Marines would follow.

Things began to go wrong almost at once. Dawson was still sorting out his battalion when Breese ordered him to bring it to the front. The Marines had barely reached the second line of rifle pits when a new order arrived. Breese had discovered that the incline where the beach sloped down to the sea furnished "splendid cover."[16] Dawson was to move his Marines there. Soon the entire brigade was lying in a long column beside the water's edge, with the Leathernecks abreast and inland of the second naval division. The next order Dawson heard was the shout, "Charge! Charge!"[17]

With a cheer, the brigade sprang up and dashed down the beach toward Fort Fisher, some six hundred yards away. Fire from riflemen on the fort's parapet halted the head of the column fifty yards short of its goal. A few sturdy souls managed to get inside the palisade. Most of their comrades threw themselves to the ground, where, in the words of an officer present, "they were packed like sheep in a pen, while the enemy was crowding the ramparts . . . and shooting into them as fast as they could fire."[18] Captain Dawson had just caught up to his leading company after a hard run through the soft sand when the sailors broke to the rear. Seeing panic spread throughout the column, he shouted to the Marines: "Lie down and fire at the parapet!"[19] Most of the men in the first two companies obeyed him; most of those in the last two

The Naval Brigade's Assault on Fort Fisher, 18 January 1865, is depicted in this late nineteenth-century chromolithograph.
Beverley R. Robinson Collection

joined the stampede. As soon as the brigade was out of range, he ordered the men who had stayed with him to retire by squads. Dawson himself and a number of officers remained outside the fort until nightfall.

All told, the naval brigade suffered 351 casualties, among them fifty-seven Marines: sixteen killed or missing and forty-one wounded. Captain Dawson and seven of his officers were breveted for gallantry. Seven enlisted Marines earned Medals of Honor (one for heroism aboard a ship on the firing line), the last of seventeen awarded to Leathernecks during the Civil War.

Yet these honors lay in the future. In the immediate aftermath of the attack, Lieutenant Commander Breese ungraciously affixed the blame for the rout on "the absence of the Marines from their [assigned] position."[20] Although Breese graciously added that he attributed their failure to insufficient time to organize "so many small squads of men from the different vessels" and "not . . . to

any want of personal valor," Captain Dawson's detailed reports make clear where the fault really lay.[21] Unfortunately, most Navy officers took Breese's view, thereby creating a point of dissension that would trouble U.S. Navy–Marine Corps relations for the next thirty years. The fundamental error, as the leader of one of the naval divisions commented years later, "was in expecting a body of sailors, collected hastily from different ships, armed with swords and pistols, to stand against veteran soldiers armed with rifles and bayonets." Future admiral George Dewey, who watched the assault from the deck of his ship, summed it up nicely: "Such an attempt was sheer, murderous madness."[22]

Well merited as these strictures were, the charge had one positive albeit unintended consequence. It served as an admirable diversion for the Army's assault. No more than 500 of Fort Fisher's defenders were involved in its repulse, but this left only 250 to hold the western land face, a late reinforcement of 350 men who had been ordered there declining to depart the bomb-proofs in which they had taken refuge. Furthermore, the attack absorbed the attention of both the fort's dynamic young commander, Col. William Lamb, and his superior officer, Maj. Gen. W. H. C. Whiting, the Wilmington district commander, who had felt honor-bound to join the garrison. Thus, glancing at the opposite end of the land face after the naval brigade had been beaten off, they were astonished to see three Union flags waving over it.

Calling on the men nearby to follow, Whiting rushed along the parapet toward the enemy. He soon went down with wounds to which he would eventually succumb, but his charge checked the Union advance. For the next five hours Fort Fisher was the scene of some of the most intense combat of the war as men fought, often with clubbed rifles, through the traverses between the land-face gun chambers. Lamb built up a front to contain the Union brigades pushing into the work from the west; Porter's fleet shifted its fire from the sea-face batteries to the struggle under way in the interior of the fort; and the sea-face batteries that could be brought to bear did the same. To his dying day, Lamb believed that had he not been disabled by a shot in the hip at the moment of launching a counterattack for which he had scraped up every available man, he could have driven its assailants out of Fort Fisher before sunset. Exactly where the Confederate Leathernecks were engaged is unknown, but that they were heavily engaged is evident from the fact that four of their six officers were wounded. Eight of the sixty-six enlisted Marines who survived had also been wounded, three mortally. Several weeks later, a midshipman who had been stationed at Wilmington recorded having heard that "our men, as a general thing, behaved well. The company of marines fought splendidly."[23]

Around 9:00 P.M., the arrival of a fourth Union brigade caused the defense to crumble. Captain Van Benthuysen, himself wounded in the head, decided that the time had come to evacuate Whiting and Lamb. A squad of his Marines carried the two officers toward Battery Buchanan. The remnants of the garrison, some four hundred men, soon followed. A terrible disappointment awaited them. The naval officer commanding the battery, a work erected in part to support a garrison in such a situation, had spiked its guns, withdrawn its men, and taken everything that could float. Fort Fisher's defenders had been abandoned to their fate.

The capture of Fort Fisher completed the Anaconda Plan's amphibious agenda. As of 16 January 1865, the eastern Confederacy was isolated from the world beyond. In the words of Rear Adm. Raphael Semmes, "The anaconda had, at last, wound its fatal folds around us."[24] Although ships' guards continued to do duty in blockaders off the southern coast and participated in the capture of the city of Mobile, for the U.S. Marine Corps the war was as good as over. It had seen its last significant Civil War combat.

This was not the case with the Confederate Marine Corps, whose most trying times lay just ahead. On 17 February 1865 Sherman's army, striking north from Savannah, forced Charleston's defenders to evacuate the city after a siege of 567 days. Commo. John R. Tucker, commanding the Charleston Squadron, destroyed his ships and led their seamen and Marines north on a circuitous journey to Richmond. There his command was combined with the Marine battalion at Drewry's Bluff to form a unit known as Tucker's Naval Brigade. Captain Tatnall's Company E withdrew into the interior of North Carolina, where it remained until the end of the war.

The end was not long in coming. Before dawn on 2 April, Union forces enjoying an overall numerical superiority in excess of two to one punched through the overextended Confederate lines south of Petersburg. Later that morning, Lee advised Davis that the Army would have to evacuate Richmond. Tucker's Naval Brigade, almost five hundred strong, was assigned to a scratch Corps commanded by Lt. Gen. Richard S. Ewell and accompanied Lee's army as it retreated to the west. An order was also sent to Admiral Semmes, commanding the James River Squadron, to join Lee with the squadron's five hundred officers and men, but by the time they had destroyed their ships and reached Richmond, the Army had withdrawn and the "last train" had departed. Putting together a train of its own at the railroad depot, the little force proceeded to Danville, Virginia, just above the North Carolina line, where Semmes expected to find Lee.

Lee hoped that his army would be able to shake off its

pursuers. His hopes were in vain. Union cavalry tore at the flanks and rear of the shrinking Confederate columns, sometimes slowing them sufficiently for enemy infantry to come up and engage them. Colonel Terrett was among a number of Confederate Leathernecks captured in the rear-guard action at Amelia Court House on 5 April. The next day, enemy pressure compelled Ewell's Corps to halt and give battle on the wooded heights overlooking a stream called Saylor's Creek.

Tucker's Naval Brigade was posted between Ewell's two divisions. The artillery continued its retreat. Following a preliminary bombardment to which the Confederates could not reply, two Union divisions deployed into a single line, waded the creek, and advanced up the slope. As they neared its crest, Ewell's men surprised them with a counterattack that hurled the Union center back in disorder. All accounts agree that the Marines, now commanded by Captain Simms, distinguished themselves in this action. In his official report, a Union division commander recorded that "the Confederate Marine Battalion fought with particular obstinacy."[25] A Confederate soldier said it more simply: "Those marines fought like tigers and against odds of at least ten to one."[26]

But the effort was in vain. Other Union forces quickly enveloped both Confederate flanks, and Ewell's divisions were obliged to lay down their arms. Not so the naval brigade. Unaware of the disaster befalling its neighbors, it retired into a densely wooded ravine where it remained undisturbed. Near dusk, a Union general investigating rumors that a Confederate formation was lurking there unwittingly rode into its lines. Narrowly escaping with his life, he returned under a flag of truce and acquainted Tucker with the hopelessness of his situation. The commodore then agreed to surrender. Afterward he told a friend that, never before having been in a land battle, he had thought "everything was going on well."[27] An incomplete return shows that Captain Simms, six other Marine officers, and forty-five NCOs and men were captured with him.

A few other Leathernecks somehow managed to slip away. For the next three days these gallant men soldiered through the death throes of the Army of Northern Virginia. Four officers and twenty-five men were present to surrender with Lee at Appomattox Court House on 9 April. Among them was 1st Lt. Richard Henderson. One suspects that his father would have been proud.

Admiral Semmes's command spent that fateful April week in Danville. Detraining around midnight on the fourth, Semmes found the Confederate government already established in the little town. The next morning he was commissioned a brigadier general, CSA, and the seamen and Marines of the James River Squadron were organized into an artillery brigade that, together with two infantry battalions, formed the garrison of the Confederacy's temporary capital. That responsibility ended the day after Appomattox, the news of which caused the government to flee south. Subsequently attached to the Confederate Army in North Carolina, the brigade surrendered at Greensboro on 1 May. The remnants of Company E had stacked arms there three days earlier.

The last Marine unit to serve under the Stars and Bars was Company C, which had been partially reconstituted following its near destruction in the Battle of Mobile Bay. Between 27 March and 11 April its members served afloat and ashore in the unsuccessful defense of Mobile against a Union offensive along the eastern side of the bay. The city fell on 12 April, and the Mobile Squadron retreated some thirty miles up the Mobile River to Nanna Hubba Bluff. At the time of its surrender on 10 May the guard detachments in the gunboats *Nashville* and *Morgan* numbered three lieutenants and twenty-four NCOs and men.

The American Marines' Civil War thereby came to an end. In the course of the conflict the U.S. Marine Corps had lost 77 men killed in action or dead of wounds, 131 wounded, and 142 captured, while 257 died of causes unrelated to combat. Aside from the approximately 250 men who are known to have been captured, the lack of records precludes a comparable determination of Confederate Marine Corps casualties.

6

At Sea in the Gilded Age, 1865–1898

Most historians of the Marine Corps have been faintly embarrassed by the Corps's performance in the Civil War, attributing its failure to cultivate an amphibious capability to a lack of institutional vision. At the restoration of peace, however, nearly everyone in high places in the Corps, the Navy, and indeed the government as a whole was well pleased with the part it had played. This became obvious as an ironic result of a congressional resolution introduced in June 1866 directing the House Naval Affairs Committee to investigate the feasibility of disbanding the Corps. Lifting a leaf from his predecessor's book, Colonel Zeilin collected encomiums to the Corps's service from no fewer than fourteen of the war's foremost admirals, including Farragut, Porter, Dahlgren, and Du Pont. The outcome was a triumph for the Marines and their supporters. Reporting adversely on the resolution in February 1867, the committee asserted:

> From the beginning, this Corps seems to have satisfactorily fulfilled the purposes of its organization, and no good reason appears for either abolishing it or transferring it to the Army; on the contrary, the Committee recommends that its organization as a separate Corps be preserved and strengthened . . . [and] that its commanding officer shall hold the rank of brigadier general.[1]

The Senate's approval of the latter recommendation made Jacob Zeilin the first Marine to attain regular rank as a general officer, Archibald Henderson having been a general by brevet. At least for the time being, the Corps also escaped the usual postwar cutbacks. Whereas the Army had enlisted most of its men "for the duration" of the war, the Corps had continued to have its recruits sign up for four years. Unless they could obtain substitutes, Marines were required to serve out that period.

Eventually, of course, the ax fell. It did not fall on the Leathernecks alone. Most Americans, their absorption in domestic affairs only rarely interrupted by fleeting war scares, saw no reason to spend large sums on armed forces for which they foresaw no need. By 1870, the number of the Navy's active ships had dwindled from a wartime peak of nearly seven hundred to barely fifty, and a few years later, the size of the Army was cut from fifty-four thousand to twenty-seven thousand men. The Corps's turn came in 1874, when its enlisted force was reduced by a third, from three thousand to two thousand men. The strength of its officer corps was capped at seventy-five, and although General Zeilin kept his star, the rank attached to the office of commandant was rolled back to colonel.

Compared with the two larger armed services, the Marine Corps got off lightly. Because the Corps was so small to begin with, however, it found the cuts particularly painful. For the next quarter century it operated in a condition of chronic overstretch. On only a handful of occasions would as many as two hundred Leathernecks be assembled in any one place. The effects of the ceiling set on the officer corps were equally unfortunate. There were years—sometimes, years in succession—when the Corps could not commission a single second lieutenant. At the same time, promotion practically

The Marine Corps recruited boys as musicians during the Civil War and the Gilded Age. William Crawford, age thirteen, appears in this photograph taken in 1866. He enlisted as a fifer in that year, and reenlisted in 1870, 1874, and 1879.

Henry Clay Cochrane, seen here about 1900, was among the most outspoken of the Corps's reformers.

ceased, especially for the bloc of company-grade officers who had joined during the Civil War.

The experiences of Henry Clay Cochrane, who had escorted President Lincoln to Gettysburg, may serve as a case in point. Cochrane had been commissioned in September 1861 and promoted to first lieutenant in August 1865. Thereafter he waited nearly fourteen years for his next promotion, and at the opening of the Gay Nineties he had yet to receive another. No wonder that in a plaintive, not to say pathetic, letter written as a white-bearded captain to Secretary of the Navy Hilary A. Herbert in 1894 Cochrane lamented that "the years are rapidly passing, my vision is fading, my hair and teeth are going, and

it has dawned on me that I am on the down hill side of life and yet doing practically the same duty that I did more than a quarter of a century ago."[2]

Just as the Civil War is often viewed as being far from the Corps's finest hour, the thirty-three years that intervened before the War with Spain are generally considered its nadir. Such an interpretation requires qualification. While it is true that the decades in question were devoid of big battles, they included no fewer than twenty-nine landings, one of which (Korea, 1871) was a sizable operation by contemporary standards. On more than a dozen other occasions, Marines were deployed in support of the civil authority within the United States. Their activities in this role ranged from escorting revenue agents in raids on illegal stills in a turbulent neighborhood known as Irishtown near the Boston Navy Yard (1867, 1868, 1871) and helping maintain order in Baltimore, Philadelphia, and Reading during the great railway strike of 1877 to guarding a quarantine camp established at Sandy Hook, New York, when cholera was discovered aboard immigrant ships (1892).

Attack of the U.S. Marines and Sailors on the Pirates on the Island of Formosa, East Indies, was the caption of this woodcut in *Harper's Weekly* for 7 September 1867. Beverley R. Robinson Collection

Thirteen of the landings, including all three in which shots were fired, took place on General Zeilin's watch. The first was a punitive expedition against the aborigines—"savages" in the less-nuanced language of the day—inhabiting the southeastern tip of Formosa (Taiwan) in retaliation for the massacre of the shipwrecked crew of the American bark *Rover* in March 1867. This turned out to be one of the few nineteenth-century operations in which a landing party found that it had bitten off more than it could comfortably chew. On the morning of 13 June, the screw sloop *Hartford,* flagship of the U.S. Asiatic Squadron, and the screw sloops *Plymouth* and *Wyoming* anchored off the landing site. From their decks officers with long glasses could see small groups of aborigines in breechclouts, their bodies painted red, musket barrels glinting in the sun, gathering on hilltops two miles away. At 9:30 A.M., the *Hartford*'s skipper, Cdr. George E. Belknap, led a force of 181 men ashore. Included in this number were forty-three Marines under Capt. James Forney, who had earned a brevet for gallantry in command of one of Farragut's guard detachments at New Orleans.

Pushing inland under a blazing sun, the expedition tried in vain to come to grips with the Formosans. The Asiatic Squadron's commander, Rear Adm. H. H. Bell, recorded the party's frustration:

> As our men marched into the hills, the savages, knowing the paths, boldly decided to meet them, and, gliding through the high grass and from cover to cover, displayed a stratagem and courage equal to our North American Indians. Delivering their fire, they retreated without being seen by our men, who, charging upon their covers, frequently fell into ambuscades. Our detachments pursued them, in this harassing manner, out of sight of the ships, until two o'clock P.M.[3]

At that time Commander Belknap called a halt to rest the men, many of whom had begun to show signs of heat prostration. So far the force had burned a few huts, but that was the extent of its accomplishments. Half an hour later, while the main body remained inert, Belknap's second-in-command, Lt. Comdr. Alexander S. Mackenzie, was killed leading the advance guard into a thicket from which shots had been fired. Mackenzie's death and the battalion's exhaustion convinced Belknap that it would be wise to fall back to the beach where the party's boats

The first photograph ever made of American Marines entering action pictures the gunboat *Palos* towing the Asiatic Squadron's landing party toward Kanghwa-do, Korea, on 10 June 1871. Naval Historical Center

were under guard. The additional exertion brought the expedition close to collapse, and by 4:00 P.M. the men were back aboard ship. Three years later, Forney was awarded a brevet for his part in the affair. No other Marine officer obtained that distinction between 1865 and 1898.

The next contested operation was smaller in scale but more successful: the seizure and burning of the pirate steamer *Forward* by six boats of sailors and Marines from the screw sloop *Mohican* in the Teacapan River on the Pacific coast of Mexico, on 17 June 1870. The last such operation was also successful, and it included the largest-scale combat in which Leathernecks participated in the three decades following the Civil War. This was the Korean Expedition of 1871.

On 23 May of that year, five vessels of Rear Adm. John Rodgers's Asiatic Fleet—the frigate *Colorado,* sloops *Alaska* and *Benicia,* and gunboats *Monocacy* and *Palos*—entered Roze Roads on the west coast of Korea not far from Chemulpo (modern-day Inchon). Aboard Admiral Rodgers's flagship, the *Colorado,* was Frederick F. Low, the U.S. minister to China, who had been sent to open diplomatic relations with the hermit kingdom of Korea. Contact was made with the local inhabitants, and on the thirty-first a small delegation of third- and fifth-rank Korean officials appeared. Low refused to receive them, directing his secretary to explain that the presence of first-rank officials qualified to conduct negotiations was required. In the meantime, the Koreans were informed, the Americans desired to chart the Salee River, as the channel of the Han River between Kanghwa-do

(island) and the Kumpo Peninsula was then called. As the Han leads to the capital city of Seoul, the Koreans might have been expected to consider such an act provocative, American assurances of goodwill notwithstanding, but they raised no objections. Twenty-four hours were allotted for them to notify the appropriate authorities.

Accordingly, at noon on 1 June, four steam launches followed by the *Monocacy* and *Palos* set out to begin the survey. As they came abreast of the fortifications on the heights of Kanghwa-do, the Koreans opened fire. The surveying party replied with gusto, shelling the forts into silence, and returned to the fleet's anchorage. American casualties were two men wounded.

Admiral Rodgers waited nine days for an apology or better tides. The former was not forthcoming, and on 10 June a punitive expedition entered the river with the mission of capturing and destroying the errant forts. The landing force numbered 686 officers and men, including 109 Marines organized into two little companies and a naval battery of seven 12-pounder howitzers. Fire support would be provided by the gunboats and four steam launches mounting 12-pounders in their bows. Cdr. L. A. Kimberly was placed in command of the landing force; Capt. McLane Tilton led its Leathernecks. Tilton was one of those unconventional characters for whom the Corps has always seemed to exercise an attraction. (Writing his wife from a Mediterranean deployment, he reported that when he first went on deck each day, "If anyone asks me how are you old fellow, I reply, 'I don't feel very well; no gentleman is ever well in the morning.'")[4]

Three forts, each with a walled water-battery, over-looked the shore of Kanghwa-do. In the course of the operation, the Americans christened them the Marine Redoubt, Fort Monocacy, and the Citadel. The *Monocacy* took the first two under fire shortly after noon. Both had been silenced by the time the *Palos* appeared with the landing party's boats in tow about an hour later. The boats cast off half a mile below the nearest fort, and at 1:45 that afternoon the bluejackets and Marines began struggling ashore across a broad, knee-deep mudflat "crossed by deep sluices," a disgusted Tilton noted, "filled with softer and still deeper mud."[5] Some men left their shoes, socks, leggings, and even trouser legs behind, and the howitzers bogged down to their barrels. Fortunately, the Koreans did not attempt to oppose the landing.

The Leathernecks had been selected to serve as the expedition's advance guard. Tilton deployed them into a skirmish line as soon as they left the boats. Once both companies reached firm ground, Commander Kimberly ordered Tilton to lead his Marines toward the fort, an elliptical stone redoubt with twelve-foot walls. Most of the sailors remained behind to manhandle the guns out of the muck. On the Marines' approach, the fort's white-robed defenders fled, firing a few parting shots. The work mounted fifty-four guns, but all except two were insignificant brass breechloaders. Tilton halted his men until the main body came up, "when we were again ordered to push forward," he wrote, "which we did, scouring the fields as far as practicable from the left of the line of march, the river being on our right, and took a position on a wooded knoll . . . commanding a fine view of the beautiful hills and inundated rice fields immediately around us."[6] At this point he received orders to hold for the night. It was 4:30 P.M. before the guns had been dragged ashore, and too few hours of daylight remained to demolish the captured fort and tackle the next. The seamen bivouacked half a mile to the rear.

The landing force moved out at 5:30 the next morning. Its fire support had been reduced by the withdrawal of the *Palos,* which had hurt herself on an uncharted rock while the landing was in progress, but that available from the *Monocacy* and the launches would prove more than sufficient. The second fort, a chipped granite structure about ninety feet square, stood on a bluff a mile up-

The Assault on the Korean Forts, 10–12 June 1871. (1) Infantry landing site; (2) artillery landing site; (3) naval encampment, night of 10 June; (4) Marine encampment, same night; (5) route of advance on 11 June; (6 and 7) points at which seamen and guns were detached to check Korean forces to the west; (8) U.S. skirmish line immediately prior to the assault on the Citadel.

stream. Tilton's men found it deserted. While a Marine bugler amused himself by rolling thirty-three little brass cannon over the bluff into the river, other members of the expedition spiked the fort's four big guns and tore down two of its walls. The march was then resumed.

The track between the first two forts had been relatively easy going, but beyond the second it became extremely difficult, "the topography of the country being indescribable," Tilton reported, "resembling a sort of 'chopped sea,' of immense hills and deep ravines lying in every conceivable position."[7] Presently the column came under long-range musket fire from a Korean force estimated to number from two to five thousand among some hills beyond the Americans' left flank. Five guns supported by three companies of seamen were deployed to hold this body in check, and the remainder of the party continued its advance. On two occasions the Koreans made a rush toward the detachment, but a few artillery shells turned them back each time.

Korean dead inside the Citadel. Naval Historical Center

The last and strongest of the Korean fortifications, the Citadel, was a stone redoubt crowning a steep, conical hill on a peninsula some two miles upstream from its neighbor. The *Monocacy* and the steam launches opened fire on the Citadel at about 11:00 A.M. At noon, Commander Kimberly halted his command six hundred yards from the fort to give the men a breather. By that time, the parties of Koreans seen falling back on the Citadel and the forest of flags in and around it left no doubt that the position would be defended.

After signaling the *Monocacy* to cease fire, the storming party, 350 seamen and Marines with fixed bayonets, dashed forward to occupy a ridgeline only 120 yards from the fort. Although Tilton's men were still armed with the model 1861 muzzle-loading Springfield rifle musket (in his words "a blasted old *Muzzle-Fuzzel*"), they quickly established fire superiority over the fort's defenders, who were armed with matchlocks, a firearm

that had disappeared from Western arsenals two hundred years before.[8] "The firing continued for only a few minutes, say four," Tilton wrote, "amidst the melancholy songs of the enemy, their bearing being courageous in the extreme."[9]

At half past twelve Lt. Cdr. Silas Casey, commanding the bluejacket battalion, gave the order to charge. "[A]nd as little parties of our forces advanced closer and closer down the deep ravine between us," Tilton continued, "some of [the Koreans] mounted the parapet and threw stones etc., at us, uttering the while exclamations seemingly of defiance."[10] The first American into the Citadel, Navy Lt. Hugh W. McKee, fell mortally wounded by a musket ball in the groin and a spear thrust in the side. The spearman also stabbed at Lt. Cdr. Winfield Scott Schley, who had followed close behind McKee. The point passed between Schley's left arm and his chest, pinning his sleeve to his coat, and he shot the man dead.

The Korean commanding general's flag and its captors aboard the *Colorado. From left to right:* Cpl. Charles Brown, Pvt. Hugh Purvis, and Capt. McLane Tilton.

Tilton was among half a dozen officers who led their men into the fort moments later. The Koreans stood their ground, and the fighting became hand to hand. Clambering over the parapet, Pvt. Michael McNamara encountered an enemy soldier pointing a matchlock at him. He wrenched the gun from the Korean's hands and clubbed him to death with it. Pvt. James Dougherty closed with and killed the man the Americans identified as the commander of the Korean forces. Tilton, Pvt. Hugh Purvis, and Cpl. Charles Brown converged on the Citadel's principal standard, a twelve-foot-square yellow cotton banner emblazoned with black characters signifying "commanding general." For five minutes the fort's interior was a scene of desperate combat. Then the remaining defenders fled downhill toward the river, under fire from the Marines, a company of seamen, and the two howitzers that had accompanied the attackers.

A total of 143 Korean dead and wounded were counted in and around the Citadel, and Lieutenant Commander Schley, the landing force's adjutant, estimated that another 100 had been killed in flight. Forty-seven flags and 481 pieces of ordnance, most quite small but including 27 sizable pieces—20-pounders and upward—were captured. The storming party lost three men killed and ten wounded, with a Marine private in each category. Captain Tilton was pleasantly surprised by his survival. In a letter home a few days later, he wrote, "I never expected to see my wife and baby any more, and if it hadn't been that the Coreans [*sic*] can't shoot true, I never should."[11] He retired as a lieutenant colonel in 1897.

Nine sailors and six Marines were awarded the Medal of Honor. Among the latter were Corporal Brown and Private Purvis, who had rendezvoused with Tilton at the Citadel's flagstaff.

The landing force reembarked early the next morning, leaving the Citadel in ruins. "Thus," wrote Admiral Rodgers, "was a treacherous attack upon our people and an insult to our flag redressed."[12] Successful as it had been from a military standpoint, however, the operation was not a masterstroke of diplomacy. Subsequent communications with Korean authorities, conducted by messages tied to a pole on an island near the anchorage, were entirely unproductive, and on 3 July the fleet withdrew. A treaty with Korea was not negotiated until 1882.

The view that the Corps spent the years from 1865 to 1898 in suspended animation must also be modified to take into account the reform movement that developed among its company-grade officers. Perhaps the most articulate of the reformers was Henry Clay Cochrane, whose promotion problems have already been noted. In a pamphlet printed for confidential circulation among his brother officers in 1875, Cochrane asserted that the Corps, "neither respected nor respectable," stood in need of "a resuscitation or a funeral."[13] The best thing might be for it to acquire a new name and mission as the U.S. Naval Artillery, with the task of manning the country's coastal fortifications. That idea found scant support among Cochrane's colleagues, most of whom cherished the Corps's link to the Navy as its key to salvation, but the remainder of his program reflected the progressive consensus. Its objective was to transform the Corps into a military elite. This was to be accomplished by improving the quality of its officers and men; providing professional education for all ranks; rationalizing its organization as a brigade composed of permanent regiments; and, especially after the cutback of 1874, increasing its authorized strength.

The officer corps would be upgraded by restricting commissions to graduates of the service academies, instituting physical and professional examinations for promotion, and lowering the mandatory retirement age to sixty-two. In addition to their purely professional benefits, the first and second of these measures would reduce

the effects of the political influence all officers deplored—at least when exerted by others. The second and third, by eliminating the unfit and infirm, would enhance the opportunities of the able, a highly attractive prospect to captains who, studying the Corps's lineal list, could expect to remain captains for twenty years.

The caliber of enlisted Marines was to be raised by similar means. These included more selective recruiting, improving the conditions of service and the quality of barracks life, instituting orderly avenues of advancement to noncommissioned rank, and standardizing drill and training, which was still largely at the whim of the barracks commanders. Reformers believed that these initiatives would not only promote discipline but also discourage desertion, which hovered around an embarrassing 20 percent per annum, the highest in the armed forces.

Contrary to what Cochrane's pamphlet implied, General Zeilin had been neither an inactive nor a reactionary commandant. Like the reformers, he was acutely concerned about the quality of the enlisted force. In fact, he coined a phrase that would serve generations of Marine recruiters, asserting that "a few good men are preferable to a number of . . . inferior material."[14] An at least moderately progressive outlook was further evidenced by Zeilin's adoption of a tactical manual embodying the lessons of the Civil War, Maj. Gen. Emory Upton's *Infantry Tactics,* and the dispatch of Capt. James Forney on a year's tour to study and report on the organization and activities of European Marine forces.

Zeilin also exerted a long-lasting influence on the Corps's insignia and accouterments. In 1868 he convened a board of officers that produced the eagle, globe, and anchor cap device that, with some stylistic revision, remains in use today. And in 1875 he approved his officers' request for the return of the Mameluke sword; the Army sword was retained for NCOs. The same set of uniform regulations also eliminated the high leather stock that had chafed Marine necks for nearly a century. Nevertheless, there is no question that Zeilin's view of the Corps was fundamentally conservative. The changes in which he had interested himself did not extend much beyond keeping the service operationally up-to-date. As if in response to the reformers' more far-reaching aims, his last annual report included the almost defiant declaration that "the present organization of the Marine Corps is the best that can be devised."[15]

On 1 November 1876 Jacob Zeilin retired, having spent forty-five of his seventy years in Marine uniform, and Charles G. McCawley became the Corps's eighth commandant. Zeilin had established McCawley as his heir apparent by appointing him commanding officer of Marine Barracks, Washington, and director of recruiting in 1871, and the transition was tranquil. The only Marine officer to have been breveted for gallantry in both the Mexican and Civil Wars (at Chapultepec and Fort Sumter, respectively), McCawley had been associated with the Corps since boyhood; his father was a Marine captain who had died on active duty in 1839.

Although at forty-nine McCawley was too old to be counted among the reformers, he shared a number of their goals. Perhaps because of his years in recruiting, he was especially interested in improving the conditions of enlisted service. He planned to provide better food, monthly rather than quarterly pay periods, more livable barracks with recreational facilities, and higher status for NCOs. McCawley also hoped to persuade Congress to increase the Corps's strength by four hundred men and to restore the rank of brigadier general to the office of commandant. He eschewed any notion of organizing the Corps into permanent units, but directed an increased emphasis on standardizing drill and training.

The results of McCawley's efforts were mixed. The professional potential of the enlisted force was enhanced by requiring recruits to be able to read, write, and speak English. Examinations became mandatory for promotion to corporal and sergeant. Two barracks were built, and Congress agreed to institute a pension for thirty years' faithful service, a benefit not extended to the Navy's enlisted men until the end of the century. Contrary to all expectations, however, the desertion rate remained as high as ever. The commandant's campaigns to obtain more men and a star were also unavailing.

As it transpired, the most important reform of the McCawley years was accomplished courtesy of the Navy. One of the points on which the commandant and the reformers agreed was that the best way to improve the quality of the officer corps would be to fill its openings with graduates of the service academies. That would require a change in existing legislation, which reserved the graduating classes of both institutions to their school's parent service. In 1880 and again in 1881, McCawley sought permission to recruit graduates of the Military Academy. Congress declined to act on his requests, but on 5 August 1882 it passed a naval appropriations bill containing a clause, inserted on the Navy's initiative, that authorized the Corps to commission Naval Academy graduates.

The Navy's motives were not altogether altruistic. By 1882 the personnel of the shrunken fleet included one officer for every four enlisted men. To check the influx of unneeded officers, the House Naval Affairs Committee had drafted a bill, sure to pass, limiting the number of appointments made each year to the number of vacancies that had occurred the year before. For the foreseeable future, many if not most academy graduates would be surplus to requirements. Allowing some of them to enter the Marine Corps would not only increase the government's return on investment, but also—so it was hoped, and so it proved—promote homogeneity among the officer corps of the sea services.

While the Act of 5 August 1882 did not restrict the Corps's intake of officers to Annapolis graduates, that was its predictable effect. Every one of the fifty-two second lieutenants commissioned from 1883 to 1897—later to be rounded off as the "Famous Fifty"—was an alumnus of the Naval Academy. Their number included five successive commandants: George Barnett, class of 1881 (1914–20); John A. Lejeune, class of 1888 (1920–29); Wendell C. Neville, class of 1890 (1929–30); Ben H. Fuller, class of 1889 (1930–34); and John H. Russell, class of 1892 (1934–36); plus thirteen other general officers. These men's influence on the evolution of the Corps would be immense.

Two of McCawley's internal initiatives also made major contributions to the Marine Corps's heritage. The first was the reinvigoration of the Marine Band, which had undergone a marked decline following Francis Scala's retirement in 1871, by the appointment of young John Philip Sousa to be its leader in 1880. The son of a

The Marine guard in the sloop *Lancaster* stands inspection, circa 1883. Naval Historical Center

sometime Marine bandsman, Sousa had originally joined the band as a thirteen-year-old "music boy" in 1868 and had gone on to conduct light-opera companies. A tireless drillmaster and prolific composer with a superb sense of theater, he quickly pulled the band out of the doldrums. In 1892 Sousa resigned his position to enter show business, in which he became internationally famous as the "March King," but by then the Marine Band had attained new heights of popularity. By that time, too, its repertoire included the rousing strains of the "Marine Hymn," first

performed shortly after the Civil War. The origin and the author of the lyrics are unknown. The melody is that of the "Gendarmes of the Queen" duet in the Offenbach opera *Geneviève de Brabant,* originally staged in Paris in 1859.

McCawley's other lasting contribution to the Corps's heritage, made in 1883, was the adoption of what was destined to become the most famous American military motto: Semper Fidelis (Always Faithful). It replaced Per Mare, Per Terram (By Sea, By Land), which General

Future "March King" John Philip Sousa reinvigorated the Marine Band during his tenure as director, 1880–1892.

Zeilin had appropriated from Britain's Royal Marines. Five years later, when John Philip Sousa composed the official Marine Corps march, he used the new motto as the title. As McCawley may or may not have been aware, the British connection continued, for Semper Fidelis was also the motto of the Devonshire Regiment.

Operationally, the fourteen years and three months McCawley served as commandant were among the quietest Marines have ever experienced. On only six occasions did disturbances ashore lead to landings, and all except one of them were minor operations involving no more than a ship's guard. The exception, however, grew into the largest deployment the Corps had yet made. The trouble began in January 1885 when Colombia withdrew its garrison from the province of Panama to combat a revolution at home. The troops' departure was a signal for two local leaders to launch revolutions of their own, sparking a three-way civil war between their followers and Colombian loyalists.

Although the United States considered transit of the isthmus a vital interest, guaranteed by treaty since 1846,

the new Democratic administration of President Grover Cleveland was determined to avoid becoming entangled in Panamanian affairs. It underwent a change of heart on learning that on 1 April 1885 one of the rebel bands had burned the city of Aspinwall (now Colón), the transisthmian railroad's Atlantic terminus.

On the morning of 2 April, the Marine barracks at Boston, Philadelphia, and Portsmouth, New Hampshire, were instructed to rush detachments to the New York Navy Yard to constitute a battalion for expeditionary service. A force of 213 officers and men under Bvt. Lt. Col. Charles Heywood, the "boy colonel" of Civil War days, sailed for Panama at 5:00 the next afternoon. A second battalion, 250 strong, with a six-gun naval battery attached, followed on the seventh. With it went the Navy officer who had been chosen to command the forces ashore, Cdr. Bowman H. "Billy Hell" McCalla.

Heywood's battalion reached Aspinwall, where landing parties from several U.S. warships had been put ashore, on 11 April. When he reported to Rear Adm. James E. Jouett, the commander of North Atlantic Station, Heywood was ordered to take his battalion across the isthmus in an armored train and protect Panama City, the railroad's Pacific terminus. The second battalion arrived four days later. McCalla kept it at Aspinwall. At the same time, however, he directed Heywood to organize the two battalions and the naval battery—an aggregate of 796 officers and men—into the first brigade the Corps had ever mustered. In addition to garrisoning Panama City, Aspinwall, and two villages on the railroad line, the Marine brigade furnished guards for the trains, which, Admiral Jouett was pleased to report, continued to run on schedule.

The intervention proved to be an unmitigated success. Despite a few tense moments, order was maintained without the need to fire a shot. At the end of the month Colombian troops landed at Panama City and the rebels melted away. A phased withdrawal of American forces was completed on 26 May.

Later historians would view the Corps's performance in the Panamanian intervention as a precursor of the rapid deployment role it would assume in the twentieth century. At the time, Colonel McCawley pointed with pride to the "extraordinary dispatch" with which the two

Marines halt on the Panama Railroad during the intervention of 1885. This sketch by T. de Thulstrup appeared in *Harper's Weekly* for 30 May 1885.   Beverley R. Robinson Collection

battalions had been organized, outfitted, and embarked; but perhaps because of the alacrity with which the movement had been improvised, no steps were taken to facilitate similar operations in the future.[16]

McCawley reached the statutory retirement age of sixty-four in January 1891. To no one's surprise Charles Heywood, whom the commandant had brought to Washington three years earlier to command the Marine barracks, was selected to succeed him. At fifty-one the "boy colonel" remained an unmistakably martial figure, tall, trim, and broad-shouldered, with strong features adorned by a majestic mustache. A member and favorite of the Corps's reformers, he immediately and energetically set out to implement their agenda. In this he would attain considerable success.

Within four months of his appointment Heywood achieved one of the reformers' key goals by persuading Secretary of the Navy Benjamin F. Tracy to sanction the establishment of a School of Application for newly joined second lieutenants and noncommissioned officers at the Washington barracks. Organized by Capt. Daniel Pratt Mannix, an ex-enlisted Civil War veteran who had spent four years on detached duty teaching at the Chinese

naval academy, the school provided instruction in seven departments: infantry, artillery, administration and sea service, law, torpedoes, engineering, and military art. Also in 1891, Heywood laid down the requirement that the commanders of Marine formations and installations write an annual fitness report—today's "fitreps"—on each of their officers. The following year he secured congressional consent to institute both professional and physical examinations for officers as a prerequisite for promotion, another of the progressives' highest priorities. Of course, the new commandant did not have everything his way. His early requests for additional manpower met the same rejection as had those of his predecessors.

Congress's unwillingness to grant the Corps even a small increase contrasted with the generosity with which it was funding the Navy's expansion. A naval renaissance had begun modestly enough in 1884 with an appropriation for the first state-of-the-art warships—three cruisers and a dispatch vessel—built since the Civil War. Produced by a combination of national aspirations and concerns quickened by the gospel of sea power proclaimed by Capt. Alfred Thayer Mahan, the buildup continued at an accelerating tempo throughout the 1890s. Before the

Col. Commandant Charles Heywood *(center)* at Marine Barracks, Boston, in 1884. Seated beside him are Maj. Robert Meade *(left),* who would briefly command U.S. forces in north China during the Boxer Rebellion; and Capt. F. C. Harrington, who would command a company at Guantánamo during the Spanish-American War. Like Heywood, both were Civil War veterans.

turn of the century, America's long-negligible Navy had become one of the four or five strongest in the world.

During these same decades the naval revolution precipitated by the machine age culminated in the appearance of heavily armored, steam-driven steel battleships and cruisers carrying their main armament in centerline turrets housing breech-loading, rifled guns with ranges measured in thousands of yards. Clearly, Marines would not be called on to contribute small arms fire to battles between ships such as these.

The institutional implications were obvious. To remain fully relevant to the new steel Navy, the Corps needed to identify a new combat mission that its guard detachments could perform in place of the one that technology had superseded. The solution espoused by the reformers was to have Marines man some of the 6-inch and smaller guns of their vessels' secondary batteries. Ships' captains had been authorized to have guards double as gun crews since 1859, and many had done so, but the

matter was left entirely at their discretion. By the late 1880s Marine progressives had concluded that the Corps must try to have this practice made mandatory.

In the meanwhile, the Navy's own progressives had conceived another, very different new mission for the Corps. They advocated reorganizing it into an amphibious force in readiness for the seizure and defense of the advanced bases that would be required by a coal-burning fleet operating outside its home waters, along with other expeditionary service as needed. The Corps's reaction was cool. Although Marines took pride in their ability to improvise rapid deployments, their receptivity to the idea of specializing in them was constrained by the fact that it usually came coupled with a demand for the elimination of the ships' guards that comprised the Corps's traditional reason for being.

Most Navy progressives viewed Marine guards as an insulting anachronism. They might concede that there had been a need for guard detachments in the days when

Bayonet drill on the dock at New London, Connecticut, about 1890. The hulk in the background is the receiving ship *New Hampshire,* which was laid down in 1819 as a ship of the line.

U.S. warships were manned by polyglot crews recruited mostly from among the riffraff populating waterfront neighborhoods in seacoast cities. Now that the Navy was deliberately and successfully recruiting adequate numbers of native-born Americans, however, the presence of a seagoing police force had become an affront to the competence of its officers and the character of its men. The practice of having guards from another service was also alleged to inhibit recruiting. Marines did not find these arguments compelling.

Both sides took their stand shortly before Heywood became commandant. In 1889 he and Captain Mannix prevailed on Colonel McCawley to submit a proposal calling for the mandatory assignment of guard detachments to secondary batteries to the Navy Board of Or-

ganization, Tactics, and Drill headed by Commo. James A. Greer. To their dismay, the Greer Board not only rejected the idea but also recommended removing Marines from the Navy's ships and transforming them into a purely expeditionary force. Although Secretary Tracy ignored these recommendations, they signaled the opening of a controversy that would percolate into the next century.

In 1890 and again in 1896 the Greer Board's findings were given new life by articles in the influential *Proceedings* of the U.S. Naval Institute, a private professional association founded in 1873. The author, a veteran of the board, was Lt. William F. Fullam, the number-one graduate of the Naval Academy class of 1877, whose long crusade to rid the fleet of Marines would cause a generation of Marine officers to regard him as the An-

Harper's Weekly published T. de Thulstrup's *A Naval Landing Party Heading for the Beach* about 1892. The early machine gun in the boat's bow is a Gatling. Beverley R. Robinson Collection

napolitan Antichrist. The letters that flowed into the *Proceedings'* lively "Comment and Discussion" department in response to Fullam's articles indicated that his views were widely shared among the Navy's officers. Some correspondents also revealed an antipathy to the Corps, exemplified by one's observation that the word *Marine* had become "a synonym for idleness, worthlessness, and vacuity of intellect."[17]

Despite such fulminations, Marines had no reason to worry as long as their commandant enjoyed the confidence of Congress and the secretary of the Navy, which Charles Heywood clearly did. In the summer of 1896, shortly after the appearance of Fullam's second article, he achieved the aim it protested. On Heywood's urging, Secretary of the Navy Herbert amended naval regulations to stipulate that whenever practical, Marine guards should be detailed to man their ships' secondary batteries. A few months later, Congress rewarded Heywood's persistent appeals for more men by authorizing him to

enlist another five hundred, the first significant increase the Marine Corps had received in more than twenty years. The boy colonel was proving to be the Corps's most effective advocate since Archibald Henderson.

Between Heywood's accession to the commandancy and the middle of February 1898, Marine detachments made ten minor landings on foreign soil. A novel deployment took place between April and October 1891, when three officers and forty men under Capt. Henry Clay Cochrane were attached to a small U.S. squadron sent to the Bering Sea to help enforce an international agreement to check the slaughter of fur seals. Of the landings, five occurred in the Caribbean or Central America, one in South America, three in East Asia, and one in the Pacific. Four were made to protect U.S. diplomatic offices during wars, revolutions, or riots; the remainder, to safeguard American lives and/or property—the same sort of missions that the Corps had been performing for close to a century.

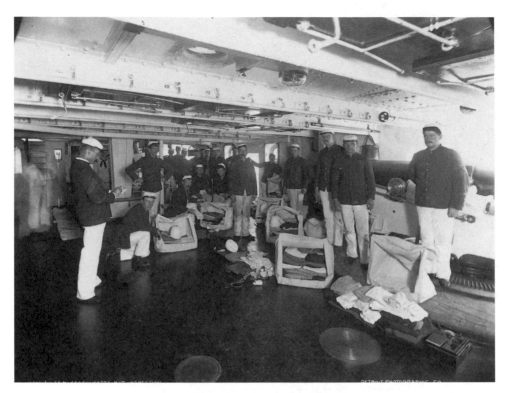

Kit inspection in the battleship *Massachusetts* in the late 1890s. The men's mess tables are triced overhead. Detroit Collection, Library of Congress

The *Massachusetts*'s Marines at mess. The youth at center is their "music boy."

The Marine reformers' goal realized: members of the *Massachusetts*'s guard detachment manning the 6-inch guns of their ship's secondary battery. The wooden tub caught the particles of unburned powder that had to be swabbed out of the bore after each shot.

The Marine guard presents arms for captain's inspection in the cruiser *San Francisco* in the mid-1890s. Detroit Collection, Library of Congress

In 1895 Cuban patriots launched the latest in a series of revolutions against Spanish colonial rule. Most Americans sympathized with the Cubans, but neither outgoing President Grover Cleveland nor incoming President William McKinley believed that the United States should intervene in the conflict. Even after the rebels purloined and publicized a personal letter in which the Spanish ambassador called McKinley "a small-time politician," the president contented himself with urging Spain to reach an accommodation with her unwilling subjects.

Early in 1898, in an attempt to improve relations between the United States and Spain, an exchange of naval goodwill visits was arranged. The United States dispatched the second-class battleship *Maine* to Havana (where, not incidentally, she would be in position to protect American interests in the event of disturbances), while Spain prepared to send the armored cruiser *Vizcaya* to New York. The *Maine* anchored in Havana harbor on 25 January. The *Vizcaya* was still en route to New York when, at 9:40 on the evening of 15 February, the battleship's forward magazine exploded, probably as a result of a fire in an adjacent coal bunker, peeling back her armored deck like the lid of a sardine can. Twenty-eight members of her Marine guard were among the 266 officers and men—exactly 75 percent of those serving in the *Maine*—who perished. Stumbling from his cabin through the pitch darkness and the dense smoke that instantly filled the ship's passageways, Capt. Charles B. Sigsbee literally bumped into his Marine orderly, Pvt. William Anthony. A veteran of fourteen years in the Corps, Anthony was equal to the occasion. "Sir, I have to inform you that the ship has been blown up and is sinking," he reported.[18] His grace under pressure made Private Anthony the first popular hero of the War with Spain—a war that catapulted the United States onto the world stage and created the conditions for the emergence of the modern Marine Corps.

7
Colonial Infantry, 1898–1917

On 25 April 1898 the United States declared war on Spain. Less than a week later the nation was electrified by the news that Commo. George Dewey's Asiatic Squadron had annihilated its Spanish counterpart at the Battle of Manila Bay in the faraway Philippines. Interest then turned to the Atlantic, into which an enemy cruiser squadron under Rear Adm. Pascual Cervera had vanished after departing the Cape Verde Islands on 29 April.

Earlier that month, in anticipation of war, the commander of the U.S. North Atlantic Squadron, Rear Adm. William T. Sampson, had requested the dispatch of two Marine battalions to Key West, Florida, for service with the fleet. On the sixteenth, Colonel Heywood was instructed to make the necessary arrangements, and within four days 450 Leathernecks had been assembled at New York. In the meantime, the Navy Department had decided that the force should be mustered as a single big battalion. Another 200 Marines were quickly collected, and on 22 April the 1st Battalion of Marines sailed for Key West. Its twenty-three officers and 621 NCOs and men—a quarter of the prewar Corps—were organized into five companies of infantry and one of artillery. In command Heywood placed fifty-seven-year-old Lt. Col. Robert W. Huntington, a veteran of the Battle of Bull Run. Second in command was Henry Clay Cochrane, who had finally been promoted to major in February. None of their company commanders was below the age of fifty.

Huntington's Battalion, as it soon came to be known, reached Key West the same day Cervera left the Cape

Verdes and remained there for more than a month. Foreseeing that the Spanish squadron would make for Cuba, Sampson sought to intercept it at the end of its voyage across the Atlantic. He was unsuccessful, and on 28 May Cervera's cruisers were discovered in port at Santiago de Cuba. Sampson decided to blockade Santiago, but for that the U.S. fleet required a sheltered anchorage to use as a coaling station. Sampson selected Guantánamo Bay, forty miles east of the city. On his orders, Huntington's Battalion sailed from Key West to undertake the Corps's first advanced base mission on 7 June.

"Billy Hell" McCalla, who had commanded in Panama in 1885, was put in charge of the operation. Fire from his ship, the cruiser *Marblehead,* had driven the Spanish from the vicinity of Guantánamo Bay by the time Huntington's Battalion arrived on 10 June. Landing unopposed on a headland on the western side of the bay, the Leathernecks entrenched a camp on a little hill some two hundred yards from shore. Tactfully, Huntington christened it Camp McCalla.

The American intrusion did not remain unopposed. The next afternoon two Marines were ambushed on outpost duty, and that night the camp came under heavy fire from Spanish troops in the dense brush around it. Although the enemy never attempted to storm the perimeter, the battalion surgeon and a sergeant were killed and two men were wounded before the enemy retired at the approach of dawn. That afternoon, amid sporadic sniping, Huntington shifted the campsite to a less exposed position nearer the bay. By the time of the move,

Lt. Col. Robert W. Huntington, center, with the colors of the 1st Battalion of Marines. He is flanked by his adjutant, 1st Lt. Herbert L. Draper *(right)* and the battalion quartermaster, Capt. Charles McCawley. McCawley, the son of the former colonel commandant, would attain the star that eluded his father—albeit in a staff appointment as the Corps's quartermaster.

nervous strain and sleeplessness had begun to take a toll on the middle-aged men commanding the battalion. Cochrane recorded that some of the company commanders advocated withdrawing. Cochrane himself argued against it; Huntington kept his own counsel. According to Cochrane, when Huntington mentioned the possibility of an evacuation to McCalla, Billy Hell retorted: "You were put there to hold that hill and you'll stay there. If you're killed, I'll come and get your dead body."[1] The Spanish returned after dark, and the battalion sergeant major died in the firing that continued throughout the night.

Then the Leathernecks' luck changed. Cuban insurgents reported that the Spanish forces—several hundred regular troops and loyalist guerrillas—were based at Cuzco Well, the only source of fresh water in the area, on a ranch approximately two miles southeast of Camp McCalla. On 14 June, Huntington sent two companies accompanied by fifty Cubans to destroy the well. With them went a dapper, tubercular young war correspondent

named Stephen Crane, who had won precocious fame as the author of *The Red Badge of Courage.* The officer in charge, Capt. W. F. Spicer, was among a number of Leathernecks toppled by sunstroke, and command devolved on the youngest of the battalion's company commanders, fifty-one-year-old Capt. George F. Elliott.

Taking cover along the crest of a ridge overlooking the ranch, the Marines opened fire. The Spanish replied vigorously from the cover of a thicket in the valley. With the outcome of the action in the balance, Elliott decided to call in fire support from the armed dispatch vessel *Dolphin.* No one had a signal flag, but Pvt. John Fitzgerald tied his neckerchief to his rifle barrel and, silhouetted on the ridgeline, making an inviting target for the enemy riflemen below, signaled Elliott's request to the ship. Unfortunately, the *Dolphin*'s first shells flew over the Spanish position to impact on a hill recently occupied by Marine reinforcements. This time lanky young Sgt. John H. Quick responded to Elliott's shout for a signalman. Knotting his neckerchief to the tip of a long stick,

A wartime photograph of the Marine battalion's camp at Guantánamo, seen from the sea. Naval Historical Center

Quick stood in full view of the Spanish to relay the captain's fire corrections to the ship—not once, but on three separate occasions. Stephen Crane watched in awe. Afterward he wrote:

> As I looked at Sergeant Quick wigwagging there against the sky, I would not have given a tin tobacco tag for his life. . . . It seemed absurd to hope that he would not be hit. I only hoped that he would be hit just a little, in the arm, or the shoulder, or the leg.
>
> I watched his face, and it was as grave and serene as that of a man writing in his own library. . . . There was not a single trace of nervousness or haste. . . . I saw Sergeant Quick betray only one sign of emotion. As he swung his clumsy flag to and fro, an end of it once caught on a cactus pillar, and he looked sharply over his shoulder to see what had it. He gave the flag an impatient jerk. He looked annoyed.[2]

The *Dolphin*'s fire did the trick. After a few minutes the Spanish broke to the east. By midafternoon the Leathernecks had occupied their objective, wrecked the well, and burned the ranch buildings. Only a single Marine had been hit. Elliott conservatively estimated Spanish losses at five men killed and wounded; another eighteen were captured by the insurgents. Camp McCalla was never seriously disturbed again.

Eight days after the fight at Cuzco Well V Army Corps, seventeen thousand men under Maj. Gen. William R. Shafter, began landing fifteen miles east of Santiago. Admiral Sampson had requested its deployment to capture the shore batteries covering the minefields that prevented his ships from entering the channel to attack the Spanish cruisers. In the event, neither operation proved necessary. The governor-general of Cuba ordered Cervera's squadron to make a suicidal sortie, and on 3 July it was destroyed in a running battle with the U.S. fleet. Santiago surrendered on the seventeenth. An armistice went into effect on 12 August, and a peace accord was signed five months later.

The Spanish-American War cost the Corps six dead and sixteen wounded. Fitzgerald, Quick, and thirteen other Marines won the Medal of Honor: one for gallantry at the Battle of Santiago and twelve for serving in boat parties that dredged up and cut the Spanish undersea telegraph cable off Cienfuegos under heavy fire from the shore. The profusion of awards resulted from the fact that

Sgt. John H. Quick won the Medal of Honor at Cuzco Well and later served with distinction in the Philippine Insurrection and World War I.

no other decoration for valor was available to American servicemen until World War I. Thirteen officers received brevet promotions: eleven for their actions at Guantánamo, and two for Santiago.

Huntington's Battalion returned home to a warm welcome soon after the armistice was signed. The stories Stephen Crane and other correspondents filed from Guantánamo had made Huntington's Leathernecks heroes. Probably for the first time, the average newspaper reader became aware that the United States had a Marine Corps—and one of which every American could be proud. On 22 September the battalion paraded through Washington to the tunes of the "Marine Hymn" and "A Hot Time in the Old Town Tonight."

In terms of its duration and human cost—114 days and 379 men killed in action—the Spanish-American War was a very minor conflict, but its consequences were immense. In the summer of 1898 the United States emerged as a world power. By year's end it was also a colonial

power, having claimed the Philippines, Guam, and Puerto Rico from Spain; annexed the Hawaiian Islands; and established a virtual protectorate over Cuba. The fact that this insular empire would require a great Navy to safeguard it, and the proof its acquisition presumably offered of Captain Mahan's sea-power gospel, confirmed the course and quickened the tempo of the American naval renaissance. During the ensuing decade the United States laid down an average of two battleships a year.

A bigger Navy gave promise of a bigger Marine Corps. In May 1898 Congress approved a wartime-only addition of 1,640 men to the Leathernecks' ranks and authorized the president to issue temporary commissions to qualified applicants from civilian life and—for the first time—meritorious NCOs. Altogether, forty-three such commissions were granted, three of them to NCOs. Even if the accessions had been permanent, however, Colonel Heywood believed them far too few to meet the demands that would result from the nation's naval expansion and imperial commitments. Late in 1898 he proposed what would have been unthinkable a year earlier: a 6,000-man Marine Corps. An exuberant Congress was amenable, and the Naval Act of 1899 increased the Corps's strength to 201 officers and 6,062 NCOs and men. It also raised the rank attached to the office of commandant to brigadier general and allowed for five colonels and five lieutenant colonels of the line—which permitted Henry Clay Cochrane, who had taken thirty-six years to reach the rank of major, to progress to full colonel in two.

Yet, Heywood did not regard the act as more than an interim measure. Asserting that in five years the Corps would need at least 10,000 men to keep pace with the Navy's growth, he continued to press Congress to reinforce its ranks. In 1902 it obliged him with another 750 men as well as a personal promotion to the rank of major general. This made the erstwhile boy colonel the first Marine ever to wear two stars. The following year the legislators allowed the Corps another seventy-seven officers and 720 men.

But the Marine Corps acquired more than additional manpower as a consequence of the Spanish-American War. It also acquired two new missions: to develop the advanced base capability that had been under discussion for a decade, and to serve as colonial infantry policing

First Lt. Constantine M. Perkins (in whites) and his Marines guard the residence of U.S. consul Osborne at Matautu Point, Apia, Upolo Island, during the Samoan Insurrection of 1899.

the peripheries of the American empire. Regrettably, the two were not compatible.

The advanced base mission was assigned to the Corps by Secretary of the Navy John D. Long on the recommendation of the General Board of the Navy in November 1900. Earlier that year Long had established the General Board, a panel of nine senior officers, to advise him on naval strategy and policy. Although the board lacked executive authority, its conclusions carried great weight, and Long and his successors often transformed them into orders. Among the board's chief concerns was the defense of America's overseas possessions, which it foresaw might require the fleet to operate hundreds if not thousands of miles from its nearest permanent base. The occupation and defense of advanced bases would be imperative. The misunderstandings that had developed between Admiral Sampson and General Shafter during the Santiago campaign made it appear unwise to rely on the Army to conduct such operations to the Navy's satisfaction. That was where the Corps came in.

Heywood's response was lukewarm. He agreed to give his Leathernecks training in advanced base activities—emplacing big guns, constructing field fortifica-

tions, laying minefields, and so on—and furnished a battalion that had undergone such training to take part in the fleet's annual winter maneuvers in the Caribbean in 1902–3. On the other hand, he declined to form the permanent units that the General Board believed should comprise an advanced base force. Too many Marines were already committed to the Corps's other new mission.

In contrast to the advanced base duty with which it had been formally tasked, the Corps's employment as colonial infantry was the child of circumstance. The American empire was basically the Navy's concern, and the Corps was the Navy's force in readiness. Thus, while Marines continued to make traditional small-scale landings for brief periods to protect American lives and property, they were also called on to carry out politically motivated interventions that might absorb a thousand men or more for months and sometimes years. These deployments would hamper the development of an advanced base capability for a third of a century. Of course, as naval progressives never tired of pointing out, manpower sufficient for both missions could have been assembled by withdrawing Marine guards from the Navy's ships; but that idea remained anathema to the Corps.

The assault on the *insurrecto* position at Novaleta, 8 October 1899, by Charles Waterhouse. Art Collection, Marine Corps Historical Center

The Leathernecks' service as colonial infantry began in the Pacific. In February 1899 the Filipino leader Emilio Aguinaldo launched an insurrection against American rule, and a month later a native revolt broke out in the Samoan Islands, which were jointly administered by the United States, Great Britain, and Germany. The major action of the Samoan Uprising took place on 1 April, when a patrol of 118 American and British bluejackets and marines was ambushed in thick brush outside Apia, on Upolu Island. The column's machine gun jammed, both contingents' commanders were killed, and the seamen fell back in disorder. Twenty U.S. Marines under 1st Lt. Constantine M. Perkins covered the retreat. Three members of his little detachment were awarded the Medal of Honor.

This reverse notwithstanding, the Samoan Uprising had been suppressed by the end of the month. The Philippine Insurrection was a different matter. It would last

more than three years and involve 125,000 troops, 4,200 of whom would be killed in action—eleven times as many as in the Spanish-American War. A Marine battalion, requested by Admiral Dewey to garrison the naval station at Cavite on Manila Bay, reached Luzon in May. Before the year's end it had been joined by two others to form a provisional regiment.

For the most part, the Leathernecks' war was limited to skirmishes fought by patrols from the installations they guarded. An exception occurred on 8 October 1899, when a 376-man battalion under George F. Elliott, a lieutenant colonel now, was detailed to cooperate with the Army in a pincers movement on Novaleta, an *insurrecto* village at the base of the Cavite Peninsula. The Marines were to storm the village; the soldiers, to intercept its fleeing defenders. Geography precluded tactical finesse. Elliott's Leathernecks carried their objective in a frontal assault along a narrow causeway and through waist-deep marshes and paddies. Surprisingly, only twelve of them were hit, three fatally. Afterward Elliott had his men gather in the shade of a giant mango tree and led them in singing "America." Two lieutenants earned brevets for their gallantry in the engagement.

The buildup in the Philippines brought into contact two of the most remarkable warriors ever to wear the globe and anchor: Smedley Darlington Butler, then a nineteen-year-old first lieutenant, and forty-four-year-old Maj. Littleton Waller Tazewell Waller, whose friends called him Tony. Butler never forgot his first sight of Waller, "a little fellow with a fiery mustache and a distinguished bearing" that made him seem to tower over taller men.[3] A descendant of several prominent Virginia families, Waller had entered the Corps in 1880. Two years later he landed with a detachment under Henry Clay Cochrane to help restore order after the British bombardment of Alexandria, Egypt, and somehow attached himself to the British Army for the start of the ensuing campaign. During the Spanish-American War he commanded the battleship *Indiana*'s guard in the Battle of Santiago. Dashing, indomitable, a magnificent campaigner, at heart a romantic, full of war stories featuring himself, he made a lasting impression on the young men who served under him. Years after Waller's death had ended their long association, Butler characterized him as "the greatest soldier I have ever known."[4] Another officer of Butler's generation who met Waller in the Philippines recalled: "The U.S. Marine Corps was his God. He never let you forget it."[5]

Like Waller, Butler was descended from several prominent families—in his case, of Pennsylvania Quakers. His father, Republican Representative Thomas S. Butler, sat in Congress from 1896 until his death in 1928. At the outbreak of the Spanish-American War Smedley added more than a year to his age and, with his parents' reluctant consent, obtained one of the Corps's temporary commissions a few months before his seventeenth birthday. The fighting was as good as over by the time he joined Huntington's Battalion at Guantánamo, but the experience whetted his martial appetite. In 1899 he secured a regular commission, passing second in an examination of thirty-two candidates. A slight, wiry man with a great beak of a nose, Butler relished the challenge of combat.

Maj. Littleton W. T. Waller in tropical service dress about the time of the Philippine Insurrection. Courtesy Vernon L. Williams

Caught in a nasty night ambush in Haiti in 1915, he exclaimed, "Isn't this great?" ("Great, hell!" a subordinate retorted. "We're all going to be killed.")[6] By that time Butler had come to disdain what he considered the "overeducated" element of the Marine officer corps, to which he consigned most Annapolis graduates. "If you have too much education," he explained, "you are acutely conscious of the risks you run and are afraid to act. . . . I never went to any military school, and so perhaps I wasn't trained to know danger when I saw it."[7] But if Butler liked to think of himself as a simple fighting man, he was also a sensitive one. Wherever he served, his sympathies were with the downtrodden, and inwardly he questioned the motives behind the interventions that brought him fame.

"Handsome Jack" Myers *(far right)*, commanded the U.S. Marines during the defense of the legations. Third from left is the Corps's old acquaintance Navy Capt. Bowman "Billy Hell" McCalla, who led the American contingent in the Seymour expedition. Charleton Heston played a somewhat contrived and fanciful characterization of Myers as Maj. Matt Lewis in the movie *55 Days to Peking* (1963).

In June 1900 Waller and Butler shared the bleak prospect of spending several years on Guam, generally considered the Corps's dreariest post. Waller had been detailed to form a detachment to take over the Marine barracks there, and Butler was one of five officers who agreed to accompany him. At the last moment, a change of orders brought what both regarded as a reprieve. The detachment was being diverted to China to fight the Boxers.

"Boxer" was the Occidental abbreviation for a member of the Fists of Righteous Harmony, a peasant movement provoked by the Western penetration of China. First tolerated, then encouraged, and finally supported by the imperial government, the Boxers aimed to purge China of foreign influences by eliminating those who bore or succumbed to them, beginning with Chinese Christians. By the late spring of 1900, two years after its inception, their sanguinary crusade had reached the outskirts of Peking, seat of the eleven foreign legations to the Manchu court.

On 28 May the eleven ministers wired a joint request for guards from the warships that had been drawn to the mouth of the Pei-Ho River by the troubles ashore. A force of 337 men representing seven nations entered Peking on 31 May. The American contingent consisted of forty-nine Leathernecks and five sailors under Capt. John T. "Handsome Jack" Myers, whose father had been the Confederacy's quartermaster general. Eighty-nine more European sailors arrived on 3 June.

Subsequent events having cast doubts on the sufficiency of this little force, on the ninth the ministers appealed for additional troops. Within twenty-four hours an international expedition of 2,130 men, headed by British Adm. Sir Edward Seymour, the senior allied officer present, set out by rail for Peking from Tientsin, a treaty port on the Pei-Ho River eighty miles to the southeast. The force included 112 American bluejackets and Marines. The telegraph line to the legations went dead that same

Marine Operations in the Boxer Rebellion, May–August 1900

day. Damage to the railroad and attacks by both Boxers and Chinese Army units slowed Seymour's projected dash to Peking to a crawl, and on the thirteenth the expedition disappeared into the limbo that enshrouded the legations after the Boxers seized control of the railroad behind it. Two days later the Foreign Settlements at Tientsin, garrisoned by 2,400 mostly Russian troops, were besieged by many times that number of Chinese. The single encouraging development in a week replete with alarming ones occurred on the morning of the seventeenth, when the allies captured the Taku Forts guarding the mouth of the Pei-Ho, thereby assuring themselves of a bridgehead into northern China.

This was the situation when Waller's minute battalion—seven officers and 131 men—landed at Tangku early on the twentieth. That afternoon, unknown to the outside world, the Chinese launched their first attack on the hastily fortified legations at Peking. By then the Leathernecks were advancing along the railroad to Tientsin. Twelve miles from the city they encountered a battalion of 440 Russian infantrymen whose commander Waller browbeat into joining in an attempt to break through to the Foreign Settlements the next morning.

The attempt did not succeed. Nearing Tientsin, the combined force came up against several thousand imperial troops in entrenched positions, and after an hour's fight the Russians began to make their way to the rear. Waller turned to Butler. "I hate to give the order," he

lamented. "But if we don't retire at once, we'll be cut off." "I vote to run," Butler interjected. "Marines never run, my boy," said Tony Waller.[8]

The conclusion of a long rear-guard action found the battalion back at its starting point. Thirteen Leathernecks had been killed or wounded. More new arrivals, mainly Russian and British, came up from Tangku that evening, raising the strength of the allied forces outside Tientsin to twenty-three hundred men. They moved forward on the twenty-third and entered the Foreign Settlements after what Butler described as "a terrible march in the face of a sand storm, and very severe fighting."[9]

The following day a Chinese courier slipped into the settlements with news of the Seymour expedition. After losing contact with Tientsin, the force had pushed on toward Peking until, on the nineteenth, mounting opposition compelled it to abandon its trains and begin a desperate retreat along the banks of the Pei-Ho. Burdened by more than two hundred wounded who could not be left to the Boxers' mercies, the expedition appeared in eminent danger of being surrounded and destroyed. Providentially, before dawn on the twenty-second, the battered column stumbled upon and succeeded in capturing the Hsiku Arsenal, a massive fortification six miles from Tientsin. It was from there that the courier had come. A relief expedition including Waller's battalion started for the arsenal the next day. The Chinese did not seriously oppose its advance, and on the twenty-sixth it escorted Seymour's force back to the Foreign Settlements.

Waller's pride in his Leathernecks' performance knew no bounds. In his official report of the week's operations, he wrote:

Our men have marched ninety-seven miles in five days, fighting all the way. They have lived on about one meal a day for six days, but have been cheerful and willing always. They have gained the highest praise from all present, and have earned my love and confidence. They are like Falstaff's army in appearance, but with brave hearts and bright weapons.[10]

A pause ensued while the forces in the Foreign Settlements awaited reinforcements to storm the city of Tientsin. Among those they received were another battalion of Marines and two battalions of the 9th Infantry from the Philippines. Accompanying them was Marine

Col. Robert L. Meade, a veteran of the boat attack on Fort Sumter, who assumed command of the U.S. forces ashore. The ad hoc American regiment, one thousand men strong, was among the sixty-eight hundred allied troops who delivered a poorly planned assault on Tientsin on 13 July. Colonel Meade, whose rheumatism had flared up, entered action with his hands and feet swathed in bandages. He and his men spent a miserable day pinned down in rice paddies by fire from the city's forty-foot-high walls. Finally, at 3:00 the next morning, the Japanese contingent blew in Tientsin's South Gate and the attackers poured into the streets. During the battle and throughout the remainder of the campaign the Leathernecks served beside a battalion of the Royal Welch Fusiliers, with whom they developed a friendship that continues to the present. On St. David's Day, Wales's national holiday (1 March), and the Marine Corps's birthday (10 November), the commandant of the Corps and the colonel of the Royal Welch exchange the traditional watchword, " . . . and Saint David."

Another pause followed the capture of Tientsin while the allies gathered strength for the advance on Peking. A third Marine battalion, hastily organized at the Washington barracks under Maj. William P. Biddle, and another infantry regiment arrived at the end of July to reinforce the Americans, who also received a flinty new commander, Maj. Gen. Adna R. Chaffee. Poor Colonel Meade had been invalided home by then, and Major Biddle, five months senior to Waller, assumed command of the Marines.

Finally, on 4 August, a relief force numbering 18,600 troops from eight nations marched from Tientsin. The 2,500-man U.S. contingent included two Marine battalions with a strength of 482 officers and men. Evidently no friend of the Corps, Chaffee left the third battalion behind with the garrison at Tientsin and assigned one of the others to guard his baggage train, leaving only a single battalion, Tony Waller's, to share in the glory at the front. As always, Waller strove to gather as much of it as possible, and his Leathernecks played a respectable part in the actions culminating on 14 August in the capture of Peking.

The relief force was delighted to find that after fifty-five days under siege the legations were still holding out.

Captain Myers's Marines had distinguished themselves in the defense, manning a breastwork on the broad Tartar Wall that bounded the south side of the legation quarter. Myers also led the defenders' only important offensive undertaking, a night attack by thirty of his own men, twenty-six Royal Marines, and fifteen Russian sailors on a bastion in which the Chinese had erected a tower overlooking the American barricade. The bastion was captured and thirty-six of its garrison killed. Allied casualties were two dead, both U.S. Marines, and three wounded, including Myers. U.S. minister Edwin Conger called the action "the bravest and most successful event of the whole siege."[11] Some years later a monument to the Royal Marines was erected outside the British Admiralty. One of its panels depicts Handsome Jack Myers leading the sortie on the Tartar Wall.

Seventeen Marines—more than a third of those present—were killed or wounded in the defense of the legations, and about twice that number in the operations leading to their relief. Thirty-three were awarded the Medal of Honor: eighteen for the defense, three for the Seymour expedition, and twelve for the fighting around Tientsin. Ten officers, including Meade, Waller, Myers, and Smedley Butler (who had helped rescue a wounded man under fire), received the last brevets awarded before that distinction became extinct.

In October the Marines returned to the Philippines, and the units there were organized into a brigade. The insurrection was still thriving, a bitter guerrilla war having developed after Aguinaldo's conventional forces were dispersed, but soon the Army's increasingly aggressive counterinsurgency began to gain the upper hand. Aguinaldo was captured in March 1901. In April he urged his supporters to give up the struggle. Thousands complied, and in July President Theodore Roosevelt proclaimed the war at an end.

The proclamation was somewhat premature. Two pockets of resistance remained: a province of Luzon and the island of Samar. The vigor of the insurrection on Samar became terribly evident on 28 September when a company of the 9th Infantry garrisoned at Balangiga, on the south coast, was almost wiped out by a Sunday-morning surprise attack in which the townsfolk joined.

Reaction to the Balangiga massacre was swift. Brig.

After raising the siege of the legations on 14 August 1900, troops of the victorious allies (American, British, French, Russian, German, Austrian, Italian, and Japanese) paraded on the grounds of Peking's Forbidden City.

Gen. Jacob H. "Hell-Roaring Jake" Smith was given the task of pacifying Samar. The Navy offered to help with a battalion of Marines, and on 22 October Tony Waller sailed from Cavite with fourteen officers and three hundred men. The verbal instructions he received in a conference with Smith the next day were at least unambiguous: "I want no prisoners. I wish you to kill and burn, the more you kill and burn the better you will please me. I want all persons killed who are capable of bearing arms in actual hostilities against the United States."[12] In response to a question from Waller, Smith defined such persons as everyone aged ten years and above. Waller was appalled. Repeating Smith's orders to his officers, he added, "But we are not making war against women and children. . . . Keep that in mind no matter what other orders you receive."[13]

The military subdistrict assigned to the Marines embraced six hundred square miles of unmapped jungle on southern Samar. To cover it, Waller stationed two companies at the coastal town of Basey, where he established his headquarters, and the other two thirty miles east at Balangiga. Small punitive expeditions immediately began to push out from both bases, burning villages, destroying foodstuffs and livestock, and killing or capturing able-bodied men.

The campaign climaxed at Sohoton Cliffs on 17 November. A supposedly impregnable stronghold occupied by several hundred *insurrectos,* the cliffs towered more than two hundred feet above the Cadacan River sixteen miles north of Basey. The *insurrectos* had carved caves reachable only by long bamboo ladders into the cliffs' soft stone face, from which they had suspended cages full of rocks that could be cut loose to cascade down on an assailant. Young Capt. David Dixon Porter, a grandson of the admiral and reputedly the handsomest man in the Corps, was to approach the cliffs overland from the

Company H, 1st Battalion, of the Marine brigade stationed in the Philippines posed for this picture outside Olongapo in 1901.

east with 125 men. Waller himself would come up the Cadacan with 75 men in boats towing a raft to which he had lashed a 3-inch field gun. The two columns were to storm the cliffs together at first light.

As it happened, the plan did not survive the first light. On reaching his position, Porter decided that Waller's detachment would be shot to pieces and attacked at once. To guarantee the quality of its covering fire, he entrusted the column's machine gun to Gunnery Sgt. John H. Quick—"one of the most competent, intelligent men I ever met in the Corps, officer or otherwise."[14] Pvt. Robert LaKaye swam the river under fire and brought back a boat in which the column began crossing. Porter and Capt. Hiram I. "Hiking Hiram" Bearss led their men up ladders the *insurrectos* had been too surprised to withdraw, while the sweep of Quick's machine gun kept anyone from getting near the rock cages above them. By the time Waller's column appeared, the battle was over. Thirty insurgents had been killed and substantial caches of gunpowder and rice as well as forty small bronze can-

non had been captured. Leatherneck casualties were nil. The insurrection on southern Samar had been dealt a mortal blow. Years later, after officers had become eligible for the decoration, Porter and Bearss received Medals of Honor for their heroism at Sohoton Cliffs.

The triumph was soon followed by a disaster. On 28 December, following instructions from General Smith, Waller left Lanang, an Army base on the east coast, to survey the route for a telegraph line to Basey, a distance of thirty-five to forty miles. His party consisted of fifty-five officers and men, two native scouts, and thirty-three bearers. They carried four days' rations, which Waller calculated would suffice to reach a supply depot inland from Basey.

Waller had miscalculated. Hacking their way through almost impenetrable jungle, clambering over the rocky ridges of the Sohoton Mountains, and crossing and recrossing meandering streams in a drenching monsoon rain, the Leathernecks traversed three or four miles for every one they advanced. Despite the dramatically swift deterioration of the party's physical condition, Waller was forced to cut rations and cut them again. Finally, two detachments of the most fit men set out to bring help—one led by Waller to Basey and the other by Captain Porter to Lanang. The remaining thirty-three Marines were left under the command of 1st Lt. Alexander S. Williams. By the time a relief column reached them on 18 January 1902, ten had died of exhaustion and exposure.

The survivors told a tale of treachery. As they had grown progressively weaker, their bearers had become increasingly unreliable, refusing to help gather firewood, keeping the sweet potatoes and other edibles they harvested from the jungle for themselves, and, according to a private who understood some of the Visayan language, plotting to kill the enfeebled Americans. When Lieutenant Williams drew his revolver to enforce an order, a bearer snatched it away from him and another struck him several times with a bolo before Williams succeeded in wrenching the knife out of his hands.

Porter, Williams, and, on being asked for his opinion, Sergeant Quick recommended that nine bearers and a scout who had idly watched the attack on Williams be shot. Waller, down with a raging fever after exertions that had prostrated men half his age, promptly ordered all ten executed, along with a bearer who had tried to steal his bolo one night. From this comfortable distance it is easy to conclude that the Marines overreacted, but their response to any hint of treachery was conditioned by the memory of the Balangiga massacre. The executions were carried out on 20 January. Waller reported them to Smith by a telegram that opened: IT BECAME NECESSARY TO EXPEND ELEVEN PRISONERS.[15]

Waller was astounded by what happened next. Embarrassed by reports of American atrocities, General Chaffee, now commanding U.S. forces in the Philippines, ordered him court-martialed for murder. Waller defended himself on the grounds that, first, the executions were justified, and, second, he had the authority to order them under the martial law then prevailing on Samar. Despite strong command pressure for conviction, the court acquitted him by a vote of eleven to two. Hell Roaring Jake Smith, whose "kill and burn" order came out at the trial, did not fare as well. He was court-martialed and forced into retirement.

Yet Waller had been hurt. At home the anti-imperialist press seized the occasion to brand him the "Butcher of Samar," a calumny he never quite lived down. But the officers of the Marine brigade understood what Waller's battalion had undergone and achieved. Whenever one of its veterans appeared in their messes, the toast was raised: "Stand, gentlemen, he served on Samar."[16]

By April 1902 the pacification of Luzon and Samar was complete. Twenty-six Leathernecks had been killed or wounded in the insurrection, and six earned the Medal of Honor. The Marine brigade remained in the Philippines until 1914, one regiment stationed at Cavite and another at Olongapo.

In addition to major deployments, the Corps made ten small landings in the opening years of the century: six in the Colombian province of Panama (1901–2), two in Honduras (1903), one in Santo Domingo (1903), and one at Beirut, then in the Turkish province of Syria (1903). All were undertaken to protect U.S. citizens and their interests at times of actual or threatened disorders.

As required by regulations, General Heywood retired on reaching age sixty-four in October 1903. His successor had already been selected. In June, President Roosevelt announced that George F. Elliott, a captain at Cuzco Well just five years earlier, would become the Corps's brigadier general commandant. An academic dropout of the Military Academy class of 1872, Elliott had spent thirty-three of his fifty-seven years in the Marine Corps. Like Heywood he was an imposing figure, broad-shouldered, wasp-waisted, and ramrod straight. Smedley Butler, who served in his battalion in the Philippines, considered Elliott "one of the kindest men in the world," despite his gruff manner and explosive temper.[17] A first-rate field soldier, Elliott was a little too impulsive to operate with maximum efficiency in the highly political environment in which his new duties placed him. But to his credit, he would steer the Corps through the most serious political challenge it had faced since the presidency of Andrew Jackson.

Elliott's policies were an extension of his predecessor's. As the Navy grew steadily larger, he appealed for corresponding additions to the Corps's strength. In 1905 and again in 1908 Congress gave him more men, establishing the ten-thousand-man Marine Corps Heywood had foreseen, and in the latter year it acknowledged the Leathernecks' increasing importance by raising their commandant's rank to major general. Yet during the same period the number of battleships in commission rose from twelve to twenty-six. This more than doubled the need for fleet Marines, and the creation of an advanced base force continued to hang fire. The advanced base mission was not altogether ignored, however. Valuable lessons were learned in exercises at Subic Bay in the Philippines in 1904 and 1907, and in 1910 the establishment of the Advanced Base School at New London, Connecticut, institutionalized training for such operations.

Two sizable interventions took place under Elliott. The first occurred within three months of his appointment. In January 1903 the United States had negotiated a treaty with Colombia, granting it a one-hundred-year lease to build and operate a canal across the Isthmus of Panama in exchange for $10 million cash on the barrelhead and an annual subsidy of $250,000. In August the Colombian senate unexpectedly rejected the treaty on the grounds that those sums were insufficient. Thereupon an outraged Theodore Roosevelt apparently entered into a secret understanding with Philippe Bunau-Varilla, a Frenchman with a financial stake in the start of an American-owned canal. From his suite in the Waldorf-Astoria Hotel in New York, Bunau-Varilla arranged for the Panama City Fire Department to revolt against Colombia.

Panamanian independence was proclaimed on 2 November. On 3 November five hundred Colombian troops came ashore at Colón to quell the uprising. Within hours the captain of the gunboat *Nashville* landed fifty seamen and Marines, and, aided by the American superintendent of the Panama Railroad, contrived to keep the Colombians from proceeding across the isthmus to Panama City. On 4 November an eight-thousand-dollar bribe from Bunau-Varilla's Panamanian confederates persuaded the Colombian commander to reembark his men. A Marine battalion that happened to have sailed from Philadelphia under Maj. John A. Lejeune on 25 October reached Colón the next day. The United States recognized the independence of Panama on 6 November. A canal treaty was signed twelve days later.

As relations between the United States and Colombia soured, three more Marine battalions were ordered to Panama. General Elliott, a veteran of the 1885 intervention, accompanied the last two. Landing at Colón on 3 January 1904, he organized the Leathernecks on the isthmus into a provisional brigade. This would be the only occasion in the twentieth century on which a serving commandant assumed personal command in the field. Happily, the crisis soon passed. Most of the Marines were on their way back to their barracks by the middle of February, but they left behind a battalion that would be garrisoned in Panama until 1914.

The other big intervention was in Cuba. On the dissolution of the American military government in 1902, the United States had dictated the insertion of a clause in Cuba's new constitution giving it the right to intervene to preserve Cuban independence, discharge treaty obligations, and maintain "a government adequate for the protection of life, property and individual liberty."[18] When in 1906 a rigged election ignited a civil war that threatened the extensive American investments on the island, Roosevelt reluctantly decided to exercise that right. Early in October the fifty-four-hundred-man Army of Cuban Pacification sailed from the United States.

The Marine Corps got there first. A battalion reached Havana onboard the transport *Dixie* on 16 September. Reinforcements followed quickly, and on 1 October Tony Waller, now a colonel, began organizing them into a brigade. At peak strength late that month his command numbered approximately twenty-nine hundred men.

The intervention accomplished its objectives without fighting. An American provisional government assumed control of Cuban affairs, and the warring factions were persuaded to surrender their arms. The Marines began withdrawing in a matter of days, but, as in the case of Panama, the movement was incomplete. A regiment remained with the Army until the end of the occupation in 1909.

A number of minor landings took place as well. At the turn of the year 1903–4 nineteen Leathernecks under Capt. George C. Thorpe escorted a diplomatic mission through hundreds of miles of dangerous territory to and from Addis Ababa, the capital city of Emperor Menelik II of Ethiopia. That January, an anti-American demonstration in Seoul prompted the dispatch of one hundred bluejackets and Marines to guard the U.S. legation.

In February a Japanese army occupied Korea in the opening moves of the Russo-Japanese War, and part of the legation guard stayed on until the restoration of peace late in 1905. Meanwhile, in May 1904 the Moroccan bandit chief Raisouli kidnapped a naturalized U.S. citizen, Ion Perdicaris. Roosevelt responded by cabling a demand to Sultan Abdul Aziz IV for "Perdicaris alive or Raisouli dead." To underscore the president's message, Handsome Jack Myers led the cruiser *Brooklyn*'s guard ashore at Tangier. The outcome was Perdicaris alive.[19]

Nearer home, a revolution in Santo Domingo (as Americans persisted in calling the Dominican Republic) occasioned four landings in 1904. Nicaragua's invasion of Honduras in 1907 prompted a gunboat to put its corporal's guard ashore there, and two subsequent deployments were undertaken in consequence of events within Nicaragua itself. In October 1909 the Nicaraguan Conservative Party launched a revolt that enjoyed American favor against the Liberal regime of President José Santos Zelaya, whose ambitions had annoyed Central America for more than a decade. To safeguard American interests should the need arise, a provisional regiment including the Panama Battalion, then commanded by Maj. Smedley Butler, was kept on a transport off Corinto from December 1909 to March 1910. The need did not arise, but by the time the Leathernecks were recalled, U.S. diplomatic pressure had forced Zelaya into exile. The Liberal government retained power, however, and in May its army pushed the Conservatives' dwindling forces back to Bluefields, on the Atlantic coast. Fearful that the city would become a combat zone, the U.S. consul called for Marines. Two gunboats promptly put landing parties ashore, and Butler's battalion was rushed to the scene. Though privately Butler deplored American involvement in what he saw as the senseless bloodshed of the Nicaraguan civil war, he knew where his duty lay. At Bluefields he informed the leaders of the opposing forces that he would not allow fighting around the city. His reluctant intervention saved the revolution from certain defeat. Disheartened, the government army withdrew, and the reinvigorated Conservatives began an advance that carried them to the presidential palace in August. Butler's Leathernecks returned to Panama a month later.

Maj. Smedley D. Butler circa 1916.

The challenges the Corps confronted in these diverse deployments paled in comparison with one it encountered in Washington, D.C. On 16 October 1908 Rear Adm. John E. Pillsbury, chief of the Bureau of Navigation (really, of personnel), wrote Secretary of the Navy Victor H. Metcalf to recommend what many Navy officers had long advocated: that Marine guards should be withdrawn from the Navy's ships. Metcalf concurred and forwarded the proposal to Roosevelt, who gave it the presidential stamp of approval. After protesting the decision to Metcalf, General Elliott appealed directly to the chief executive. He found the president inflexible; the guard detachments would have to go, and he was not to make trouble over it. On a happier note, Roosevelt agreed to put the Corps's future on a firmer footing by allowing Elliott to prepare a formal statement of its duties for his consideration. The resultant document was signed into law as Executive Order 969 on 12 November. Mention of ships' guards was conspicuous by its absence. Soon the fleet began sending its Marines ashore.

Elliott thought he had achieved everything possible under the circumstances. That satisfaction was soon dispelled by reports that the president wanted to do more than take the Marines off ships: he wanted to merge them into the Army. The reports were true. In conversation with his military aide, Army Capt. Archie Butt, Roosevelt declared: "[The Marines] have augmented to themselves such importance, and their influence, which they have gained by pandering to every political influence, has given them such an abnormal position for the size of their Corps that they have simply invited their own destruction. . . . [N]o vestige of their organization should be allowed to remain."[20]

Elliott now went to action stations. For once the sea services showed a united front; even naval progressives were aghast at the prospect of losing the Marine Corps altogether. From 7 to 15 January 1909 a subcommittee of the House Naval Affairs Committee under the friendly chairmanship of Smedley Butler's father investigated the removal of guard detachments from the Navy's big ships. Elliott, his senior staff officers, Tony Waller, and others delivered predictably impassioned testimony in favor of their retention. The House found the Marines' arguments persuasive. On 3 March it attached what was called the Butler Rider to the Naval Act of 1910, stipulating that none of the monies allocated to the Marine Corps should be spent unless the ships' guards were restored. With only days left in office and otherwise satisfied with the contents of the act, Roosevelt chose not to continue the contest. The Marines returned to the fleet.

As Elliott approached retirement, most observers assumed that he would be succeeded by Tony Waller, the officer the Corps itself undoubtedly would have chosen. There were other contenders, but none could match Waller's record of service. As expected, Secretary Meyer recommended his appointment to President William Howard Taft. The president in turn told Archie Butt that he intended to name Waller to the post—"and this in spite of the fact," Butt wrote his sister-in-law, "that Waller was court-martialed for shooting a few of the little Brown Brothers in the Philippines. . . . But Waller is the idol of the Corps and certainly the only man in the entire body who has any fitness for the position at the present time."[21]

At this point Boise Penrose, Pennsylvania's influential senior senator, paid the president a call. Penrose's message was blunt. His candidate for commandant was Col. William P. Biddle, a member of the prominent Philadelphia family. Unless Biddle received the appointment, Penrose would withdraw his support for Taft's legislative program. "[I]n five minutes," Butt noted sadly, "Waller was sidetracked and Colonel Biddle elevated to the place of command. . . . Presidents have always used the army and navy for trading stamps, but I had hoped that the President would throw down the glove to Penrose or rather pick up the one Penrose threw at his feet; but it was not to be."[22] On 13 February 1911 Biddle became the Corps's eleventh commandant.

A veteran of almost thirty-six years of active duty, Biddle had been Dewey's fleet Marine officer at Manila Bay, led the Leathernecks in the march on Peking, and later commanded the brigade in the Philippines. This rather impressive résumé notwithstanding, most contemporaries found the new commandant lacking in drive. In China his staff had dubbed him "Sitting Bull," having concluded, as one of its members wrote, "that Major Biddle's dominant characteristic was love of a comfortable chair."[23] Josephus Daniels, the second of the navy secretaries under whom Biddle served, described him as "an agreeable gentleman . . . not noted for vigor and initiative."[24]

Whatever Biddle's energy level, his years as commandant were eventful. In March 1911, less than a month after his appointment, the threat that the opening spasms of the Mexican Revolution posed to American residents led to the formation of an expeditionary brigade under Waller at the U.S. base at Guantánamo, Cuba, ready to intervene at a moment's notice. The call to do so never came, and in a few months the brigade was disbanded, but its brief existence had an important consequence.

Concerned about the recent exhibitions of hostility to the Corps in high places, and unhappy with the selection of Biddle as commandant, the brigade's officers met on 26 April and established the Marine Corps Association, an unofficial, self-supporting organization with the mission of representing their corporate interests and stimulating their professional development. Two years later the association received a written charter, and in 1916 it commenced publication of the *Marine Corps Gazette,* "a periodical journal for the dissemination of information concerning the aims, purposes and deeds of the Corps, and the interchange of ideas for the betterment and improvement of its officers and men."[25] The *Gazette* has discharged those duties ever since.

A new outbreak of violence led to the deployment of another expeditionary brigade to Cuba in May 1912. This time the trouble was in Cuba itself, where the government's refusal to allow the organization of a political party along racial lines provoked the Negro Rebellion. The Leathernecks guarded towns, railroads, and American properties, freeing the Cuban Army to search out the rebel bands. The fighting had ended by mid-July, and the brigade was dissolved later that month.

The Nicaraguan kettle also continued to boil. That same July, Gen. Luis Mena, an erstwhile ox driver who had become minister of war in the Conservative government, launched a revolt against President Adolfo Díaz. Highly pleased with Díaz and apprehensive about the danger to American citizens and investments, the United States intervened. On 4 August the gunboat *Annapolis* sent one hundred seamen and Marines to guard the U.S. legation at Managua. Smedley Butler's Panama Battalion reached the capital ten days later. By the end of the month naval landing parties had gone ashore at Bluefields, Corinto, and San Juan del Sur, and the 1st Provisional Regiment, 780 Leathernecks under portly, bespectacled Col. Joseph H. "Uncle Joe" Pendleton, was on the way from Philadelphia. One of the Naval Academy's "Famous Fifty" Marine graduates, Uncle Joe was among the best-loved officers in the Corps. Even Butler, who had no use for Annapolitans, was pleased to call "that sturdy old soldier and genial companion" a friend.[26] Arriving at Corinto on 4 September, Pendleton assumed command of the Marines ashore in western Nicaragua.

The campaign was waged along the railroad that ran in a southeasterly direction from Corinto through León, Managua, and Masaya to Grenada on Lake Nicaragua. At the beginning of the intervention, all except Corinto and Managua were in rebel hands. Butler kept going throughout the ensuing operations despite an attack of

"Uncle Joe" Pendleton at the capture of Coyotepe Hill, Nicaragua, in October 1912.

malaria that sent his temperature soaring to 104 degrees. His feverish, bloodshot stare inspired his men to give him the enduring nickname "Old Gimlet Eye."

The decisive action was fought on 4 October. By then Butler had talked Mena into surrendering, but another rebel general, Benjamín Zeledón, remained in arms. Just north of Masaya the railway ran between two hills, Coyotepe and Barranca; Coyotepe, with an elevation of about five hundred feet, was the higher and steeper. Zeledón held both summits with approximately a thousand men in trenches protected by barbed wire and supported by a few small field guns. Following his rejection of Pendleton's summons to surrender by 8:00 A.M. on 3 October, two Marine batteries shelled the rebel positions throughout the day. At 5:15 the next morning the Americans attacked Coyotepe: Pendleton with 600 bluejackets and Marines from the east and Butler with 250 Marines from the southeast. Exactly thirty-seven minutes later and at a price of four dead (all Marines) and fourteen wounded they were in possession of the hilltop. Twenty-seven Nicaraguans had been killed and nine captured.

The Nicaraguan Campaigns, 1912 and 1927–1932

Barranca's defenders decamped when the Americans on Coyotepe took them under fire. The Nicaraguan Army, which had awaited the outcome of the fight, captured Masaya that same day.

León was occupied by another American force on 6 October. Mopping-up operations ended on 2 November, and except for a hundred-man legation guard, the Leathernecks were withdrawn by the end of January. All

told, the Nicaraguan intervention cost the Corps thirty-seven casualties. This was the first time Marines had been committed to combat to uphold or install a Latin American government of which the United States approved. It would not be the last.

Meanwhile, the Corps had finally begun to take serious steps toward developing the capability to perform its advanced base mission. Much of the impetus for its new interest was external. By 1910 the General Board had become highly dissatisfied with the spasmodic efforts that had been made to create an advanced base force during the past decade. So, too, were the Navy reformers, most notably the Corps's old scourge, William F. Fullam, now a captain who had attained an influential position as an aide to Secretary Meyer. Yet it seems clear that Headquarters Marine Corps was not merely reacting to outside pressures. While Biddle had never been an exponent of the advanced base mission, he was clearly more receptive to it than his predecessors had been. This receptivity was reflected by his appointment of Maj. Eli K. Cole, arguably the foremost advocate of that mission, to the newly established post of assistant to the commandant, with special responsibility for readiness and training. Within a year, one or more permanent companies had been organized at every Marine barracks and the Advanced Base School relocated to Philadelphia, where its enrollment included both officers and men. By the end of 1912 almost a fifth of the Corps had passed through it.

Biddle also evidenced an openness to innovation by approving 1st Lt. Alfred A. Cunningham's request for permission to attend the Navy's fledgling flight school in Annapolis. Cunningham's reporting date, 22 May 1912, would become the official birthday of Marine aviation. A second Marine, 1st Lt. Bernard L. Smith, also earned his wings that year, and a third, 2nd Lt. William M. McIlvain, in 1913. Together with seven ground crewmen, Smith and McIlvain formed the Aviation Detachment, Advanced Base Force, in the fleet maneuvers of 1913–14, which proved to be a watershed in the evolution of the modern Marine Corps.

Planning to have the maneuvers include a major advanced base exercise had begun in January 1913. The experience gained at Subic Bay in 1907 had convinced the Corps that an advanced base force should consist of two regiments: a fixed defense regiment to man the base's big guns and fortifications, and a mobile defense regiment with infantry and field artillery to deal with any enemy forces that succeeded in getting ashore. Because of the usual manpower shortage, the regiments formed for the exercise numbered eight hundred rather than the approximately thirteen hundred men they were to count at full strength.

The Leathernecks began to ship out from Philadelphia on 27 November, and the 1st Advanced Base Brigade was formally constituted on 23 December. Its mission was to hold Culebra, a small island off the coast of Puerto Rico, against an assault by an enemy—"Black"— fleet. Col. George Barnett, who commanded the Philadelphia barracks, was named the brigade commander. From 10 to 18 January 1914 the brigade dragged its guns into position, built emplacements and entrenchments, strung wire, laid minefields, and otherwise prepared the island for defense. After two days of mock bombardments, the Black fleet began landing a force of twelve hundred seamen and Marines before dawn on 21 January. Within hours the chief umpire, Navy Capt. William S. Sims, ruled that the attackers had failed to crack Culebra's defenses. The Corps had demonstrated the feasibility of advanced base operations to the Navy and to itself.

Biddle's tour as commandant ended the following month. In March 1913 newly elected Democratic President Woodrow Wilson had named Josephus Daniels, an energetic southern populist, to be secretary of the Navy. Determined to destroy what he considered the undue influence of officers who homesteaded positions in Washington, Daniels announced that henceforth such assignments would be made for a single, four-year term. Some months thereafter Biddle put in for retirement. Daniels ascribed the commandant's decision to the introduction of the single-term policy, which would have prevented his reappointment, but it may well be that Biddle was loath to spend another year, much less face another four, under the iconoclastic secretary.

Biddle's action presented the Wilson administration with an unexpectedly early opportunity to install a commandant of its own choosing. Once again, most observers thought that Tony Waller, still the Corps's favorite, enjoyed the inside track. But once again, most observers were wrong. This time Waller was undone by the shadow of Samar. Daniels decided that his appointment would be incompatible with the administration's policy of promoting cordial relations with the Philippines, although in his memoirs Daniels acknowledged Waller's "high qualities as a man and an officer." Nevertheless, he recalled,

First Lt. Alfred A. Cunningham *(left)*, the Corps's first pilot, cranking up the trainer known as Noisy Nan at Philadelphia in 1911. He became interested in aviation while assigned to the Advanced Base School a year before obtaining orders to flight school.

it seemed to me unwise to appoint as head of the Marine Corps an officer who was alleged to have needlessly caused the death of Philippine soldiers [*sic*], though in the trial he had been acquitted. . . . Except for my intense hostility to the war upon the Filipinos and my zeal that they be given the right of self-government, I would have favored him.[27]

On 25 February 1914, President Wilson announced that he had selected George Barnett as the major general commandant of the Marine Corps. Despite the disappointment some Leathernecks felt over his selection, the polished and charming Barnett proved to be an effective commandant. Whereas his predecessors had merely accepted the advanced base mission, Barnett embraced it. In testimony before Congress he declared that "the fortification and defense of naval advance or temporary bases for the use of the fleet has been made the principal wartime mission of the Marine Corps."[28] To ensure that this was well understood, Barnett emphasized the importance of the Advanced Base School and detailed the captains and majors who had interested themselves in advanced base operations to serve as instructors-evangelists at the Naval War College.

Unfortunately, the Corps's rival mission repeatedly frustrated Barnett's efforts to implement more than doctrinal change. On assuming his duties, Barnett planned to establish the permanent brigade the General Board had decided would be needed for advanced base duty in time for the next fleet maneuvers. The intervening occupation of Veracruz, Mexico, prevented him from carrying out that intention. In 1915 he was able to organize the fixed defense regiment, but the following year the Caribbean claimed it, too.

Trouble had been brewing between the U.S. and Mexican governments since February 1913, when Gen. Victoriano Huerta shot his way into power, only to be challenged by a revolution that President Wilson applauded. To increase its chances of success, Wilson refused to recognize Huerta and declared an arms embargo of Mexico. He also deployed naval forces to protect Americans along the Mexican Gulf coast. On 9 April 1914 the tension was brought to a head by Mexican troops who briefly detained a party of U.S. seamen at Tampico. Although Huerta apologized for the incident, he refused to fire the twenty-one-gun salute the United States de-

The first Marine landing party leaves the *Prairie* at Veracruz on the morning of 21 April 1914.

manded without an assurance that it would be returned. The reservation was unacceptable to Wilson. On 20 April the president asked Congress for authority to use armed force in Mexico, but the Senate adjourned without taking action on the measure.

At 2:30 the next morning Wilson was awakened and informed that the German steamer *Ypiranga* was expected to dock at Veracruz that day with a huge shipment of American-made arms and ammunition. Wilson decided that her cargo must not reach Huerta. Orders were sent to Rear Adm. Frank F. Fletcher, commander of the naval forces off Veracruz, to seize the city's customhouse and intercept the arms as they were landed.

In an attempt to avert bloodshed, Fletcher notified the military commandant of Veracruz, Gen. Gustavo Maass, and the municipal authorities of his orders and urged them not to offer resistance. For his part, Huerta replied to Maass's request for instructions with orders to withdraw peaceably, but his message arrived too late. The general had already sent an officer to exhort, arm, and release the inmates of the city jail and had dispatched one

hundred regulars to the harbor area to "repel the invasion." Their efforts to carry out his order were supported by the cadets of the Mexican Naval Academy, policemen, members of the home guard, and ordinary Veracruzanos who took arms in defense of their city.

The landing party came ashore at 11:30 A.M. It numbered 787 men: 285 seamen from the battleship *Florida* and 502 Marines from the understrength 2nd Advanced Base Regiment, which had remained on call since the Culebra maneuvers, and a provisional battalion composed of the guard detachments from the *Florida* and her sister ship, the *Utah*. The bluejackets were to occupy the customhouse and the post and telegraph office; the Leathernecks, the railroad terminal, roundhouse, and yard, the cable office, and the power plant.

The landing was unopposed, but as the Americans marched into the city they were greeted by a fusillade of small arms and machine-gun fire from street corners, windows, and parapet roofs. Suddenly, Veracruz became a battleground. While the forces ashore slowly fought their way forward, Fletcher landed the *Utah*'s 384-man

The senior officers of the 1st Marine Brigade pose with their commander, Col. Littleton W. T. Waller, at Veracruz. *Front row, from left to right:* Lt. Col. Wendell C. Neville, Col. John A. Lejeune, Waller, Maj. Smedley D. Butler, and Maj. Randolph C. Berkeley.

bluejacket battalion, the only other unit at his disposal. By mid-afternoon the Americans had occupied all of their objectives. Fletcher then called the advance to a halt, initially in the hope that it would be possible to arrange a cease-fire. It was late in the day before that hope faded, and he instructed the landing party to remain on the defensive pending the arrival of reinforcements.

Five battleships and two cruisers reached Veracruz during the hours of darkness. The battleships' seaman battalions were organized into a regiment twelve hundred strong, and their Marine detachments into a three-hundred-man battalion. After another vain attempt to contact Mexican officials, the advance got under way at 7:45 A.M. Street fighting was as much a novelty to the Leathernecks as to the sailors, but they quickly adapted. Smedley Butler, who landed about midnight, recalled that, "stationing a machine gunner at one end of a street as a lookout, we advanced under cover, cutting our way

through adobe walls from one house to another with axes and picks. We drove everybody from the houses and then climbed up on the flat roofs to wipe out the snipers."[29] By noon Veracruz had been secured, although scattered sniping persisted for several days. American losses totaled seventeen dead and sixty-three wounded; four of the former and thirteen of the latter were Marines. Mexican casualties must have numbered upward of five hundred.

The 1st Advanced Base Regiment, originally ordered to Tampico, went ashore that afternoon. A third, provisional regiment assembled at Philadelphia disembarked on the twenty-ninth, and on 1 May, Tony Waller arrived to assume command of a brigade of 3,141 officers and men. By then the sailors and fleet Marines had returned to their ships and an Army brigade had landed. Leathernecks and soldiers garrisoned the city until the U.S. withdrawal on 23 November. Huerta had entered exile in July.

Nine Marines, including Butler, were among the fifty-

The Haitian and Dominican Campaigns, 1915, 1916, and 1919–1922

five men awarded the Medal of Honor for their actions at Veracruz. All of the Marines and most of the others were officers, who finally became eligible for the decoration in March 1915. Butler returned his medal to the Navy Department, protesting that he had done nothing heroic. He was told to keep and wear it.

Seven months after the evacuation of Veracruz, the Corps was committed to an occupation destined to last almost two decades. In a region wracked by what Theodore Roosevelt called "the revolutionary habit," Haiti held the revolutionary record. Between December 1908 and July 1915, seven presidents had been either overthrown or assassinated. The U.S. State Department took a dim view of such high jinks, fearing that sooner or later they would cause Haiti to precipitate an international crisis by defaulting on her foreign loans.

Nevertheless, the American intervention was unplanned. When on 27 July 1915 a mob tore an eighth president quite literally to pieces, 330 bluejackets and Marines were landed at Port-au-Prince to preserve order. Once the capital had been occupied, however, Wilson was unable to resist the temptation to take matters in hand. Five companies of Leathernecks plucked from Barnett's fixed defense regiment disembarked at Port-au-Prince on 4 August, and on the fifteenth Tony Waller came ashore with a full regiment and embodied the 1st Provisional Marine Brigade, then numbering 2,029 men. Rear Adm. William B. Caperton, the senior U.S. officer present, stage-managed the Haitian National Assembly's acceptance of a handpicked new president and a treaty effectively transforming the country into an American protectorate. Waller set about to eliminate the bane of the Haitian political process, the *cacos*.

Named for an indigenous bird of prey, the *cacos* were bandits who inhabited the mountains and jungles of northeastern Haiti. They eked out their livelihood by shaking down the peasantry and by helping presidential aspirants realize their ambitions—"for a certain sum," as Waller put, "to be paid out of the Haitian treasury . . . [and] also the privilege of looting some of the towns on the way down."[30] To induce the *cacos* to disband, Waller offered a subsidy of one hundred Haitian gourdes—about twenty dollars—to each chief who would turn in himself and his weapon, and ten gourdes to each rank-and-file *caco*. At the same time, he began to push combat patrols inland from the coastal towns in American hands. Several skirmishes ensued, and by early October the hardcore *cacos* had retired deep into the interior.

Smedley Butler was delighted to have Waller give his battalion the task of penetrating their refuges. On 22 October Butler set out to locate a *caco* stronghold called Fort Capois with a mounted patrol of forty men that included Gunnery Sgt. Dan Daly, who had won the Medal of Honor at Peking. After nightfall on the twenty-fourth, the patrol was ambushed by a force Butler estimated at four hundred *cacos* while fording a river in a heavy rain. A packhorse went down, but the Marines made it safely across the river. Butler called a halt on reaching high ground a mile from the ambush site and set about organizing a defensive perimeter. Sergeant Daly was told to break out the patrol's machine gun.

"It was lost in the river, sir," Daly replied. Butler masked his disappointment with a casual remark and moved on. An hour later, Daly approached him. "I've set up the machine gun, major," he reported.[31] Acting on his own initiative and alone, Daly had slipped through the *caco* band to the ford, found the dead packhorse, retrieved the machine gun and ammunition, and returned to the perimeter before anyone realized that he was gone.

Repeatedly shifting position to avoid being submerged by the *caco* rushes, the Leathernecks survived the night. At first light Butler divided his command into three squads and ordered each to charge outward. The result of this unconventional tactic was a rout in which the Marines not only put the *cacos* to flight but went on to capture their base, Fort Dipitié, which dawn revealed several hundred yards away. Two Leathernecks were wounded in the fray; the *cacos* lost eighteen killed and wounded. On Butler's recommendation, two of his officers received the Medal of Honor, and Sgt. Dan Daly became the first Marine to be awarded a second.

In the following weeks Butler's columns captured and destroyed Fort Capois and two lesser fortifications, Selon and Berthol, with little or no opposition. His final objective was Fort Rivière, an old French masonry work some two hundred feet square crowning the remote summit of Montagne Noir. The *cacos* considered the position impregnable, and some Marine officers believed that its reduction would require a regiment supported by field artillery. Butler chose to tackle it with about one hundred men divided into four companies and eight machine guns.

On three sides the ground dropped away from the fort too sharply for an assault to be possible. The only practicable approach was along the slope extending to the sally port on its western face. At 7:30 A.M. on 17 November, Butler led a company up the slope while the expedition's machine gunners laid down covering fire. When he arrived at the sally port with his orderly, Pvt. Samuel Gross (real name: Samuel Marguilies), and Sgt. Ross L. Iams, Butler discovered that it had been bricked up. The only way into Fort Rivière was through a drain four feet high, three feet wide, and fifteen feet long, into the mouth of which a *caco* was firing.

For a few seconds the Marines flattened themselves against the wall, Butler on one side of the drain, Iams and Gross on the other. Then Iams said, "Oh, hell, I'm going through," and ducked into the opening.[32] Gross shouldered Butler aside to follow directly behind Iams. The *caco* snapped off a shot, but somehow his bullet missed all three men. Iams's aim was better, and the Leathernecks emerged from the drain to find themselves facing a mob of screaming *cacos*. Iams and Gross each shot one of the leaders, and Gross also dropped a giant, club-wielding *caco* who was about to brain Butler.

In the meantime, other Leathernecks had begun scrambling out of the drain. "Hand to hand fighting, even with rocks, was going on," one recalled. "It was Sergeant Grimm, I believe, who exchanged rock for rock with some unknown *caco;* the two of them pitching big stones at each other over a wall gave a comical twist to the otherwise confused melee of bayonets and machetes."[33] In a quarter of an hour it was over. More than fifty *cacos,* including several *gros chefs,* died in the struggle. Not a single American was killed or seriously wounded. Butler, Iams, and Gross were awarded Medals of Honor, and this time Butler accepted his without complaint. He and Dan Daly remain the only Marines to share the remarkable distinction of having won the medal twice.

Even before the capture of Fort Rivière signaled the

A modern painting by Lt. Col. Donna Neary, USMCR, portrays the capture of Fort Rivière. The Marines are *(from left to right)* Sgt. Ross L. Iams, Maj. Smedley D. Butler, and Pvt. Samuel Gross.
Art Collection, Marine Corps Historical Center

pacification of the *cacos,* the Marines had undertaken their other major mission: the creation of a national constabulary, the Gendarmerie d'Haiti, to replace the disbanded Haitian Army. Until adequate numbers of native aspirants could be trained, the Gendarmerie would be officered by Marine officers and NCOs seconded to the Haitian service at a higher rank than they held in the Corps. On 3 December Butler became its first major general commandant. Originally the force's numbers were fixed at fifty-five officers and 1,530 gendarmes. Under Butler's energetic leadership, progress was rapid. In February 1916 the Gendarmerie formally assumed the responsibility of policing the country, relegating the Marine brigade to a supporting role, and in August a supplementary U.S. agreement with the Haitian government increased its authorized strength by 60 percent.

Haiti's neighbor, the Dominican Republic, passed under American control the following year. As usual, the intervention came about in reaction to a revolution. This one was provoked by President Juan Isidro Jiménez's dismissal of a political rival, Gen. Desiderio Arias, as minister of war. Arias responded by having his troops seize control of Santo Domingo, the country's capital.

Well content with Jiménez, who had recently accepted an American plan for reforming the republic's finances and army, the United States attempted to negotiate an end to the confrontation. On 14 May 1916 Arias agreed to evacuate Santo Domingo, where the first Marines had landed nine days earlier, and withdrew ninety miles north across the mountains to Santiago de los Caballeros. In the interim, Jiménez had resigned office rather than accept American assistance against his countrymen, but that solved nothing. In common with many other Dominicans, Arias was opposed to the reforms the United States wanted made. To allow his revolution to succeed, even by default, would hardly be compatible with American aims. If Dominican authorities declined to act against Arias, very well: the United States would act alone.

The job was given to Uncle Joe Pendleton, whose 4th Marine Regiment was ordered from San Diego to the Dominican Republic on 4 June. Pendleton set out for Santiago from Monte Cristi, on the northern coast, with about 850 men on the twenty-sixth. The same day a smaller column jumped off from Puerto Plata, fifty miles to the east. The two forces were to unite at Navarette, twelve miles from Santiago.

A Marine mounted patrol sets out into *caco* territory with a Haitian guide in 1915.

Leatherneck transport in the Dominican campaign extended from burros to Model Ts requisitioned from Santo Domingo's Ford agency.

Pendleton's column fought two actions during its advance. Like the engagement at Coyotepe, both called for assaults on entrenched hilltops. The first took place at Las Trencheras on 27 June. After the Leatherneck artillery gave the summit a good pasting, the infantry stormed it with fixed bayonets. The second clash occurred at Guayacanas on 3 July. This time dense brush impeded the artillery, but the rebel position was hosed down by machine gunners, two of whom earned the Medal of Honor for their work. Marine casualties in these encounters totaled two killed and twelve wounded. The American columns met at Navarette on 4 July, and a surrender delegation from Santiago appeared the next day.

During the following months the 2nd Provisional Marine Brigade, as Pendleton's command had been designated, established garrisons in ten cities, disarmed the Dominican Army, and, as in Haiti, paid private citizens to turn in their firearms, eventually collecting fifty-three thousand guns of various sorts. These activities precipitated several small shootouts and a daring coup in Pacificador Province, where Governor Juan Perez refused to recognize American authority. Apprehensive that Perez would free and arm the hundred convicts being held in the *fortaleza* at San Francisco de Macorís, 1st Lt. Ernest C. Williams, the commander of the company stationed there, decided to take charge of their custody. On the evening of 20 November, Williams led twelve picked men in a rush for the gate. The fort's forty-man garrison greeted them with a burst of fire. Eight Leathernecks fell wounded, but Williams and the others succeeded in pushing their way through the gate before it could be closed. Two Dominicans died in a point-blank exchange of shots inside the fort, and the remainder laid down their arms. The exploit earned Williams the Medal of Honor.

U.S. officials had hoped that the reforms they envisioned could be carried out with the cooperation of the Dominican government. By November it was obvious that such cooperation would not be forthcoming, and on the twenty-ninth the United States reluctantly announced the installation of a military government headed by Navy Capt. Harry S. Knapp. (Pendleton became the minister of war and the navy, the interior, and the police.) As in Haiti, the American intervention had become indefinite; but also as in Haiti, the Marine brigade was quickly

Who wouldn't want to join the Marines after encountering Sgt. Michael Fitzgerald at the recruiting station on 23rd Street in New York City in 1916?

charged with creating its replacement. On 7 April 1917 Knapp directed Pendleton to raise and train a force to which the maintenance of order could one day be relinquished, the Guardia Nacional Dominica. Like the Gendarmerie d'Haiti, it would initially be officered by Marine volunteers.

Open-ended though it was, the occupation of Hispaniola did not threaten to impose as great a strain on Marine manpower as it would have two years earlier. In 1916, influenced by the Great War under way in Europe, President Wilson asked Congress to approve a great construction program calculated to produce a Navy "second to none." To man the 157 ships to be built in three years would require the number of naval personnel to jump from 50,000 to 75,000. Arguing that the Marines' manning level should be a fifth as large as the Navy's, HQMC successfully appealed for a proportionate increase. The Naval Act of 1916 provided for a Marine Corps of 597 officers and 14,981 men and upgraded its rank structure to include seven brigadier generals. Tony Waller, Uncle

Joe Pendleton, and John A. Lejeune were among the colonels who pinned on stars as a result. Of great long-term significance, the act also created the Marine Corps Reserve.

Another of the act's provisions empowered the president to augment the Corps by 2,515 officers and men in the event of war. That event was guaranteed by Germany's resort to unrestricted U-boat warfare in February 1917. But even then the Caribbean made another claim on the Corps's resources. Defeated in a corrupt election, the Cuban Liberal Party launched an insurrection in which a number of American-owned sugar plantations were promptly torched. The first Marines committed to the Sugar Intervention landed on 25 February. Others followed, and from August 1917 to August 1919 at least one and usually two regiments were stationed in Cuba. As they had during the Negro Rebellion, the Leathernecks performed guard duties while the Cuban Army operated in the field. The last Marine outposts would not stand down until 1922.

8
Over There, 1917–1918

At the time America entered the world war on 6 April 1917, the Corps numbered only 511 officers and 13,214 men. The possibility that Marines might serve in France did not seem likely—except, that is, to General Barnett, who realized that the absence of Leathernecks from the American Expeditionary Forces (AEF) would give a hollow ring to the Corps's cherished recruiting slogan, "First to Fight." Barnett pressed his case on Capitol Hill, and when the naval appropriation bill for 1918 became law it included a provision for an increase in the number of men wearing forest green to more than thirty thousand; by war's end, that figure would double.

Close on the heels of the declaration of war, Barnett approached Secretary of the Navy Josephus Daniels and asked him to offer a brigade of combat-ready Marines to Secretary of War Newton D. Baker. At first, Daniels appeared reluctant to accompany the commandant to see Baker. He may have suspected that Barnett wanted the additional commitment to justify his persistent requests for personnel increases. On second thought, however, Daniels sagely concluded that the addition of a few Marines to the AEF could bring political dividends to the Navy in its annual budgetary battle with the Army.

At the War Department, Barnett, Daniels, and Chief of Naval Operations William S. Benson found Secretary Baker loath to allow the Marine Corps to insinuate itself into what his constituency insisted should be a purely "U.S. Army show." Baker made it clear that a token force of Marines would be an administrative and logistical em-

barrassment. He quizzed Barnett on details of uniform and equipment, stressing the necessity for commonality among U.S. ground forces in the interests of economy of supply. In each instance Barnett agreed to the necessary changes, leaving Baker no excuse to refuse his offer. Even the organization of the Marine contingent had to be modified. Because Army regiments numbered twice as many men as the Marine Corps equivalent, the Corps had to muster the proposed two-regiment brigade (5th and 6th Marines) into a single regiment—the 5th—in order to have an Army-style regiment ready to join the first troops leaving for France.

To give the outfit polish and grit, Barnett ordered eight companies of veteran Leathernecks home from the Caribbean to form the backbone of the regiment. Among the fledgling officers of the 5th Marines was a twenty-five-year-old platoon leader from Texas, 2nd Lt. John W. Thomason Jr., whose writings were destined to make him the Kipling of the old Corps. Thomason noted that the regiment included men from every part of the country and every walk of life: store clerks and lumberjacks, farmhands and college graduates. But at the same time he observed that there were

diverse people who ran curiously to type, with drilled shoulders and bone-deep sunburn, and a tolerant scorn of nearly everything on earth. Their speech was flavored with Navy words, and words culled from all the folk who live on the seas and ports where our warships go. They were the old breed of American regular, regarding the service as home and

The children of Menaucourt cheer as the 5th Marines arrive to enter cantonment there in June 1917.

war as an occupation; and they transmitted their temper and character and viewpoint to the high-hearted volunteer mass which filled the ranks.[1]

The force sailed from New York in June 1917, arriving at St. Nazaire, France, at the end of the month. By 3 July the entire Marine regiment was under canvas ashore, and on 15 July it joined the 1st Division to be reviewed by the AEF's commander-in-chief, Gen. John J. Pershing. The sharp-eyed Pershing was mortified to note that the intrusive Leathernecks seemed better trained and looked more military than the soldiers of his beloved regular Army. This discovery notwithstanding, he assigned the Marines to military police duties along the lines of communications while the soldiers began training for frontline service. At the same time, he moved to forestall the assignment of additional Leathernecks to his command. In a terse cablegram to Washington, Pershing cited his concerns for commonality, arguing that Marines did not assimilate well into the organizational structure of the AEF. Finally, he asked that "no more Marines be sent to France."[2]

To Pershing's dismay, the War Department informed him that President Wilson had already directed the de-

ployment of more Marines to France; in fact, another regiment of Marine infantry and a battalion of machine gunners would soon sail to join the AEF. Then, Brig. Gen. Henry P. McCain, the adjutant general of the Army, dictated their organization in an order that must have made Pershing bridle: "This regiment [6th Marines] to combine with the other one [5th Marines] to a brigade in the 2nd Division commanded by a Marine Corps general about to be nominated, and will be part of the Army under your command."[3]

Back home, eager enlistees underwent a strict regimen of training that ensured that every Leatherneck scheduled to go "over there" was fit. For most of the nineteenth century, the training of Marine recruits had been left to the whims of the various barracks commanders. By the time America entered the world war, however, it had been standardized and localized on an isolated island off the coast of South Carolina. Parris Island became a name synonymous with military toughness, providing an experience that thousands of young men would never forget. One alumnus captured the essence of the ordeal in a letter home: "The first day at camp I was afraid I was

Off-duty Leathernecks befriend a French farm girl at Menaucourt in the summer of 1917.

On the way to France in November 1917, members of the 6th Machine Gun Battalion crowd the rails of the *Von Steuben* as another transport, the *Agamemnon,* steams past.

Marine recruits perform physical training at the newly acquired training camp at Parris Island, South Carolina.

going to die. The next two weeks my sole fear was that I wasn't going to die. And after that I knew I'd never die because I'd become so hard that nothing could kill me."[4]

Barnett also established an advanced combat-training program at the newly acquired base at Quantico, Virginia. Every Leatherneck slated for duty in the AEF received additional weeks of rugged indoctrination to life on the Western Front, including valuable instruction from veteran British and French officers. In addition, candidates seeking a commission had to complete the demanding program of officer candidate school. With such a program to ensure preparedness, no one should have been surprised to find that the Leathernecks appeared more polished than the doughboys.

By February 1918 the 6th Marines and the 6th Machine Gun Battalion had joined the 5th Marines to form a brigade under Brig. Gen. Charles A. Doyen, USMC. Doyen appealed to Pershing to allow the unit's name to reflect its parentage: thus, the 4th Brigade (Marine), 2nd Division, AEF, was born. Each AEF division contained two infantry brigades of two regiments each, a brigade of ar-

tillery, and a regiment of combat engineers, plus support and headquarters elements. The strength of these formations averaged 25,500 men, more than twice the number in a British, French, or German division.

In May, General Doyen became ill and AEF Headquarters sent him home, along with a message that no replacement was required. Command of the Marine brigade went to an Army officer, Brig. Gen. James G. Harbord, an old friend of the AEF's commander. On giving Harbord the Marines, Pershing is said to have told him, "You are to have charge of the finest body of troops in France, and if they fail to live up to that reputation I will know whom to blame."[5] The first test for Harbord and his Marines—an elite force of 280 officers and 9,164 NCOs and men—lay ahead at Belleau Wood.

By then, the war had reached its climacteric. Having knocked out Russia in late 1917, Germany resolved to make a desperate double-or-nothing gamble to achieve victory in France before the reservoir of American manpower could be tapped. The German spring offensive opened on 21 March 1918 with a mighty blow that sent

Marine Operations on the Western Front, 1918. Front line as of 9 June.

the British Expeditionary Force staggering back some forty miles. For a few days the Allies were face-to-face with disaster, but in the end the breach was sealed. Unwilling to concede the defeat this foreboded, on 9 April the German high command launched a second, slightly less formidable assault on the British front. It, too, scored substantial gains, but eventually it, too, was contained.

Still determined to force the war to a triumphant conclusion—unlikely as that had become—the Germans turned their attention to the French. On 27 May the third of the German spring offensives struck surprised French forces north of the Aisne, previously thinned to reinforce the British sector, and achieved a stunning breakthrough. By 31 May the Germans had reached the Marne at Château-Thierry—barely forty miles northeast of Paris, and had driven a two-and-a-half-mile wedge into the Allied front. Not since 1914 had the enemy stood so close to the French capital. Although in fact the losses sustained in its previous offensives had severely weakened the German Army, to the Allies the crisis of the war appeared to be at hand.

Previously, Pershing had steadfastly resisted appeals to integrate American formations into the French and British armies. In accordance with his instructions from President Wilson, he was determined to retain control of his troops until enough of them reached France to form a "separate and distinct" American Army. The German onslaught caused him to relent, and on 28 March he offered to place all American combat troops in France—approximately four divisions—temporarily at the disposal of the French high command. A regiment of the 1st Division entered action at Cantigny on 28 May, the same day the 2nd Division was moving forward to help stem the German advance below the Marne.

Harbord ordered Col. Albertus W. Catlin's 6th Marines to take up positions along the Paris–Metz highway just south of a little forest called Belleau Wood. His instructions left no doubt as to the seriousness of the situation: the Marines and the soldiers of the 9th Infantry on their right were to dig in and hold at all costs: "No retirement will be thought of on any pretext whatsoever."[6] Entrenching tools had not been issued, so the Leathernecks and doughboys used their mess kits and bayonets to burrow into the ground. Meanwhile, retreating French troops streamed past on their way to the rear. Capt. Lloyd W. Williams marched his company through shattered

The 55th Company, 5th Marines, rests in a village on the way to the front before the Battle of Belleau Wood.

Meaux, twenty-five miles northeast of Paris, on 1 June. A French officer proceeding in the opposite direction invited Williams and his Marines to join his dispirited column. The gallant Leatherneck responded tersely: "Retreat? Hell! We just got here."[7]

A day later, German forces approached the American position for their first major encounter with fresh troops from across the Atlantic. Allowing the columns of *feld-grau* infantry to advance to within one hundred yards of their lines, the Marines cut them down like ninepins with well-aimed rifle fire. For two days the Kaiser's troops attempted to pierce their front, to no avail. By 5 June the German offensive had stalled.

Then, on the afternoon of 6 June, the Marines received orders to eject the Germans from Belleau Wood. Their objective stood on a fold of rocky ground in the midst of rolling farm country, extending approximately a mile and a half from north to south and half a mile from east

to west. Colonel Catlin described it as "a typical piece of well kept French woodland."[8] The trees, tall but averaging only five to six inches in diameter, grew so close together that in places visibility was limited to fifteen or twenty feet. Inside, the wood bristled with machine-gun nests. Since the initial contact, the Germans had learned that they were facing American regulars. The German high command did not consider Belleau Wood of great strategic significance, but it decided to assert a moral superiority over the new enemy by repulsing the American assault. The stage was set for the fiercest battle the Corps had ever fought.

A short, savage artillery barrage preceded the Leathernecks' attack. At 5:00 P.M., waves of Marines fixed bayonets and crossed wheat fields dotted with poppies. As withering German fire tore through their ranks, the Americans wavered but continued to advance. Gunnery Sgt. Dan Daly, the only enlisted Marine to have won two

Medals of Honor, swung his rifle toward the enemy lines and shouted to his platoon, "Come on, you sons-of-bitches! Do you want to live forever?"[9] (After the battle, he would be cited for three separate acts of heroism, recommended for a third Medal of Honor, and awarded both the Navy Cross and the Army's Distinguished Service Cross.) Colonel Catlin, watching the attack through his field glasses from a little rise three hundred yards from the woods, was shot through the right lung. "I suffered but little pain and I never for a moment lost consciousness," he recalled, "nor did any thoughts of death occur to me. I was merely annoyed at my inability to move and carry on."[10] Lt. Col. Harry Lee assumed command.

By nightfall Leatherneck blood dotted the landscape, matching the color of the poppies, but the Marines had a foothold in the woods. Later, a battalion commander declared that "the only thing that drove these Marines through those woods in the face of such resistance was their individual, elemental guts, plus the hardening of the training."[11] That night Sgt. John H. Quick won a Navy Cross and a Distinguished Service Cross to wear beside his Medal of Honor. Learning that a battalion on the edge of the woods was low on ammunition, Quick and 2nd Lt. William B. Moore, a Princeton football hero, drove one of Henry Ford's tin lizzies through a curtain of fire to resupply it. The butcher's bill for the day was 1,087 Leatherneck casualties, more than the Corps had lost in all the other battles it had fought since 1775.

The next morning the advance continued in the face of bitter opposition. By the close of 12 June, the entire wood except a small area along its northern fringe was in American hands. At dawn the Germans counterattacked behind a barrage of artillery and mustard gas. Although the gas alone caused 450 Marine casualties, the brigade held its ground in a desperate day's fighting. Late on 15 June, depleted Marine columns moved to the rear, leaving it to the U.S. 7th Infantry Regiment and French forces to mop up the remaining Germans. But the Leathernecks' battle for Belleau Wood had not ended. When the Germans reinforced the defenders, the Allied attack stalled. On 23 June the Marines returned to the scene with newly replenished ranks. Three days later Maj. Maurice Shearer, commanding the 3rd Battalion, 5th

Sgt. Dan Daly wearing the Medals of Honor he won in China and Haiti, and the Distinguished Service Cross he earned in France.

Marines, was able to report: "Woods now U.S. Marine Corps entirely."[12]

From first to last, the forest had cost the Marine Brigade 5,183 killed and wounded, a casualty rate of more than 50 percent.[13] Among the dead were Captain Williams, who had declined the French officer's invitation to join the retreat, and Capt. Edward C. Fuller, the son of a future commandant. A grateful France announced that Belleau Wood henceforth would be named Bois de la Brigade Marine. In a petulant gesture, AEF Headquarters altered the name to Bois de la Brigade des Americains. Just as forthrightly, the French changed it back. And the French were not the only ones impressed by the prowess and élan of the Marines; the Germans began to refer to them as *Teufelhunden*—"devil dogs."

Along with the victory came an outburst of interservice acrimony that persisted throughout the war.[14] Although Pershing had issued orders that American war correspondents should not identify units in their dispatches, those covering the Battle of Belleau Wood re-

The savagery of the Battle of Belleau Wood is chillingly evoked in this painting by Frank Schoonover. Art Collection, Marine Corps Historical Center

ported the attacking units to be Marines. Then Floyd Gibbons of the *Chicago Tribune* fell gravely wounded while accompanying Dan Daly's platoon. Believing that his wound was mortal, friends among the censors at AEF Headquarters let Gibbons's "last," particularly vivid, dispatch go through unaltered. Because tiny Belleau Wood was unknown to his readership, Gibbons used the name of the entire region—Château-Thierry—for the site of the encounter. Thus, to the consternation of every soldier in the AEF—especially the doughboys of the 1st and 3rd Divisions fighting gallantly to stem the German offensive— the Marines became the beneficiaries of a public relations bonanza. For the remainder of the war, soldiers taunted them with a musical doggerel, sung to the tune of "Mademoiselle from Armentières," that resulted in a full share of black eyes and broken noses:

> The Marines have won the Croix de Guerre, parlez-vous?
> The Marines have won the Croix de Guerre, parlez-vous?
> The Marines have won the Croix de Guerre,
> But the sons-of-bitches were never there.
> Hinky dinky parlez-vous?[15]

The Army's resentment was also evidenced in official snubs. After the capture of the woods, a beaming French President Clemenceau visited the headquarters of the 2nd Division. Neither Harbord nor any of his Marines were invited to meet him.

Despite the terrible losses the German army had already suffered, its high command launched another offensive on 15 July. The blow fell on the French front in Champagne. This time the Allies were ready. Intelligence had obtained complete details of the enemy plans and in most areas the offensive was stopped in its tracks. Only eight of the forty-seven divisions committed to the operation succeeded in crossing the Marne, and on 17 July the Germans called off the attack.

Profiting from the enemy's discomfiture, the Allies immediately counterattacked. Their principal objective was to cut the highway from Soissons to Château-Thierry, which was used to supply German forces in the salient. The key role in the assault was assigned to the French XX Corps, consisting of the 1st and 2nd Divisions, AEF, and a French Moroccan division. Harbord had

The 4th Brigade on the march through the French countryside.

taken over the 2nd Division, Pershing having sacked its original commander, and Marine Col. Wendell C. Neville succeeded him in command of the 4th Brigade.

The Leathernecks moved into the pocket south of Soissons on 18 July with fixed bayonets. Once again they attacked into a wood, the Forêt de Retz, which Lieutenant Thomason thought "was like Dante's wood, so shattered and tortured and horrible." He remembered that "machine-guns raved everywhere . . . it was every man for himself, an irregular, broken line, clawing through the tangles, climbing over fallen trees, plunging heavily into Boche rifle-pits." Mostly, Thomason recalled the dying as the gallant Marines took position after position: "Some guns were silenced by blind, furious rushes that left a trail of writhing, khaki figures, but always carried two or three frenzied marines into the emplacement; from whence would come shooting and other clotted unpleasant sounds and then silence."[16]

In two days of bitter fighting the brigade suffered 1,972 casualties, of which the 6th Marines took two-thirds.[17] During the hours of desperate combat one young company commander, 1st Lt. Clifton B. Cates, sent a runner to his battalion commander to report: "I am in an old abandoned French trench. . . . I have only two men left out of my company and twenty out of other companies. . . . I have no one on my left, and only a few on my right. I will hold."[18] On the evening of the nineteenth, the Germans pulled back across the Marne. With their withdrawal, the initiative passed to the Allies, who never relinquished it.

Two Central European sergeants serving in the same company of the 5th Marines, Louis Cukela and Matej Kocak, won the Medal of Honor on 18 July. Kocak, an Austrian by birth, personally captured an enemy machine-gun nest and then led twenty-five stray Moroccans in an attack that overran another. Cukela, a Serb, had joined the U.S. Army in 1914 and had been stationed in the Philippines. Two years later, the news that the Germans had captured his native village inflamed his indignation to the point that he purchased his discharge and returned to the United States with the intention of enlisting in the Canadian Army, which was already fighting in Europe. But like many another belligerent young man, he was seduced by the slogan "First to Fight" and

John W. Thomason as a captain during World War I. Thomason's writings, especially *Fix Bayonets!,* made him the Rudyard Kipling of the old Corps. He served as a Marine from 1917 until his death in 1944.

reached France in June 1917 as a U.S. Marine. According to the citation for his Navy Medal of Honor, when his company's advance was checked, "Sergeant Cukela advanced alone. . . . Disregarding the warnings of his comrades, he crawled out from the flank under a heavy fire and worked his way to the rear of the enemy position." Cukela then "[rushed] a machine gun emplacement, killed or drove off the crew with his bayonet, bombed the remaining part of the strong point with German hand grenades, and captured two enemy machine guns and four men."[19]

Soon after Soissons, command of both the 2nd Division and the 4th Brigade (Marine) changed again. Late in July Pershing appointed Harbord to straighten out the muddle behind the lines in the Services of Supply. Harbord proved a success as the chief of the SOS, but his reassignment left the 2nd Division without a commander. Its senior officer was Brig. Gen. John A. Lejeune, whom Barnett had sent to France in June in the hope that he could persuade Pershing to approve the formation of a Marine division. After serving briefly as commander of an Army infantry brigade, Lejeune had taken over the Marine Brigade from Neville.

A grizzled Cajun whose down-home manner masked a shrewd intelligence, Lejeune was placed in temporary command of the division while Pershing looked for a successor to Harbord. After a few days, Pershing decided to leave him in the job, and in August "Gabe" Lejeune pinned on his second star. He was the first Marine Corps officer ever to lead a unit larger than a brigade in combat. His selection was undoubtedly influenced by the fact that he was one of the few Marines of his generation to have attended the Army War College, where he made many friends among classmates and faculty now occupying important positions in the AEF.[20] At the same time, Pershing and senior Army officers probably hoped that giving Lejeune command of the 2nd Division would silence entreaties by Barnett and the Navy Department for a Marine division within the AEF. Even as these important changes were being made, Pershing and Brig. Gen. Henry P. McCain, adjutant general of the Army, exchanged secret cablegrams on the subject; they concluded that the AEF could do without more Marines. Neville, given his first star, resumed command of the Marine Brigade.

In early August, the 2nd Division occupied a quiet

Maj. Gen. John A. Lejeune *(center, facing camera directly)* and Brig. Gen. Wendell C. Neville *(to his right).* This photograph was taken in Germany in 1919.

sector around Marbache in the Moselle Valley, readying itself for the next push. That month, the Marine Brigade was inspected by Assistant Secretary of the Navy Franklin D. Roosevelt, who had just visited the battlefield of Belleau Wood. Deeply impressed by what he had seen there, Roosevelt declared that, effective immediately, the right to wear the Marine Corps collar emblem, previously restricted to officers, was extended to enlisted men. No doubt he would have agreed with a German intelligence report prepared around the same time that explained that "the Marines are . . . a sort of elite corps. . . . Prisoners . . . consider their membership in the Marine Corps to be something of an honor. They proudly resent any attempt to place their regiments on a par with other infantry regiments."[21] Marines themselves relished the story of the philanthropic American lady who visited a French field hospital. Spying a clean-shaven face among the rows of bewhiskered French casualties, she exclaimed, "Oh, surely you are an American?" "No, ma'am," came the answer, "I'm a Marine."[22]

On 20 August the 2nd Division assembled at Colombey-les-Belles, south of Toul, in preparation for the Saint-Mihiel offensive. This battle was the payoff of Pershing's repeated refusals to allow his units to be frittered away as fillers for French and British formations: an operation conducted by an American field army—the First Army, officially constituted on 10 August—under American command. Its objective was the elimination of the Saint-Mihiel salient, a wedge-shaped indentation in the Allied front, sixteen miles deep and twenty-five miles wide at its base, that had been occupied by the Germans since the beginning of the war. Besides displaying the AEF's capabilities to friend and foe, the reduction of the salient would open important rail communications to Allied use. To carry out the operation Pershing assembled fourteen U.S. divisions—including the 2nd—and borrowed four from the French.

At 1:00 A.M. on 12 September, Allied artillery began an intense bombardment of the German lines. For four hours American and French gunners blasted the enemy's trenches and dugouts. Pershing's men pushed into the salient from east and west at 5:00 A.M. By chance, the Germans were in the process of evacuating their positions. The attacking forces encountered relatively little resistance, and by nightfall on 13 September the occupation of the salient was complete. The fruits of victory included sixteen thousand prisoners and 443 guns. By the horrific standards of the Western Front, American casualties were light, just under seven thousand; the Marine Brigade's share totaled 132 dead and 574 wounded.

The Saint-Mihiel offensive proved that an American army could fight effectively under American command. The AEF had little time to savor its triumph, however, for ten days before the attack Pershing had pledged that it would be ready to join in an Allied general offensive no later than 25 September. In the north, the British would push east toward Cambrai; in the center, the French would thrust across the Aisne; and in the south, the Americans would strike north through the wooded heights of the Meuse-Argonne toward Sedan with the objective of severing the Metz-to-Bruges railroad, which linked the northern and southern wings of the German Army on the Western Front. Should this connection be broken, the enemy would find it difficult if not impossible to conduct an orderly withdrawal from France and Belgium. As the AEF's next battleground lay forty miles west of Saint-Mihiel, two weeks were consumed by the complex task of moving 600,000 American troops to relieve the 220,000 French in the lines there.

The 2nd Division did not participate in this redeployment. Together with the 36th Division, it was loaned to the French to reinforce an offensive in Champagne between the Argonne Forest and Reims. From 24 to 30 September, the Marine Brigade traveled by rail with its parent division to take up a position behind the French Fourth Army. The keystone of the German front in this sector was Blanc Mont Ridge, a heavily fortified eminence that dominated the last natural defensive position south of the Aisne, some sixteen miles to its rear. Its capture would compel the enemy to fall back all the way to the river.

Lejeune met his new commander, one-armed, red-bearded Gen. Henri Gouraud, at Châlons-sur-Marne on 25 September. Lejeune formed an excellent opinion of the French officer, and thus two days later he was shocked to hear rumors that Gouraud planned to use American units piecemeal. As Pershing had done on so many similar occasions, Lejeune bridled. The 2nd Division, he argued, should be kept intact. "General," he promised, "if you do not divide the Second Division, but put it in line as a unit on a narrow front, I am confident that it will be able to take Blanc Mont Ridge, advance beyond it, and hold its position."[23] He would soon be called on to make this promise good.

The Fourth Army had begun its attack on 26 September, the same day on which the AEF launched the Meuse-Argonne offensive. During the opening days of the attack, French troops advanced three and a half miles, but by 28 September XXI Corps had ground to a halt against German trenches and concrete pillboxes on the desolate, chalky ground at the foot of Blanc Mont. After another conference with Lejeune, Gouraud decided to give the 2nd Division a chance to show what it could do. During the night of 1–2 October, the Americans entered the front line.

Spearheaded by the 2nd Division, XXI Corps renewed its attack on 3 October. The 4th Brigade (Marine) attacked on the left and the 3rd Brigade on the right. A company of French tanks supported each brigade. The artillery barrage began at 5:45 A.M. Lieutenant Thomason recalled that "the heavens seemed roofed over with long, keening noises—sounds like the sharp ripping of silk, magnified, running in swift arcs from horizon to horizon. . . . Almost, one expected to look up and see them, like swift, deadly birds, some small, some enormous, all terrible."[24] Following the barrage within 330 yards of the first objective, by mid-morning units of the 2nd Division had advanced three and a half miles. Three Medals of Honor were won during the day's fighting: two by Marines and one by a soldier, all for the single-handed destruction of machine-gun nests.

The Yanks resumed the advance on 4 October. Unfortunately, the French units on the Marines' left failed to keep pace and the brigade was repeatedly required to beat off German counterattacks on its exposed flank. At 6:00 the next morning the 6th Marines and the French 17th Infantry captured the machine-gun strongpoint on Blanc Mont, taking more than two hundred prisoners and sixty-five machine guns. The next day the Marines pushed down the ridge into the hasty fortifications beyond. Lejeune's promise had been kept.

On the night of 6 October the 2nd Division was relieved by the U.S. 36th Division. The battle had cost the Marines 2,538 men killed and wounded. The grateful French presented two thousand Croix de Guerre to the officers and men of the division and appointed Lejeune

5th Marines at Champagne, 4 October 1918, by John W. Thomason Jr., a talented artist as well as author, illustrates the assault on Blanc Mont. Heavy machine-gun fire tore into the regiment's left flank, where French troops had failed to keep pace, and came close to destroying it. Many American officers, like the one shown, adopted the French officers' custom of carrying a cane. Virginia Military Institute Museum, Lexington, Va.

a Commander of the Legion of Honor. Pershing later praised the victory as having been won "against a persistent defense worthy of the grimmest period of trench warfare."[25] But however impressive its resistance appeared, the German Army was approaching exhaustion. Although Lejeune's troops had been opposed by elements of eight divisions, only two of those divisions were considered fit for combat by the German high command. By mid-October the Central Powers had begun to disintegrate. Bulgaria surrendered on 29 September; the German government dispatched the first of a series of armistice notes to President Wilson on 4 October; Turkey dropped out of the war on 31 October; Austria-Hungary, on 3 November; and on 7 November, the mutiny of the German High Seas Fleet sparked a revolution ashore. Yet even with the inevitable end in sight, the combatants continued to flail away at each other, with deadly results.

Following the battle of Blanc Mont, the 2nd Division rejoined the AEF to take part in the final phase of the Meuse-Argonne offensive. Between 26 September and 16 October, when the First Army was compelled to halt to reorganize, Pershing's troops advanced ten of the thirty-five miles they needed to cover to reach the railroad on which the maintenance of the German front depended. Assigned to V Corps in the left center of the American front, the 2nd Division occupied a two-and-a-half-mile-wide sector west of the Meuse River facing the Hindenburg Line. As the AEF wheeled into position for the final battle of the war, it numbered more than a million Americans fighting in nineteen divisions, plus eight French divisions placed under Pershing's command.

At 5:30 A.M. on 1 November, the American Army attacked in strength, with the Marines moving forward on the left of the 2nd Division. The next day, the division's 3rd Brigade took the lead. In a daring thrust on the night of 3–4 November, soldiers of the 9th Infantry, followed by the 23rd Infantry and a battalion of the 5th Marines, marched for six hours and fifteen minutes in total dark-

Marines advance across open country in the Meuse-Argonne offensive. Note the rifle-grenadier *(left center)*.

ness and driving rain to surprise sleeping German units four miles behind the front without suffering a single casualty. The intrepid doughboys and Leathernecks missed capturing a German general and his headquarters by a bare fifteen minutes.

The advance continued although rations ran short. Marines foraged for discarded German rations, scrounged food from French civilians, and even devoured the remnants of a cabbage patch planted by the retreating enemy. Lejeune ordered another night march similar to the earlier one; it, too, brought spectacular results. By 6 November the AEF was close enough to the vital railroad to take it under artillery fire. But while the enemy's resistance crumbled, it never collapsed. In the last eleven days of the war, 273 Marines were killed and 1,363 were wounded.[26]

When the armistice went into effect at 11:00 on the morning of 11 November 1918, most of the combat-weary Leathernecks and doughboys sat down in numb disbelief. Warming fires appeared in the shell-pocked meadows and the patriotic songs that had been the emotional staple of fighting men on both sides echoed eerily across the scarred landscape. More than a decade later Lejeune recalled the emotional impact of the cease-fire: "A few minutes before eleven o'clock, there were tremendous bursts of fire from the two antagonists and then—suddenly—there was complete silence." He thought "it was the most impressive celebration of the armistice that could have possibly taken place. There was a solemn and an earnest joy in the hearts of every man at the front. . . . We were happy because fighting, death, and destruction had ceased. I offered up a prayer of thanksgiving to Almighty God."

For soldiers and Marines alike, however, hope for a swift passage home proved fleeting; AEF Headquarters had other plans. Fearful that with the cease-fire America's volunteer Army would unravel, Pershing chose the units for occupation duty in Germany carefully. The 2nd Division was among those he selected. In mid-November the bone-weary troops began the long, cold march to the Rhine. Hiking along muddy roads for ten hours a day, Lejeune's men wound their way through France, Belgium, and Luxembourg to the German border. On reach-

In the Argonne, two Leathernecks man a 37-mm gun, an infantry close-support weapon, while riflemen push ahead.

ing the Rhine, the officers of one Leatherneck battalion marched in formation to the water's edge and urinated in it. On 31 December 1918, after a grueling march of two hundred miles, the 2nd Division crossed the bridge at Remagen and moved upriver to Koblenz. The 5th Marines took up position in the Wied Valley while the 6th Marines occupied the towns across the Rhine. A docile populace accepted the inevitable, and the occupation proceeded without serious incident. Marines and soldiers became tourists, fought boredom, and complained about the inadequate delousing facilities. Peacetime routines of training, more training, and endless inspections filled their days.

At long last, the order came to return home. In midsummer 1919 the division boarded railway cars for Camp Pontanezen, near Brest on the Atlantic coast of France. The men of the 2nd Division marched together for the last time on 9 August when they paraded through the streets of New York to the thunderous acclaim of its citizenry. En route to Quantico, the 4th Brigade (Marine), AEF—never to be called that again—marched past the White House to be reviewed by President Wilson. Reservists and wartime-only enlistees returned to civilian pursuits, and regulars took up old duties at familiar posts and stations.

Few Leathernecks would ever forget the thrill of their first step onto the soil of France or their first time under fire. For others, the agony of old wounds or the sear of gas-scarred lungs lingered as painful reminders. The cost of being "First to Fight" had been heavy: 11,366 casualties.

Cpl. Robert G. Robinson in his flying suit.

Of the Marines who served in France, 1 out of 6 was wounded; 2,459 made the supreme sacrifice. Only 25 Marines were taken prisoner, however. Six Marines serving in the 4th Brigade won the Medal of Honor, and 744 received the Navy Cross or the Distinguished Service Cross. In addition, the citations the 2nd Division had received in the French Army's orders of the day entitled the members—present and future—of its units to wear the green-and-red fourragère of the Croix de Guerre. The 5th and 6th Marines wear it still. Of the 78,839 men who belonged to the Corps during the war, approximately 32,000 served in France.[27]

Sadly, a second brigade of combat-ready Marines failed to see action. Early in 1918 General Barnett had ordered the organization and training of the 5th Brigade at Quantico; composed of the 11th and 13th Regiments and the 5th Machine Gun Battalion, it went to France under the command of Brig. Gen. Eli K. Cole in September. Pershing had accepted one brigade of Marines, but he made it clear that he could do without another. To its members' dismay, the 5th Brigade was broken up and assigned to rear-area duties or used as replacements for the 4th Brigade. Both Cole and Brig. Gen. Smedley D. Butler received orders to command AEF depot divisions or processing facilities. Butler managed to straighten out the problem-ridden Camp Pontanezen near Brest, but he felt left out. To his congressman father Butler fumed: "For over twenty years, I worked hard to fit myself to take part in this war . . . and when the supreme test came my country did not want me."[28] But at least Butler made it to France. His idol, Tony Waller, spent his war commanding the skeleton of the Advanced Base Force at Philadelphia and retired, a major general, in 1921. Two future commandants, Ben H. Fuller and John Russell, also failed to receive orders to France and served in posts in the Caribbean.

Butler blamed HQMC for his failure to gain a combat assignment. Others believed that the friction that had developed within the AEF was the result of anti–Marine Corps prejudice of senior Army officers. One of Lejeune's regimental commanders went so far as to refer to the Marines as "a bunch of adventurers, illiterates, and drunkards" in official correspondence.[29] Another senior Army officer privately declared that the letters "USMC" stood for "Useless Sons-of-bitches Made Comfortable."[30] The seeds of intense interservice rivalry had been sown on the Western Front, and the fruits of controversy would ripen during the interwar years.

Like the Corps's ground forces, its newly hatched aviation community had to overcome major obstacles to take an active part in the war. American intervention found the 1st Aviation Company located in Philadelphia with the Advanced Base Force. Renamed the 1st Marine Aeronautic Company, from October through December 1917 the Marine aviators flew antisubmarine patrols from Cape May, New Jersey. On 9 January 1918 the company deployed to Ponto Delgada on São Miguel Island in the Azores to patrol the waters of the eastern Atlantic with a force of eighteen single-engine seaplanes. The operations were generally uneventful and most of the aviators yearned to join the fight in France. Senior Marine Corps officers wanted to see Leatherneck aviators in France, too. The problem, predictably, was that AEF Headquarters wanted no part of naval aviation. In February 1918, however, the Navy decided to form a unit,

In the early fall of 1919 Maj. Gen. Commandant George Barnett *(left)* accepted the return of the unit colors of the 4th Brigade (Marine), AEF. Lt. Col. Thomas Holcomb, 6th Marines, a future commandant, is the second officer to Barnett's left. Barnett Papers, Marine Corps Research Center, Quantico, Va.

designated the Northern Bombing Group, to attack the German submarine pens along the Belgian coast. The group would consist of a Navy night wing and a Marine day wing.

The Corps's pioneer pilot, 1st Lt. Alfred A. Cunningham, received permission to cull sufficient Navy pilot trainees from the pool at Pensacola to man the four squadrons of the newly established 1st Marine Aviation Force. Eager to join the fight, the Navy pilots—mostly wartime-only reservists—applied for transfers and accepted commissions in the Corps. Cunningham and his band of 149 aviators disembarked at Brest on 30 July 1918, only to discover that their bombers had been shipped to England. Rising to the occasion, Cunningham worked out a deal with the British to trade him bombers for American-built aircraft engines, at the rate of one for

three, and, until he had enough planes to commence operations, to allow his men to gain experience by flying missions with the Royal Air Force. It was 14 October before eight DeHavilland (DH) bombers—lumbering, single-engine two-seaters with a top speed of 120 miles per hour—from Squadron 9 climbed into the air on the first all-Marine raid. By then the Germans had abandoned the submarine pens, so the Marines' target was the railway yards at Thielt, Belgium.

One plane was piloted by 2nd Lt. Ralph Talbot, who had become a naval aviator after completing his freshman year at Yale and then accepted Cunningham's invitation to transfer to the Corps. On the return flight, Talbot became separated from the formation and was jumped by a dozen German fighters. His gunner, Cpl. Robert G. Robinson, shot one down before being hit in

Marinettes and Yeomen (F) at their mustering-out ceremony after World War I. In the center (bareheaded) is Secretary of the Navy Josephus Daniels; to his right is Assistant Secretary of the Navy Franklin D. Roosevelt; to Daniels's left is Chief of Naval Operations William S. Benson.

the arm, stomach, and hip. Talbot downed another German with his forward-firing machine guns and, with Robinson unconscious in the rear seat, shook off his pursuers in a steep dive, skimming over enemy trenches at an altitude of fifty feet to land his gunner at the nearest hospital. Both men were awarded the Medal of Honor. Ironically, the riddled Robinson lived to wear his medal, but Talbot died in a crash during takeoff eleven days later.

By the end of the war, Marine aviators had flown fifty-seven missions—forty-three with the RAF and fourteen on their own—dropping fifty-two thousand pounds of bombs and scoring four confirmed victories and eight others claimed. Four Marines were killed in action or died of wounds, and, besides the two Medals of Honor, they earned another twenty-eight decorations.

Much to his men's dismay, Cunningham requested an early return home for the 1st Aviation Force. After the signing of the armistice, there seemed little reason for Leatherneck aviators to remain in Europe—especially since they were not wanted by the AEF. An officer of vision, Cunningham believed that "we could accomplish much more at home, getting our aviation service established under the new conditions of peace."[31] In December 1918, the 1st Aviation Force sailed for the States. Some senior Marine officers were disappointed that the aviators did not have the opportunity to join their comrades-in-arms in an air-ground combat team and questioned the utility of aviation for the Corps.

In terms of public relations, the Marine Corps's service with the AEF hit the bull's-eye. In fact, less than half of its men had reached France. Yet to most Americans, the Marines' claim to be the "First to Fight" rang solid and true. The legionary romance that had enveloped the Corps during its campaigns in tropic climes was complemented by the glory of having beaten the Kaiser's crack troops in the greatest European war in a century. In the postwar decade this shining image would be kept bright by popular works such as Thomason's *Fix Bayonets!*, a narrative of the 4th Brigade's battles, and *What Price Glory?*, a hit Broadway play by a disabled Marine officer, Capt. Lawrence Stallings.

Yet most of the men who served in the Corps in 1917–18 never got "over there." In making his pitch to send Marines to France, Barnett had promised to meet the Corps's traditional commitments as well. Throughout the war, Leathernecks continued to serve in small detachments in the Navy's warships; naval stations at home and overseas kept their trusty Marine sentries; weak brigades remained in Santo Domingo, Cuba, and Haiti; and three regiments stayed in the States to constitute the Advanced Base Force or guard vital oilfields along the border between Texas and Mexico.

The requirement for expeditionary duty also involved the Corps in the periphery of the Russian Revolution. In June 1918 the Czech Legion, an anti-Bolshevik army of freed prisoners of war that had fought its way east along the Trans-Siberian Railroad, seized the port of Vladi-vostok on the Pacific coast of Siberia. Leathernecks and bluejackets from the flagship of the Asiatic Fleet, the cruiser *Brooklyn,* joined landing parties from British and French ships to maintain order in the city. Most of the Marines were withdrawn in August, but a detail stayed behind to guard a Navy radio station on an island in Vladivostok Bay until November 1922.

Another body of Marines was never intended to enter the firing line. On 12 August 1918 the egalitarian secretary of the Navy, Josephus Daniels, authorized the enlistment of women reservists into the previously all-male Corps. Mrs. Opha M. Johnson became the first of 277 "Marinettes" to don forest green, freeing combat-trained Leathernecks from clerical duties to join their comrades in France. While HQMC limited the women Marines to administrative assignments, a barrier had been broken. *Leatherneck* magazine praised them, if a bit condescendingly: "Everyone is proud of the Marine girls. They carried themselves like real Marines . . . and proved they were ready to go anywhere and conduct themselves with honor to the Marine Corps."[32] As the Marinettes mustered out of uniform, Secretary Daniels paid them a memorably maladroit tribute. "We will not forget you," he declared. "As we embrace you in uniform today, we will embrace you without uniform tomorrow."[33]

9
Between the Wars, 1919–1941

For most Americans the armistice signified the return of peace. That was not the case for the U.S. Marines, who, in the midst of demobilization, found themselves with two guerrilla wars to fight. At the same time, scandal and a political dogfight buffeted the Corps. Together, these events made its transition into the postwar world a stormy passage.

The guerrilla wars began even before the Great War ended. Both took place on Hispaniola, where the effectiveness of the brigades occupying Haiti and the Dominican Republic had been diminished by the flow of troops to France. In Haiti, the calm that had prevailed since 1915 was shattered when a band of one hundred *cacos* led by Charlemagne Masséna Péralte attacked the Gendarmerie post at Hinche on 17 October 1918. The French-educated son of a prominent local family, Péralte had recently escaped from a humiliating sentence of five years' hard labor imposed for his part in the attempted robbery of a Gendarmerie payroll. Although the assault failed, in Péralte the *cacos* had found a leader—and, as a Marine officer recalled, "a damned good one."[1] The people's resentment of the *corvée* forced labor program—suspended, too late, in the summer of 1918—and rumors that the whites planned to reintroduce slavery gave him a broad base of support. Soon the insurrection spread throughout central and northern Haiti, several thousand full-time *cacos* were active in various bands, and Péralte began signing himself "Chief of the Revolutionary Forces Against the Americans on the Soil of Haiti."[2]

At first, Marine Col. Alexander S. Williams, major general commandant of the Gendarmerie, tried to meet the emergency with the forces at his disposal. These proved unequal to the task, and in March 1919 he requested the help of the 1st Marine Brigade. Reinforced by six companies of infantry and an observation squadron of thirteen biplanes, the Leathernecks launched a campaign of combat patrols deep into the interior. A new command team also arrived, with Lt. Col. Frederick M. "Fritz" Wise relieving Williams as commandant of the Gendarmerie in July and Col. John H. Russell taking over the 1st Brigade in October.

The tempo of operations increased throughout the year, from fewer than forty hostile contacts from January through June to more than eighty from July through September. The first instance of a coordinated air-ground attack, later to become a Marine Corps specialty, occurred in August, when a Curtis Jenny and a DH-4 cooperated with an infantry company to surprise a big *caco* camp on a mountain near Mirebalais. The planes' bombs drove the startled *cacos* off the mountaintop into ambushes set by the ground forces, who killed or wounded more than two hundred of them. Marine aviators also began to develop dive-bombing techniques that would enable them to place their ordnance in the confined target areas of jungle clearings.

Despite mounting losses, the rebels remained in arms. On 7 October three hundred of Péralte's *cacos* delivered an audacious attack on Port-au-Prince. Forewarned of the action, the Marines and gendarmes beat them off without difficulty. By that time, Fritz Wise had concluded that the only way to wind up the war would be, as he put it, to "get Charlemagne."[3] He recognized that this would not be easy, requiring as it did the removal of one heavily guarded individual constantly on the move through a population of several millions, largely sympathetic to him, in a country the size of the state of New York.

Wise's order was carried out by Herman H. Hanneken, a twenty-four-year-old Marine sergeant serving as a Gendarmerie captain in command of the post at Grande Rivière du Nord. A native of St. Louis, Hanneken had enlisted in the Corps in 1914 after brief stints as a divinity student and a cowpoke. In Haiti he learned to speak the native patois as fluently as any *papaloi*. John W. Thomason described him as "long-legged, with big bones and a square, powerful frame. . . . He has high cheekbones and lean jaws, . . . and the feature most men notice is his eye. It is an eye singularly direct, deep-set, pale, and cold, like a cat's."[4]

With the cooperation of two Haitian agents, Hanneken concocted an elaborate scheme to entice Péralte to attack Grande Rivière, where a warm reception was prepared. The *caco* chieftain took the bait, assembling seven hundred men for the operation, but at the last moment elected to remain behind. Informed of this development by one of their agents, Hanneken and his second in command, Gendarmerie 1st Lt. (Marine Cpl.) William R. Button, decided that if Charlemagne would not come to them, they would go to him. The agent agreed to guide them. Faces blackened with burnt cork, after nightfall on 31 October they led sixteen handpicked gendarmes through six *caco* checkpoints to Péralte's camp. As they approached the circle of firelight, the guide pointed out Charlemagne. Hanneken drew his .45 and put two slugs through the Chief of the Revolutionary Forces. An instant later, a *caco* camp follower threw a blanket over the fire. Button sprayed the area with his Browning automatic rifle as Péralte's surviving supporters departed in haste.

The next morning, after the assault on Grande Rivière had been shattered, Hanneken brought Péralte's body into town. To dispel any doubts of the *caco*'s demise, the Marines photographed the corpse and exhibited prints throughout Haiti. Péralte was then given a Christian bur-

Sgt. Herman Hanneken, who would retire as a brigadier general, executed Col. Fritz Wise's order to "get Charlemagne" Péralte.

ial—beneath the Marine sentry post at the entrance to the headquarters of the Department of the North.

Both Hanneken and Button were awarded the Medal of Honor and Haiti's highest decoration, the Médaille Militaire. A few months later Hanneken earned the Navy Cross by eliminating another guerrilla chief, Osiris Joseph. Button died of fever at Cap Haitien in 1920. Hanneken, commissioned the same year, went on to command a regiment at Peleliu and retired a brigadier general.

Charlemagne Péralte's mantle fell briefly on the shoulders of his principal lieutenant, Benoit Batraville, but only one sizable engagement remained to be fought. It took place on 15 January 1920, when Batraville replicated Péralte's attack on Port-au-Prince, with the same lack of success. He achieved a small triumph in April with the capture of Gendarmerie Lt. (Marine Sgt.) Lawrence Muth, who had been badly wounded and left for dead by his men. Following the prescription of a voodoo wizard, Batraville cut out and ate the young

The Gendarmerie d'Haiti palace guard at Port-au-Prince, 1921. Col. John A. Rossel Collection, Marine Corps Historical Center

officer's heart and liver in order to absorb his courage and wisdom, and smeared Muth's brains on his men's rifles to improve their accuracy. These precautions proved unavailing. On 19 May he was killed in an action with a Marine patrol led by Gendarmerie Capt. J. L. "Si" Perkins.

Batraville's death rang down the curtain on the *caco* rebellion. The Marines estimated that approximately two thousand insurgents had been killed in the course of the conflict: 35 in 1918, 1,881 in 1919, and 90 in 1920. The Gendarmerie lost approximately seventy-five officers and men killed and wounded, while the 1st Brigade suffered twenty-three casualties.

The campaign had a sensational aftermath. In 1919 Colonel Russell court-martialed three enlisted men, including a private serving as a Gendarmerie lieutenant, on charges of shooting a prisoner "just for excitement."[5] All were found guilty, but in scanning the trial transcripts General Barnett was shocked to read that an officer defending one of the men had asserted, in extenuation of the crime, that "indiscriminate killings of natives by

Marines were commonplace."[6] The commandant thereupon wrote Russell that indiscriminate killings must cease. In 1920 his order became public knowledge, provoking the predictable outcry. An American journalist who hurried to Haiti did nothing to calm the furor by reporting, "I have heard officers wearing the United States uniform [Marines seconded to the Gendarmerie] talking of 'bumping off gooks' as if it were a variety of sport—like duck-hunting."[7] Critics of "bayonet rule" in the Caribbean seized on the issue as an example of Yankee imperialism at its worst.

That summer, Secretary Daniels dispatched Maj. Gen. John A. Lejeune and Brig. Gen. Smedley D. Butler to Haiti to investigate the allegations of Marine atrocities. They returned to report that cases of misconduct had been few and had resulted in long prison terms. A naval court of inquiry convened a few months later reached the same conclusion, as did a Senate select committee that visited Hispaniola in 1921 and 1922. Perhaps the best summing up was offered by Col. Fritz Wise, who noted in his memoirs: "There was no question that some rough stuff had been pulled in Haiti. . . . But that was all over now. Haiti was at peace. Haiti had been brought to peace by men fighting and living amid conditions that people back home could never even picture."[8]

The trouble in the Dominican Republic was less an insurrection than a persistence of banditry in the unruly eastern provinces of Macorís and Seibo. Intelligence placed the combined strength of the bands involved at from six hundred to one thousand men. Real battles were few and Marine casualties light, but firefights were frequent. In 1918 the 2nd Brigade's patrols made forty-four serious contacts, losing five men killed and thirteen wounded. When the incidence of violence increased early in 1919, Brig. Gen. Ben H. Fuller, who had relieved Uncle Joe Pendleton the previous October, asked for more troops. The 15th Regiment arrived in February 1919, and an observation squadron joined it in March, raising the brigade's strength to more than one hundred officers and twenty-five hundred men. The deployment marked the organization of the first task-organized Marine air-ground team. As in Haiti, the aircraft—six Jennies—proved a valuable asset in the campaign, reporting hostile movements, supporting Marine columns in the field, and experimenting with dive-bombing techniques. That year, Marine units were involved in more than 150 skirmishes. Casualties were low (three dead and four wounded), but the bandits remained active.

There were also rumors of Marine atrocities in the Dominican Republic, but they never attracted the attention given to reports of misdeeds in Haiti. The potential for major embarrassment was avoided by the suicide of Capt. Charles F. Merkel, a German-born ex–enlisted man who had clearly gone beyond the pale to acquire the sobriquet "the Tiger of Seibo."[9] Arrested and confined to quarters awaiting trial, Merkel shot himself in October 1918 with a pistol that, according to the official account, he had hidden on his person. Scuttlebutt held that he was visited by two fellow officers who left him the traditional alternative to disgrace: a pistol loaded with a single round.

By 1919 President Wilson had begun to reconsider the wisdom of occupying the Dominican Republic. Late in 1920 his outgoing administration announced that the Marines would soon be withdrawn. The military government was charged with executing this decision in an orderly manner. It responded by initiating a vigorous program to train the hitherto neglected Guardia Nacional (soon renamed the Policia Nacional) and redoubling its efforts to pacify Macorís and Seibo. A combination of intensive patrolling, the screening of virtually the entire male population of the two provinces, and an offer of amnesty finally accomplished the latter, and by May 1922 the country was at peace. In August 1924 the Marines finally began an exodus from Santo Domingo; the last Leatherneck departed on 16 September 1924.

The Corps's first major postwar political controversy arose in June 1920, when Secretary Daniels ousted Major General Barnett as commandant and replaced him with John A. Lejeune. Barnett's Republican supporters cried "Foul!" and rallied to prevent Lejeune's confirmation. Daniels believed that the redoubtable Mrs. Barnett had encouraged her husband to dig in his heels. Privately, he said that if the commandant was an Indian, his name would be "Man-Afraid-of-His-Wife."[10] Publicly, Daniels claimed that when he reappointed Barnett in 1918, the commandant promised—like each of the Navy's bureau chiefs—to step down after the war. Barnett denied it. When the secretary tried to explain his policy of limiting the tenure of senior officers in Washington to single four-year tours, even his most strident supporters had difficulty stifling yawns. Then Daniels began to argue that he believed in rewarding men "who had been at the cannon's mouth." Lejeune had the requisite tropical sweat stains and powder burns on his uniform to meet that criterion. The new secretary of the Navy, Edwin H. Denby, accepted Lejeune as commandant and put at least that controversy to rest.

The new commandant took the reins of the Corps firmly in hand. In an open letter to its officers, Lejeune left no doubt as to the standards he expected: "I want each of you to feel that the Commandant of the Corps is your friend. . . . At the same time, it is his duty to the Government and to the Marine Corps to exact a high standard of conduct, a strict performance of duty, and a rigid compliance with orders on the part of all officers." He added: "You are the permanent part of the Marine Corps, and the efficiency, the good name, and the esprit of the Corps are in your hands. You can make it or mar it."[11]

Lt. Col. Earl H. "Pete" Ellis as a lieutenant colonel in 1918 while serving as adjutant, 4th Brigade (Marine), AEF. Courtesy Dorothy Ellis Gatz

Throughout the nine years of his commandancy Lejeune argued in vain for a system of selection boards to examine officers for promotion at each rank to replace the traditional scheme of seniority. With the support of Smedley Butler's father, Congressman Thomas S. Butler, Lejeune's proposal moved swiftly through the House Naval Affairs Committee during each session of Congress. But it never cleared the Senate Naval Affairs Committee, where skeptics argued that a system of promotion based on examination by a selection board offered the potential for a misuse of administrative power. It would be up to Lejeune's successors to convince their civilian superiors that the Corps would have better leaders if its officers were promoted on merit rather than seniority.

Lejeune did not need to consult Congress to alter the traditional focus of Headquarters Marine Corps (HQMC). Since the founding of the Corps, designated staff officers

had guided the day-to-day functioning of HQMC while the commandants mostly tended to political or ceremonial duties. Lejeune believed that HQMC should be involved in planning and organizing for expeditionary duty and war, not merely "housekeeping." While serving as assistant to the commandant, Lejeune had convinced Barnett to establish a planning section. Now he took his vision a step further. On 1 December 1920 Lejeune expanded the Planning Section into the Division of Operations and Training to manage all matters relating to operations, training, education, intelligence, and aviation. He also brought in a protégé and friend dating from his tour in the Philippines more than a decade before—Lt. Col. Earl H. "Pete" Ellis.

A lanky midwesterner, Ellis had enlisted in the Corps at age twenty in 1900 and obtained his commission a year later. His effulgent intellect and boundless energy impressed everyone with whom he came in contact. As a junior captain he had served with distinction as an instructor at the Naval War College. In France, Ellis performed brilliantly as the adjutant of the Marine Brigade from July 1918 until the end of the war, supervising its staff work so ably that he was generally regarded as the man most responsible for the efficiency of its operations. Supposedly, Lejeune even entrusted him with the task of planning the 2nd Division's assault on Blanc Mont.

Tragically, Ellis's professional performance caused his superiors to overlook the fact that he was an alcoholic of exceptional instability whose recorded eccentricities included bringing a dinner party to a close by blasting the plates off the table with his .45. By 1920 acute alcoholism had seriously undermined his health. During his sober interludes, however, he became intrigued with the prospect of a conflict in the Central Pacific. At the end of the world war, Japan had been given League of Nations mandates over the formerly German islands in the region—suzerainty, in effect, under the Empire of Japan. Ellis began a monumental study of the potential for amphibious operations should war break out with Japan.

On 23 July 1921 Ellis submitted the result of his labors to Lejeune: a thirty-thousand-word plan for "Advanced Base Operations in Micronesia, 1921." Anticipating the loss of the Philippines, Ellis's plan called for an amphibious advance northward across the Japanese-held islands in the Central Pacific, beginning with the establishment of an advanced base in the Marshall Islands. To an uncanny extent, the tactics and procedures Ellis prescribed—the use of underwater demolition teams, the organization of assault forces, and the role of naval air and gunfire support—foreshadowed the techniques that would actually be employed in World War II. Even in specifics his projections often proved accurate; the four thousand troops who seized Eniwetok Atoll in the Marshalls in February 1944 closely corresponded to the number he allocated to the operation.

Well before completing his study, Ellis approached Lejeune with a request for permission to visit the Central Pacific in the guise of an American businessman. Although the terms of the mandates prohibited the Japanese from fortifying their islands, it was widely—albeit erroneously—assumed that they were doing so. Ellis felt impelled to see for himself. As a bachelor, he would not need to account for his movements to anyone except the commandant. Lejeune approved his proposal, Ellis gave him an undated letter of resignation to be used if needed, and Lejeune assisted him in establishing a fake identity. In the summer of 1921, Ellis set out on his lonely mission, posing as a representative of a New York firm owned by a retired Marine lieutenant colonel.

Traveling to Japan and then on to the Central Pacific, Ellis died at Koror in the Palau Islands on 12 May 1923. The Japanese government notified the American embassy, and arrangements were made for Chief Pharmacist's Mate Lawrence Zembsch to travel in a Japanese ship from Yokohama to Koror to retrieve Ellis's ashes. When the vessel returned in mid-August 1923, Zembsch was found to be in a catatonic state. He was taken to the U.S. naval hospital in Yokohama and by the end of the month had recovered sufficiently to report that the Japanese had known that Ellis was an American agent. Before Zembsch could elaborate on this story, the hospital was leveled by the great Kanto earthquake of September 1923; he died in its ruins.

Here were the ingredients of a first-rate mystery. Friends believed that Ellis had been killed by the Japanese secret police. After World War II, the Marine Corps tried to solve the puzzle. An investigating officer interviewed a number of people who had known Ellis on Koror, including a native woman with whom he had lived. Their testimony indicated that although the Japanese suspected Ellis to be a spy, they did not kill him. In all probability, he simply drank himself into the grave.[12]

Informed of Ellis's death, Lejeune decided not to use his friend's letter of resignation and instead issued a terse statement that Ellis had been absent without leave. His disavowal of official responsibility for Ellis's activities averted the threat of a scandal. The entire bizarre affair could easily have mushroomed into a cause célèbre because the Department of the Navy had supported, if not actually concocted, the risky venture; the Office of Naval Intelligence even paid Ellis's travel expenses.

Lejeune also interested himself in the Corps's newest component. At the end of the Great War, the Marine air wing numbered 282 officers and 2,180 men. Its future was highly uncertain. Many senior officers, disgusted that the 1st Aviation Force had not been deployed in support of Leatherneck operations in France, saw no point in maintaining air units. As resourceful in peace as he had been in war, Alfred E. Cunningham met the opposition on its own terms, conceding that the only justification for aviation was to assist ground forces and arguing that it had great potential to do so. Those sharing his views included Lejeune, who declared that "a modern force without aviation is inconceivable."[13] In the outcome, the progressives prevailed. The manning levels established for the Corps by Congress in 1920 authorized an aviation force of 1,020 men, and in October of that year four squadrons were established: two at Quantico, one in the Dominican Republic, and one in Haiti.

To ensure that America did not forget its Marines, Lejeune—ably supported by the irrepressible Butler, commanding at Quantico—kept Leatherneck prowess in a variety of activities in the public eye. The Corps's first opportunity to shine came with the annual interservice rifle and pistol matches, which Marines had dominated since 1910. In the first postwar competition, Leatherneck "dingers" swept the events. Beginning in the fall of 1921, Butler took his Quantico-based expeditionary brigade into the field to join National Guard troops in annual reenactments of Civil War battles. The first of these events took place near Chancellorsville, Virginia. More than three thousand Marines marched to the battlefield in a column five miles long. Trucks, aircraft, balloons, armored cars, searchlights, tractors, and artillery pieces added to the display.

The performance drew giant crowds of the curious and the influential. President Harding and Secretary Denby attended, giving the spectacle an official stamp of approval. Besides being great publicity, these events provided fun-filled physical fitness training for the Quantico Marines. Butler added to his legend during the march: the hawk-beaked warrior's favorite ploy was to take a straggler's rifle and pack and carry them along with his own gear. "Old Gimlet Eye" was then thirty-nine years old and weighed less than 140 pounds. Following this success, the Quantico Marines returned to the field for two further reenactments before the expense of other commitments caused Lejeune to cancel the annual pageants.

When not on maneuvers, Quantico Marines fielded a series of superb athletic teams that contributed to the Corps's can-do image. Inspired by Butler, in four seasons the football team won thirty-eight games, tied two, and lost two against the other services, colleges, and the service academies. To the spectators' delight, Butler acted as head cheerleader, supported by the post band blaring away in the background.

The publicity generated by the reenactments, athletic achievements, marksmanship awards, and businesslike management of the Corps's meager budget lent a rosy hue to the early 1920s. In 1921 a dramatic increase in armed robberies of railway mail cars gave the Marines another opportunity to be of service to their country— and, in the process, add luster to an already glowing image. Alarmed by the growing number of mail robberies, Postmaster General Will H. Harp asked President Harding for the assistance of federal troops. Harding responded by directing Secretary Denby to "send in the Marines." In their first stint at guarding the mails, fifty-three officers and twenty-two hundred enlisted men began their new duties on 11 November, their ears ringing with the secretary's stirring words: "If attacked, shoot, and shoot to kill." The colorful Denby added that if the mail did not get through, "there must be a Marine dead at the post of duty."[14] The robberies promptly ceased and after four months the Marines were withdrawn. Five years later, a new rash of attacks on the mails led to the reintroduction of Marine guards, with equally gratifying results.

Yet as the Corps undertook this new mission, Congress continued to slash away at its strength. Near the end of the congressional session in 1919, budget cutters pruned the smaller of the naval services to 1,093 officers and 27,400 enlisted Marines. By 1921 these numbers had dropped to 962 officers and 16,085 men. Lejeune promised to reduce expenses by 40 percent that year and by 50 percent the next. Two-thirds of the recruiting stations were closed and the minimum age for enlistees was raised to twenty-one. For a while the Corps was obliged to cease recruiting altogether and accept only applicants for reenlistment.

While meeting its existing obligations and assuming new commitments, the Corps sought to develop its long-stillborn specialty of amphibious warfare and to correct shortcomings evident in fleet maneuvers. The consensus of military opinion regarded this effort as a waste of time. Instructors at Army schools asserted that opposed landings offered little chance of success. As proof, they pointed to the failure of the largest amphibious operation of the Great War, the British assault on Turkey's Gallipoli Peninsula in April 1915. Although the attacking forces had managed to fight their way ashore, the defenders quickly sealed the beachheads and after eight ghastly months the British withdrew. Unopposed landings, on the other hand, need not be naval in character. The Army could easily absorb that mission.

The fleet exercises of 1922, held at Guantánamo Bay and Culebra, differed little from the Advanced Base Force maneuvers of 1913–14. As before, bluejackets ferried Leathernecks to the beach, where the latter wrestled huge naval guns ashore and built emplacements. A year after this uninspiring exercise, Lejeune ordered the name of the organization changed from Advanced Base Force to Expeditionary Force. The mission to defend advanced bases for the fleet remained the same.

When the fleet put to sea for the next set of maneuvers, from December 1923 to February 1924, the amphibious exercises increased markedly. This time, the entire East Coast Expeditionary Force—more than thirty-three hundred Marines—embarked under the command of Brig. Gen. Eli K. Cole and Col. Dion Williams,

Problems evident in interwar exercises, such as this one in Culebra in 1924, led to the development of amphibious doctrine and equipment used in World War II.

senior officers with intelligence and vision. But the landings in the Caribbean underscored the problems that had plagued the practice of amphibious warfare since the Gallipoli fiasco. Forces still landed on the wrong beaches, naval gunfire support remained sporadic and inadequate, and supplies that had been improperly loaded were unloaded in similar fashion. Cole and Williams returned to Quantico with much to report.

In 1925 fleet maneuvers were conducted in the Hawaiian Islands, and a contingent of fifteen hundred Marines was assembled from Quantico, Mare Island, and ships' detachments. The participants included the faculty and students of the Quantico schools, who arrived to operate in the field as an ad hoc staff. As part of the "Blue" force, the Marines assaulted "Black" defenders in the islands. For a welcome change, the fleet provided sufficient gunfire support. Although a radical improvement over the clumsy attempt in the Caribbean the year before,

the exercise identified additional problems: ordinary ship's boats did not appear suitable for amphibious operations; naval air and shore-based air support remained inadequate to support a major landing; troops required extensive training in at-sea transfers to facilitate ship-to-shore movement; and effective communications equipment was needed, the existing apparatus having proven unfit for amphibious employment.

Unfortunately, increasing commitments abroad precluded significant participation by the Corps in fleet maneuvers for almost a decade thereafter. In 1927, however, the Joint Board of the Army and Navy confirmed the Marine Corps's responsibility for the conduct of amphibious warfare. Thus, although responding to day-to-day problems kept most Leathernecks busy overseas, the Corps retained its amphibious mission.

One of the Corps's new commitments arose on the other side of the Pacific. When Generalissimo Chiang

For unabashed swagger, nothing could surpass this private first class of the Mounted Platoon, U.S. Legation Guard, Peking, in 1935. Peacetime promotions were notoriously slow, and this Marine most likely made PFC after reenlisting.

Kai-shek and the Chinese nationalist party, the Kuomintang, broke ranks with the Communists and set out to unify China in the mid-1920s, foreign lives and properties once again appeared to be threatened. In July 1926, the Kuomintang Army began to move north into the Yangtze Valley. Landing parties of bluejackets and Leathernecks from the Asiatic Fleet streamed ashore in answer to the pleas of missionaries and businessmen. As the situation worsened, the secretary of state advised President Calvin Coolidge to take stronger action.

Late in January 1927 Coolidge approved the assembling of the 4th Marine Regiment in San Diego; on 3 February the unit sailed for Shanghai. A brigade headquarters, two more battalions for the 4th Marines, an artillery battalion, a tank platoon, and aviation elements followed three weeks later. Smedley Butler was placed in command. The year before, Butler had brought

charges against Col. Alexander S. Williams—his second in command at San Diego—for drunken behavior. Recalling that incident and Butler's strident prohibitionist views, Will Rogers provided a pungent observation: "Smedley Butler has arrived in China. The war may continue but the parties will stop."[15]

At Shanghai and Tientsin, the 3rd Marine Brigade contributed to the maintenance of order by sheer presence. Realizing that his men's real mission was to look imposing, Butler gave his instinct for showmanship free rein, staging what amounted to a continuous military pageant enhanced by imaginative if nonregulation touches such as having the brigade's machine guns, mortars, and antitank guns nickel-plated. During one exhibition of America's military might, an aircraft buzzed the grandstand and then performed a daring roll. Unfortunately, the maneuver sheared both wings off the aircraft, which crashed into a nearby lake. As the pilot floated to the ground in front of the crowd, a lady was heard to remark: "Trust Smedley, he always puts on a wonderful show."[16] Soon young officers who had hoped to see action began quipping that the "China expedition" should have been named the "China exhibition." Butler did not share their bellicosity. To Lejeune he wrote, "General, it is all shadow boxing. There is nothing to hit. It will positively do no good to shoot a lot of Chinese coolies."[17]

Late in May the newly reconstituted 6th Marines and the 1st Battalion of the 10th Marines reinforced the units at Shanghai. By then the center of American concern had shifted to northern China, where the political situation provoked fears of another attack on the legations at Peking. In June the bulk of the brigade moved to Tientsin. There Butler organized a mechanized "emergency flying column" of two thousand men ready to set out for the capital on two hours' notice. The call never came, and early in 1929 Butler and most of the force returned to the States. Although the apparent triumph of Chiang Kai-shek's Kuomintang promised to initiate an era of stability in China, the 4th Marines were left behind to help garrison the International Settlements at Shanghai.

One of the Corps's most charming traditions, Mess Night, has its origins in China. While serving as adjutant of the 4th Marines in 1927, Capt. Lemuel C. Shepherd Jr. developed a friendship with a British officer. Young Shepherd and his commanding officer, Col. Henry C. Davis, were invited to attend a mess night as guests of the 2nd Battalion, Scots Guards. "It was an impressive evening," Shepherd recalled later. "The battalion had brought out its beautiful silver to adorn the dinner table, which was lighted with handsome candelabra. During the evening, the Pipe Major played Scottish ballads on his bagpipe and a Guardsman danced the Highland fling and other Scottish dances."[18] Shepherd was not the only Marine impressed. The next morning, Colonel Davis instructed him to arrange a similar event and to invite the British, stipulating that the ceremonial procedure follow that which had been observed the previous evening. The China Marines had given birth to the Marine Corps Mess Night.

While the exhibition force was conducting its imperial tattoo, nearer home the Corps became engaged in the last and longest of the banana wars. The timing was ironic, for the United States had almost wound down its Caribbean empire. The last company of Marines had sailed from the Dominican Republic in September 1924. Not quite a year later, in August 1925, the one-hundred-man legation guard was withdrawn from Managua, Nicaragua. The only country in which Marines remained was Haiti, which the State Department did not expect to be ready for self-government—at least, by American standards—until around 1935.

To facilitate the achievement of that goal, the position of U.S. high commissioner to Haiti, with both civil and military authority, had been created in 1922. Lejeune recommended Butler for the assignment, but the Department of State considered him too controversial and the assignment went to Brig. Gen. John H. Russell, the 1st Brigade's commander. Under Russell's proconsulship Haiti made steady progress toward independence throughout the remainder of the decade. Special emphasis was placed on developing the Gendarmerie (renamed the Garde d'Haiti in 1928) into an efficient, apolitical force capable of preserving order after the protectorate ended.

The pattern of disengagement was interrupted by developments in Nicaragua. Later, an American author calculated that, following the departure of the legation guard, three weeks, four days, and thirteen hours passed before civil war broke out between the Conservative Party in power and its Liberal opponents. In May 1926

the Marine detachment in the cruiser *Cleveland* occupied Bluefields for a month to protect the American colony from the conflict. Leathernecks and bluejackets returned to establish a neutral zone around the city in August, and in October another detachment landed at Corinto to keep peace during an abortive, American-sponsored meeting between Liberal and Conservative leaders.

So far, U.S. involvement in the Nicaraguan imbroglio had been limited to little more than the traditional defense of American lives and property. In November, an event occurred that led to large-scale intervention. Concluding that it would be impossible to remain in power without American support, President Emiliano Chamorro resigned in favor of another Conservative, Gen. Adolfo Díaz, who was to hold office until an election scheduled for 1928. Intent on promoting the restoration of peace in Nicaragua, the Coolidge administration decided to support this solution. By March 1927, more than two thousand Marines, including Maj. Ross E. "Rusty" Rowell's Observation Squadron 1 (VO-1M), had been landed in Nicaragua. Designated the 2nd Marine Brigade and placed under the command of Brig. Gen. Logan Feland, this force assumed responsibility for the defense of Managua, the security of the railway from Corinto to the capital, and the maintenance of neutral zones around major cities.

Although the Leathernecks did not join in the fighting, their presence was clearly to the advantage of the Díaz regime. Yet the revolution showed no sign of subsiding, and in April Coolidge dispatched former secretary of war Henry L. Stimson to negotiate a settlement between the Nicaraguan antagonists. A man of great ability, Stimson did just that. According to the terms of the Peace of Tipitapa, concluded on 4 May 1927, the warring factions agreed to lay down their arms, disband their forces (to include the Nicaraguan Army), and abide by the outcome of an American-supervised election in November 1928. In the meantime, the Marines would maintain order and begin training a national constabulary, the Guardia Nacional de Nicaragua, which Stimson believed would stabilize the country's political process by deterring presidential hopefuls from trying their hand at revolution.

Endorsed by the chiefs of the Conservative and Liberal Parties, the occupation proceeded with only one

Nicaraguan rebel leader Augusto Sandino.

cheeky letters to the Marines, Sandino was the illegitimate offspring of a member of the landowning elite and an Indian servant girl. Keenly aware of the weight of public opinion, he cultivated good relations with the press. One of his greatest successes was an interview with American correspondent Carleton Beals in which he compared himself and his followers to George Washington. As a result of such coverage, Sandino soon became an international symbol of resistance to *yanqui* imperialism and the beneficiary of fund-raisers held in Manhattan as well as Mexico City. To most Marines, though, he was just another bandit.

That Sandino meant to fight became clear shortly past 1:00 on the morning of 16 July 1927, when he led eight hundred men in a determined assault on thirty-seven Marines and forty-seven *guardias* garrisoning the little town of Ocotal, the capital of Nueva Segovia. The fighting was still going on at 2:35 that afternoon when Maj. Rusty Rowell appeared overhead with five World War I DH-4s from Managua, each carrying four fragmentation bombs. Unaccustomed to aerial intervention, the Sandinistas neglected to take cover and were decimated by what was probably the first sustained dive-bombing attack in history. At the end of the action, the Marines collected fifty-six bodies and calculated that the retreating enemy had carried off twice that number of dead and wounded. The garrison had lost one man killed and four wounded.

Some officers believed that this debacle would be the last heard of Sandino. They were wrong. At 1:00 A.M. on 19 September, a band of his followers attempted to storm a barracks occupied by forty-six Marines and *guardias* at Telepaneca, a village ten miles from Ocotal. The attack was repulsed and the Sandinistas withdrew at dawn, having suffered an estimated fifty casualties. Two Marines were killed and one *guardia* wounded.

Thus far, the honors belonged to the Leathernecks; but Sandino was learning. Never again would his forces hurl themselves against a fortified position. Instead, they would employ the less costly tactics of ambush and evasion. The opportunity to put these into practice came early in October, after engine failure forced a Marine reconnaissance plane down on Sapotillal Ridge in the wilds of northern Nueva Segovia. Later the same day, a twenty-man patrol advanced from the nearest Marine outpost to

serious incident—a bandit raid on a railway town in which two Marines were killed. True, one relatively minor Liberal leader, thirty-two-year-old Augusto C. Sandino, denounced the Tipitapa agreement and led a band of 150 intransigents into the jungles of remote Nueva Segovia Province on the Honduran frontier. But negotiations were under way to persuade him to surrender. By the end of June, the strength of the 2nd Brigade had been reduced to fifteen hundred men. To all appearances, the situation was well in hand.

Appearances were deceptive. Augusto Sandino would soon emerge as by far the most formidable of the Corps's Caribbean adversaries. A dapper, diminutive mestizo who indulged an irreverent sense of humor by penning

A DH-4 of VMO-7 over El Chipote, where Sandino had his headquarters, on 26 January 1928. This is probably the earliest photograph of a Marine aircraft in combat.

Leathernecks paddle a dugout canoe through a stretch of white water during the Coco River patrol.

Marine Capt. Victor F. Bleasdale, a major in the Guardia Nacional de Nicaragua, on campaign in Nueva Segovia province in 1928. A former enlisted man who had won the Navy Cross in France in 1918, he would go on to command a regiment in the Pacific in World War II.

In Nicaragua, Marines airlifted supplies to remote garrisons in Fokker Trimotors, the Corps's first transport plane. These two were photographed at Ocotal in 1929.

Members of the garrison of Ocotal display a flag captured from the Sandinistas during the action of 16 July 1927. The Leatherneck commander, Capt. Gilbert D. Hatfield, stands third from left.

rescue the two aviators. Surprised by several hundred Sandinistas as they approached the ridge the next morning, the Americans were forced to fall back, leaving behind three dead. Toward the end of the month—by which time the airmen had been captured and hanged—a second patrol reached the ridge but was immediately attacked and pinned down until the arrival of a third patrol two days later. During the return march, the combined column was again ambushed by a sizable Sandinista force.

These events naturally focused attention on Nueva Segovia. On 23 November one of Rowell's reconnaissance flights located Sandino's stronghold, a fortified mountaintop called El Chipote twenty-six miles from the Honduran border. On receiving this intelligence, Col. Louis M. Gulick—who had relieved General Feland in August—made plans to carry the war to Sandino. Un-

fortunately, they were not very good plans. Grossly underestimating the Sandinistas' capability, Gulick committed fewer than 200 men to the offensive. Two columns, one of 115 men, the other of 65, were to advance from Marine outposts, rendezvous at the deserted village of Quilali, establish a base there, and push on to capture El Chipote. This scenario did not survive ambushes sprung by more than a thousand Sandinistas on 30–31 December. The badly battered columns fought their way to Quilali, where they were surrounded, having lost 8 men killed and 30 wounded, including both column commanders.

Aviation saved the day. The Marines in Quilali cleared the grass-grown main street, and 1st Lt. Christian F. "Frank" Schilt, a thirty-two-year-old ex-enlisted pilot in Observation Squadron 7, volunteered to land on it. Be-

A Marine patrol in Nicaragua in 1927. Note the firepower in the front row: two submachine guns and an automatic rifle.

tween 6 and 8 January 1928, Schilt made ten flights into Quilali, hauling out eighteen badly wounded men and bringing in fourteen hundred pounds of supplies and a new commanding officer. Every landing and takeoff was made under fire on a runway so short—barely five hundred feet—that men on the ground had to dash out and grab Schilt's plane to prevent it from hurtling into a ravine at the end. Relieved of the burden of their wounded, the Leathernecks withdrew. Schilt was awarded the Medal of Honor. Like so many junior officers who won their spurs in Nicaragua, he went on to a distinguished career in the Corps, retiring as chief of Marine Corps aviation in 1957.

Stung by this setback, Gulick concentrated a battalion to go after Sandino. It occupied El Chipote later in January; as was to be expected, Sandino had decamped. No doubt now remained of the seriousness of the insurgency. Logan Feland returned to resume command of the 2nd Brigade, which was quickly brought up to a strength of thirty-seven hundred men, and General Lejeune came to make a personal tour of inspection. The mission of

First Lt. Christian Schilt at Quantico in 1926.

A DH-4 of VMO-7 over El Chipote, where Sandino had his headquarters, on 26 January 1928. This is probably the earliest photograph of a Marine aircraft in combat.

Leathernecks paddle a dugout canoe through a stretch of white water during the Coco River patrol.

Marine Capt. Victor F. Bleasdale, a major in the Guardia Nacional de Nicaragua, on campaign in Nueva Segovia province in 1928. A former enlisted man who had won the Navy Cross in France in 1918, he would go on to command a regiment in the Pacific in World War II.

In Nicaragua, Marines airlifted supplies to remote garrisons in Fokker Trimotors, the Corps's first transport plane. These two were photographed at Ocotal in 1929.

driving the rebels out of Nueva Segovia was assigned to the newly arrived 11th Marines. They had accomplished that trying task by the start of summer, but Sandino simply shifted his area of operations to the eastern lowlands. Marine forces there responded with thrusts deep into the interior, most notably a forty-six-man expedition led by Capt. Merritt A. "Red Mike" Edson that paddled dugout canoes four hundred miles up the Coco River to seize an enemy base camp at Poteca. All of these operations ended in what soon became a frustratingly familiar pattern, with the Sandinistas fading into the bush.

On the other hand, if the Marines were unable to grasp the will-o'-the-wisp, the will-o'-the-wisp was unable to shake their control of the country. The American-supervised election of November 1928 was acclaimed as the most honest ever held in Nicaragua and produced the first peaceful transition of power in that nation's history. The Liberal candidate, Gen. José M. Moncado, won handily. In hopes that this outcome would satisfy Sandino, American authorities promised him amnesty if he would disband his followers. He spurned the offer, vowing to remain in arms as long as U.S. troops remained in Nicaragua.

Thus no end of the intervention appeared to be in sight when Henry Stimson reentered the play as secretary of state in the Hoover administration in 1929. At that date five thousand Marines—nearly a third of the Corps—were serving in Nicaragua. Stimson considered this commitment excessive; but he also believed that to complete the stabilization of that country it would be necessary to supervise the election of 1932. Immediately on assuming office, he initiated a program of disengagement in which the war against Sandino was gradually transferred to the Guardia Nacional. By midsummer the strength of the 2nd Brigade had been reduced to twenty-five hundred men, and at year's end it stood at eighteen hundred.

Few Marine officers were disappointed by Stimson's decision. Most had come to regard the war as a stalemate. Despite their numerical advantage over the Sandinistas, usually no more than one thousand to fifteen hundred strong, the Marines lacked the manpower both to garrison settlements and to field patrols of the force and frequency needed to harry the enemy from his sanctuaries. In any event, hard-pressed Sandinistas could slip over the border into Honduras. Finally, the Marines realized that they did not possess the support of the civilian population, over whom they had no jurisdiction. As one officer wrote, "the shifting of the *guardias* into the bandit area was acclaimed as a probable solution to the difficulty, as they could control the civil population and force them to cooperate."[19]

Turning the war over to the Guardia, almost wholly Marine officered in the beginning, proved a ticklish business. Commanding Nicaraguan troops called for a high order of leadership. No fewer than seven Marines were killed by their own men in mutinies between 1927 and mid-1932. Such setbacks notwithstanding, the Guardia's efficiency increased from year to year, as did its complement of Marine-trained Nicaraguan officers. In 1932 it assumed full responsibility for offensive patrolling. The election held that November resulted in the victory of the Liberal candidate, Dr. Juan B. Sacasa. His inauguration took place peacefully on 1 January 1933. The remnant of the 2nd Brigade was dissolved the next day. In five and a half years of conflict, forty-seven Marines had been killed in action or died of wounds and sixty-six others wounded.

Sandino, still in arms when the Marines withdrew, accepted the Liberal government's offer of amnesty a few months later. In 1934 he was assassinated on the order of the *jefe* of the Guardia, Col. Anastasio Somoza, who then overthrew Dr. Sacasa and erected a family dictatorship that endured for almost half a century.

Despite its clouded outcome, the Nicaraguan campaign brought two benefits to the Corps. First, it promoted the development of the Marine air-ground team. In Robert D. Heinl's deft summation: "Most of the things done by Marine aviation in Nicaragua had been done or experimented with before. But never before had they been done simultaneously and routinely, and never before had combat and logistic air support been woven into the fabric of a campaign."[20]

Second, the Sandino chase provided a generation of officers with valuable experience in jungle warfare and small-unit tactics. Among them was a pugnacious, pipe-smoking Virginian destined to become a legend in the Corps, Capt. Lewis Burwell "Chesty" Puller. A cousin of George Patton, Puller had joined the Marine Corps in

First Lt. Lewis B. "Chesty" Puller, with pipe, was serving as a captain in the Guardia Nacional de Nicaragua and Gunnery Sgt. Willis Lee as a first lieutenant when this photograph of them and two of their NCOs was made in the field in 1931.

June 1918, at the end of his freshman year at VMI. Selection for NCO and then officer's school kept him from getting to France, and in June 1919, two weeks after receiving a reserve commission, he was discharged. Nothing daunted, he reenlisted as a private for service in the Gendarmerie d'Haiti. The *caco* rebellion was then at its height. Before it was over, Puller had been in forty actions, risen to the rank of captain in the Gendarmerie (and corporal in the Corps), and won the first of his lifetime total of twenty-two decorations. In 1924 he obtained a regular commission as a second lieutenant, USMC. Glancing at his new gold bars, he told a friend, "Well, I've got 'em. Now, all I need is a war."[21] He found his war in Nicaragua, where in two tours as a Guardia company commander he fought in another sixty actions, earned two Navy Crosses, and cemented his reputation as an exceptionally able and aggressive combat officer.

Meanwhile, the leadership of the Corps underwent a succession of changes. In February 1929 General Lejeune announced that he would not seek reappointment the following month. Few were surprised when Maj. Gen. Wendell C. Neville got the nod as his replacement. A Naval Academy graduate like Lejeune, Neville shared his predecessor's commitment to a Corps tied to the needs of the fleet. Butler, who heartily approved of Neville's appointment, was not forgotten. In July 1929 he received his second star, making him, at age forty-nine, the youngest major general in the American armed forces.

After barely a year in office Neville suffered a debilitating stroke and died in July 1930. Many Marines expected Butler, the Corps's ranking major general, to become the fifteenth commandant. But the cantankerous Quaker had accumulated too many enemies; moreover, his powerful congressman father had died in 1928. To head the Corps, Hoover and Secretary of the Navy Charles F. Adams chose sixty-year-old Brig. Gen. Ben H. Fuller, who had been running HQMC since Neville's incapacitation. Apparently, Hoover and Adams concluded that Fuller would be a better team player in the administration's plans for drastic defense reductions.

Controversial as this decision has remained, it was probably for the best. Butler's view of the Corps's role was still basically that of colonial infantry fighting little wars on the frontiers of American influence. For all his ability, he represented the past. It is difficult to imagine him working constructively with the admirals he loathed to develop the Corps's big-war, amphibious mission. Fuller and his successors represented the future.[22]

Deeply disappointed, Butler remained in uniform for less than a year. In January 1931 he was threatened with a court-martial for having told an unflattering story about Italian dictator Benito Mussolini in an address to a Philadelphia civic club. An outpouring of public support and the shrewd attorney Butler engaged—a one-armed ex-Marine—forced the Hoover administration to back off, and in the end Butler was allowed to draft his own letter of minimal reprimand. The incident sealed Butler's estrangement from officialdom, and in September, aged just fifty, the Corps's stormy petrel marched noisily into retirement at his own request. In retirement he was free to lash out at his nemeses: Naval Academy graduates, admirals, the Navy in general, and the "headquarties toadies" who seemed to be leading the Corps.

General Fuller, the new commandant, was a quiet, kindly man affectionately known as Uncle Ben. The Corps's senior officer in length of service as well as position, he had graduated from the Naval Academy in 1889, the same year as the chief of naval operations, Adm. William Veazie Pratt. This fact had figured in his appointment, for Hoover and Secretary Adams anticipated—correctly, as it turned out—that the two classmates would foster interservice cooperation. As commandant, Fuller concentrated his efforts on shielding the Corps's already attenuated ranks from the impact of the Great Depression and strengthening its ties to the Navy. In the first of these endeavors he was reasonably successful. Although authorized enlisted strength was reduced from 18,000 in 1930 to 15,350 in 1932, the following year his testimony to Congress was instrumental in heading off an administration proposal to cut it even further to 13,600. Of far greater consequence was the outcome of his efforts to emphasize that Marines were a component of the naval service and not, as even some of their officers had begun to call them, "State Department troops."

Much of the progress in this direction came about through Fuller's support of his energetic deputy, Maj. Gen. John H. Russell, who had returned to duty in 1930 after eight years as high commissioner in Haiti. Appointed assistant to the commandant in February 1933, Russell was certain that the future of the Corps lay in the conduct of amphibious operations. Together, he and Fuller made three major contributions to readying it for that role: the formation of the Fleet Marine Force (FMF); the establishment of the Marine Corps Equipment Board; and the sponsorship of studies that produced the *Tentative Landing Operations Manual.*

Fuller had secured the backing of the General Board in reinforcing the Corps's connection to the Navy in 1931. On Russell's suggestion, in 1933 he wrote to Admiral Pratt proposing that the name of the two Marine expeditionary forces be changed to Fleet Marine Force. Pratt concurred, and the FMF was created by Navy Department Order 241 of 7 December 1933. The effect was more than cosmetic. Its charter made the FMF an integral element of the U.S. fleet, with primary responsibility for the seizure and defense of advanced bases. Fuller declared that the development of this force must be the Corps's top priority. The Marine Corps Equipment Board was also activated in late 1933. Its mission was to identify and then persuade the Navy to procure improved landing craft, the need for which had been repeatedly demonstrated. The compilation of the *Tentative Landing Operations Manual,* a distillation of the principles of amphibious warfare, began at the Quantico schools in 1931. While he was acting commandant in November 1933, Russell suspended classes and set students and faculty to work on completing the project. Based in part on a pamphlet entitled *Joint Overseas Expeditions* recently issued by the Joint Army-Navy Board, the manual was ready in January 1934. Although not without shortcomings, it provided a firm foundation on which the Corps could build its amphibious expertise.

Fuller's commandancy also witnessed another of the recurrent proposals to have the Corps absorbed by another armed service. In 1931 Maj. Gen. George S. Simonds, a confidant of Gen. Douglas MacArthur, the Army chief of staff, prepared a lengthy memorandum arguing that the Army should incorporate the amphibious mission of the Marine Corps. Simonds noted that of all the Western nations, only the United States and Great Britain still maintained separate Marine forces, and even the British had taken away the combined arms capabilities of their Royal Marines. The Army, he asserted, could provide the Corps's administrative, supply, and schools support, and in the process save the taxpayers a whopping twenty-five million dollars. With the nation engulfed in the worst depression in its history, the Army's argument won immediate favor. However, the Corps's friends rose to the occasion, and the legislation died in Congress.[23]

Retiring after a little less than forty-five years' commissioned service in March 1934, Fuller was succeeded by General Russell, whose tour, through brief, proved highly productive. Overlooking no opportunity to emphasize the importance of the Fleet Marine Force, Russell even banned the use of the term *expeditionary,* which he considered old-fashioned, in the title of Marine Corps formations. The withdrawal of Marine forces from Haiti in August 1934 finally freed the Corps from its

China Marines take positions to assist in quelling a coolie riot at a flour mill in Shanghai, 14 September 1937.

Caribbean commitments and gave Russell the personnel to begin putting the amphibious doctrine developed at Quantico into practice.

The first large-scale landing exercises since the late 1920s were held from 5 to 10 May 1934. A much more ambitious series of problems, Fleet Landing Exercise (FLEX) I, took place from 15 January until 15 March 1935. Other FLEXes followed annually until the outbreak of war. On Capitol Hill, Russell achieved an objective that had eluded Lejeune, Neville, and Fuller, persuading Congress to allow the Corps to promote officers on the basis of merit (as determined by selection boards) rather than seniority. Finally, he revitalized the moribund Marine Corps Reserve and instituted the Platoon Leaders Class program of reserve officer training for college undergraduates.

Russell reached the mandatory retirement age in 1936. As his successor he recommended fifty-seven-year-old Brig. Gen. Thomas Holcomb. There were other contenders, but Russell's long-standing friendship with President Roosevelt guaranteed that Holcomb got the job. It was the first time since 1914 that an officer who had not graduated from the Naval Academy came to head the Corps. But Holcomb, a battalion commander at Belleau Wood and a graduate of both the Army and Navy War Colleges, was a thorough professional. Like his predecessors, he assigned top priority to strengthening and training the FMF. And he, too, was an old acquaintance of Roosevelt, whom he had met while the chief executive was a youthful assistant secretary of the Navy.

Under Holcomb's leadership the Corps continued to improve its amphibious capabilities. The hands-on experience gathered in the yearly FLEXes was carefully analyzed to refine the doctrine formulated at Quantico. One of the chief difficulties, already identified in the mid-1920s, proved to be the unsuitability of standard ships' boats as landing craft. The problem was solved, largely through the perseverance of the Marine Corps Equipment Board, by the adoption of three specialized craft. The first was a troop carrier based on the "Eureka" boat, a shallow-draft, broad-bowed craft manufactured by Andrew Higgins, a civilian boat builder in New Orleans, for use in the Louisiana bayous. Modified in various ways, Higgins's boat became the Landing Craft, Vehicle and Personnel (LCVP), of World War II. The success of this project encouraged Higgins to design an amphibian carrier to ferry tanks to a beachhead. The result was the Landing Craft, Mechanized (LCM). The last of the new vehicles also derived from a civilian product, Donald Roebling's "Alligator." An amphibian tractor able to trundle over coral reefs and onto dry land, it entered inventory as the Landing Vehicle, Tracked (LVT). The contribution these craft made to victory in the war against Japan would be impossible to exaggerate.[24]

Even before Pearl Harbor, Marines stood toe to toe with the Japanese. When war broke out between China and Japan in 1937, the headquarters of the 2nd Brigade and the 6th Marines deployed to the Shanghai-Tientsin area to reinforce the 4th Marines. This time, the Leathernecks found themselves facing an adversary determined to break the Western hold on the International Settlements in Shanghai. In one memorable confrontation in the summer of 1940, Maj. Chesty Puller, executive officer of the 2nd Battalion, 4th Marines, drew his pistol on a Japanese Army officer who had led a detachment into the American sector to seize some Chinese. The Japanese released their captives and withdrew.

A generation of Marines remembered China duty with tears in their eyes. Although a private earned only twenty-one dollars a month, he could live like a king. Chinese room boys shined shoes, washed clothes, and even cleaned rifles and equipment. A steak in town cost only thirty cents, a bottle of Chinese beer to wash it down—two cents a quart! And then there were the girls, White Russian as well as Chinese: beautiful, accommodating, and, like everything else, affordably priced.[25]

But the curtain was coming down. In September 1939 the German invasion of Poland ignited World War II. France fell to Hitler's armies the following summer. In response to the pleas of British Prime Minister Winston Churchill, Roosevelt ordered Marines to lonely, frozen Iceland in the North Atlantic. Earlier, Roosevelt had anticipated using the 1st Marine Division to secure the Azores. Instead, the chief executive decided to send the 1st Provisional Brigade—4,095 Marines—to relieve the British garrison of Iceland. Landing there on 7 July 1941, the Leathernecks ate unfamiliar English chow and adopted the custom of the rum ration while enduring the unenthusiastic hospitality of the population. An Army brigade began to arrive in August 1941, and by 8 March 1942 the last Marine had departed.

The previous July, Japan had occupied French Indochina. The United States responded to this act of aggression by imposing economic sanctions that set it on a collision course with the island empire. As war clouds gathered over East Asia, American leaders grew increasingly apprehensive about the defense of the Philippines. On 28 November 1941, the last of the 4th Marines, band playing, marched down Bubbling Well and Nanking Roads through Shanghai to the docks. The headquarters of the 2nd Brigade and the 6th Marines had already returned home in February 1938. As the fifes and drums played "China Night" one last time, the Leathernecks filed aboard ship. An era had ended.

Worldwide, the Corps numbered scarcely more than it had two decades earlier. But they were a hard lot. Few Leathernecks made private first class in one enlistment; most stayed because they had nowhere else to turn in the harsh economic climate of the depression. The officers were a mix of Naval Academy alumni, distinguished graduates of college and university ROTC programs, and outstanding NCOs selected for officer training. The Leathernecks of 1941 still wore the dishpan helmets of World War I and carried much of the equipment of an earlier era, but the lean interwar years had spawned an earnest and tough Marine Corps ready to wrestle with any adversary.[26]

10
World War Two

The South Pacific Campaign, 1942–1943

A bright, warm sun greeted the occasional Hawaii-based Leatherneck resolute enough to get out of bed in time for morning chow on Sunday, 7 December 1941. At the Ewa Mooring Mast Field, near Barbers Point and four miles west of the huge Navy base at Pearl Harbor on the island of Oahu, the startled duty officer of Marine Air Group One (later, MAG-21) saw squadrons of Japanese torpedo planes thunder over the strip, headed in the direction of the base. Half an hour later, Nakajima fighters strafed the Marine aircraft—parked wing tip to wing tip to prevent sabotage—destroying all forty-seven planes. As the enemy aircraft returned, a new wave of strafing runs by Mitsubishi Zeroes set barracks and hangars afire. Planeless pilots and ground personnel responded with a fruitless fusillade of rifle and pistol fire.

A few minutes earlier, Japanese fighters and torpedo planes had rendezvoused to the northwest of the Hawaiian Islands. They flew off six carriers, part of a task force that had departed the Kurile Islands on 26 November and steamed through the less-transited region of the North Pacific. Except for a few clouds clinging to the mountaintops of Oahu, the attackers had unlimited visibility. At 7:35 A.M., Cdr. Fuchida Mitsuo signaled his admiral, "Tora! Tora! Tora!"—complete surprise had been achieved and the attack was on. Fuchida fired a signal flare, and the Japanese torpedo planes went for the capital ships tied up or at anchor in Pearl Harbor. In minutes, the attackers sank four battleships and damaged four others. Fortunately, the carriers *Enterprise, Lexington,* and *Saratoga* were safe at sea.

As bugles and alarms called Marines, soldiers, and sailors to their stations, smoke from burning ships and buildings billowed skyward. Marines from the barracks and others assigned to the 3rd and 4th Defense Battalions drew rifles and ammunition. Only when the Leathernecks mounted machine guns on the roof of the barracks were they able to shoot down three enemy aircraft. In general, the Japanese encountered little opposition. Marines serving in the ships of the fleet manned antiaircraft batteries and managed to inflict occasional damage on the foe. Fifteen ships tied up at Pearl Harbor had Marine detachments onboard. When the battleship *Arizona* blew up, the commander of her Marine detachment, Maj. Alan Shapley, swam through the debris and burning oil to save a fellow Leatherneck. PFC Willard Darling's plunge into the harbor to rescue a drowning Navy officer earned him the Navy Cross.

While the Japanese planes returned to their carriers, Marines counted their casualties: 108 dead and another 49 wounded. Officers formed barracks Marines and Leathernecks from the two defense battalions into units prepared to counter an enemy landing, but the Japanese had accomplished their mission and were steaming home. The attack had lasted only 110 minutes; more than 2,403 Americans had died.

As news of the attack reached the Western Pacific, Marines in lonely outposts found themselves already surrounded or under siege. More than two hundred Leathernecks stationed in Tientsin and Peking, hopelessly outnumbered and outgunned, received orders to surrender

Smoke from burning warships blackens the sky above these Marines deployed on the parade ground outside their barracks at Pearl Harbor on the morning of 7 December 1941. They hope to get a shot at low-flying Japanese aircraft.

without firing a shot. A garrison of 153 Marines, 277 sailors, and 326 native police on Guam gave up after a short struggle following a Japanese landing on 10 December.

On tiny Wake Island, Maj. James P. S. Devereux's 1st Defense Battalion made an epic stand in the face of impossible odds. Supporting it in the air were twelve F4F Grumman Wildcats of Maj. Paul A. Putnam's VMF-211, which had been flown off the *Enterprise* on 4 December. At 5:00 on the morning of 11 December, Japanese transports escorted by a cruiser attempted to land troops on the island—actually, three islands, located 450 miles from their nearest neighbor. Devereux held his fire until 6:15; by then, the light cruiser *Yubari* and six destroyers

had closed to within forty-five hundred yards of the beach. Leatherneck shore batteries opened fire, sinking the destroyer *Hayate* and several transports and sending the cruiser limping away. A Marine aviator sank a second enemy destroyer, the *Kisaragi*. Wake's planes also shot down three Japanese bombers and damaged four others. The enemy force withdrew.

But Devereux knew that his tiny force was doomed. In Hawaii, a relief force centered on the carriers *Lexington, Saratoga,* and *Enterprise* was organized and steamed hurriedly toward the beleaguered island. Fear of losing the ships prompted their recall and, with them, the last hope for Devereux's garrison. By the seventeenth, Wake was down to four Wildcats; only by cannibalizing

The War in the Pacific, 1941–1945

damaged planes were ground crews able to get these few into the air. On 23 December, by which date the last Wildcat had been lost, greatly superior Japanese forces succeeded in fighting their way ashore. Realizing that further resistance would be futile, Cdr. Winfield S. Cunningham, the atoll commander, authorized Devereux to lay down his arms. Wake's last, Spartan message to the outside world, "Enemy on island issue in doubt," became a source of grim pride to the American people.[1] Contrary to a story widely believed during the war, however, Devereux never transmitted a request to "send us more Japs."[2] As he recalled years later, "Japs were one thing we didn't need any more of."[3]

Wake Island cost the Japanese 820 dead and 330 more wounded, as well as two ships and seven planes. American losses included 49 Marines, 3 sailors, and 70 civilian construction workers killed. The 470 Marines and sailors, 5 soldiers, and 1,146 civilians made prisoner were taken on the *Nitta Maru* to Shanghai. En route, Japanese guards beheaded 2 Marines and 3 sailors, and abused the other captives. The cruel treatment foreshadowed the bitter struggle to wrest the Pacific from the empire of Japan. But the little garrison's gallant stand would not be forgotten. Capt. Henry T. "Hank" Elrod, the pilot who sank the *Kisagari,* was awarded the Medal of Honor—the Corps's first in World War II.

In the Philippines, Leathernecks assigned to the barracks at Olongapo and Cavite mounted out to reinforce the 4th Marines on Corregidor. China Marines had little respect for the Japanese soldiers they had encountered in Shanghai and Tientsin. But the enemy they faced in the Philippines was cut from the same cloth as the tireless troops who would shortly take Malaya, Singapore, and the Dutch East Indies. Despite stubborn resistance by the

American and Filipino forces, the Japanese closed in on the gaunt defenders. On 29 April 1942 a bombardment of Corregidor signaled the beginning of the final push to seize the Philippines. Lt. Gen. Jonathan M. Wainwright—left in command after the departure of Gen. Douglas MacArthur—ordered his forces to lay down their arms on 6 May. Burning his regimental colors, Col. Samuel L. Howard, commander of the 4th Marines, wept to think that he would become the first Leatherneck to surrender an entire regiment.

Although the Japanese attack on Pearl Harbor caught the base's Marine defenders as unaware as anyone else, the Corps had been practicing its amphibious assault mission for more than a decade in the belief that it would one day be tested against Japan. Despite the miserly appropriations and isolationist thinking of the interwar years, by 7 December 1941 the Marine Corps had grown to more than sixty-five thousand men organized into two divisions, two air wings, and several defense battalions. The Corps was readier for war than at any time in its history.

In early 1942, two brigades of Marines sailed for Samoa in the South Pacific, the region where strategists assumed that the Japanese would strike next. Instead, the enemy attempted to seize Midway, a tiny American island in the Central Pacific. Taking advantage of a brilliant piece of code breaking, U.S. naval forces intercepted the Japanese task force. On 4 June 1942, fifty-two partly obsolete, Midway-based Marine aircraft—twenty-five fighters of VMF-221 and twenty-seven dive bombers of VMSB-241—took off to attack the Japanese carriers and to defend against inbound strikes. Twenty-three of the intrepid Leathernecks did not return, but their sacrifice helped to set the stage for the great American victory that followed. The next day, eleven of the surviving Marine dive bombers joined in the pursuit of the Japanese. Hit by flak after releasing his bomb at the cruiser *Mikuma,* Capt. Richard E. Fleming crashed his plane into the ship's after turret to win a posthumous Medal of Honor.

Midway cost the Americans the carrier *Yorktown* and 98 aircraft, but the Japanese lost four carriers and 322 planes. Elated with their victory at Midway and in an earlier encounter in the Coral Sea, the Navy's leaders pressed to seize the initiative in the Pacific. In Hawaii,

Adm. Chester A. Nimitz, commander of the Pacific Fleet, proposed sending the 1st Marine Raider Battalion to Tulagi in the Solomon Islands to destroy a Japanese seaplane facility. But in Washington, the Joint Chiefs of Staff (JCS)—goaded by Adm. Ernest J. King, the chief of naval operations—proposed a much larger operation.

Although the United States and Great Britain had agreed on a "Germany first" strategy, Admiral King argued that U.S. forces should maintain the momentum against the Japanese. By tacit agreement, the war in Europe would remain an "Army show" while the fight in the Pacific rested in Navy hands. Intelligence reports of the construction of a Japanese airfield near Lunga Point on Guadalcanal in the Solomons supported King's argument for offensive action in the South Pacific. Although the Battle of the Coral Sea had forestalled a Japanese amphibious assault on Port Moresby, the Allied supply base in eastern New Guinea, completion of the airfield might signal the beginning of a renewed advance to the south. Thus was born Operation Watchtower, the seizure of Tulagi and Guadalcanal.

At midnight on 6–7 August 1942, officers on the bridge watch of the transport *McCawley* peered anxiously into the murky darkness. In less than three hours, the amphibious force to which the ship belonged hoped to pass undetected through the center of a seven-mile passage between the nearest of the Russell Islands and Guadalcanal. The embarked troops came mostly from the 1st Marine Division, commanded by Maj. Gen. Alexander A. Vandegrift. The core of the division was composed of the ramrod-straight, sunburned Leathernecks who had formed the backbone of the lean interwar Marine Corps, supplemented by young enlistees eager to be "first to fight." Vandegrift, commissioned in 1909, had earned the reputation of an intelligent and determined officer. In 1928 he had commanded a battalion in the brigade sent to China under Smedley Butler, a close personal friend. Later in the interwar period, Vandegrift served as military secretary to General Holcomb, and was expected to succeed him at the helm of the Corps. The operation in the Solomons would task his skills like no previous assignment.

When Vandegrift learned of the division's assignment from Vice Adm. Robert L. Ghormley, commander, South Pacific Force and Area, the news came as a shock. Short one regiment, he had expected to spend the winter months in New Zealand, where he planned to train his troops in battalion tactics and absorb sorely needed additions to the division's ranks. Just before the move to the Solomons, Vandegrift received reinforcements: the 1st Raider Battalion and the 1st Marine Parachute Battalion—units with far fewer men and less firepower than a typical infantry battalion—the 2nd Marines, and the 3rd Defense Battalion.

While in numbers Vandegrift now had a division, that division lacked the cohesiveness and training of an effective combat force. Vandegrift's overworked staff pleaded for more time, but to little avail; D-day was moved back only one week—from 1 August to 7 August 1942. The lack of information on the Japanese in the Solomons troubled both Vandegrift and the amphibious task force commander, Rear Adm. Richmond Kelly Turner. When the task force left New Zealand on 22 July, Watchtower more resembled a leap of blind faith than a carefully considered and timed example of amphibious professionalism.

At 3:00 A.M., the shrill cry of a bosun's whistle roused the men from their bunks. More than one sleepy Leatherneck muttered the timeless lament: "Gahd! The only people up this time of the night are burglars and bad women!" While the troops wolfed down a heavy preassault breakfast, their commanders pondered the formidable task that lay ahead. Combat veterans of World War I led the two infantry regiments: Col. Clifton B. Cates, the 1st Marines; Col. Leroy P. Hunt, the 5th Marines. Both had fought guerrillas in Haiti and Nicaragua, and more recently had confronted the Japanese in diplomatic face-offs in China. The division's third infantry regiment—the 7th Marines—had been left behind to defend Samoa. Cates recalled that his regiment had never even conducted a command-post exercise: "We were short on equipment and short on training . . . maybe we [thought we could] make up in guts what we lacked otherwise."[4]

The fifteen ships of Transport Group X-ray hove to four miles east of Lunga Point, anchoring off Red Beach. Vandegrift ordered the 5th Marines to seize the eighteen-hundred-yard strip, which was backed by dense jungle foliage, and drive seven hundred yards inland. The 1st Marines would pass through them to strike toward a prominent terrain feature, Mount Austen, which overlooked the Japanese airfield. A canny tactician, Vandegrift believed that the Tenaru, a small, unfordable river on the right flank of the beachhead, gave him natural protection from the main body of Japanese troops.

The first landing craft touched down at 9:10 A.M. To the Leathernecks' surprise, no Japanese appeared to resist the landing. As the troops pushed through the jungle, supplies began to pour ashore from the anchored transports. By early afternoon on 8 August, the 1st and 5th Marines had overrun both the airfield and the Japanese encampment with little opposition from the defenders, who were apparently dumbfounded by the audacity of Operation Watchtower. The Japanese Special Naval Landing Force battalion—an estimated 430 marines—and a labor force of some seventeen hundred Koreans had fled inland when the preassault bombardment began the day before. To the Marines' delight, the enemy left behind a considerable stockpile of ordnance and equipment.

On nearby Tulagi, the assistant division commander, Brig. Gen. William H. Rupertus, and Landing Group Yoke found that the Special Naval Landing Force troops there intended to fight a vicious, no-surrender battle in defense of the island. Lt. Col. Merritt A. Edson's 1st Raider Battalion and Lt. Col. Harold E. Rosecrans's 2nd Battalion, 5th Marines, landed on Tulagi's south coast and struck toward the ridge that ran lengthwise through the island to the native townsite and government center.

By nightfall Edson had established his command post in the former British residency. The Japanese defenders had withdrawn into a ravine southeast of Hill 281, on Tulagi's eastern tip. Rosecrans's battalion swept the northern portion of the island, then moved into position to support Edson along the crest of Hill 281. As darkness closed in, the Marines anticipated attack by the Japanese naval infantry.

Throughout the long night, the Japanese swarmed from hillside caves in repeated but unsuccessful attempts to penetrate the Raiders' lines. Edson's rules—don't panic, stay in position, count on fellow Marines for support, and avoid indiscriminate firing—kept the Raiders' lines intact. Nevertheless, it required heroism to face the Japanese onslaughts throughout the black night. PFC Edward H. Ahrens of Company A took on a Japanese patrol

The Opening Months of the Struggle for Guadalcanal, August–October 1942. *Note:* Both map and text identify terrain features according to the names used at the time, which as a result of faulty intelligence were sometimes incorrect. The "Tenaru River" was actually Alligator Creek, and the "Ilu River" was the Tenaru.

single-handed. Ahrens's company commander, burly Capt. Lewis H. "Lew" Walt, found him at first light, dying from his wounds. Ahrens's foes lay across him in a frozen catafalque of death. In the hand-to-hand combat during the previous night, Ahrens had been shot twice and bayoneted three times. By mid-afternoon of 8 August, Japanese opposition on Tulagi had ended.

That night, a cruiser-destroyer force of the Imperial Japanese Navy responded to the American intrusion with a stinging riposte. Rear Admiral Richmond Kelly Turner, the commander of the invasion force, had positioned three cruiser-destroyer forces to bar the Tulagi-Guadalcanal approaches. At the Battle of Savo Island the Japanese demonstrated their superiority in night fighting at this stage of the war, shattering two of Turner's covering forces without loss to themselves. Four heavy cruisers went to the bottom—three American, one Australian—and another lost her bow. As the sun came up

over "Ironbottom Bay," Marines watched grimly as Higgins boats swarmed out to rescue survivors.

Earlier on the evening of the naval calamity, at a shipboard command conference, Turner had announced that Vice Adm. Frank Jack Fletcher, the tactical commander of Operation Watchtower, had obtained Ghormley's permission to withdraw his carriers from the amphibious objective area. Fletcher had already lost one carrier at Coral Sea and another at Midway; he could not risk the loss of a third. After a miserly seventy-two hours off Guadalcanal-Tulagi, he intended to steam away. Turner went on to say that without the covering umbrella of Fletcher's aircraft he could not guarantee the safety of his own ships; he intended to depart as well. Vandegrift left the conference visibly stunned.

As promised, Turner withdrew his ships on 9 August. The unloading of supplies ended abruptly, and hulls still half full steamed away. Vandegrift pressed Turner for a

Senior officers of the 1st Marine Division following a briefing four days after the landing on Guadalcanal: General Vandegrift *(front row, fourth from left);* Col. Pedro A. del Valle, CO of the 11th Marines, the division's artillery regiment *(second from left);* Lt. Col. Gerald C. Thomas, division operations officer *(fifth from left);* Col. Clifton B. Cates, CO of the 1st Marines and, like Vandegrift, a future commandant *(sixth from left);* and Lt. Col. Randolph M. Pate, division logistics officer and another future commandant *(seventh from left).*

firm estimate on his time of return, but the admiral had no answer. The 1st Marine Division had been cast adrift. The hoard of Japanese supplies captured at Lunga Point looked better than ever. When rations fell to two meals a day, hungry Marines consumed rice, assorted seafood, and strange edibles courtesy of Emperor Hirohito.

Most of the division's heavy engineering equipment had disappeared with the Navy transports, but the resourceful Marines completed the runway with captured Japanese gear. On 12 August, a Navy PBY-5 amphibian landed to signal the opening of Henderson Field, named in honor of

Maj. Lofton R. Henderson, a Marine aviator killed at the Battle of Midway. The PBY departed carrying a load of wounded Marines, the first of more than two thousand to be evacuated. Henderson Field became the centerpiece of Vandegrift's strategy: to hold the airstrip at all costs. With it, supplies could come in and wounded could be taken out; no longer must he depend on the Navy. The determined Vandegrift instructed his commanders not to conceal their setbacks from the troops. He anticipated no repeat of Wake Island or Corregidor if every Marine did his job.

While Vandegrift's two regiments dug in east and west

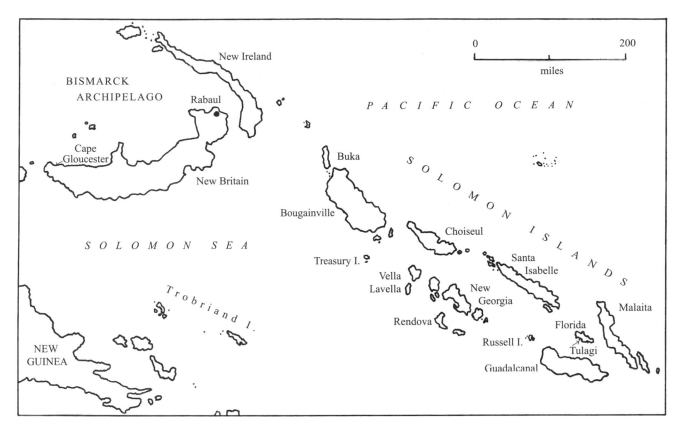

The Southwest Pacific Campaign, 1942–1944

of Henderson Field, Japanese headquarters in Rabaul, on New Britain, planned a response to this unexpected display of American offensive-mindedness. Although the officers there were surprised by the landing, they were not alarmed. Misled by intelligence estimates that placed Marine numbers at perhaps two thousand men—one-fifth of their real strength—they believed that a modest force if quickly sent could overwhelm the invaders. Their superiors in Tokyo were equally sanguine. Buoyed by the optimism of Imperial General Headquarters, a Japanese journalist proclaimed that the Marines in the Solomons were like "summer insects which have dropped into the fire by themselves."

Confident of victory, Imperial General Headquarters ordered Lt. Gen. Hyakutake Haruyoshi's 17th Army at Rabaul to attack the Marine perimeter with a reinforced infantry brigade under Maj. Gen. Kawaguchi Kiyotake. Hyakutake selected a crack infantry battalion from the 35th Brigade—commanded by a veteran of the war in China, Col. Ichiki Kiyono—to land first. Ichiki personally led his men ashore at Taivu Point, east of the Marine

perimeter, on the evening of 18 August. A notorious fire-brand, Ichiki once boasted that it took only swords and sabers to defeat Americans.

Eleven days after the landing of the Ichiki Detachment, the Kawaguchi Detachment—more than thirty-five hundred troops—would follow. Fortuitously, a heroic native scout, Jacob C. Vouza, encountered Ichiki's force as it wove through the jungle toward Henderson Field. Although he was captured, tortured, and left for dead, the gallant islander escaped and crawled back to the Marine lines to report the enemy formation.

Meanwhile, on 20 August, Vandegrift greeted the arrival of Marine Air Group 23's two squadrons at Henderson Field. A jeep carrier, the *Long Island,* catapulted off nineteen Grumman F4F-4 Wildcat fighters led by Capt. John L. Smith. Twelve Douglas SBD-3 dive-bombers commanded by Maj. Richard C. Mangrum followed. The Marine aviators dubbed Henderson Field "Cactus Base" in radio jargon, and the appellation "Cactus" stuck for the remainder of the operation. The arrival of MAG-23 gave Vandegrift's force a much-needed sting.

Both sides realized that Henderson Field represented the key to victory on Guadalcanal. Dispersed aircraft appear as white specks to the left and right of the runway, and Fighter One can be seen in the background.

During the night of 20–21 August, Ichiki's troops stormed the Marines' lines in a screaming, frenzied display of the "spiritual strength" that they had been assured would sweep aside their Occidental enemies. As the Japanese charged across the sandbar astride the Tenaru toward the lines of the 1st Marines, Lt. Col. Edwin A. Pollock's 2nd Battalion cut them down. Lt. Col. Lenard B. Creswell's 1st Battalion moved upstream on the Tenaru at daybreak, waded across, and moved on Ichiki's flank. After a mortar preparation, the Japanese tried again to storm the sandbar. A section of 37-mm guns sprayed the enemy force with deadly canister shells. By daylight, however, the Japanese still held the coconut grove on the east bank of the river. Pollock's infantrymen moved toward the trees, cutting down Japanese soldiers with well-aimed rifle fire. Col. Pedro A. del Valle's artillerymen swept the east bank and beyond with their 75-mm pack howitzers.

Trapped between the two Marine battalions, Ichiki burned his colors after soaking them in his own blood, and then committed seppuku. Leatherneck mortars and artillery pounded the survivors as they attempted to flee into the jungle. Tanks rolled over the enemy bodies, grinding them into their treads; crocodiles fed on the corpses that clogged the river. Marines counted 777 dead Japanese outside the barbed-wire perimeter; many more dead and wounded were probably dragged away. Only fifteen prisoners were taken, a grim testimony to the fury of the enemy assault. Leatherneck casualties included thirty-five killed and another seventy-five wounded. Reflecting on the defeat, a senior Japanese officer, noting that the attack was sheer folly, concluded that "this tragedy should have taught us the hopelessness of 'bamboo spear tactics.'"[5]

Taking prisoners proved to be risky business. "Dead" and wounded enemies rose up to shoot down Marines or throw a grenade. The ground war in the Pacific began to take on a grim, "no quarter" aspect. In a letter to General Holcomb, Vandegrift wrote starkly: "I have never heard or read of this kind of fighting. . . . The wounded will wait

Japanese dead of the Ichiki Detachment litter the beach near the mouth of the Tenaru River after the bloody battle on the night of 20 to 21 August 1942.

until men come up to examine them and blow themselves and the other fellow to pieces with a hand grenade."[6]

While the 1st Marine Division had a well-earned breathing spell as the Japanese regrouped for another onslaught, the action in the air over the Solomons intensified. Almost every day, Japanese aircraft arrived around noon to bomb the perimeter. Marine fighters found the twin-engine Betty bombers easy targets. Zero fighters were another story. Although the Leathernecks' Wildcats were much sturdier aircraft, the Zeroes' superior speed and maneuverability gave them a distinct edge in aerial combat. The Leatherneck aviators therefore avoided dogfights wherever possible and attacked by making single firing runs from high-speed dives. Those tactics made the airspace over the Solomons dangerous for the Japanese.

From Tulagi, General Rupertus sent 2/5, Edson's Raiders, and the 1st Parachute Battalion back to Guadalcanal to reinforce the main body of the division. In the meantime, the remainder of General Kawaguchi's troops—at least, those whose transports had not been sunk by American aircraft—had reached the island. An-

alyzing available intelligence, Vandegrift concluded that the Japanese brigade—now down to approximately three thousand effectives—intended to attack Henderson Field. He was correct. Kawaguchi did intend to attack, and had selected three points for his thrust: the southeastern face of the perimeter near the Ilu Plain, the western face where the 5th Marines held the line, and the center with his main body. Assembling his men in the foothills of Mount Austen, Kawaguchi ordered them to charge down the grassy slopes and burst onto the Lunga Plain only a mile from Henderson Field. Edson correctly predicted the point of attack and positioned his now-combined Raider-Paratroop force to block it. Del Valle ordered 105-mm howitzers closer to support Edson.

As the Marines readied themselves for the attack, Kelly Turner returned bearing both good and bad news. The good news was that he believed he could spirit in a convoy from Samoa and return the 7th Marines to Vandegrift. Through Turner, Admiral Ghormley sent the bad news, informing Vandegrift that in the opinion of his staff, naval forces could no longer support the Marines

Gunners serve a 105-mm howitzer at Guadalcanal. Leatherneck artillery, both the 75-mm and 105-mm howitzers, played a vital role in the campaign.

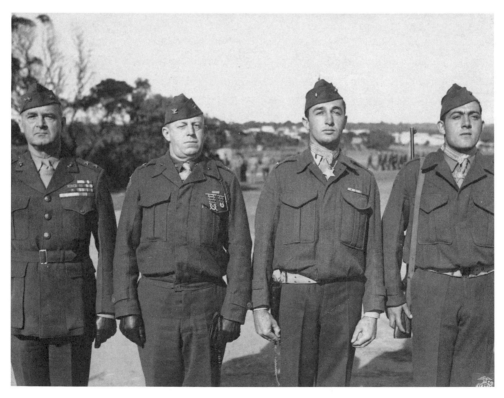

Four of the heroes of Guadalcanal. *From left to right:* Maj. Gen. Alexander A. Vandegrift, Col. Merritt A. Edson, 1st Lt. Mitchell Paige, and Sgt. John Basilone, shown at the ceremony at which they were decorated with the Medal of Honor.

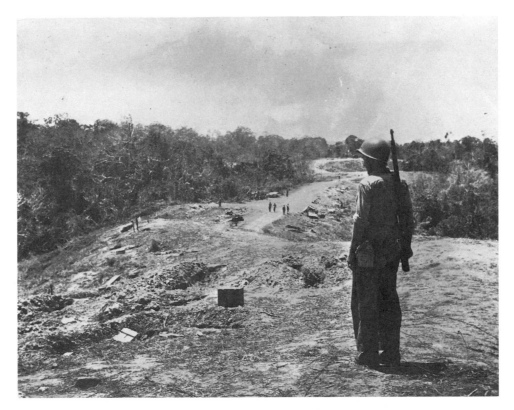

Bloody Ridge was the scene of perhaps the most savage fighting in the struggle for Guadalcanal.

on Guadalcanal. Vandegrift allowed only his operations officer, Col. Gerald C. Thomas, to know of Ghormley's gloomy prediction. Then he ordered Thomas to prepare a contingency plan to withdraw from the perimeter and fight guerrilla fashion at the headwaters of the Lunga River.

The first blow came during the night of 12–13 September, as the Japanese began to probe Vandegrift's lines. At 9:00 the following evening Kawaguchi attacked Edson's left flank. In desperate hand-to-hand combat, the 840 Raiders and Paratroopers held. Eleven more attempts followed in a night that seemed endless. By 2:30 the next morning, Edson could tell Vandegrift and Thomas: "We can hold!"[7] Kawaguchi had been stopped, but barely. Early in the morning Vandegrift added 2/5 to Edson's force on the ridge.

Much of the Japanese failure lay in Edson's heroics. Already a legend, Red Mike roamed his battalion's forward perimeter encouraging Marines to hold on. When dawn finally came, the defenders observed hundreds of Japanese bodies strewn over the landscape—almost half the enemy force. Sixty-nine Marines had been killed and

194 wounded; the terrain had a new name: "Bloody Ridge." Edson's force had held the last hill short of the division command post. Japanese stragglers continued to pose a problem, albeit a minor one. The morning after the assault, Marines shot several infiltrators near Vandegrift's headquarters; the division sergeant major himself killed one. The struggle for Bloody Ridge became a moral turning point of the entire Pacific war.

The battle for Bloody Ridge convinced Japanese planners that the campaign to eject the Americans from the Solomons must be stepped up. From Pearl Harbor to Washington, American commanders grew increasingly apprehensive as they scanned decrypted messages that revealed the flow of enemy aircraft, ships, and troops to the Solomons. President Roosevelt noted his "anxiety about the Southwest Pacific" and directed the Joint Chiefs of Staff to "make sure that every possible weapon gets into that area to hold Guadalcanal."[8] Secretary of the Navy Frank Knox replied to a journalist's question with a candor not likely to bolster the flagging morale of the beleaguered Marines ashore in the Solomons: "I will not make any predictions, but every man will give a good

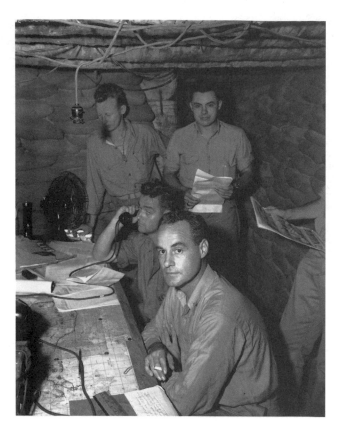

Lt. Col. Merrill B. Twining *(front)* and Maj. Henry W. Buse *(directly behind him)* in the command post of the 1st Marine Division on Guadalcanal.

account of himself. There is a good, stiff fight going on. Everybody hopes we can hold on."[9]

While the cryptanalysis picture evoked trepidation at the strategic level, Vandegrift's problems defending the perimeter had eased. The 6th Seabee Battalion completed an alternate airstrip, dubbed "Fighter One." Turner made good on his pledge to return the 7th Marines, and the transports brought in much-needed supplies. Air operations continued undiminished. Two pioneers of Marine Corps aviation, Brig. Gen. Roy S. Geiger and Col. Louis E. Woods, freed Vandegrift of the burden of managing air defenses. Geiger and Woods tightened procedures, enhanced morale, and began a study of Japanese air tactics to increase the effectiveness of Marine Corps aviation. The efforts of Leatherneck aviators slowed the enemy buildup significantly.

Fearing the landing of additional Japanese artillery, Vandegrift moved to push the western boundary of the perimeter to the Matanikau River. On 23 September

Leatherneck units jumped off to make a flanking movement from the interior to trap enemy units along the coast. A new battalion, Lt. Col. Chesty Puller's 1/7, found Japanese resistance strong. Much to their dismay, the Marines made little progress. Mistaken orders, garbled reports, and a communications failure contributed to friendly casualties of sixty killed and one hundred wounded.

Vandegrift could ill afford such losses. He had learned the hard way that the Japanese remained on the island in force. In order to prevent them from placing artillery on the Matanikau—where it would command his entire perimeter—he launched another offensive on 7 October. Two battalions advanced along the coast; three others, including Puller's, pivoted to the left in a hooking maneuver to cross the river and fall on the enemy's right flank and rear. Puller's battalion caught a Japanese unit bivouacked in a ravine and shattered it with mortar and artillery fire. Two companies of Raiders wiped out an enemy force left behind as a bridgehead in a savage night action punctuated by intense hand-to-hand combat. The classic spoiling operation forestalled Japanese attempts to position their artillery to support an assault on Vandegrift's perimeter. To guard against a recurrence of the threat, the 5th Marines, now commanded by Red Mike Edson, dug in along the east bank of the Matanikau.

Disease now hit the Marines with full force. Hundreds of Leathernecks already harassed by attacks of gastroenteritis and tropical fungus infections were toppled by malaria. Mosquito discipline had been poor, mostly because the men were reluctant to use the antimalarial drug, Atabrine, which turned their skin yellow. Many Marines believed that the drug caused impotence. It took a temperature of 103 degrees or higher to earn a ticket to the hospital. Otherwise, bluejackets and Leathernecks shivered with chills or burned with fever on the line.

Above all else, Vandegrift yearned for the division to be withdrawn to New Zealand. His weary Marines were in desperate need of a rest. The gaunt stares, Atabrineyellow faces, and blank spaces on unit rosters made him fearful. Meanwhile, Hyakutake was planning another attack. Still underestimating Vandegrift's strength—at seventy-five hundred rather than the actual nineteen thousand—the Japanese high command planned to neutralize Henderson Field with naval gunfire. Under cover of the

A Marine patrol moves out on Guadalcanal.

bombardment, Lt. Gen. Maruyama Masao's 2nd (Sendai) Division would be landed at night. Hyakutake moved to Guadalcanal to direct the operation in person. Crypt-analysts discovered the main ingredients of the Japanese plan and provided details of the forthcoming attack. But senior officers in Washington remained apprehensive. Gen. Henry H. "Hap" Arnold, the U.S. Army Air Forces' wartime leader, returned from a visit to the Southwest Pacific with a prediction of defeat from his senior air commander.

Vandegrift examined his options carefully. The Cactus Air Force provided only a partial solution. Leather-neck aviators performed well in air-to-air combat, but the SBD dive-bombers failed to deter the nightly Japanese destroyer runs. Three times during October the seaplane tender *Nisshin* ran the gauntlet to land material for the Japanese—including eight howitzers and sixteen tanks. It was the Navy's job to control the waters off Guadal-canal, and that had yet to happen.

Vandegrift petitioned for reinforcements, and Ghorm-ley sanctioned his request on 6 October. The 164th In-fantry Regiment—the first increment of the Americal Division—landed at Lunga Point. The fresh soldiers im-pressed the gaunt, battle-weary Marines—not for their élan, but because of their equipment. Each trooper carried a new M1 Garand rifle, wore a new pack, and seemed to have an unlimited supply of Hershey Bars. Transports disgorged seventy days of rations. Brisk trad-ing followed until an early afternoon air raid disrupted the bazaar.

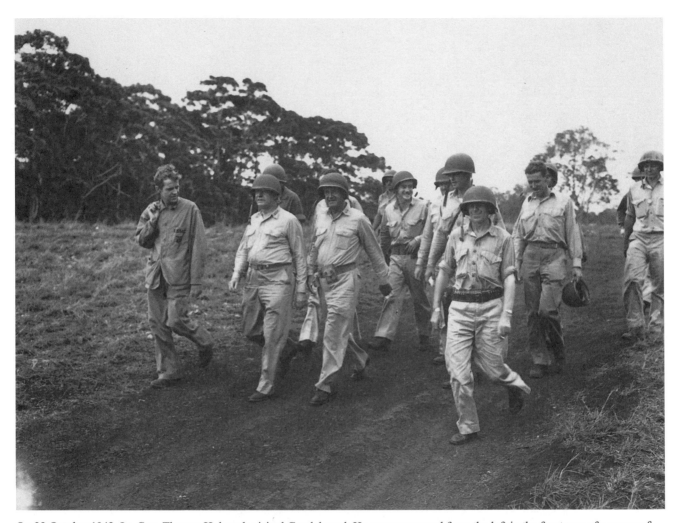

On 22 October 1942, Lt. Gen. Thomas Holcomb visited Guadalcanal. He appears second from the left in the front row of a group of officers. Maj. Gen. Alexander A. Vandegrift is to the immediate left of Holcomb, and Col. Merritt A. Edson is to the left of Vandegrift in the front row.

In the early morning hours of 14 October, enemy flares illuminated the perimeter as the Japanese began an intense artillery and naval bombardment of Henderson Field. The entire Lunga area shook as the battleships *Kongo* and *Haruna* poured 14-inch shells into the Leatherneck positions. Under cover of the bombardment Vice Adm. Kurita Takeo hoped to land the rear echelon of the Sendai Division. Fortunately for the Marines, the Japanese fired mostly armor-piercing rounds left over from naval actions; the shells buried themselves in the ground and did little harm unless they scored a direct hit. Nevertheless, many aircraft suffered damage and only seven SBDs could fly the next morning.

Vandegrift knew that a Japanese attack was forthcoming. Expecting the assault to come from the west, he strengthened his forces there at the expense of the defenses to the east. Additional wire was strung outside the brittle front line, and machine guns were presighted to cover every approach. But when the Japanese attack came, it was from the south. On the eve of what he and his superiors in Rabaul and Tokyo hoped would be the final ground offensive, the commanding general of the 2nd (Sendai) Division harangued his troops: "The ensuing operation for the capture of Guadalcanal, engaging the attention of all the world, is the decisive battle between Japan and America . . . if we are not successful . . . not one man should expect to return alive."[10]

In the jungle west of Bloody Ridge, Maruyama ordered the six thousand men of the Sendais forward. The dense foliage offered concealment as the Japanese began their fifteen-mile trek behind Mount Austen on 16 October. Slowed by heavy packs and burdened with artillery shells, the soldiers struggled up and down the rain-slicked slopes. The assault began in driblets at the mouth of the Matanikau on 21 October. Leatherneck 37-mm guns knocked out Japanese tanks sent to support the infantry. Del Valle's artillery destroyed another three tanks and leveled the advancing infantry. Marine commanders counted more than 650 enemy bodies in front of their lines.

The main attack began at 9:30 P.M. on 24 October, striking Puller's 1/7 just south of Bloody Ridge and the 3rd Battalion of the 164th Infantry on his left. The Sendai's 29th Infantry Regiment hit and then bypassed an outpost thirty-three hundred yards east of Puller's battalion. As the heavens released a torrential downpour, Maruyama's attack force of six infantry battalions became disorganized and failed to mass for the assault. Japanese infantry charged the Leatherneck lines piecemeal. Some shouted "Marine, you die!" and "Blood for the Emperor!" only to hear a defiant "Blood for Franklin and Eleanor!" in return.[11] Lt. Col. Herman H. Hanneken's 2/7, holding a line running eastward from the Matanikau, bore the brunt of the Japanese assault the next night.

Sgt. "Manila John" Basilone was one reason why the Japanese failed to penetrate the Marine lines. His exploits earned him the first Medal of Honor won by an enlisted Marine in World War II. "While the enemy was hammering at [Puller's] defensive positions," his citation read, "Sergeant Basilone, in charge of two sections of heavy machine guns, fought valiantly to check the savage and determined assault. In a fierce frontal attack with the Japanese blasting his guns with grenades and mortar fire, one of Sergeant Basilone's sections, with its gun crews, was put out of action, leaving only two men able to carry on. Moving an extra gun into position, he placed it in action." Then Basilone, "under continual fire, repaired another and personally manned it, gallantly holding his line until replacements arrived."[12] With his ammunition running low and supply lines cut off, Basilone battled his way through hostile lines to resupply the machine-gun section. Manila John Basilone's actions that day contributed to the virtual annihilation of an entire Japanese regiment. Basilone was offered a battlefield commission but turned it down.

Japanese aircraft appeared over Guadalcanal in increasing numbers on 25 October. Leatherneck pilots flying from Fighter One's strip kept them from providing significant support for the enemy ground forces. Newly arrived Capt. Joseph J. Foss, a lanky farm boy from South Dakota, became an ace, adding four kills to a like number scored the previous day. By the time Foss left Guadalcanal in January 1943 he had shot down twenty-six enemy aircraft, tying Eddie Rickenbacker's World War I record and earning the Medal of Honor.

While Maruyama prepared to renew his attack, Marine battalion commanders adjusted their positions. An estimated thousand enemy dead lay in front of their lines. Puller had lost only nineteen Marines dead and another thirty wounded. The enemy's new effort also failed, and Maruyama's force melted away into the jungle. Another thousand enemy corpses added to the carnage. Noncombat deaths and illness completed the destruction of the Sendais as an offensive threat.

The final Japanese attack against the western flank on 25 October fared no better. Hanneken's 2/7 held firmly to its anchor on a ridgeline. Another enlisted Marine, Sgt. Mitchell Paige, won the Medal of Honor on that day: "When the enemy broke through the line directly in front of his position . . . [he] continued to direct the fire of his gunners until all his men were either killed or wounded." Despite the intense enemy fire and the loss of his comrades, Paige "never [ceased] his withering fire against the advancing hordes until reinforcements finally arrived. Then, forming a new line, he dauntlessly and aggressively led a bayonet charge, driving the enemy back and preventing a breakthrough in our lines."[13] Unlike Basilone, Paige accepted his battlefield commission.

After the abortive Japanese attempts to pierce the Marines' lines during October, the primary burden of the defense of Guadalcanal-Tulagi fell to the Navy and the Cactus Air Force. The new COMSOPAC, Vice Adm. William F. "Bull" Halsey, sent his carrier forces to attack Japanese surface and air units in the Solomons. On 9 November the Japanese ordered the 38th (Hiroshima) Division ashore at Tassafaronga Point. But in the naval battle for Guadalcanal, most of the force went to the bottom as American aircraft sank seven of the eleven troop transports. The naval battle and the successful disruption of

Capt. Joe Foss, the Cactus Air Force's leading ace. His distinguished postwar career included terms as governor of his native South Dakota and president of the National Rifle Association.

the landing of the Hiroshima Division marked the turning point in the campaign for Guadalcanal; no longer could the enemy reinforce his troops ashore with impunity or operate freely in the waters off Guadalcanal. By late November enemy naval forces in the region had been defeated. Halsey brought welcome gifts to the haggard, malaria-ridden, and exhausted Leathernecks on Thanksgiving Day: a turkey dinner with cranberry sauce and orders to withdraw from the Solomons.

The Army's Americal Division—already in place—would garrison Guadalcanal, joined by the 25th Infantry Division from Hawaii. Instead of returning to New Zealand, the 1st Marine Division would recover and retrain in Australia. On 9 December 1942 the 5th Marines crawled up the cargo nets of the *Hunter Liggett* for transport south. Many were so weak they could scarcely climb aboard. Others collapsed on deck. Vandegrift paid them a final tribute: "At all times you have faced without flinching the worst that the enemy could do to us and have thrown back the best that he could send against us."[14] After visiting the 1st Marine Division cemetery,

Vandegrift passed command of ground forces on the 'Canal to Maj. Gen. Alexander M. Patch of the Americal Division and boarded a plane for Brisbane. Along with Raider commander Red Mike Edson, Vandegrift earned the Medal of Honor for his leadership on Guadalcanal. Leatherneck losses numbered 1,044 dead, 2,894 wounded, and 55 missing. Navy surgeons recorded more than nine thousand cases of malaria. An estimated 25,600 Japanese soldiers died for their emperor out of the 31,400 sent to evict the Americans from the island.

While Marines everywhere basked in the heroic aura earned by the Leathernecks in the Solomons, few realized that a daring mission undertaken just a month prior to the launching of Operation Watchtower briefly threatened to tarnish the Corps's image. On 8 August 1942, pressure to show results against the Japanese—however meager—resulted in the dispatch of two companies of the 2nd Raider Battalion under Lt. Col. Evans P. Carlson to attack Makin Atoll in the Gilbert Islands. The gaunt, craggy-faced Carlson, a veteran of the Nicaraguan campaign, was among the Corps's most unorthodox officers.

Lt. Col. Evans Carlson, kneeling second from left, and some of his Raiders with a Japanese flag and weapons captured at Makin.

In 1938 he had spent three months with Mao Tse-tung's Eighth Route Army and had become enamored with the tactics and esprit de corps of the Chinese Communist forces. One result of this experience was his contribution of the term *gung ho* (pull together)—which would acquire a somewhat derisive connotation—to the Corps's vocabulary. Afterward, he had resigned his commission to undertake a personal crusade for American aid to China. In April 1941, convinced that war was coming, he returned to forest green with a determined belief in the efficacy of guerrilla operations.

Adding to the impetus for the operation was the presence of Maj. James Roosevelt, Carlson's executive officer and the president's son. Landing in rubber boats from the submarines *Nautilus* and *Argonaut* on 17 August, Carlson's Raiders found fewer than 70 Japanese rather than the estimated 250. A fierce Japanese counterattack convinced Carlson that he was greatly outnumbered, however, and the Raiders prepared to withdraw. But the rough surf swamped their rubber boats. Apparently, at this point Carlson considered surrendering. Then, learning the actual number of Japanese he faced from a prisoner, he renewed his assault on the atoll and blew up an enemy radio station. After reembarking on the submarines, Carlson discovered to his horror that nine Marines had been left behind in the confusion. Captured by the Japanese, the luckless Leathernecks were beheaded. Despite the mixed outcome of the operation, both Carlson and Roosevelt won Navy Crosses.

During the Guadalcanal campaign, American planners ordered the formation of the I Marine Amphibious Corps to include all Leatherneck ground forces in the South Pa-

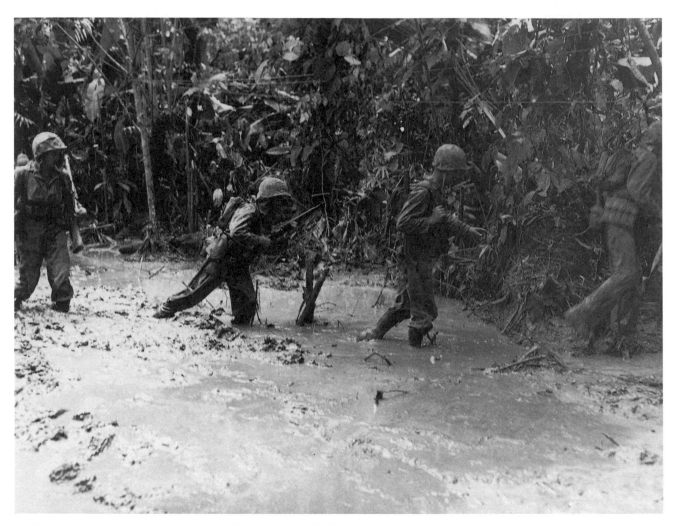

Leathernecks move to the front on Bougainville, 4 December 1943.

cific. Vandegrift, newly promoted to lieutenant general, became its commander in July 1943 with the mission of seizing Bougainville in the northern Solomons. In the meantime, Marine units had supported Army troops in the occupation of the undefended Russell Islands in February and the landings on fiercely defended New Georgia, midway up the Solomons, in June and July. For his new task, Vandegrift had the 3rd Marine Division for the assault and the 37th Infantry Division in reserve. As a diversion, the 2nd Parachute Battalion under Lt. Col. Victor H. Krulak —725 Marines—would land at Choiseul on the night of 27–28 October. If things went as planned, the Japanese would mistake the battalion for the entire Marine division and reinforce the garrison with troops from Bougainville. As another diversion, the New Zealand 8th Brigade Group landed in the Treasury Islands on 27 October.

H-hour was set for 6:45 A.M. on 1 November, with the 9th Marines landing on the left and the 3rd Marines (reinforced with the 2nd Raider Battalion) on the right. Naval transports would retire after discharging their cargo, then return with the 21st Marines (the 3rd Marine Division's third infantry regiment) and the 37th Infantry Division. The confused Japanese high command failed to reinforce its meager garrison on Bougainville until it was too late. At the end of the first day, more than fourteen thousand troops and sixty-two hundred tons of supplies had been moved ashore. The only interruptions came from occasional enemy air attacks.

The American assault drove the Japanese 23rd Infantry onto the only high ground, renamed "Hellzapoppin Ridge" by the Marines. It took until 18 December for the 21st Marines to wipe out the enemy unit. When the

World War Two

The Central Pacific Drive, 1943–1945

The series of Orange plans developed during the interwar years to guide American strategy in a conflict with Japan envisioned an offensive across the Central Pacific. In the event, the Japanese onslaught threw U.S. forces on the defensive for six months following the attack on Pearl Harbor. After the victory at Midway put the war on balance, the enemy threat to the lines of communications to Australia drew American resources to the southwest Pacific—itself a strategically defensive deployment. The turning point came in the grueling struggle for Guadalcanal, where the Japanese effort to regain the initiative was defeated. American strategists then faced the question of what to do next.

Gen. Douglas MacArthur urged mounting an offensive under his command along the "New Guinea–Mindanao Axis" to liberate the Philippines at the earliest opportunity. Adm. Ernest J. King argued with equal vehemence in favor of launching a drive under naval command through the islands of the Central Pacific: in effect, a revival of the Orange plans. Amphibious forces, spearheaded by fast-carrier task groups, would prevent the Japanese from reinforcing or mutually supporting the links in their far-flung defensive perimeter. In the end, the Joint Chiefs of Staff decided that the supply of men and material was sufficient to support a dual advance and approved both proposals. MacArthur would push up the coast of New Guinea toward the Philippines while naval forces under Adm. Chester A. Nimitz, commander in chief, Pacific Fleet, struck across the expanse of the Central Pacific.

Nimitz's forces would be supported by carrier aircraft, MacArthur's by land-based planes. To the displeasure of the Corps's leaders and senior Navy officers, the JCS allowed MacArthur to retain the 1st and 3rd Marine Divisions, at least initially. This left only the 2nd and 4th Marine Divisions for V Amphibious Corps in the Central Pacific. But HQMC contemplated the formation of two additional divisions—a 470,000-man Marine Corps by mid-1944. The Army objected, but to no avail.

Originally, the Central Pacific offensive was to begin with an attack on the Marshall Islands. As the planning developed, however, strategists concluded that the more southerly Gilberts would provide airfields and anchorages to support the advance northward. The Gilberts, a former British protectorate, consisted of sixteen scattered atolls lying athwart the equator. Betio, the main island in Tarawa Atoll, would constitute the first large-scale test of Marine Corps amphibious doctrine against a strongly fortified beachhead. To lead the campaign Nimitz selected Vice Adm. Raymond A. Spruance, whose command was designated the Fifth Fleet. Rear Adm. Richmond Kelly Turner headed Spruance's amphibious forces, with the ground troops of V Amphibious Corps led by Maj. Gen. Holland M. "Howlin' Mad" Smith, USMC.

A short, thickset, jowly man who wore horn-rimmed glasses and a close-cropped mustache, Smith had been born at Hatcheechubbee, Alabama, sixty-one years before. Educated to join his father's law practice, he had escaped the paternal program by obtaining a direct commission in the Corps in 1905. As a junior officer he saw

3rd Marine Division departed, it had suffered 423 dead and 1,418 wounded. The 3rd Defense Battalion and the Army's XIV Corps remained to garrison the island. A Seabee battalion constructed an airstrip on Bougainville. On 9 March 1944 the Japanese attempted to regain the area with six major assaults from the interior over a two-week period, losing 6,843 soldiers in the futile effort.

Most Leatherneck air units continued to operate in the South Pacific as ground elements prepared to participate in the drive to seize the Central Pacific from the Japanese. Flying from Henderson Field, Marine aviators—VMF-112, VMF-121, VMSB-144, and VMSB-234—hammered the Japanese units that remained. Their operations contributed heavily to the enemy's decision to abandon the region. In more than six months of aerial combat, ninety-four of them lost their lives, but they earned an impressive one-to-three kill ratio against Japanese pilots.

A number of Marine aviators became aces in the Solomons. The most celebrated, following Joe Foss, was Maj. Gregory R. "Pappy" Boyington, the hard-drinking, hell-raising commanding officer of the "Black Sheep" of VMF-214. A prewar pilot, Boyington had resigned from the Corps early in 1941 to join the Flying Tigers, a group of American volunteers flying for the Nationalist Chinese against the Japanese. In China he chalked up his first six victories. Returning home to rejoin the Corps on the outbreak of war, he found that his foreign service had made him an object of suspicion and spent a year parking cars before he was allowed back in uniform.

By the time Boyington reached the southwestern Pacific, Leatherneck squadrons were equipped with the bent-wing F4U Corsair, the premier American naval fighter of the war. He was then twenty-nine, a relatively advanced age for a fighter pilot. His men called him "Grandpappy" or "Gramps," and reporters settled on "Pappy." Between 16 September 1943 and 3 January 1944, the old man knocked down twenty-two Japanese aircraft; adding his China kills to that number gave him a total of twenty-eight and made him the leading Leatherneck ace of World War II. Forced to bail out of his damaged aircraft after downing two Zeroes during his last mission, he spent the next twenty months as a prisoner of war. Only on his release did he learn that he had been

The legendary Gregory "Pappy" Boyington, the highest-scoring ace in the Corps's history, commanded the Black Sheep Squadron (VMF-214) in the Solomons.

awarded what everyone thought was a posthumous Medal of Honor.

The third-ranking Marine ace, twenty-three-year-old 1st Lt. Robert M. Hanson, the son of a missionary couple, piloted a Corsair in VMF-215. He ran up the startling score of twenty-five confirmed victories between 1 November 1943 and 3 February 1944, when his plane was hit while attacking a Japanese flak tower and he crashed into the sea. Of the eleven Leatherneck pilots who earned the Medal of Honor in World War II, nine won them in the Solomons.

Command of Leatherneck ground forces in the South Pacific had passed to Gen. Douglas MacArthur, and his Sixth Army staff had alerted the 1st Marine Division, now commanded by Maj. Gen. William H. Rupertus, to its next target in July 1943: Cape Gloucester, at the northwest corner of New Britain. In contrast to the poorly supplied and supported Guadalcanal-Tulagi operation, new equipment and replacements poured into the division. Leathernecks turned in their trusty, time-honored Spring-

The Black Sheep Squadron scrambles at the Turtle Bay fighter strip on Espíritu Santo Island in the New Hebrides, 11 September 1943.

field '03 rifles for new Garand M1s. The temperamental Reising submachine guns went to the surplus pile, replaced by the heavier but reliable Thompson. For the ship-to-shore movement, the Navy provided an impressive array of twenty-four LSTs, fourteen LCMs, and fifteen LCIs. Only the lead battalions in the assault would land from the familiar LCVPs, launched from high-speed destroyer transports.

On 26 December 1943 the initial assault waves—composed of the battalions of the 7th Marines—headed for the beach. Advancing cautiously into thick jungle growing right up to the water's edge, the keyed-up Leathernecks found a series of well-constructed but unmanned bunkers. Two additional battalions (1/1 and 3/1) marched seven miles from the main landing site to seize the Japanese airfield on the island. Once ashore, the

Marines dug into the slimy jungle muck and waited for the Japanese counterattack they knew would come.

Violent winds and heavy rains plagued the attackers. Despite the foul weather, however, the Japanese were unable to eject the Marines from the island. A spirited assault against the lines of the 2nd Battalion, 7th Marines, on the night of D-day resulted in more than two hundred dead Japanese. Four times on 2 January 1944 the 3/5 and 3/7 tried to cross a formidable obstacle—dubbed "Suicide Creek"—but failed. Finally, three Sherman tanks unlocked the barrier by knocking out the Japanese bunkers that blocked the Marines' advance.

Next, the Leathernecks turned to Aogiri Ridge, held by an estimated one thousand well-dug-in defenders. The initial attacks failed, but Lt. Col. Lew Walt's 3rd Battalion, 5th Marines, finally broke through. Walt almost in-

dividually turned the tide of battle, throwing his weight behind a 37-mm gun to move it into firing position so violently that he dislocated his shoulder. After reaching the crest of the hill, his battalion repulsed five screaming banzai charges during the night of 9–10 January; Aogiri Ridge became "Walt's Ridge."

Only one significant height remained in enemy hands, Hill 660. Its defenders were the Japanese high command's last hope. A Leatherneck battalion swarmed straight up the steep slope on a wide front while another exploited the diversion to approach the position from the rear. Lt. Col. Henry W. Buse Jr.'s 3rd Battalion, 7th Marines, gained the northwest summit by literally pulling itself up, surprising the few defenders holding the rearward high ground. By dusk on 16 January the perimeter had been tightened and the final feeble Japanese counterattacks beaten off.

Chesty Puller added to his renown at Cape Gloucester. Now the executive officer of the 7th Marines, he prowled the front outside the wire, cheering countless Leathernecks with his jocular, "How's things going, Old Man?"[15] His fearlessness and seeming invulnerability kept many a frightened and exhausted Marine going. To the surprise of General Rupertus and the division staff, the enemy began to vanish. Later reports revealed that the Japanese withdrew along the jungle trails that led the three hundred miles back to Rabaul, eluding the Leatherneck patrols that pursued them. By early February, little combat remained. An attempt by the 5th Marines to outflank the enemy by landing ahead of the retreating columns largely failed. On 28 April 1944 the 40th Infantry Division relieved the Marines at Cape Gloucester. The offensive had cost 310 Leathernecks killed and another 1,083 wounded.

Without regret, Marines of the 1st Division watched the volcanic cone of Cape Gloucester's Mount Talawe

fade into the distance. The camp had worn them down. Malaria and almost epidemic. Optimists belie would return to Australia, where th revisiting their old liberty haunts. In idence at Pavuvu, the largest of the R miles north of Guadalcanal, to prepa sault. Encamping in a coconut planta underwent drastic personnel changes joined and combat-experienced veterans

The grim contest to wrest the southwe the Japanese had ended. MacArthur was lo Marines, the amphibious cutting edge of h He attempted to flatter Vandegrift by arguir the 1st Marine Division left the southwest Pa Central Pacific drive, they would simply be ' If they remained, however, they would be "Ma Marines." To Washington, MacArthur thundere icism: "By using Army troops to garrison the is the Pacific under Navy command, the Navy retai rine [Corps] forces always available, giving them ently an army of their own."[16] But Admiral King's to get Vandegrift's Marines back under Navy control vailed.

Despite their severe losses in the South Pacific, sen Japanese commanders remained sanguine in their beli in racial superiority. A communiqué from Hyakutake headquarters on Rabaul, released during the Guadalcanal campaign, spoke reams about the enemy's unbridled optimism: "Westerners—being very haughty, effeminate, and cowardly—intensely dislike fighting in the rain or mist or dark. They cannot conceive [of the] night as a proper time for battle—though it is excellent for dancing." Hyakutake concluded that "in these weaknesses, lie our greatest opportunity."[17] The long journey to Tokyo had barely begun.

combat in Santo Domingo and served in a succession of staff appointments in France during World War I. Between the wars he became increasingly involved in the development of the Corps's amphibious capabilities, holding major commands in the big exercises of 1939–41. Admiral Nimitz had personally selected him to command the Marine forces in the Central Pacific. In his outspoken autobiography, "Howlin' Mad" protested that his sobriquet was unwarranted. "I am not given to sudden, uncontrollable bursts of temper or to bawling out without cause," he insisted. "However, I do speak frankly, freely and emphatically when injustices occur, when official stupidity obstructs plans, or when the brass . . . tries to take liberties with my Marines."[1] To the surprise of many, Smith and the acerbic "Terrible" Turner worked well as a team.

For the assault on the Gilberts—Operation Galvanic—Smith had the 2nd Marine Division, commanded by Maj. Gen. Julian C. Smith, and the 27th Infantry Division, a New York National Guard outfit under Maj. Gen. Ralph C. Smith. On 20 November 1943, the 27th Division's 165th Infantry Regiment waded ashore at Makin, the northernmost atoll in the Gilberts. Although opposed by fewer than eight hundred Japanese, it took the 6,470 soldiers—led by overaged officers practicing World War I tactics—four long days to capture the island at a cost of sixty-six dead. Howlin' Mad Smith began to have doubts about the effectiveness of Ralph Smith's division.

The real contest for the Gilberts lay 105 miles south of Makin on Tarawa Atoll. The Japanese had built their defenses on Betio, a palm-fringed islet two miles long and at most half a mile wide at the southwestern corner of the atoll. To hold it, Rear Adm. Shibasaki Keijo had 4,836 men, including 2,619 elite troops of the Sasebo 7th Special Naval Landing Force. Betio bristled with more than five hundred heavy gun emplacements, pillboxes, and blockhouses. Shibasaki bragged that the Americans could not take the island with a million men in a hundred years, and exhorted his forces to "defend to the last man all vital areas and destroy the enemy at the water's edge."[2] The welcome the landing force received at Tarawa would be very different from that experienced at Guadalcanal.

General Holland M. "Howlin' Mad" Smith, one of the Corps's pioneers in amphibious operations, commanded the landing forces at the seizure of the Gilberts, the Marshalls, and the Marianas.

The Marines planned to land on the north shore of the reef. Only LVTs could cross the barrier, and the landing force had only 125 of this new craft, which meant that the remaining Leathernecks would be forced to get out and wade ashore if their boats failed to clear the reef. The pre-D-day softening up consisted of fifteen hundred tons of bombs and two thousand tons of naval ordnance—sufficient according to the Navy; not nearly enough in the opinion of Howlin' Mad Smith. H-hour was scheduled for 8:30 A.M. on 20 November, then postponed to 9:00 to allow time for silencing the shore batteries with naval gunfire. Despite the bombardment, the initial assault waves began taking fire three to four thousand yards from the beach.

First ashore into the maelstrom of exploding shells and withering small arms fire was 1st Lt. William Dean Hawkins and the Scout-Sniper Platoon, 2nd Marines. A quarter of an hour ahead of the first assault wave, the lean six-footer from Texas led his Marines up the seaplane ramp at the end of Betio's pier. Fighting their way down

D-Day on Betio Island, Tarawa Atoll, 20 November 1943

the jetty, the platoon used flamethrowers to torch pier-side shacks concealing machine-gun emplacements. Throughout the day, Hawkins and his men roamed the seawall destroying Japanese positions. Riding an LVT, Hawkins personally knocked out six machine-gun nests; even with two bullets in his shoulder, he kept fighting to gain a foothold on the beach for the 2nd Marines.

Concerned that in the smoke shrouding the island his ships' shells might hit the landing craft, the commander of the attack force lifted the bombardment almost twenty minutes before the first wave touched down. Thus Shibasaki was given ample time to reposition his troops to oppose the assault. The 2nd and 3rd Battalions, 2nd Marines, and 2/8 hit the beach first, ferried in LVTs. Behind 2/2, the 1st Battalion of the 2nd Marines waded across the reef, just as 3/8 waded in behind 2/8; both battalions incurred heavy casualties from enemy gun emplacements. Once they reached

shore the Leathernecks found themselves pinned behind a coconut-log seawall by enemy fire.

After three waves of Marines made it to the beach, the niggardly quota of LVTs had been used up. The remaining assault waves landed on the reef, disgorging their human cargo to be swallowed up in the carnage created by the enemy fire sweeping the lagoon. When the commanding officer of the 2nd Marines became ill prior to the invasion, Lt. Col. David M. Shoup received a spot promotion to colonel and led the regiment in the assault. Although wounded in the leg, Shoup—a stocky farm boy from Indiana—positioned himself and a makeshift staff next to the pier and directed the action from there. His heroic leadership would be rewarded by the Medal of Honor.

By noon the assault had stalled. Marines still hugged the narrow beaches and the seawall. Landing craft of all types remained stranded on the reef, piled high with dead

The northern shore of Betio Island, Tarawa atoll, immediately after the battle. Bodies float in the water beside knocked-out amtracs (amphibious tractors).

and wounded, while reinforcements failed to cross the formidable barrier. Julian Smith asked Holland Smith to release the Corps reserve, the 6th Marines. Smith passed the urgent request on to Turner, who approved it without hesitation; the battle for the atoll appeared to be in doubt. Even as the order crackled over the radio nets, Julian Smith ordered 1/8—his divisional reserve—into the crucible of Tarawa.

As the sun slipped over the horizon, some five thousand Leathernecks had reached shore; another fifteen hundred had been killed or wounded. Fearing the worst, Marines dug into their shallow perimeter to await a long night of Japanese counterattacks. Their thin line of resistance offered no possibility of falling back to regroup; this was a bitter fight to the finish. The pungent smell of

decaying bodies clogged the nostrils of both attackers and defenders. Fortunately for the Marines, the pre-assault bombardment had severed Japanese communications, preventing Shibasaki from organizing an effective counterattack.

Any number of fearless Marines contributed to the victory on Tarawa, but correspondent Robert Sherrod credited Hawkins with the ultimate success of the landing. Wounded again on the second day of the landing, he destroyed four more pillboxes before an enemy bullet cut him down for the last time. Hawkins earned one of the four Medals of Honor awarded to Marines for Tarawa—three posthumously—and his citation stands as an epic saga of human bravery in the face of the fiercest odds.

On D+1 Shoup ordered his four battalions to attack to

First Lt. William D. Hawkins led the Scout-Sniper Platoon, 2nd Marines, in the first wave at Tarawa. His heroism was instrumental in the success of the assault.

the south. By late afternoon, elements of the 1/2 and 2/2 had driven across the airfield and reached the south coast, while 3/2 had secured the western edge of the island. Two new battalions, 1/6 and 1/8, had come ashore, and a battalion of artillery had been emplaced on nearby Bairiki Atoll. As the Leathernecks gained ground, Shibasaki was killed in the shelling of his command post. At 1706 Shoup buoyed the spirits of Turner and Smith with a message: "Casualties many. Percentage dead not known. Combat efficiency—we are winning."[3] A few hours later Col. Red Mike Edson, the division chief of staff, landed and assumed command on Betio, allowing Shoup to concentrate on leading his regiment.

The Marines renewed their yard-by-yard advance the next day, eliminating a Japanese strong point between Red Beach 1 and Red Beach 2 and, for the first time, inflicting more casualties than they were absorbing. By nightfall they had cleared all except the eastern third of the island. Survivors at the Japanese headquarters sent a final message to Tokyo: "Our weapons have been destroyed and from now on everyone is attempting a final charge."[4] Three times between 7:30 P.M. and 4:00 A.M. the remnants of the garrison dashed forward in futile efforts to break through the Marine lines.

Early on the morning of D+3 a fresh battalion, 3/6, moved up to spearhead the advance. It reached the eastern tip of the island around noon, and at 1:30 Julian Smith, who had transferred his headquarters ashore the previous day, declared Betio secure. In seventy-six hours of intense fighting, 984 Marines and 59 Navy men lost their lives; another 2,072 suffered wounds, and 88 were missing. The casualty rate amounted to 19 percent. Only seventeen Japanese prisoners were taken—all wounded —plus 129 terrified Korean laborers. An estimated 4,690 Japanese had died for their emperor.[5]

Seizure of the Gilberts cost the Navy–Marine Corps team dearly. The casualty figures shocked Americans at home, and supporters of MacArthur—led by the Hearst newspapers—trumpeted their view that direction of the Pacific war should be vested in him. Less partisan observers concluded that too few Marines had been assigned for the assault, artillery should have been positioned on Bairiki from the beginning, planners should never have gambled on crossing the reef in ships' landing craft, and the Corps had an insufficient number of LVTs available for the operation. Closer to the fighting, Howlin' Mad Smith considered the seizure of the Gilberts a tragic error: "Was Tarawa worth it? My answer is an unqualified: No! From the very beginning the decision of the Joint Chiefs to seize Tarawa was a mistake and from their initial mistake grew the terrible drama . . . resulting in these needless casualties. . . . Tarawa should have been bypassed."[6]

The conquered Gilberts provided sites for much-needed airfields. Four new landing strips appeared following the seizure of Tarawa, and by early 1944 B-24s were flying from them in support of further operations against Japan. General Smith asked for at least one Marine air wing (MAW) to support his amphibious corps. His request was denied; the Navy did not want to provide the escort carriers necessary to make a MAW available to the landing force. Thus, Leatherneck flyers remained in the southwest Pacific until Christmas 1943; only then did

Ashore on Tarawa, Marines use all available cover as they push deeper into the Japanese defenses.

squadrons move forward to operate out of airstrips in the Gilberts. The 1st MAW remained in the Solomons until the fall of 1944, when it was deployed to support MacArthur's forces in the liberation of the Philippines.

On 1 January 1944 Lieutenant General Vandegrift replaced Thomas Holcomb, who was approaching the statutory retirement age of sixty-four, as commandant of the Marine Corps. The succession surprised no one; Holcomb had been grooming Vandegrift as his successor since the late 1930s. On stepping down, Holcomb was awarded his fourth star, thereby becoming the first Marine officer to reach the rank of full general. The Corps that Vandegrift inherited numbered more than 390,000 personnel.

In 1944 the Marine Corps's attention was focused on the Pacific. The war there had become the "Navy's war,"

and Leathernecks provided the bulk of the Navy's "army" to fight it. Five divisions had been formed, and four air wings joined in support of the forces in the field. The 1st Marine Division was at Cape Gloucester, the 2nd was recovering and retraining in Hawaii, the 3rd was leaving Bougainville, the 4th was en route from San Diego to the Central Pacific, and the 5th Marine Division was forming at Camp Pendleton. The Corps was still mostly an all-white, male outfit. But traditional barriers had been broken. The Women Marine Corps Reserve, activated in February 1943, reached its authorized strength of one thousand officers and eighteen thousand enlisted personnel in June 1944. And a handful of black Marines, enlisted for the first time in June 1942, served in service and support units.

The Marshall Islands were the next step in the struggle

In an obviously staged photograph, Col. David M. Shoup, who commanded the assault forces on the bloody beaches of Tarawa, sits amid Japanese corpses reading Dale Carnegie's *How to Win Friends and Influence People.* The original caption was simply, "We aren't interested in their friendship."

to wrest the Pacific from the enemy. Located 620 miles northwest of Tarawa, the Marshalls consisted of more than two thousand small islands and thirty-two atolls scattered over an eight-hundred-square-mile area. They had been held by the Japanese since World War I. Navy planners recommended simultaneous assaults on Kwajalein Atoll, site of the Japanese headquarters, and several other of the more important atolls. Intelligence reports indicated that the Japanese were constructing airstrips on the islands and that there was a seaplane base on Jaluit Atoll. Recalling all too well the high casualties at Tarawa, Holland Smith recommended assaulting Maleolap and Wotje first, then taking Kwajalein. Turner disagreed, causing a predictable outburst from Howlin' Mad: "I don't try to run your ships and you'd better by a goddamn sight lay off my troops!"[7] Although Smith's vituperative analysis proved correct, Nimitz settled the dispute—predictably—in favor of his admirals, and Operation Flintlock, the seizure of the Marshalls, followed the original plan.

Intelligence analysts noted that only Kwajalein appeared to be defended heavily, by an estimated eight thousand Japanese; however, of that number barely twenty-two hundred were combat troops. Prior to D-day, Army Air Forces planes from the Gilberts dropped two thousand tons of bombs on the archipelago while Spruance's battleships, cruisers, and destroyers pounded the islands with thirty-six thousand shells, four times the number expended on Tarawa. Carrier aircraft took control of the skies, destroying every Japanese plane in the Marshalls before D-day. Spruance had an impressive array of three hundred ships and more than eighty-four thousand troops at his disposal. Turner's amphibious force—two new command ships, seven old battleships, eleven carriers, seventeen cruisers, seventy-five destroyers and destroyer escorts, ninety-six transports, twenty-seven cargo vessels, five LSDs, and forty-five LSTs—comprised the heaviest amphibious lift in history to that date.

For his landing force Smith had only the newly formed 4th Marine Division commanded by Maj. Gen. Harry Schmidt and the 7th Infantry Division under Maj. Gen. Charles H. Corlett. V Amphibious Corps also included the 22nd Marines and the 106th Infantry Regiment. The 1st and 15th Defense Battalions tagged along to garrison the Marshalls once the operation concluded. The infantry division assigned for the operation to seize the Marshalls came from Hawaii. The 22nd Marines deployed from Samoa, while the rest of the 4th Marine Division sailed from Camp Pendleton.

Intelligence estimates indicated approximately three thousand defenders on Roi and Namur, but the islets were not heavily fortified. Only a single pair of 5.5-inch naval rifles covered the approaches to the beach. For the assault, the Marines had three times as many LVTs as at Tarawa. Prior to D-day, Turner's forces occupied undefended Majuro Atoll, two hundred miles southeast of Kwajalein, for use as an advanced base. The 4th Marine Division would seize Roi and Namur Islands in the northern end of the Marshalls, and the 7th Infantry Division would storm ashore on Kwajalein in the southern end of the chain. Three weeks after the initial phase of the operation, the 22nd Marines and the Army's 106th Infantry would seize Eniwetok Atoll in Operation Catchpole.

On D-day, 31 January 1944, the 25th Marines landed on the islets around Roi and Namur; the 14th Marines followed to provide fire support. On D+1 Col. Louis R. Jones and two battalions of the 23rd Marines assaulted Roi while Col. Franklin A. Hart's 24th Marines came ashore on Namur. H-hour was 11:00 A.M., an unusual hour caused by delays in coordinating the ship-to-shore movement. On Roi, the Leathernecks slaughtered the dazed defenders easily, but on Namur they found the Japanese more determined. The 24th Marines repulsed a banzai attack on the night of D-day, and on the morning of D+2 Smith declared both islets secure. More than 3,563 Japanese had died; Marine casualties numbered 313 killed and 502 wounded.

To the south, soldiers of the 7th Infantry Division landed on Kwajalein on 1 February and completed the conquest of the island four days later. The success of these operations allowed Smith to activate Operation Catchpole, which used the V Corps reserve to take Eniwetok Atoll, 360 miles from Kwajalein in the northwest corner of the Marshalls. On 18 February, after a particularly heavy bombardment, Tactical Group I—the 22nd Marines and the 106th Infantry, commanded by Brig. Gen. Thomas E. "Terrible Tommy" Watson, USMC—stormed ashore to seize the three islands in the atoll.

Once again, a day prior to the landing, Marines had emplaced artillery batteries on nearby islets to support the main landings. On the morning of D+2, the 106th Infantry hit the beach in the face of characteristically obstinate resistance. After two days of bitter fighting, the atoll's defenders were overcome. On 22 February the 22nd Marines seized nearby Parry Island in a fierce battle with a well-dug-in enemy; thirty-four hundred Japanese troops died and sixty-six chose to surrender. Spruance declared the Marshalls secured on 7 March. Operations planners elected to bypass the Japanese bases remaining in the Marshalls. Cut off from resupply and reinforcement by Marine and Navy air attacks, the tiny outposts withered quickly.

MAG-31 began flight operations from the small airstrip on Roi on 15 March, and MAG-13 from Majuro on the twenty-first. That same month, the 4th Marine Base Defense Wing set up headquarters on Kwajalein. MAG-22 arrived from Midway to join the units in the Marshalls. A total of ten fighter and four bomber squadrons flew out of the newly acquired airfields. From the spring of 1944 until the end of the war, Leatherneck aviators dropped more than 6,920 tons of bombs on enemy installations on the four main atolls of the Marshalls. Naval gunfire added another 2,340 tons of ordnance to the devastation. Of a Japanese garrison estimated at more than thirteen thousand troops and laborers, more than half died as a result.

The successes in the Gilberts and Marshalls convinced Nimitz that the Fifth Fleet could continue the amphibious advance across the Central Pacific. Sufficient naval forces were available to invade the Marianas while continuing to support MacArthur in his advance toward the

Leathernecks in the front lines on Eniwetok Island in the Marshalls, 23 February 1944.

Philippines. Nimitz even considered bypassing the Marianas in his eagerness to press on to the home islands of Japan, but the Army—speaking through Hap Arnold—objected. Unexpectedly, considering the ordinary course of Army-Navy wrangling, Admiral King agreed with Arnold on the importance of occupying the islands. Arnold viewed the Marianas as airfields that could be used to launch B-29s against Japan. The new bombers could carry ten thousand pounds of ordnance to targets fifteen hundred miles distant. King regarded the islands as advanced bases for the assault on the enemy's homeland.

Convinced, the JCS turned aside MacArthur's argument for putting the full weight of American resources behind the southwestern Pacific drive and advanced the timetable for the war in the Central Pacific. Washington directed Nimitz to bypass Truk and the Carolines and as-

sault the Marianas—Operation Forager—by late spring. MacArthur's force was increased from six divisions to twelve, leaving Nimitz with four Marine and six Army divisions. Both King and Nimitz believed that a landing in the Marianas would force the Japanese fleet to offer battle for the first time since 1942.

Of the fifteen islands in the Marianas, Nimitz's staff considered only Saipan, Tinian, and Guam of importance. In both size and geography these islands presented a marked contrast to the tiny, flat coral atolls of the Gilberts and Marshalls. Saipan, 14 miles in length, had an area of approximately 72 square miles; Tinian was 50 square miles in area; and Guam, 209. Fields of sugarcane grew on all three, but Saipan and Guam had rugged, wooded interiors—good for defending. As the American drive through the Central Pacific gained momentum, it

Bomb-laden Corsairs of VMF-1 outbound in the Marshalls, 15 March 1944.

stimulated Tokyo to reinforce the Japanese garrison in the Marianas. By the late spring of 1944 there were approximately 30,000 Japanese troops on Saipan; 9,000 on Tinian; and 18,500 on Guam.

Saipan contained the headquarters of the Japanese Central Pacific Fleet, commanded by Adm. Nagumo Chuichi. Subordinate to him was Lt. Gen. Saito Yoshitsugu, commanding the Thirty-first Army. Saito had at his disposal 29,662 defenders, including the Yokosuka Special Naval Landing Force. Although the Japanese were capable of a mobile defense, they elected to wage the traditional fixed defense at the water's edge.

Spruance as fleet commander retained command of the operation to seize the Marianas. Kelly Turner still commanded all amphibious forces under Spruance's Fifth Fleet—a massive armada of more than eight hundred ships and 162,000 soldiers, sailors, and Marines. Holland Smith, newly promoted to lieutenant general, was designated commanding general, expeditionary forces. Tactically, Howlin' Mad functioned as commanding general of the Northern Troops and Landing Force, which consisted of the 2nd Marine Division under

Tommy Watson, Harry Schmidt's 4th Marine Division, and Ralph Smith's 27th Infantry Division. Far to the east, the 77th Infantry Division rested in strategic reserve in Hawaii. Roy S. Geiger commanded the Southern Troops and Landing Force, composed of Allen H. Turnage's 3rd Marine Division, Brig. Gen. Lemuel C. Shepherd Jr.'s 1st Provisional Marine Brigade, and the 9th and 14th Defense Battalions. The last two units were to garrison the Marianas once they had been taken.

Since the campaign to seize the Marshalls, HQMC had reduced the size of a division from 19,965 to 17,465 men; however, it had increased the number of flame-throwers, mortars, and tanks, and added an amphibious tractor battalion. The twelve-man infantry squad disappeared in favor of a thirteen-man variety composed of three four-man fire teams—with one man in each armed with a Browning automatic rifle—and a squad leader.

On 11 June carrier aircraft attacked targets in the Marianas. Two days later the naval gunfire preparation began. Seven fast battleships and eleven destroyers hurled fifteen thousand shells at Saipan; the next day,

A contemporary painting by Hashimoto Yaeji titled *Fierce Fighting of the Lt. Otsu Unit on Saipan* portrays the ferocity of the Pacific war through Japanese eyes.

eight old battleships relieved the modern battleships on the gun line. Despite the fierce pounding by ships and aircraft, enemy coastal artillery survived to strike the landing craft as they hit the beaches. The night before the invasion, Tokyo Rose tormented her listeners in the landing force: "I've got some swell recordings for you, just in from the States. You'd better enjoy them while you can, because tomorrow at oh-six-hundred you're hitting Saipan and we're ready for you. So, while you're still alive, let's listen to . . . "[8]

Two and one-half hours before the actual landing, the 24th Marines and 1/29 conducted a feint off Tanapag harbor. Initially, the ruse worked and an enemy regiment deployed to the area, but the main force was not fooled. At 8:30 A.M. on D-day, 15 June, two divisions of Leathernecks landed abreast on the beaches of Saipan: the 2nd Marine Division on the left, the 6th and 8th Marines in

the assault waves; the 4th Marine Division on the right, the 23rd and 25th Marines leading; with the 27th Infantry Division in reserve. Thirty-four LSTs dropped the assault waves in seven hundred LVTs.

Within twenty minutes more than eight thousand Marines were ashore, even though enemy machine-gun and mortar fire raked the landing force when it came within nine hundred yards of the shoreline. Casualties mounted swiftly—five battalion commanders were hit, and 2/6 went through four commanding officers during the first day. A third of the 8th Marines suffered wounds, and Japanese fire killed or wounded 35 percent of the 6th Marines. By dark, twenty thousand Marines had reached shore, at a cost of 10 percent casualties. Undaunted, General Saito voiced his defiance in a message to Imperial Headquarters in Tokyo: "After dark, this division will launch a night attack in force, and expect to annihilate

Marine dead await burial on Saipan, 17 June 1944.

the enemy at one swoop."[9] But he had only thirty-six tanks and fewer than a thousand infantry available to carry out his boast. They did not succeed.

As anticipated, the Japanese fleet came out in a desperate attempt to repel the invasion. It did not succeed, either. In the Battle of the Philippine Sea, which exuberant American pilots dubbed the "Marianas Turkey Shoot," the Japanese lost three of their nine carriers and more than four hundred aircraft. When Spruance broke off the pursuit after sunset on 21 June, the enemy carrier air arm had been reduced to thirty-five planes. By then, there were seventy-eight thousand Americans on Saipan.

Howlin' Mad Smith sent the 27th Division's 165th Infantry ashore on 17 June, directing the 2nd and 4th Ma-

rine Divisions to move aside to allow the National Guard division to fit between them. All three divisions were to jump off in an attack to the north the following morning. Almost immediately a sag appeared in the center of the advance as the 27th Division—slow and methodical in its tactics—lagged behind the aggressive Leathernecks. Already disappointed in the performance of the 27th Division and its commander, Smith sought the counsel of Admirals Turner and Spruance. Both agreed with him that Ralph Smith should be relieved of command. Howlin' Mad lost no time in so doing. Ralph Smith was transferred to a new command in the European Theater, and outraged senior Army officers vowed that Army troops would never again be placed under Marine Corps command. Surprisingly, Nimitz, Spruance, and Turner failed to support Holland Smith in the brouhaha that followed. The affair poisoned Army–Marine Corps relations for the remainder of the war, leaving a bitter aftertaste that lingered into the Korean conflict.

Meanwhile, the battle for Saipan continued. On 25 June, 3/8 and 1/29 captured Mount Tapotchau after a bitter struggle. During the fighting a bystander overheard "Terrible Tommy" Watson exhorting a subordinate to take the height with the encouraging observation that there was nothing on it except some Japanese with machine guns and mortars. Five days later, the surviving Japanese—military and civilian—poured into the northern end of the island to commit mass suicide. In its final transmission to the embattled garrison, Tokyo continued to ask the impossible: "Because the fate of the Japanese Empire depends on the result of your operations, inspire the spirit of the officers and men and to the very end continue to destroy the enemy gallantly and persistently, thus assuaging the anxiety of our emperor."[10]

The wishful response of the senior surviving officer on Saipan foreshadowed the bitter struggles remaining for Marines as they assaulted yet other hellish beaches: "Have received your honorable words and we are grateful for boundless magnanimity of the imperial favor. By becoming the bulwark of the Pacific with 10,000 deaths, we hope to requite the imperial favor."[11] In a final display of devotion, a handful of Japanese troops, led by officers brandishing samurai swords, launched a banzai attack on 7 July. The fanatical force managed to shatter the lines of two battalions of the 105th Infantry before the artillerymen of 3/10 stopped them in their tracks with fuses for their howitzers cut to explode only fifty-five yards in front of their guns.

At 4:15 on the afternoon of 9 July, Turner declared Saipan secured. More than 28,811 Japanese defenders were known to have perished, and countless other charred bodies remained sealed in caves and bunkers. Only 736 prisoners were taken, and 438 of that number were Korean laborers; U.S. casualties totaled 3,225 dead, 13,099 wounded, and 326 missing. The loss of Saipan, part of Japan's main line of defense, brought down the Japanese government. On 18 July Prime Minister Tojo

Hideki and his cabinet resigned. On 24 November, 110 B-29s flew from Saipan to bomb Tokyo.

On 21 July—"Liberation Day"—Geiger's Southern Force invaded Guam, the southernmost inhabited island in the Marianas. The naval gunfire preparation had begun on 8 July, with six battleships and nine cruisers pummeling the island. Three days later, air strikes added to the destruction of Japanese forces and installations. The landing force faced a total of thirteen thousand Japanese soldiers reinforced by fifty-five hundred sailors. Charging ashore at 8:29 A.M. on D-day, Geiger's Marines met stiff resistance at the water's edge from coastal guns that had survived the preassault bombardment. Although the Japanese launched a spirited counterattack that night, the Leathernecks held their ground and reached their first objective on the morning of D+1.

On the night of 25–26 July, Lt. Col. Robert E. Cushman's 2/9 (attached to the 3rd Marines) beat off no fewer than seven major enemy attacks. More than half of Cushman's command were killed or wounded, and their commander earned a Navy Cross. The commanding officer of Company F, Capt. Louis H. Wilson Jr., a future commandant, earned the Medal of Honor. His citation noted that he and his company fought "fiercely in hand-to-hand encounters . . . in furiously waged battle for approximately ten hours."[12] On 10 August, Geiger declared the island secure. By then, approximately 17,300 Japanese had died. The Americans counted 1,919 dead, 7,122 wounded, and seventy missing.[13]

Two weeks earlier, the 4th Marine Division had invaded Tinian, only three miles southwest of Saipan. The island had been bombarded by air and sea strikes for six weeks before the first Leatherneck stepped ashore. Col. Keishi Ogata, commanding a garrison of forty-seven hundred soldiers and 4,110 sailors, was clearly surprised by the audacious assault. Moving by LVTs directly from Saipan in a shore-to-shore amphibious operation, the Leathernecks landed on 24 July. Although battered by the intense combat to seize Saipan, the 2nd and 4th Marine Divisions took up the assault. The 27th Infantry Division remained on Saipan in reserve. Even though the Japanese attempted to defend the island at the water's edge, Geiger's force quickly established a beachhead. A counterattack at 2:00 A.M. on D+1 failed to dislodge it. By the end of the day, the 2nd Marine Division had joined the forces ashore and overrun the island's airfield with little difficulty. Tinian was declared secure on 1 August: Marine casualties numbered 1,860. Japanese losses were approximately 6,050 dead and 255 captured, with thousands more believed buried in caves and bunkers.

Ten Leathernecks earned Medals of Honor on Saipan, Tinian, and Guam; but only two lived to wear them. An estimated thirty thousand Japanese troops and twenty-two thousand civilians perished in the cauldron of the Marianas. American casualties totaled more than twenty-seven thousand. Three quarters of them were Marines, again causing MacArthur's admirers to clamor for his elevation to command the entire Pacific war. Just as stridently, Nimitz's supporters continued to back the Navy-Marine drive across the Central Pacific.

Meanwhile, the grim contest to seize the southwest Pacific came to its climacteric. In July 1944 Maj. Gen. William H. Rupertus's 1st Marine Division staged two rehearsals at Cape Esperance in preparation for Operation Stalemate II, the seizure of Peleliu, an island in the Palau group 470 miles east of Mindanao in the southern Philippines. Nimitz favored a landing on Peleliu to provide an air base to support the advance across the Central Pacific. Although tropical, Peleliu was not shrouded in jungle foliage. Aerial photographs supplied by naval intelligence showed a cover of scrub brush across the island's limestone ridges. But they did not show the hundreds of caves—some natural, some man-made—dotting the island. Even though the number of defenders exceeded that of the landing force, the American commanders hoped the preinvasion bombardment would kill enough Japanese to even the odds. Unknown to General Rupertus, the enemy planned to allow the attackers to seize the beaches and then counterattack. There would be none of the reckless banzai attacks characteristic of the Guadalcanal campaign. The core of the enemy troops facing the 1st Marine Division was Col. Nakagawa Kunio's 2nd Infantry Regiment, fresh from Manchuria. By the time the amphibious craft entered the waters around Peleliu, Nakagawa had machine guns and mortars sited to cover every avenue of approach to the heart of his defense.

The amphibious force commander, Vice Adm. Theodore S. Wilkinson, elected to bypass the largest island in the Palaus, Babelthuap. Tiny Koror Island, where Pete Ellis had died two decades earlier, was also ignored. Another island in the chain, Angaur, lay nine miles south and four miles west of Peleliu. Believed to be lightly held, it would be secured by the 81st Infantry Division, the landing force reserve for the Peleliu operation. Marine planners conceived a conventional amphibious assault on Peleliu's western shore facing the airfield. Chesty Puller, now commanding the 1st Marines, would strike at the upper fringes of the airfield and then push north. Col. Harold D. "Bucky" Harris would drive with his 5th Marines straight across the airstrip and hold it. Col. Herman Hanneken received orders to land his 7th Marines in the south and overrun that end of Peleliu.

The ten-minute ship-to-shore run proved as perilous as expected. Japanese guns, concealed in caves and protected from the naval bombardment, sank twenty-six LVTs and damaged twice that number. It took until noon for the Marines to establish a firm—albeit shallow and crowded—beachhead. The platoons of Capt. George P. Hunt's Company K, 1st Marines, crossed the beach on the left and faced a coral outcropping honeycombed with caves and alive with defenders. Despite heavy casualties, Hunt's men worked their way behind the fortifications and rushed the outcrop from the rear to seize the crest. Second Lt. William A. Willis slid down a rope and tossed a smoke grenade into the aperture of a 47-mm gun emplacement, blinding the defenders and allowing one of his Marines to fire a rifle grenade into the position. The exploding ammunition drove the defenders out, clothing ablaze, to be gunned down. But the cost to take Peleliu was high; after two days' time Hunt's company had only 78 men left out of its original 235.

Temperatures on the island rose to 100 degrees, and drinking water—often contaminated with rust or oil—ran short. As the fighting continued, critics wondered why Peleliu had not simply been bypassed. By 15 October, when Marine commanders turned the mopping up over to Army units, Peleliu had exacted a cost of 1,794

Leathernecks on Peleliu wait in their fighting holes while combat engineers blast a Japanese cave sometime in late September or early October 1944.

dead Americans—including 1,241 Marines—and another 7,800 wounded. Leathernecks contributed 5,024 of the latter total, along with 117 missing in action. The 1st Marines took the heaviest casualties; in Maj. Raymond G. Davis's 1/1, only 74 men out of almost 500 remained unscathed. Intelligence sources estimated Japanese losses to be more than ten thousand, while Army and Marine infantrymen took only 302 prisoners. Of the eight Medals of Honor won by Marines on Peleliu, six were earned posthumously by recipients who hurled themselves on enemy grenades.[14]

For more than a year Admiral King had been arguing that American forces should bypass the Philippines and seize Formosa as a base of operations against the Japanese homeland. General MacArthur insisted that the United States was politically and morally obligated to liberate the Philippines at the earliest possible moment. In October 1944 the Joint Chiefs of Staff finally shelved plans to invade Formosa and directed MacArthur to complete his campaign to liberate the Philippines. Nimitz was ordered to assault the islands of Iwo Jima and Okinawa in early 1945.

Code-named Operation Detachment, the seizure of Iwo Jima—eight square miles of wasteland in the Bonin Archipelago—would provide a base for P-51 fighters needed to escort B-29s flying from the Marianas to strike the Japanese home islands. Only 660 miles south of Tokyo, Iwo Jima was 625 miles from Saipan. The Japanese had completed two airfields on the island and another strip was under construction. Radar installations on the island provided a two-hour warning for Tokyo when B-29s flew past from the Marianas on the way to bomb targets in the home islands. The Japanese called the foul-smelling islet "sulfur island." No source of fresh water existed, and the Japanese garrison collected rainwater in concrete cisterns to sustain itself; by D-day, the enemy force had been on a half ration of water for months.

A once-important factor that American planners no longer needed to take into account was the Imperial Japanese Navy. When MacArthur's troops landed in the Philippines at the end of September, the enemy fleet had come out in a do-or-die attempt to break up the invasion; and in the four interlocking engagements that comprised the Battle of Leyte Gulf, the greatest naval action ever

A Corsair of the 1st MAW makes a bombing run on Peleliu.

fought, it had died. The remnants of Japanese sea power no longer entered the strategic equation.

When the Americans launched their assault on the Marianas, the Japanese began to strengthen Iwo Jima in earnest. Lt. Gen. Kuribayashi Tadamichi had more than eight months to fortify the island. For the task, Tokyo gave him some twenty-one thousand troops—fourteen thousand Army, seven thousand Navy—plus ample artillery and a tank regiment. Guns ranging from naval rifles to 8-inch coastal artillery—361 in all—covered the approaches from the beaches, and the Japanese constructed hundreds of concrete blockhouses and fortified caves. Kuribayashi planned to destroy the invaders with a positional defense rather than attempting to stop them at the water's edge. He knew that this was a fight to the finish; no reinforcement or relief was possible. Posters adorning the walls of the bunkers and caves exhorted his troops to die in place: "Once the enemy invades the island, every man will resist until the end, making his position his tomb. Every man will do his best to kill ten enemy soldiers."[15]

Most of Kuribayashi's senior officers seem to have been ignorant of the Japanese defeat at the Battle of Leyte Gulf and continued to believe that the Navy would somehow come to their rescue once the assault on Iwo Jima began. On 13 February 1945 a Japanese patrol plane spotted the American task force as it left Saipan. On Iwo Jima, no hysteria followed the report. Most of the defenders knew that the Americans would arrive eventually. But when the news of the sighting reached Tokyo, a mob of Japanese schoolboys toppled Commodore Perry's statue to the ground in a frenzy of anti-Americanism.

Overall responsibility for the invasion was vested in Admiral Spruance, commanding the Fifth Fleet. Kelly Turner, recently promoted to vice admiral, remained at the head of the amphibious forces. In an apparent sop to his Army critics, Holland Smith became commanding general, Fleet Marine Force, Pacific, with no tactical control over the landing force. Maj. Gen. Harry Schmidt commanded V Amphibious Corps, consisting of Graves B. Erskine's 3rd Marine Division, Clifton B. Cates's 4th Marine Division, and Keller E. Rockey's 5th Marine Division. Each infantry battalion had an assault platoon armed with rockets, flamethrowers, and demolition charges. The tank battalions had additional flame tanks. Training prior to D-day stressed the assault of fortified positions. Howlin' Mad Smith stunned his commanders and staff with a gloomy estimate of exorbitant casualties: before the battle ended, more than fifteen thousand Americans would lose their lives. Present when Smith made his pessimistic prediction, Secretary of the Navy James V. Forrestal exclaimed that "Iwo Jima, like Tarawa, leaves us very little choice except to take it by force of arms, by character, and courage."[16]

Bombers from Saipan and the guns of the fleet blasted Iwo Jima for an unprecedented seventy-four days—but the immediate pre-D-day shelling lasted only three days. Once again, Howlin' Mad Smith scored the Navy: "not enough!" He wanted ten days. Task Force 58—which included eight Leatherneck squadrons of Corsairs—steamed to within sixty miles of the Japanese homeland and bombed Tokyo, destroying aircraft that might interfere with the landing. When Smith and fellow critics charged that the Navy showed more interest in upstaging the Army Air Forces' B-29 raids on Japan than in continuing to support the amphibious drive, Navy officers countered that the attacks diverted attention from the forthcoming assault.

Nevertheless, the D-day shelling was the heaviest of the Pacific war. Eighty-five minutes of uninterrupted pounding was followed by fighter-bomber runs from Task Force 58, then another intense round of bombardment from the ships offshore. Leatherneck aviators from VMO-4 and VMO-5 flew from makeshift platforms mounted on the LSTs and helped direct the shelling. The Japanese defenders sustained few casualties because they had burrowed deep underground, but they suffered. A survivor recalled the horror of the bombardment for his captors: "For two days we cowered like rats, trying to dig ourselves deeper into the acrid volcanic dust and ash of Iwo Jima. Never have I felt so helpless, so puny, as I did during those two days. There was nothing we could do, there was no way in which we could strike back."

As his Marines stormed the most terrible beaches in the Corps's history, Smith's prediction of immense casualties—one out of every four assault troops—was

borne out. In a letter to Vandegrift, Smith shared his frustrations and uneasiness on the eve of the landing:

> On two separate occasions I protested that naval gunfire is insufficient, with the result that it has been increased to some extent, but not enough, in my opinion, to suffice. I can only go so far. We have done all we can to get ready . . . and I believe it will be successful, but the thought of the probable casualties causes me extreme unhappiness . . . would to God that something might happen to cancel the operation altogether.[17]

At 3:30 A.M. on 19 February, Leathernecks on the ships of the amphibious force ate what had become the traditional meal before a landing—steak and eggs. Beginning at 6:45 battleships and cruisers blasted the landing beaches. Five rocket ships heaped more than five tons of ordnance on the Motoyama Plateau. Kuribayashi signaled his superiors that "the violence of the enemy's bombardment is far beyond description."[18] Most observers offshore concluded that few Japanese could survive the flaming death. "Nobody can live through this," correspondent Robert Sherrod reflected hopefully, "but I know better."[19] The defenders huddled in caves, bunkers, and concrete pillboxes and waited. An awesome armada of death—495 ships of the Fifth Fleet's amphibious force—lay offshore. At 8:30 the first assault wave left the line of departure.

At 9:02 A.M. sixty-nine LVTs—twenty Marines in each—touched down on the southern end of the island: the 5th Marine Division on Green and Red Beaches, the 28th Marines on the left and the 27th Marines on the right; the 4th Marine Division on Yellow and Blue Beaches, the 23rd Marines on the left and the 25th Marines on the right. The 3rd Marine Division remained offshore as a floating reserve. The 4th Marine Division would drive up the eastern side of Iwo Jima, and the 5th Marine Division would assault up the western flank of V Amphibious Corps's front. There were 482 amtracs in the initial assault, enough to transport eight battalions of infantry. In ten waves at five-minute intervals, nine thousand Marines rushed ashore. The assault divisions had as their initial objectives the enemy airfields and Mount Suribachi—a 556-foot-high extinct volcano at the island's southern tip. Having taken them, they were to turn and attack in line to the north along the island's steep

The massive assault on Iwo Jima began on 19 February 1945 with two divisions storming ashore. This photograph shows lines of landing craft approaching the invasion beaches with Mount Suribachi in the background.

central plateau to its rocky northern beaches, at which the conquest of the island would be complete.

Guns and mortars opened up as the Leathernecks came ashore. Horrified correspondents observed human body parts scattered about in the filthy volcanic ash. Sherrod described the scene as "a beachhead in hell."[20] Casualties in the first assault battalions were high. Medical personnel attempted to treat the wounded as close to the front as possible. By the time the island was declared secure, twenty-three doctors and 827 corpsmen lay dead on the volcanic ash of Iwo Jima.

Manila John Basilone, winner of the Medal of Honor at Guadalcanal, rallied his machine-gun platoon in 1/27 with characteristic aggressiveness: "Come on, you guys, we got to get these guns off the beach!"[21] That night, Basilone died a warrior's death, struck down by a mortar shell that exploded behind him. For his heroism on

Iwo Jima, he was posthumously awarded the Navy Cross.

By 6:00 P.M. the landing force had carved out a small beachhead four thousand yards wide and less than eleven hundred yards deep in the face of the most stubborn Japanese resistance encountered in the war. But more than thirty thousand Marines—six infantry regiments and six artillery battalions—had made it ashore. Late that afternoon, Schmidt and Turner agreed to draw on the force reserve and land most of the 3rd Marine Division. After that, only the 3rd Marines remained in reserve. As the outcome appeared in doubt, Schmidt asked Turner to release that regiment as well. The amphibious task force commander refused, replying rather tartly that there were sufficient Marines ashore already. Critics later charged that Turner's decision increased the casualties among the landing force. Almost six hundred Leathernecks lay dead or dying, with the survivors clinging to the beachhead.

The Assault on Iwo Jima, 19 February 1945

Instead of delivering the expected counterattack under cover of darkness, however, the Japanese stayed in their caves and bunkers while mortar and artillery shells rained on the narrow beaches throughout the endless night.

On D+1 the 28th Marines under Col. Harry B. Liversedge fought their way, inch by inch, up Mount Suribachi after an intense naval bombardment had peppered its slopes. An estimated sixteen hundred Japanese defenders had burrowed into Suribachi's sides, concealed in well-camouflaged positions. Liversedge's battalions gained only two hundred yards in that first bloody day. It took four days of bitter fighting to take the height and overrun the adjacent airfield. Hearing Japanese voices

coming from fissures in the volcanic rock, Leathernecks poured gasoline into the openings and turned the caves and hideouts into flaming tombs. By then, the combat efficiency of the regiment had declined to less than 75 percent.

At 10:15 A.M. on 23 February, the 28th Marines took the crest and raised a small flag. Watching from offshore, Secretary of the Navy James V. Forrestal turned to Smith and remarked that "the raising of the flag on Suribachi means that there will be a Marine Corps for the next five hundred years."[22] Two hours later, a larger flag was found and raised on the summit. An Associated Press photographer, Joe Rosenthal, captured the event in a pic-

Men of the 5th Marine Division cross the black sand beach of Iwo Jima. Mount Suribachi looms to their left.

ture that has come to symbolize the valor of the Corps. Sadly, half of the Leathernecks who raised the famous flag would not survive the battle for Iwo Jima. The sight of the Stars and Stripes flying over Suribachi disturbed the Japanese defenders. The height was supposed to have been held for two weeks; instead, it had fallen in only three days. But it had cost the 28th Marines 519 men.

By 1 March the 23rd Marines had been shattered as a combat unit and were replaced by the 24th Marines. Elements of the landing force continued to root out pockets of enemy resistance. Casualties remained high. In one battalion of the 25th Marines, only 150 men remained uninjured out of more than 900 who began the invasion. Of the twenty-four assault battalion commanders, nineteen became casualties. By the end of the second week

on Iwo Jima, V Amphibious Corps had sustained more than thirteen thousand casualties, including three thousand dead.

On 3 March the first U.S. aircraft landed on one of the captured airfields—refurbished and repaired by a Seabee battalion. The Navy C-47 brought in medical supplies and mail and departed with litters of critically wounded Leathernecks. A day later, the first crippled B-29 landed after a bombing run to Tokyo. By then, the surviving Japanese were backed into enclaves on the northern coast. On 7 March units of the 3rd Marine Division conducted a predawn attack and effectively wiped out the Japanese tank regiment. By D+19 the Leathernecks finally held the entire plateau. Kuribayashi sent his last message to Tokyo on 16 March: "I humbly apologize to

This 4th Marine Division Leatherneck never made it off the beach.

His Majesty that I have failed to live up to expectations. Bullets are gone and water exhausted. Permit me to say farewell."[23] His body was never found.

On 19 March two Japanese bombs struck the carrier *Franklin*. Included among the ship's 772 dead were sixty-five Marines. The blasts knocked two Marine squadrons, VMF-214 and VMF-452, out of the war. The carrier *Wasp* departed the area around the same time, leaving only four squadrons of Leatherneck fighters on the *Bennington* and the *Bunker Hill*.

Although the seizure of Iwo Jima was supposed to take no more than four days, it could not be declared secure until 26 March. The final enemy cave was not snuffed out until D+34. An Army regiment came ashore to mop up. More than twenty-two thousand Japanese soldiers had died; fewer than three hundred survived the assault. In all, 71,245 Marines landed at Iwo Jima; 5,931 of them were killed and another 17,372 were wounded. There was one Leatherneck casualty for every dead Japanese soldier; one out of every three Leathernecks was wounded or killed. Howlin' Mad Smith, not easily moved, stood in awe of the toll: "Iwo Jima was the most savage and the most costly battle in the history of the Marine Corps. Indeed, it has few parallels in military annals."[24] Nimitz added his postscript to the epic assault: "Uncommon valor was a common virtue."[25] Of the 82 Marines who earned Medals of Honor in World War II, 22 did so on Iwo Jima. Among them was PFC Jacklyn H. Lucas, 1st Battalion, 26th Marines, the youngest Leatherneck—only six days over seventeen years old—to win the nation's highest award for valor. At the dedication of his division's cemetery, General Erskine spoke of the human cost to take Iwo Jima: "Victory was never in doubt, its cost was. What was in doubt, in all our minds, was whether there would be any of us left to dedicate our cemetery at the end, or whether the last Marine would be knocking out the last Japanese gunner."[26]

The next order of business was Okinawa. Spruance remained in overall command; Turner continued to head the amphibious force. Code-named Operation Iceberg, the invasion would be the largest of the Pacific war: more than thirteen hundred ships of all types and a landing force of 182,112 men—including 81,165 Marines. Because for the first time in the Central Pacific drive Army

Associated Press photographer Joe Rosenthal captured five Marines and a Navy hospital corpsman raising an American flag atop Mount Suribachi on 23 February 1945 in the most famous photograph ever taken of Marines. The men are *(from left to right)* PFC Ira H. Hayes, PFC Franklin R. Sousley, Sgt. Michael Strank, Pharmacist's Mate 2/C John H. Bradley, PFC Rene A. Cagnon, and Cpl. Harlan H. Block. Sousley, Strank, and Block were killed in action before the island was secured.

The invasion beach on Iwo Jima on the same day as the flag-raising seen from the 4th Marine Division's command post.

troops outnumbered Marines, an Army officer was assigned to command the landing force. Lt. Gen. Simon Bolivar Buckner's Tenth Army consisted of two corps: Maj. Gen. John R. Hodge's XXIV Corps (7th, 77th, and 96th Infantry Divisions); and Maj. Gen. Keller E. Rockey's III Amphibious Corps (1st and 6th Marine Divisions). The 1st Marine Division had recovered from Peleliu, and the 6th Marine Division, although newly formed, contained a core of veterans from earlier Pacific campaigns. The 2nd Marine Division, rested and reequipped from the rigors of the Marianas campaign, provided the demonstration force, while the 27th Infantry Division formed the reserve. Four air groups joined in the formation of a Marine tactical air force commanded by Maj. Gen. Francis P. Mulcahy. Another eight squadrons of Marine aviators flew from the carriers *Bunker Hill, Bennington, Essex,* and *Wasp.*

Okinawa, which lies in the center of the Ryukyus, an island chain stretching for more than 790 miles between Japan and Formosa, offered the amphibians two deep-water bays for the landings and a level interior with at least two large airfields. Only 325 miles from Kyushu, the southernmost of the Japanese home islands, Okinawa measures sixty miles in length and varies in width between two and eighteen miles. One of the forty-seven prefectures of Japan, the island was the home of more than 450,000 people, mostly farmers.

On 26 March 1945 the preinvasion bombardment began. Rear Adm. Morton L. Deyo's Task Force 54 shrouded Okinawa in a blanket of fire from ten battleships, seven heavy cruisers, three light cruisers, and thirty-two destroyers and destroyer escorts. On the same day, two regiments from the Army's 77th Infantry Division and a Leatherneck reconnaissance battalion landed on the five small islands of the Kerama group, fifteen miles west of Okinawa. This minor adjunct to the main assault to the north served to screen Turner's southern flank and provided a protected anchorage for Spruance's Fifth Fleet.

On 1 April—both Easter Sunday and April Fool's Day—Buckner's landing force stormed ashore, the two corps landing abreast over the Hagushi beaches on the west coast of Okinawa between Yontan and Kadena. The assault was preceded by an attack by five hundred carrier aircraft that strafed and napalmed the landing sites. Soldiers took the southern beaches while Marines seized the northern beaches. XXIV Corps then wheeled to the south, III Amphibious Corps to the north. The 2nd Marine Division feinted off the southern coast, leading the Japanese to believe that another landing might take place there. Then the veterans of Saipan returned to their ships to become a floating reserve for the remainder of the campaign.

Flawlessly executed, the landing split the island in two. By the evening of L-day more than fifty thousand Americans were holding a beachhead three miles wide and more than a mile deep. Miraculously, the landing force suffered only twenty-eight men killed and another twenty-seven missing. Lt. Gen. Ushijima Mitsuru, the Japanese commander, hoped to confront the enemy in the south in a final, desperate bid to delay or prevent the impending invasion of the home islands. The slogan he had coined for his Thirty-second Army appeared everywhere on the walls of bunkers and barracks: "One plane for every warship. One boat for every ship. One man for every ten enemy. One man for every tank."[27]

Ushijima's army consisted of two divisions, the 24th and the 62nd, plus the 44th Independent Brigade, a tank regiment, and artillery units. Two shipping engineer regiments, service units, and the Boeitai—a sort of Okinawan home guard—rounded out his command. Concentrated in the rocky southern third of the island was Rear Adm. Ota Minoru's naval base force. Total Japanese troop strength in the Ryukyus was estimated at more than 155,000 men.

Soldiers and Marines swept aside the defenders without difficulty during the early stages of Operation Iceberg. XXIV Corps took Kadena on 2 April and its commanders declared the airstrip ready to receive planes that

The Campaign for Okinawa, April–June 1945

night. General Mulcahy established a tactical air command post ashore the same day. Two days later, Maj. Gen. Pedro del Valle's 1st Marine Division cut across the narrow island to the east coast. On 14 April the 4th Marines attacked the Yaetake hill mass. Cpl. Richard E. Bush, a squad leader, earned a Medal of Honor in the bitter fighting on the Motobu Peninsula—and lived to wear it. His citation read:

Rallying his men forward with indomitable determination, Corporal Bush boldly defied the slashing fury of concentrated Japanese artillery fire pouring down from the gun-studded mountain fortress to lead his squad up the face of the rock precipice, sweep over the ridge, and drive the defending troops from their deeply entrenched position . . . he fought relentlessly in the forefront of the action until seriously wounded and evacuated with others under protecting rocks. Although prostrate under medical care when a Japanese hand grenade landed in the midst of the group . . . [he] unhesitatingly pulled the deadly missile to himself and absorbed the shattering violence of the exploding charge in his own body.[28]

Meanwhile, on 4 April, XXIV Corps struck to the south against stiffening resistance. Two days later, in a

Smoke billows from the mouth of an enemy-occupied cave into which Marines have just tossed an explosive charge during the contest for Okinawa.

hopeless attempt to disrupt the assault, Tokyo dispatched the remnants of the Japanese fleet. Vice Adm. Ito Seiichi steamed south in the superbattleship *Yamato* in company with nine other warships on a suicidal mission to break up the invasion. On 7 April, aircraft from Vice Adm. Marc A. Mitscher's Task Force 58 spotted the Japanese force and attacked it, sinking a cruiser and four destroyers. The mighty *Yamato* capsized after being hit by at least sixteen bombs and torpedoes. Less than a tenth of her crew of 2,769 survived the last sortie of the Imperial Japanese Navy.

On the day the *Yamato* sailed, Japanese suicide planes appeared in the skies off Okinawa. An estimated 699 aircraft attacked the invasion force that day—including 355 kamikazes. Two American destroyers, a destroyer escort, and two cargo ships went down. Twelve other vessels suffered damage. The kamikaze raids continued throughout the campaign; for the first time in an amphibious operation, the Navy lost more men killed in action than the Marines or the Army.

On land, the bloody contest continued. In the north,

Maj. Gen. Lemuel C. Shepherd Jr.'s 6th Marine Division cleared the Motobu Peninsula. By 12 April—the day of President Roosevelt's death—the advance in the south had ground to a halt. The addition of a third infantry division to the two already in the line failed to break the stalemate. On 19 April the largest single artillery concentration of the Pacific war took place. XXIV Corps amassed 324 guns and fired nineteen thousand shells in an attempt to breach the Japanese defenses—in vain. Leatherneck commanders urged Buckner to land the 2nd Marine Division behind the Japanese line of resistance in an amphibious end-run. General Vandegrift, who was visiting the island on an inspection tour, added his support to the idea. Buckner rejected it nonetheless. His decision widened the Army–Marine Corps rift and exacerbated the tensions generated in the Marianas the year before.

Opting for a battle of attrition, Buckner ordered the 6th Marine Division to join III Amphibious Corps in the south. Both corps struck toward Naha on 11 May against formidable resistance. On the thirteenth, Leathernecks

A flame-throwing tank of the 6th Marine Division douses a Japanese position on Shuri Ridge.

began thrusting their way up the deadly saddle they called Sugar Loaf. By 23 May the 6th Marine Division had reached the outskirts of Naha, the island's most populous city; a week later, the 1st Marine Division stormed Shuri Ridge and the ruins of medieval Shuri Castle. Most of Ushijima's troops retreated to the south, joined by hordes of terrified civilians desperately fleeing the falling bombs and shells.

The struggle had shifted in favor of the attackers by the end of May. By then, the Japanese had lost an estimated sixty-two thousand troops. The early summer rains that began on the twenty-first turned roads into oozy seas of muck. Filthy water and slime jammed weapons, contaminated wounds, and fouled clothing and food. On 4 June the 6th Marine Division sealed off the base of the Oroku Peninsula. The 22nd Marines assaulted the promontory a day later while the 4th Marines executed a skillful shore-to-shore amphibious movement. On the same day, MAG-14 arrived to bring the number of Leatherneck aircraft ashore to more than seven hundred. Maj. Gen. Louis E. Woods relieved Mulcahy as commanding general, 2nd

Two Leathernecks from the 29th Marines share their fighting hole and ponchos with an Okinawan war orphan.

Units of the 6th Marine Division advance on Naha, Okinawa's provincial capital, early in June 1945.

MAW. On 14 June units of the 6th Marine Division broke into Oroku village and destroyed the naval defense force. Admiral Ota provided Tokyo with a typical final message: "The naval base force is dying gloriously!"[29]

By 17 June the attacking Americans had shattered Ushijima's army. Discipline gone, Japanese soldiers fought among themselves or turned on the civilian populace in an orgy of pillage and rape. The slippage in Japanese morale was also evident in the seventy-four hundred surrenders 6 percent of the island's garrison. One enemy officer approached the lines of the 7th Infantry Division dressed only in a loincloth and presented his sword. Consulting two dictionaries—one, English-Japanese, the other, Japanese-English—he pronounced solemnly to his captors: "Me vanquished, miserable, dishonorable, depraved."[30]

On 18 June an exploding Japanese shell sent a fragment of coral into General Buckner, killing the landing force commander as he observed an assault by the 8th Marines—brought hurriedly from the 2nd Marine Division in the Marianas. Command passed to Maj. Gen. Roy S. Geiger, USMC, but only for as long as it took the Army to act. In what must have been the most expeditious personnel action of the war, Army chief of staff George C. Marshall ordered Lt. Gen. Joseph H. "Vinegar Joe" Stilwell of China fame to Okinawa as a replacement for Buckner. Obviously, the Army's leaders had not forgotten the Smith versus Smith imbroglio at Saipan.

Still in command on 21 June, Geiger announced that all resistance on Okinawa had ceased; on the next day, Ushijima committed seppuku. By then, MAG-31 was operating out of Yontan and MAG-33 from Kadena. MAG-22 established its headquarters at Ie Shima and MAG-14 arrived from the Philippines. Thirty-two squadrons of Marine aviators eventually flew in support of the battle for Okinawa.

An estimated 107,539 Japanese and Okinawans died during the eighty-two days of intense combat. The U.S. Navy lost 36 ships, and another 243 were damaged—exceeding the losses at Pearl Harbor. Almost five thousand sailors died—more than the number of soldiers or Marines. More than 3,200 Marines paid the supreme price for victory; another 11,677 Marines wounded added to the grisly total. Altogether, the Tenth Army suffered 65,631 casualties, making Okinawa the most costly campaign of the Pacific war.

Even before the landings on Okinawa, the Joint Chiefs had set plans in motion for the invasion of the Japanese home islands. Operation Olympic, the landing on Kyushu, was scheduled for 1 November 1945; three Marine divisions and three air wings would join ten Army divisions in the attack. Operation Coronet, the landing on Honshu, would take place in March 1946; eleven Army divisions and III Amphibious Corps would provide the assault forces. Even as the guns fell silent on Okinawa, B-29s from island bases were flying twelve hundred sorties a week to turn Japan's wood-and-paper cities into charcoal.

On 26 July the Allies presented the Japanese government with the Potsdam Declaration, calling for unconditional surrender. As American leaders considered their options, all were painfully cognizant of the fact that an estimated 4.7 million Japanese remained under arms, including 1.5 million stationed in the home islands. U.S. casualties in the planned invasion of Japan were expected to be a minimum of one hundred thousand men. On 16 July the first test of an atomic bomb took place at Alamogordo, New Mexico. On 6 August a B-29 flying from Tinian dropped a duplicate bomb on Hiroshima; two days later, the Soviet Union declared war on Japan. A second atomic bomb obliterated Nagasaki on 9 August, and a day later the Japanese government sued for peace. On 15 August the most costly war in the history of the U.S. Marine Corps came to an end.

When the Allied commanders gathered on the deck of the battleship *Missouri* in Tokyo Bay on 2 September, Lieutenant General Geiger represented the thousands of Leathernecks who had paid for the surrender ceremony with their sweat and blood; in a sop to Army-Navy rivalry, Nimitz did not invite Howlin' Mad Smith to the ceremony. Of the almost 500,000 Americans who had worn forest green or jungle camouflage since 7 December 1941, half were serving in the Pacific or in the ships of the fleet on V-J Day. World War II cost the Marine Corps 19,733 dead and 67,207 wounded. Of the 2,270 Marines captured by the Japanese, 1,756 survived.[31] The naval war in the Pacific brilliantly vindicated the dedicated planning by senior Leatherneck officers during the interwar years, many of whom foresaw both war with Japan and a lengthy amphibious campaign as a result.

12

The Unification Struggle and Korea, 1945–1953

At the end of World War II the Marine Corps numbered more than 485,000 men and women. Six divisions and five air wings had served in the Pacific against Japan. After V-J Day, the 1st and 6th Divisions deployed to China to disarm Japanese garrisons. A skeletal 2nd Division took up residence at Camp Lejeune as part of the peacetime establishment. The remaining divisions cased their colors. By the summer of 1946 the number of Marines on active duty had been reduced to 155,000. The Corps proposed to stabilize its strength at seven to eight thousand officers and one hundred thousand NCOs and men, approximately a third of whom would form a Fleet Marine Force (FMF) of two divisions and two air wings.[1]

But just as the Corps was reveling in its greatest triumph, it unexpectedly found itself fighting for its life—not on foreign soil but in the halls of Congress. The conflict arose during the unification struggle brought about by plans made by the Army's leaders to reorganize the American armed forces. Enthusiastically endorsed by President Harry S. Truman, these plans called for the transformation of the Air Force, then a branch of the Army, into a separate service; the creation of an umbrella department of defense, with its own secretary, to administer the entire military establishment; and the reduction of the Marine Corps to a force of light infantry units no larger than a regiment, without an air component and with a maximum strength of sixty thousand men. The chief of naval operations, Adm. Chester W. Nimitz, declared indignantly that the adoption of this program would "eliminate the Marine Corps as an effective combat force."[2]

The Army's plan formed the substance of a Senate bill (S. 2044) introduced in January 1946. Well aware of what was coming, General Vandegrift had already appointed a strategy board headed by Brig. Gens. Merritt A. Edson and Gerald C. Thomas to map out the Corps's legislative goals and defenses. They in turn activated two groups of mid-ranking officers to monitor political developments, lobby sympathetic congressmen and journalists, and draft position papers. Among those so tasked were two of the Corps's brightest young men: Lt. Col. Victor H. Krulak—better known as "Brute," the nickname he had received as the shortest member of the Naval Academy class of 1934—and Lt. Col. Merrill B. Twining. Both men were destined for three stars and consideration for commandant.

On 6 May 1946 Vandegrift appeared before the Senate Naval Affairs Committee to testify on S. 2044. In a highly publicized statement drafted by Krulak and Twining, he declared that the passage of the bill would "in all probability spell extinction for the Marine Corps." Despite the Corps's 170 years of service, however, and all that should have counted for, the commandant urged Congress to decide its fate purely on the grounds of military effectiveness. "We have pride in ourselves and our past," he continued, "but we do not rest our case on any presumed ground of gratitude owing us from the nation. The bended knee is not a tradition of our Corps."[3]

Vandegrift's "bended knee speech" demolished S. 2044. Congress adjourned without acting on the unification question.

When the Eightieth Congress convened in January 1947, the administration reentered the fray with a bill that was, from the Corps's standpoint, no improvement over its predecessor. The president also issued a gag order prohibiting officers from testifying against the measure. Edson thereupon requested immediate retirement in order to be able to tell Congress what he thought of the proposed legislation—which he did, in no uncertain terms. By then, Vandegrift's political action team had concluded that the only way to safeguard the Corps's identity would be to have its functions prescribed by law. The highly effective opposition this group orchestrated to the new bill forced the administration reluctantly to conclude that unification could not be accomplished over the Corps's objections. Yet another bill was therefore introduced, this time including a definition of the armed services' roles and responsibilities. The section relating to the Marine Corps was written largely by Krulak, Twining, and Lt. Col. James C. Hittle. It defined the Corps as a separate service—not a branch of the Navy—within the Navy Department, with the principal responsibility for developing amphibious doctrine and equipment and the primary mission of providing "fleet Marine forces of combined arms, together with supporting arms components, for service with the fleet in the seizure or defense of advanced naval bases and for the conduct of . . . land operations . . . essential to . . . a naval campaign."[4] This legislation passed into law as the National Security Act of 1947. The Corps had achieved a dazzling victory in the fiercest of the many bureaucratic battles in its long history.

One of the arguments that had been advanced for reducing the Corps to light infantry was that the advent of atomic weapons had rendered amphibious assaults obsolete; an enemy with such weapons would vaporize the attackers in their transports before they even reached the beaches. This prospect was also, and understandably, of concern to the Corps. After witnessing the Bikini A-bomb tests in July 1946, Lt. Gen. Roy S. Geiger, commanding general, Fleet Marine Force–Pacific, wrote Vandegrift expressing his opinion "that a complete re-view and study of our concept of amphibious operations will have to be made."[5]

The commandant responded by convening a special board headed by Lt. Gen. Lemuel C. Shepherd Jr. to investigate the future of amphibious warfare in the atomic age. The board's report, submitted on 16 December 1946, conceded that conventional landings would indeed be impossible against an enemy armed with nuclear weapons. Unlike the Corps's critics, however, the board did not conclude that this finding signaled the end of amphibious operations. Instead, it proposed developing means to make unconventional landings that would deprive the enemy of massed targets for atomic bombs until the attackers were in such close contact that the defenders could not use them without obliterating their own troops as well. The most promising of such means seemed to be transport seaplanes and, especially, helicopters. As the Corps had none of the latter, the board recommended the immediate organization of an experimental squadron. Vandegrift approved the report three days after receiving it.

Follow-up studies determined that the Corps should concentrate on helicopters, and the Marine Helicopter Experimental Squadron (HMX-1) was activated at Quantico in December 1947. Meanwhile, in a ferment reminiscent of that of 1933–34, officers assigned to the Marine Corps schools began to formulate a "New Concept" that would later become known as "vertical envelopment." The first simulated helicopter assault was made at Camp Lejeune in May 1948. Although only five two-passenger helicopters were available to carry sixty-six Marines ashore from the escort carrier *Palau,* the results buoyed the optimism of the operation's planners. Negotiations were opened with manufacturers for the production of a craft capable of transporting fifteen to twenty combat-loaded Marines for distances of up to three hundred miles. In November the Quantico schools issued a landmark manual in the Amphibious Operations series titled *Employment of Helicopters (Tentative)—PHIB 31.* Like the *Tentative Landing Operations Manual* of the preceding generation, it provided the starting point for the development of a doctrine in which the Corps saw the key to its future.[6]

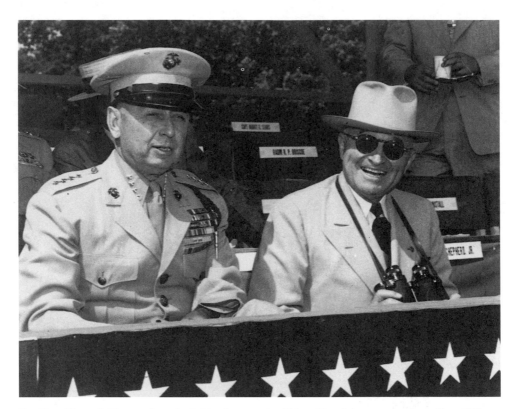

President Harry S. Truman inscribed this photograph of himself and the commandant, Gen. Clifton B. Cates, "with kindest regards," but the chief executive was outraged when Cates and other senior officers urged Marine Corps supporters in Congress to thwart Truman's plans to emasculate the smaller of the naval services.

While these events were in progress, a number of changes occurred in the Corps. As Vandegrift approached retirement in late 1947, the choice of his successor quickly narrowed to Cliff Cates and Lem Shepherd. Both had fought at Belleau Wood and commanded divisions in the war against Japan. Deeming their qualifications equal, Truman picked Cates, who was three years older and slightly senior in date of rank. The president announced his decision in an interview with both men, promising Shepherd that "you . . . will have your chance next time"; and he proved as good as his word.[7]

Two significant changes in the Corps's personnel composition were mandated during Cates's first year as commandant. The passage of the Women's Armed Forces Integration Act on 12 June 1948 required all the services to accept women into their regular as well as reserve components. A month later, a presidential order abolished racial segregation throughout the military. Neither ruling was welcomed by traditionalists within the

Corps, and neither had much immediate effect. There were only fifteen hundred African American Marines on active duty (serving in all-black service or security companies or performing stewards' duties), and women regulars were limited to a strength of eleven hundred and restricted to chair-borne duty.[8]

In the course of the year it became apparent that despite the Corps's success in defining the terms of the National Security Act of 1947, the Truman administration's determination to slash the defense budget had put the FMF at peril. The conflict this foreboded crystallized following the appointment of Louis A. Johnson as secretary of defense on 28 March 1949. A personal friend of President Truman, Johnson viewed the sea services as expensive anachronisms. As he explained to an appalled admiral, "There's no reason for having a Navy and Marine Corps. . . . We'll never have any more amphibious operations. That does away with the Marine Corps. And the Air Force can do anything the Navy can do nowadays, so that does away with the Navy."[9] Johnson's views were similar to those of the chairman of the Joint Chiefs of Staff, General of the Army Omar N. Bradley, who informed the House Armed Services Committee in October: "I am wondering whether we shall ever have another large-scale amphibious operation. Frankly, the atomic bomb, properly delivered, almost precludes such a possibility."[10]

Under Cates's leadership the Corps struggled to resist the erosion of its strength and status. Recognizing that in itself the National Security Act provided adequate protection for neither, HQMC sought to underpin it by securing the passage of two additional acts, the most important of which was to make the commandant a member of the Joint Chiefs of Staff. In this position he would have direct access to the secretary of defense and an immediate influence on the formulation of strategic and budgetary policy. The second was to prescribe the strength of the FMF at two divisions, each consisting of six battalion landing teams (BLTs), and two air wings, each of twelve squadrons. The Corps succeeded in marshaling considerable congressional and public support for both aims. In January 1950 bills were introduced to give the commandant a seat on the Joint Chiefs and to guarantee the Corps manpower to maintain the FMF at the desired level. Befuddled by four years of fratricide among the armed forces, Congress failed to take action on either proposal.

In the meantime, Secretary Johnson had been busy. In 1948 the FMF had numbered 35,086 men organized into eleven BLTs and twenty-three air squadrons. Johnson's first Defense Department budget, for Fiscal Year 1950 (beginning in July 1949), allocated 29,415 men to the FMF, compelling General Cates to reduce the number of BLTs to eight. That same year the secretary decommissioned eleven of the FMF's twenty-three air squadrons. In testimony to Congress in October, Cates asserted: "It appears . . . that the power of the budget, the power of coordination, and the power of strategic direction . . . have been used to destroy the operating forces of the Marine Corps."[11] But worse was to follow. In early June 1950 Secretary Johnson announced that the budget for Fiscal Year 1951 would cut the FMF to 23,952 men in six BLTs and twelve squadrons. The announced retrenchment meant a drop in the enlisted ranks from 78,715 men to 67,025. Three weeks later, on 25 June 1950, eight divisions of the Communist North Korean People's Army, spearheaded by 150 Soviet-made T-34 tanks, crossed the thirty-eighth parallel and invaded South Korea. At that time, HQMC counted only 74,279 Marines on the rolls.

The ill-equipped Republic of Korea (ROK) forces, lacking armor and heavy artillery, proved no match for the attackers. Seoul, the country's capital, fell on 28 June. By that date President Truman had decided that although the United States had no treaty obligation to defend South Korea, its role as the leader of the free world required it to do so. The Soviets were staging one of their recurrent boycotts of the United Nations, which made it possible for the American delegation to obtain passage of a resolution condemning the invasion as an act of aggression and calling on member nations to aid in repulsing it. Command of the U.S.—and, a few days later, UN—forces was vested in Gen. Douglas MacArthur.

In the frantic opening days of a war that had taken Washington policy makers unawares, no one seemed to have time for General Cates. Senior Army and Air Force officers on the staff of the JCS even suggested leaving the U.S. Marines off the troop list in Korea. Nevertheless, the commandant continued to press his case for Leatherneck participation in the conflict. On 1 July the chief of naval operations, Adm. Forrest P. Sherman, offered MacArthur a brigade of combat-ready Marines. MacArthur, who had learned the value of Marines in the Pacific war, immediately asked the JCS to assign the unit to his command. Even before the Joint Chiefs received MacArthur's enthusiastic response, Cates had alerted Maj. Gen. Graves B. Erskine at Camp Pendleton to place the 1st Marine Division on alert for possible deployment.

On 2 August Brig. Gen. Edward A. Craig's 1st Provisional Marine Brigade marched ashore at Pusan, on the southeastern tip of the Korean peninsula. At the time of the Communist invasion there were only 27,656 men serving in FMF units. But on 19 July 1950 President Truman authorized the call-up of the Marine Corps Reserve. Eventually, more than 35,000 men answered the call to the colors—many of them veterans of World War II.

In Korea, the events of the intervening month had been little less than catastrophic. Three understrength U.S. Army divisions, hurriedly deployed from occupation duty

Brig. Gen. Edward A. Craig *(right)* commanded the 1st Provisional Marine Brigade in the Pusan perimeter and then served as assistant division commander of the 1st Marine Division. Here he is seen conferring with Col. Chesty Puller outside Seoul following the Inchon invasion.

in Japan, displayed the effects of soft living. Without mines and effective antitank weapons, the poorly trained GIS barely managed to slow the North Koreans' advance. By the end of July, however, U.S. forces (now organized as the Eighth Army under the command of Lt. Gen. Walton H. Walker) had established a leaky perimeter around Pusan. Another American division had entered the lines since the invasion, increasing the Army total to four. The Eighth Army also included five ROK divisions, but these lacked the heavy armaments to stand up against the North Koreans hammering Walker's thinly held fifty-mile front.

The Marine brigade was built around Lt. Col. Raymond L. Murray's 5th Marines, one battalion of artillery from the 11th Marines, and Brig. Gen. Thomas H. Cushman's MAG-33. The lean and determined Craig, who had once served as an aide-de-camp to John A. Lejeune, had laid out the parameters of the desperate situation to his troops in no uncertain terms before leaving California: "It has been necessary for troops now fighting in Korea to pull back at times, but I am stating now that no

unit in the brigade will retreat except on orders from an authority higher than the 1st Marine Brigade. You will never receive an order to retreat from me."[12]

Craig's 6,534 cocksure Marines exuded a confidence not shared by senior Army officers and officials within the Department of Defense. But the Leathernecks, most of them veterans of World War II, surprised their enemy. Used to confronting the dispirited ranks of the ROK Army or the out-of-shape American troops deployed hurriedly from Japan, the invaders found to their alarm and dismay that the Marines fought and fought well. Marines were easy to spot on the battlefield because, unlike the other forces in the United Nations command, they wore camouflaged covers on their helmets and leggings instead of high-top boots. More important, they refused to give ground no matter the odds, and they always carried their dead and wounded from the battlefield.

Ground troops were not the Corps's only contribution to the struggle. Marine aviators sailed from San Diego on 12 July. MAG-33 crossed the Pacific in the escort carrier *Badoeng Strait*. When Craig's brigade landed at

The Korean War, 1950–1953

Pusan, VMF-214 began flight operations from the carrier. One of the first helicopter rescues of the war occurred within a week. First Lt. Gustave F. Lueddeke picked up Capt. Vivian M. Moses of VMF-323 after enemy ground fire downed the latter's Corsair. The dauntless Moses volunteered for another mission the following day and was again shot down. This time, he drowned in a rice paddy after being thrown from his aircraft.

On the day the Marines landed, North Korean attacks threatened to break through the southern sector of the Pusan perimeter. Many commanders feared the fall of Pusan and an American Dunkirk. On 3 August the Marine brigade was attached to the 25th Infantry Division as part of Task Force Kean, replacing the badly mauled 24th Infantry Division at the southern end of the perimeter. Walker hoped that with the support of the Marines, he could launch the first UN offensive of the war, break the back of the North Korean 6th Division, and retake Chinju. Walker ordered the Leathernecks to seize the enemy-held ridges near Chindong-ni and advance south to Kosong and west to Sachon until they reached Chinju.

The UN offensive went amiss almost from the beginning as uncoordinated Army and Marine units became lost and attacked the wrong objectives. North Korean soldiers and infiltrating columns of refugees snarled the lines of communications. Hundred-degree-plus temperatures felled many of the unacclimated U.S. troops. The first success for the Leathernecks came on 11 August when the artillerymen of 1/11 blasted a convoy of the North Korean 83rd Motorized Rifle Regiment. Marine Corsairs strafed the enemy troops as they attempted to flee. Although the Marines were diverted to counter a new crisis before reaching Sachon, they had blunted the enemy's assault on the southern face of the perimeter. Intense combat continued through the remainder of a scorching August. Once again, Craig's Marines prevented a North Korean breakthrough across the Naktong. Reluctantly, on 5 September, Walker released the brigade to MacArthur, who had plans of his own for it. In thirty-eight days of fighting, the token force of Leathernecks had inflicted more than ten thousand casualties on the invaders while suffering only 902 of their own (172 killed, none captured).

Meanwhile, the Corps came under attack from a new quarter. On 29 August, in reply to a letter from Congressman Gordon L. McDonough urging that General Cates be included in the JCS, President Truman wrote: "For your information the Marine Corps is the Navy's police force and as long as I am President that is what it will remain. They have a propaganda machine that is almost equal to Stalin's."[13] Both letters appeared in the newspapers on 5 September. The furor they provoked was so great that the next day Truman tendered two handsome apologies, the first in a letter to Cates and the second at a personal appearance at the annual convention of the Marine Corps League. "I sincerely regret the unfortunate choice of language . . . in my letter of 29 August," the president told the commandant. "I am profoundly aware of the magnificent history of the United States Marine Corps."[14]

A new chapter was about to be added to that history. From the opening days of the war, MacArthur had been convinced that an amphibious landing behind the North Korean front line would turn the tide of battle in favor of the United Nations forces. MacArthur reasoned that an assault at Inchon, the port city of Seoul, would cut the supply lines to the enemy forces besieging the Pusan perimeter and liberate the South Korean capital and its important airfield at Kimpo. Only twenty-five miles from Seoul, the seaport was part of the vital network connecting the capital and the airfield with the road and rail system across the Han River. MacArthur's intelligence officers estimated that the North Korean garrisons in the area consisted of only 2,200 second-rate troops at Inchon, and 21,500 better trained and equipped soldiers around Seoul.

Few persons outside his staff shared MacArthur's enthusiasm. Inchon offered an assortment of an amphibian invader's worst nightmares: a narrow channel, easily mined, twisting its way through extensive mudflats; a high seawall; an island (Wolmi-do) blocking the harbor entrance; and the most extreme tidal range—thirty-two feet—in the world. Because of the tidal conditions, there was only one day during the month of September—the fifteenth—on which an amphibious assault was even remotely feasible. To add a final complicating factor, MacArthur's planners concluded that Wolmi-do would have to be secured before a landing could be made at Inchon itself, and that both operations could not be carried out on the same tide. This meant that more than eleven hours must elapse between the attack on Wolmi-do, made on the morning tide, and the landing at Inchon, which would go in on the evening tide, with just ninety-nine minutes of daylight remaining.

Faced with these daunting circumstances, MacArthur chose to gamble on the element of surprise. In the end, he had to exploit his enormous prestige and formidable rhetorical skills to persuade the Joint Chiefs to approve the operation. "We shall land at Inchon," he intoned in his characteristically majestic manner, "and I shall crush them!"[15] Even then, the most that dubious Navy and Marine commanders would concede was that the invasion was "not impossible."

On the suggestion of General Shepherd, then commanding FMFPAC, MacArthur asked for the 1st Marine Division for the task. The Joint Chiefs approved his request; the 1st and 7th Marines received orders to deploy to South Korea with sufficient replacements and attachments to build the division's strength to more than twenty-four thousand. Maj. Gen. O. P. Smith, a lean, white-haired fifty-six-year-old, commanded. Chesty Puller, commanding the 1st Marines, added a rousing postscript to the briefing his officers received on the upcoming deployment to Korea. "You young people are lucky," he growled. "We used to have to wait every ten or fifteen years for a war. You get one every five years! You people have been living by the sword. By God, you better be ready to die by it!"[16]

MacArthur assigned the 1st Marine Division, along with the 7th Infantry Division, to X Corps, to be commanded by his chief of staff, Maj. Gen. Edward M. Almond, USA. More than one Leatherneck questioned MacArthur's choice of Almond when he could have employed the more experienced Shepherd. Senior Marines suggested that the decision was yet another example of Army–Marine Corps rivalry.

To support the operation, the 1st Marine Air Wing (MAW) left El Toro, California, on 1 September with MAG-12 (three squadrons of aircraft). By the time of the landing, there were six aircraft carriers off the west coast of Korea, and some of them contained squadrons of Marine aircraft. On the first day of Operation Chromite (as the invasion of Inchon was named), the Corsairs of

The Inchon Invasion, 15 September 1950

VMF-323 and VMF-214 hit the island of Wolmi-do. At 6:30 on the morning of 15 September, Lt. Col. Robert D. Taplett's 3/5 stormed ashore on the island. The surprised enemy offered little opposition. As Taplett's Marines advanced to the high ground, they shot down scattered North Korean troops and collected dazed and deafened prisoners. Grenades and satchel charges quickly reduced the lightly manned caves and pillboxes. Less than sixty minutes after H-hour, Sgt. Alvin E. Smith of Company G raised a flag from a shattered tree stump atop the island's highest hill. Taplett declared the island secured at 11:00 A.M. and requested permission to strike down the causeway connecting Wolmi-do with Inchon. General Smith declined the aggressive Taplett's offer because the remainder of the division was still aboard ship waiting for the evening high tide.

Aboard the flagship *Mount McKinley,* MacArthur saw the flag go up over Wolmi-do. To the officers around him on the bridge, he said, "That's it. Let's get a cup of coffee." To the fleet, he radioed: "The Navy and Marines have never shone more brightly than this morning."[17] Taplett's Leathernecks counted 180 dead North Koreans, estimated that another 100 lay entombed in caves and bunkers, and displayed 136 dejected captives. Not a single Marine had been killed, and only eighteen were wounded.

Late that afternoon, Murray and the remaining two

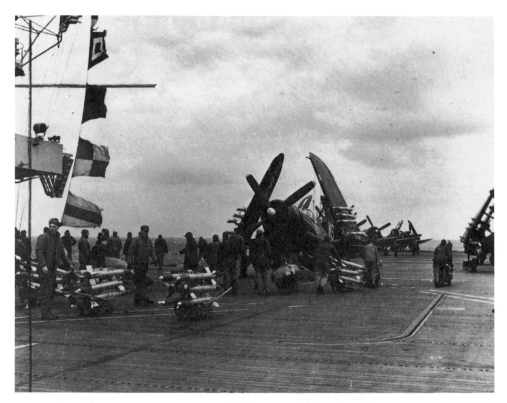

Leatherneck flight deck crews load rockets onto the Corsairs of VMF-323 aboard the *Badoeng Strait* off the west coast of Korea in September 1950.

battalions of his 5th Marines landed over Red Beach, a stretch of seawall located squarely on the Inchon waterfront. Puller's 1st Marines came ashore on Blue Beach, three miles south of the downtown area, in hopes of encircling the port district. As the Leathernecks stormed ashore, fires from the old Asahi Brewery, railroad yards, and factories on the outskirts of the city lit the sky.

Although a handful of North Koreans offered a short, sharp fight, most of the enemy on the high ground surrounding Inchon opted to surrender. By D+1 (16 September) the Leathernecks had punched through the outskirts of Inchon and had left the mopping up to ROK Marines. The North Korean command's decision to commit only a single infantry regiment to the defense of Inchon allowed MacArthur to take the port cheaply. Allied losses on D-day numbered only 22 men dead and 174 wounded; the following day saw only 3 dead and 21 wounded. On 18 September, soldiers of the 7th Infantry Division filed ashore, followed by the 7th Marines.[18]

General Smith ordered Murray's 5th Marines to seize Kimpo airfield, then cross the Han River and march up its right bank to Seoul. Puller's 1st Marines were to punch straight up the Inchon–Seoul highway, seize Yongdungpo on the Han opposite Seoul, and ford the river to link up with the 5th Marines entering the city from the north. While waiting to jump off, the Leathernecks of 1st Lt. H. J. "Hog Jaw" Smith's Company D, 5th Marines, spotted six T-34 tanks approaching their lines accompanied by an estimated two hundred enemy soldiers. Waiting until the enemy had closed to point-blank range, the Marines fired every weapon at their disposal at once. Five accompanying M26 Pershing tanks contributed to the carnage. In seconds, all of the T-34s began to burn and the corpses of North Korean infantry littered the road. Eight Corsairs of VMF-214 inundated another file of T-34s with napalm. The first round of the battle of Seoul had gone to the UN forces, spearheaded by the U.S. Marines.

In the following days, the battle toughened. Although the North Koreans had lightly garrisoned the capital city with headquarters and service troops, thousands of the seasoned soldiers besieging the Pusan perimeter hurried

Members of the 5th Marines use scaling ladders to scramble over a seawall on Red Beach at Inchon.

Amtracs carry Chesty Puller's 1st Marines toward Blue Beach at Inchon.

Marines spring from their landing craft and an LST beaches itself at Inchon on D-day, 15 September 1950.

This view of the Inchon beachhead on 16 September, with three LSTs beached and offloading in the background, testifies to the logistical scale of the operation.

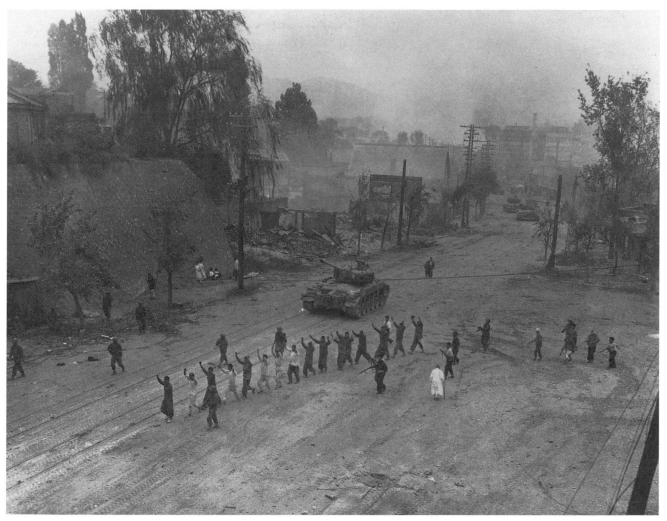

Marine tanks and South Korean forces, apparently including armed civilians, round up North Korean troops in Seoul on 26 September 1950.

to meet the assault on their rear. With their arrival, North Korean strength around Seoul approached that of the invasion force. Nevertheless, the enemy proved unable to organize an effective defense of the capital. Kimpo airfield and Yongdungpo fell to the Leathernecks. Assaulting Marines found only two understrength and demoralized North Korean regiments defending the airfield. Most enemy soldiers had been issued white civilian clothing so that they could meld easily into the crowds of civilian noncombatants clogging the roads to the south.

MAG-33 occupied the airfield on 19 September. Between 7 September and 9 October, four Leatherneck F4U squadrons—two flying from carriers and two operating out of Kimpo—flew 2,163 sorties in support of X Corps, losing eleven planes and six pilots during this period.

Puller's 1st Marines found themselves tangling with a regiment of the North Korean 18th Division. The fracas ended in a wild fight between Capt. Robert H. Barrow's Company A and at least a battalion of enemy troops. Barrow, a future commandant, dug his men in beside a dike on Yongdungpo's riverfront. At 9:00 P.M. on 21 September the North Koreans attacked behind five T-34 tanks. As the tanks rumbled up the street parallel to the dike, Barrow's Marines replied with 3.5-inch rocket fire to stall the advance. The riflemen of Company A, fighting from deep holes, drove back five separate enemy attacks during the night; before dawn, the enemy force abandoned its assault. Barrow's men counted 310 dead North Koreans.

On 24 September the battle for Seoul began in earnest.

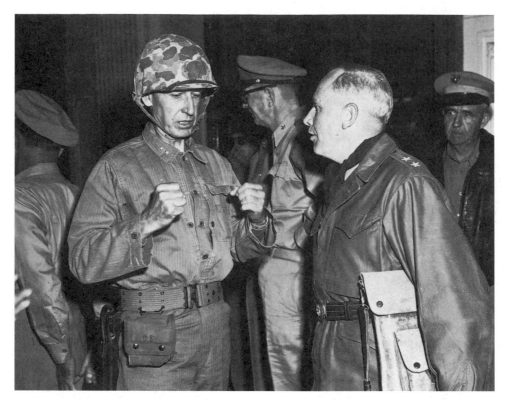

Maj. Gen. Oliver P. Smith, commanding general, 1st Marine Division *(left),* confers with Maj. Gen. Edward M. Almond, commanding general, X Corps, shortly after the capture of Seoul. Behind Almond to the right is Maj. Gen. Field Harris, commanding general, 1st MAW.

By then the 5th Marines had reduced the crack North Korean 25th Brigade to near impotence. The commander of Company I, Capt. Robert A. McMullen, suffered his seventh wound in two wars. Nineteen-year-old PFC Eugene A. Obregon earned the Medal of Honor for covering a fellow Marine with his own body while fighting off attackers with a carbine. And Puller added to his personal legend, appearing wherever the fighting was fiercest with his trademark pipe clenched between his teeth and a crumpled utility cap on his head (he disliked wearing a helmet). A corporal recalled that "whenever he saw a Marine walking away from the front, whether for ammo or to an aid station or whatnot, Puller would frown at him with a hard, unfriendly stare. When he saw one of us going toward the front, for any reason, he'd wave and smile and call, 'How things doin', old man?'"[19]

By 27 September American flags were fluttering from many of Seoul's shattered buildings. North Korean defenders began an abrupt withdrawal from the city, pursued by Col. Homer L. Litzenberg's 7th Marines, who had circled around the capital from the north. Litzenberg's seizure of Uijongbu on 3 October marked the end of the Inchon–Seoul campaign, a masterstroke of amphibious strategy costing less than two thousand Leatherneck casualties. During the same period, the Eighth Army broke out of the Pusan perimeter and drove north. On 26 September the 1st Cavalry Division, leading the advance from the south, linked up with elements of X Corps at Osan, thirty miles below Seoul. By the beginning of October eight of the approximately fourteen enemy divisions in South Korea had been destroyed and the others were fleeing north in disorder. As an effective fighting force, the North Korean Army had ceased to exist. To the surprise of senior Marine commanders, MacArthur did not order the Leathernecks to rejoin the main body of UN forces following the amphibious landing at Inchon; he had another mission for them.

On 1 October, two days before withdrawing the Marines from combat, MacArthur called on all North Korean forces to surrender unconditionally. Two events transpired on the day of his appeal that augured grave consequences for the conduct of the war: a South Korean Army division crossed the thirty-eighth parallel into North Korea, a penetration authorized by President Truman and the Joint Chiefs of Staff; and Communist China's premier, Chou En-lai, warned that the Chinese people would not "supinely tolerate North Korea being savagely invaded by the imperialists."[20] In the aftermath of the victory at Inchon, however, no one took the threat of Chinese intervention seriously. With the enemy on the ropes, American policy makers became beguiled by the possibility of seizing the moment to do more than merely defend South Korea.

A new and more ambitious aim became official policy on 7 October, when the UN General Assembly adopted a U.S.-sponsored resolution establishing the objective of reunifying the entire Korean peninsula under an "independent and democratic government." Thus MacArthur eyed the Yalu River, the boundary between North Korea and the Chinese province of Manchuria, as the limit of advance for UN forces. Ignoring the warnings from Communist China, MacArthur ordered the I ROK Corps, 1st Cavalry and 24th Infantry Divisions, and the British Commonwealth Brigade to advance up the east coast and across the thirty-eighth parallel. The ROK II Corps maneuvered in the center of the peninsula, while the ROK Capital and 3rd Divisions advanced along the west coast. At the same time, MacArthur sought a repeat of his success at Inchon.

MacArthur's strategy called for Smith to reassemble the 1st Marine Division at Inchon by 7 October, then travel by Navy transport around the Korean peninsula for a landing at Wonsan, North Korea's major port. Rapidly advancing ROK troops captured Wonsan just three days later, eliminating the need for an amphibious assault. MAG-12 moved from Kimpo to Wonsan; VMF-312 and VMF(N)-513 arrived on 14 October and began flight operations immediately. After waiting onboard their transports until the Navy cleared the harbor of mines, the Marine infantrymen filed ashore on 26 October. Smith ordered the 1st Marines to clear the area around Wonsan of enemy stragglers and infiltrators. The 5th and 7th Marines began the drive north to Hamhung and Hungnam in preparation for the advance by UN troops to the

Yalu. MacArthur envisioned an easy push to the border, with little opposition from the dispirited North Koreans.

Smith did not share MacArthur's optimism. The possibility of Chinese intervention worried the normally imperturbable Leatherneck. MacArthur's orders required the Marine division to advance inland from Hungnam north and west, traveling seventy-eight miles along a single road through narrow valleys between steep mountains to Yudam-ni near the Chosin Reservoir. From the reservoir it was only seventy miles to the Chinese border. Tactically, MacArthur's plans made little sense. Advancing in a column of infantry battalions along the mountainous road denied the Leathernecks the opportunity to maintain links with friendly units; nearly eighty miles of rugged terrain separated them from the soldiers of the Eighth Army to the west.

Litzenberg's 7th Marines led the column, followed by Murray's 5th Marines and Puller's 1st Marines. A savvy, hard-driving officer, Litzenberg ordered heavy patrols to scour the hilltops along his flanks. Marine Corsairs flew continuous cover for the regiment, and the battalion of 105-mm howitzers supporting the 1st Marines blasted the terrain to their front. On 1 November the 1st Cavalry Division encountered large numbers of Chinese troops in the Eighth Army's sector. The following day, Smith learned that an ROK division operating near Hamhung had reported taking several prisoners claiming to belong to the 124th Division of the Chinese People's Liberation Army. At midnight on 2 November, the forward companies of the 7th Marines made contact with elements of the 124th Division. General Lin Pao, the veteran commander of China's Fourth Field Army, had deployed his Ninth Army Group, one hundred thousand troops organized into ten divisions, across the border from Manchuria.

The enemy attack began with bugle calls, green flares, and the screeching of whistles. Litzenberg's Marines held their ground and the Chinese left the field in disarray. Captured documents and the number of enemy dead— 662 in front of one Leatherneck battalion alone—suggested that the Marines had mauled at least two of the three Chinese regiments. Despite Smith's cautionary reports to X Corps headquarters, his orders to advance to the Yalu remained unchanged.

For the next five days the 7th Marines fought through

a series of Chinese strong points manned all the way to the plateau on which lies the Chosin Reservoir. By 13 November advance elements of the Marine division had entered Hagaru-ri, a sizable town at the southern end of the reservoir. Although Smith had not reached his objective, he ordered the 7th Marines to halt in the vicinity of Hagaru until the 5th Marines joined them and Puller's 1st Marines could report that the main supply route to the rear had been secured.

Despite the reports of Chinese units reaching his headquarters in Tokyo, MacArthur refused to alter his plan for an advance to the Yalu. Earlier, he had opined that Communist forces could not or would not launch a counteroffensive; he even predicted victory by Christmas. MacArthur's unbridled optimism meant a further advance to the north for the weary 1st Marine Division.

In mid-November the weather grew increasingly colder. A piercing wind from the wastes of Siberia swept the four-thousand-foot-high Chosin Plateau. Streams iced over, as did the reservoir. Surgeons treating wounded men in frigid hospital tents were appalled to find that blood froze to their gloves. On 23 November Smith sent the 5th and 7th Marines forward to Yudam-ni. Both regiments made the fourteen-mile trek in two days, fighting through lightly held Chinese roadblocks. On 27 November the 5th Marines began the fifty-five-mile march from Yudam-ni to Mupyong-ni—the next leg of MacArthur's drive to the Yalu. A starless and moonless night engulfed the weary Marines as they shivered and ached in the –20-degree cold.[21]

As the Leathernecks bedded down in a tight perimeter, dire news reached Smith's headquarters at Hagaru. Units throughout the Eighth Army reported a major Chinese offensive in progress. Entire UN divisions had been either halted or forced to give ground; ominously, some units—notably, ROK outfits—had been routed and had fled the battlefield. On the night of 27–28 November, the Marine division came under attack all along the route from Chinhung-ni to the perimeter at Yudam-ni. By the morning of the twenty-eighth the division found itself facing the prospect of annihilation.

The Marines confronted an estimated eight Chinese divisions. Moving under cover of darkness, the enemy had slipped through the hills undetected to envelop the Marine main supply route. The Chinese tactics stunned the UN forces. Usually, Chinese units deployed in columns of battalions and rushed their opponents' lines in night attacks with utter disregard for their losses. Other than infantry mortars, the Chinese possessed few supporting arms. But Leatherneck artillery and Marine close air support kept the Communists off the high ground to lessen the threat.

Smith understood all too well that his division held four separate perimeters from Chinhung-ni north to Yudam-ni. He ordered the 5th and 7th Marines to break out and join him at Hagaru, after which the division would withdraw to Koto-ri and Chinhung-ni. Initially, the retreating regiments had to make their way through high, bitterly cold Toktong Pass halfway between Hagaru and Yudam-ni. Litzenberg ordered Capt. William E. Barber's F/2/7 to guard the pass and prevent the Chinese from establishing a roadblock; underscoring the gravity of the situation, he reinforced Company F with heavy machine guns and 81-mm mortars.

At 2:30 A.M. on 28 November, a battalion of the Chinese 59th Division hurled itself at Barber's lonely outpost. Although the Chinese overran three of its positions during the night, Company F still held the pass at daybreak. The Leathernecks had lost twenty men killed and fifty-four wounded, while an estimated 450 Chinese troops had died. Air drops provided munitions to keep the surrounded Marines going in the face of superior numbers. Hit in the hip on the second day of the assault, Barber—decorated for heroism at Iwo Jima—commanded his company from a stretcher. His gallantry at Toktong Pass earned Barber the Medal of Honor.

On 30 November Litzenberg and Murray decided to break out. Carrying their wounded and accompanied by their vehicles and artillery, the Marines began to fight their way down the fourteen miles of the main supply route across Toktong Pass to Hagaru. Lt. Col. Robert D. Taplett's 3/5 led the advance and broke through the encirclement by nightfall on 3 December. Meanwhile, Lt. Col. Raymond G. Davis's 1st Battalion, 7th Marines, began a desperate night march across the barren landscape toward Barber's perimeter at Toktong Pass. At first light, an air strike and mortar fire cleared the way for 1/7 to join Barber's company. Only 82 Leathernecks of the

Capt. William E. Barber *(left)* earned the Medal of Honor while commanding Company F, 7th Marines, in the defense of Toktong Pass. Lt. Col. Raymond G. Davis *(right)* won the nation's highest award for heroism for leading 1/7 across the frozen hills of North Korea to break the Chinese siege of the vital pass. *Leatherneck* (November 1990) and *Officer Review* (November 1998)

original 240 in F/2/7 could walk. Like Barber, Davis earned the Medal of Honor.

The squadrons of MAG-33 supported the beleaguered riflemen with air strikes from Wonsan and Yonpo, near Hungnam. VMF-214 and VMF-323, flying from Navy carriers, added to the power of the air-ground team while VMO-6 flew artillery spotting missions. Parachutes from Marine and Air Force transports kept the weary columns supplied with food and ammunition: eight hundred thousand pounds at Hagaru and more than a million at Kotori. Even boxes of PX goods came fluttering down in the parachute drops; when the irrepressible Puller learned that one such parcel contained packages of condoms, he supposedly snarled: "What the hell do they think we're doing to these Chinese?"[22]

With Toktong Pass relieved, the retreat could begin. The 5th and 7th Marines fought their way through the Chinese encirclement with Lt. Col. Harold S. Roise's 2/5

acting as rear guard. Finally, seventy-nine hours after setting out, Murray's 5th Marines reached the Hagaru perimeter. The Leathernecks had brought along all of their equipment except for eight 155-mm howitzers abandoned after their diesel-powered prime movers ran out of fuel. The new arrivals joined a scratch force that had fought two Chinese infantry divisions to a standstill. By the time the retreating Marines arrived, engineers had the Hagaru airstrip in operation. Transport aircraft flew supplies and ammunition in and casualties out. More than three thousand disabled Marines left via the air pipeline, along with a thousand wounded and frostbitten soldiers from the 7th Infantry Division, which had been cut to pieces on the eastern side of the Chosin Reservoir.

The breakout of the two regiments from Yudam-ni buoyed Smith's confidence. He and his staff now began planning in earnest for the withdrawal of all Leathernecks from Hagaru. Refusing to call the division's

Leatherneck infantrymen pause while a Marine Corsair napalms a Chinese roadblock during the retreat from the Chosin Reservoir.

retrograde movement a retreat, Smith referred to the maneuver as an attack to the rear. Down the main supply route he intended to take the survivors of assorted Army units, ROK stragglers, and 235 Royal Marines of 41st Independent Commando. Smith waited two days before setting out, allowing the 5th and 7th Marines time to rest and eat warm food. Five hundred replacements, many of them previously wounded men returning from hospitals in Japan, arrived on incoming transports.

On the starry, bitterly cold night of 6 December, a Chinese division slammed into the 5th Marines at Hagaru. Fire discipline and heavy use of supporting arms paid dividends; hundreds of Chinese fell in the worst slaughter of the Chosin Reservoir campaign. The next night, eight hundred Chinese soldiers jumped Maj. Fran-

cis F. "Fox" Parry's 3rd Battalion, 11th Marines. Parry deployed his artillerymen as infantry to beat off the attack. When a second Chinese assault stalled his column, Parry's Marines unlimbered their howitzers and fired point-blank into the onrushing horde; the time-fused shells exploded as close as forty-five yards in front of the guns. In another action that evening, a Chinese unit hit the division's command post. Headquarters Marines walking alongside their vehicles took the attackers under fire as a Corsair from VMF(N)-513 made strafing runs to within yards of the road. By then, the 7th Marines had reached Puller's perimeter at Koto-ri.

On 7 December the 5th Marines set fire to all supplies and ammunition remaining at Hagaru. Then they, too, joined the weary column marching away from the reser-

A Marine column winds its way through the mountains toward Hungnam.

voir. The grim procession stretched for more than eleven miles. Six squadrons of Marine Corsairs wheeling above the force made any attempt by the Chinese to interfere with it suicidal. More than ten thousand men and in excess of a thousand vehicles made it down the main supply route. Smith's commanders reported 7 missing Leathernecks and bluejackets, 103 killed, and 506 wounded.

The 1st Marine Division, with assorted attachments and stragglers, now numbered more than fourteen thousand men. Before the division pulled out of Koto-ri, General Shepherd flew in with the intention of accompanying it on its breakthrough to the sea, but Smith persuaded him not to add the worry of having a three-star Marine killed or captured to all those he already carried. Chesty Puller put Mag-

gie Higgins, the courageous woman war correspondent, on Shepherd's plane for the flight out, despite her protests—delivered with a vehement profanity that startled even the usually unflappable Puller—that she wanted to stay with the troops. Smith then ordered the division on the road for the last leg of the withdrawal, through Funchilin Pass to the perimeter at Chinhung-ni, which was being held by Puller's 1st Battalion. Litzenberg's regiment moved out first and in two days of hard fighting narrowed the gap to just six miles. The two battalions with Puller at Koto-ri formed the rear guard. Their fifty-two-year-old colonel circulated among his men, encouraging young Leathernecks by his outrageous assurance: "You're the 1st Marine Division," he told them with characteristic bravado, "and don't you forget it. We're

Chesty Puller commanded the 1st Marines during the Chosin Reservoir campaign. Informed that his outfit was surrounded by enemy troops near Hagaru-ri, he is reputed to have growled, "Fine, that will make it easier to kill them."

the greatest military outfit that ever walked on this earth. Not all the Communists in hell can stop you. We'll go down to the sea at our own pace and nothing is going to get in our way. If it does, we'll blow hell out of it."[23] The 7th Marines took the point and fought southward to the pass. Lt. Col. Donald M. Schmuck's 1st Battalion, 1st Marines, advanced from Chinhung-ni to seize Hill 1081 overlooking Funchilin Pass. A swirling snowstorm and –14-degree temperatures aided Schmuck's Leathernecks as they mounted the key terrain apparently unseen and took the enemy bunkers in savage hand-to-hand fighting.

By nightfall on 10 December, units of the Marine division were flowing easily from Koto-ri to Chinhung-ni. The lack of serious opposition made it obvious that the Chinese forces had been bested. American correspondents waiting to interview the arriving Marines were astonished to learn that the Leathernecks had never doubted their ability to break out. In the early hours of 12 December, the Marines and stragglers boarded ships for Pusan.

The Chosin campaign cost the Corps 4,418 casualties, including 718 dead. Not included in that number were those suffering from illness, frostbite, or intestinal problems caused by eating frozen C-rations. American intelligence estimates put Chinese losses at a staggering 37,500, with 25,000 killed—more than 50 percent of the troops engaged. Perhaps 35–40 percent of the enemy casualties resulted from the close air support furnished by Leatherneck pilots, air support hitherto unequaled in warfare. The Marine aviators offered a tuneful tribute to their faithful Corsairs:

> Up in Korea 'midst rocks, ice, and snow,
> The poor Chinese Commie is feeling so low,
> As our Corsairs roar by overhead,
> He knows that his buddies will all soon be dead.
>
> Lin Pao went way up to cold Koto-ri,
> His prize Chinese Army in action to see,
> He said that his soldiers no battle could lose,
> But all that he found was their hats and their shoes.[24]

O. P. Smith deserved all of the praise heaped on him. Unlike the overconfident MacArthur and his fawning subordinates, Smith foresaw what might happen and endeavored all along to be ready for the worst, even while obeying orders with which he disagreed. By smashing the Chinese Ninth Army Group, he had saved not only his division but also the port of Hungnam and probably the entire X Corps. The Marines had destroyed no less than seven Chinese divisions. Marching out of the Chosin Reservoir in the swirling snow of a subzero north Asian winter, the half-frozen Leathernecks gave their fellow UN troops and the American people a badly needed morale boost. Chesty Puller emerged with his fifth Navy Cross—the most ever awarded to a single individual—and his first star, although the latter had been selected before the Chosin campaign.

Christmas Day 1950 found the 1st Marine Division at Pusan, bivouacked in the same bean patch where the brigade had encamped six months before. There, the Leathernecks—ostensibly in reserve—thawed, showered, and removed the lice from their clothing. Thirty-four hundred replacements swelled the division's ranks.

Weary Marines gather the bodies of other American Marines, British Royal Marines, and U.S. Army and Republic of Korea troops for a mass burial at Koto-ri, 8 December 1950.

By then, U.S. war aims had come full circle. No longer did Washington dream of unifying Korea under a pro-Western government. From now on, the fight would continue simply to preserve the prewar status quo.

On New Year's Day 1951, Chinese forces launched their second major offensive of the war. Twenty-one Chinese and twelve North Korean divisions struck south. Several ROK divisions were overrun, and on 4 January Seoul fell. The Eighth Army's new commander, Gen. Matthew B. Ridgway—Walker having died in a jeep wreck on 23 December—placed his troops along a defense line running from Pyongtaek to Samchok. Ridgway ordered Smith's Marines—bolstered by another eighteen hundred replacements—to deal with North Korean guerrillas operating behind his lines and harrying a triangular area on the east coast between Pohang, Andong, and Yongdok. While farther to the north UN forces engaged in pitched battles against the Chinese and North Korean troops, the Leathernecks patrolled endless rice paddies and hunted down small bands of Communist irregulars.

Grimmer work began anew on 11 February 1951,

when Ridgway attached the 1st Marine Division to Maj. Gen. Bryant E. Moore's IX Corps in the center of the peninsula. Ten days later the Leathernecks jumped off as part of two successive operations Ridgway dubbed "Killer" and "Ripper." This time, the UN command sought not to gain ground in the north but to expel Chinese forces from South Korea. Ridgway hoped to force the Communist armies to mass, thus making them easy targets for artillery and air strikes. Instead, the Chinese withdrew slowly in front of the Marines for the next four weeks. Rough terrain and wet weather gave the Leathernecks their greatest problem. By 14 March the 1st Marine Division had driven past Hoengsong and now brushed up against an enemy hill defense replete with bunkers. By then, UN forces had outflanked the Communists, recapturing Seoul that same day.

Still determined to prevail, the Communist forces organized for a new offensive, which the UN command expected in the so-called Iron Triangle between Chorwon, Pyonggang, and Kumhwa. In anticipation of the enemy offensive, Ridgway ordered the Marines to advance to a new phase line, "Kansas," above the thirty-eighth parallel. On 4 April the 7th Marines—now commanded by Col. Herman R. Nickerson Jr.—was among the first of the Eighth Army units to recross the thirty-eighth parallel. Three days later, the simmering conflict between Truman and MacArthur reached a dramatic climax when the president relieved the general as UN commander and replaced him with Ridgway. Lt. Gen. James A. Van Fleet assumed command of the Eighth Army.

By late April the Marine division had fought its way north to the Hwachon Reservoir, just above the thirty-eighth parallel. ROK units flanked the Leathernecks. On the night of 22–23 April the Chinese counterattacked. A human torrent poured over the ROK division on the left of the Marines. Within minutes the South Korean lines broke as terrified soldiers fled south, leaving a ten-mile-wide gap in the Eighth Army's front. At daybreak Chinese troops were surging past the Marine division's dangling flank. To divert the tide, General Smith committed his division reserve, the 1st Marine Regiment, and echeloned the 7th Marines to form a new front angling back to the left rear. On the other side of the gap, the 24th Infantry Division reacted in similar fashion, refusing and reinforcing its right flank. With the Eighth Army's entire line under heavy attack, however, General Van Fleet directed both units to fall back. Meanwhile, American and British forces took position to stem the advance of the Chinese who had moved through the gap, and in a few days a firm new front was established twenty miles below the old line. On 26 April, the crisis past, Smith relinquished command of the division to Maj. Gen. Gerald C. Thomas, a distinguished Leatherneck who had worn forest green since World War I. Chesty Puller rotated home in May. Korea was Puller's last war. He retired a lieutenant general in 1955.

The beginning of June found the 1st Marine Division approaching Yanggu and the Soyang River valley. Communist forces occupied the series of ridges overlooking the large valley, named "the Punchbowl" by the Leathernecks. Hill 1316, a sizable enemy ammunition and supply center, dominated the terrain, and Thomas expected a hard fight. Reinforced with the ROK 1st Marine Regiment, the division hammered at the approaches of Hill 1316 and the southern rim of the Punchbowl in an of-

fensive that took most of June but denied the area to the enemy. For the next six months, Communist forces attempted in vain to retake the contested ground.

Chinese and North Korean losses in the first year of the war stunned leaders in both nations, and on 10 July 1951 cease-fire talks began; they would drag on for two long years. From the outset, the Communists appeared unwilling to bargain in good faith. In a bid to apply military pressure at the bargaining table, General Van Fleet ordered the Marines back into the line on 27 August. This time, the Leathernecks prepared to seize the enemy-held hills on the north side of the Punchbowl. In contrast to the earlier stages of the conflict, Communist forces now appeared on the battlefield supplied with ample artillery, mortars, machine guns, and ammunition. More ominous for the Leatherneck riflemen, much of their close air support disappeared when the Air Force demanded and obtained operational control of all fixed-wing aircraft in the theater. On 20 September Van Fleet called a halt to the offensive, concluding that casualties were running too high. Nevertheless, the Leathernecks held the northern rim of the Punchbowl.

In that same month, Helicopter Transport Squadron (HMR)-161 arrived with the new Sikorsky HRS-1 helicopter, a five-passenger craft with a top speed of ninety knots. HMR-161 demonstrated its utility on 13 September by transporting 18,848 pounds of rations to infantry battalions on the forward edge of the battle area and evacuating seventy-four wounded men on the return trip. A few days later, HMR-161 transported the entire divisional reconnaissance company to the top of Hill 884. Old-timers scoffed, but a Marine who did not have to climb a thousand feet with a full pack arrived fresh and ready to fight. The hopes that the Corps's planners had pinned on the helicopter had not been misplaced.

After September 1951 the war in Korea settled into a positional conflict reminiscent of World War I. Leathernecks and soldiers constructed bunkers on the reverse slopes of the steep hills, while Communist forces dug tunnels into the hillsides. Patrol actions and small attacks dominated the next twenty-two months. While not as intensive as the opening phases of the war, this period accounted for 40 percent of the division's total casualties. General Thomas did what he could to relieve the boredom of the outpost war. On 10 November 1951, at exactly noon, he ordered every weapon in the division—from rifle to heavy artillery—to fire a single round in one tremendous thunderclap to celebrate the Marine Corps's birthday.

On 23 March 1952, the division—now commanded by Maj. Gen. John T. Selden—moved from the Punchbowl area to a stretch of front along Korea's west coast, with the mission of defending the vital corridor to Seoul, Kimpo, and Inchon. Between 26 and 29 March 1953 the Chinese made one last, desperate attempt to take a series of Marine outposts called Carson, Reno, and Vegas. These names were inspired by the realization that holding the positions would be a gamble, which proved the case. Although Carson breasted the enemy tide, the other two outposts were overrun. Lew Walt's 5th Marines quickly recaptured Vegas, but Reno remained in Communist hands. By the time the fighting died down, Marine casualties totaled 1,015 men; Chinese losses were estimated to be twice that number.

Aerial combat pitting Leathernecks against Communist pilots occurred only infrequently. The first encounter took place on 21 April 1951, when two aviators of VMF-312 flying from the *Bataan,* Capt. Phillip C. De-Long and 1st Lt. Harold Daigh, were jumped by four North Korean Yaks. Daigh shot down one enemy aircraft immediately while DeLong—a World War II ace with eleven victories—destroyed two others. Daigh damaged the fourth Yak, which limped home. A little more than six months later, on 4 November, Capt. William F. Guss, a Marine aviator flying an F-86 Sabrejet on exchange duty with the U.S. Air Force, downed the first of twenty-six MiGs that would fall to Leathernecks in the course of the war. The Corps's only ace of the Korean War, Maj. John F. Bolt, downed six MiG-15s between May and July 1953 while on exchange duty with the 51st Fighter Interceptor Wing. Two other Marines flying with the Air Force each scored three confirmed victories: Maj. Alexander J. Gillis and Maj. John H. Glenn, who would later gain fame as the first American astronaut to orbit the earth.

On the morning of 17 May 1951, Chinese Communist troops assaulted positions held by the 3rd Battalion, 7th Marines. The mountain of bodies stacked in a ravine opposite the Leatherneck lines attest to their failure to breach the perimeter.

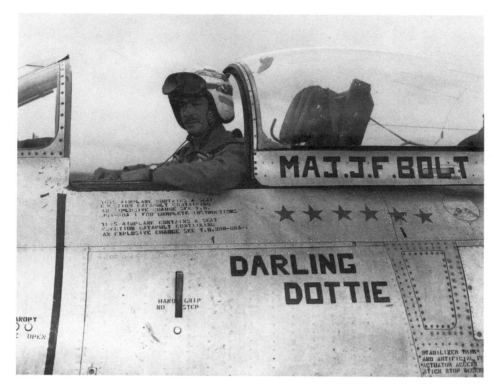

Major John F. Bolt Jr. in the cockpit of his F-86 Sabrejet, "Darling Dottie," on 13 July 1953, two days after downing his fifth and sixth MiG-15s to become the Corps's first jet ace. He was also a six-victory ace in World War II.

Josef Stalin's death on 5 March 1953 probably encouraged Communist China's desire to end a conflict it knew it could not win. The incoming Eisenhower administration's thinly veiled threats to go nuclear also may have influenced enemy thinking. The war ended with the signing of a truce—not a peace—at Panmunjom on 27 July 1953. By that date, 4,262 Marines had lost their lives in Korea, and another 21,781 suffered wounds—twice the total for World War I. These figures represented approximately 18 percent of the overall 136,913 American casualties. Forty-two Leathernecks earned the Medal of Honor, 28 of them posthumously. Only 227 Marines were captured out of a total of 7,190 U.S. personnel in enemy hands.[25] Even the Corps's critics had to admit that the Marine Corps's performance in Korea was far superior to that of the Eighth Army and X Corps. In Korea, the Marines could not claim to have been among the "first to fight," but few could dispute their claim to have been "the best." Hanson Baldwin's terse comment in one of his columns for the New York Times spoke reams about Marine Corps esprit and professionalism: "The Marines were ready."[26]

13

The Vietnam War, 1954–1975

As the war in Korea ground to its unsatisfactory conclusion, the Marine Corps faced cuts in both manpower and dollars. President Truman's budget for Fiscal Year 1954 called for a reduction in the number of Leathernecks from 248,000 to 225,000. The following year, the administration of President Dwight D. Eisenhower reduced the size of the Corps even further to 205,000 men and women. In January 1952 the 3rd Marine Division was activated at Camp Pendleton, and in August 1953 it deployed to Japan as a strategic reserve for the winding down of the Korean War. In 1955 the 1st Marine Division left Korea and returned to Camp Pendleton while the 1st MAW deployed to Japan. An infantry regiment left the 3rd Marine Division when it redeployed to Okinawa and became the main component of the 1st Marine Brigade at Kaneoe Bay, Hawaii. The 2nd Marine Division remained at Camp Lejeune, North Carolina, where it had been since the end of World War II.

On 31 December 1955 General Shepherd retired. The Eisenhower administration accepted his recommendation for a successor: Randolph McCall Pate, fourth in seniority among the Marine lieutenant generals. Lacking the extensive combat command experience of his immediate predecessors, Pate brought a new style of leadership and executive management to the Corps's highest post; in the process, he created more controversy than the Marine Corps had experienced since the ouster of General Barnett in 1920.

When Eisenhower's secretary of defense, Charles E. Wilson, decreed that all officers serving in the Washington area would work in mufti, Pate—a traditionalist—embellished the edict by requiring his officers to wear hats. The new commandant also made such anachronisms as swagger sticks almost mandatory for all officers and senior NCOs. Many officers close to Pate suggested that he suffered from mental lapses that affected his judgment. Nevertheless, Pate survived a serious controversy surrounding a tragedy that involved the Corps's time-honored method of recruit training.

Leatherneck élan during the Korean War remained in the memories of most citizens in the mid-1950s. But a tragedy at Parris Island cast a pall of gloom over the Corps's leadership and the tradition of tough military training. During the night of 8 April 1956, an inexperienced drill instructor marched the seventy-four recruits of Platoon 71 into the murky waters of Ribbon Creek on an unauthorized punishment hike. Six recruits drowned. The drill instructor, SSgt. Matthew C. McKeon, admitted that he had been drinking. The outcry following the deaths suggested to many observers that the Corps's senior leadership had lost control. To regain command, and to prevent future training accidents, HQMC ordered the creation of a recruit training regiment at both depots, with their commanding officers reporting directly to an inspector general of recruit training at HQMC.[1]

Leatherneck commitments overseas remained significant. In the summer of 1958, competing factions in the Lebanese presidential election brought that Middle Eastern nation close to anarchy. Troops from nearby Syria loomed menacingly, exacerbating the situation, and the government of Lebanon asked the United States and Great Britain to intervene. A sizable force of Marines was in the Mediterranean at the time: BLT 1/8 aboard ships just north of Malta, BLT 3/6 at sea between Athens and Crete, and BLT 2/2 steaming between Cyprus and Beirut. The headquarters of the 2nd Provisional Marine Force was in the area, ostensibly to conduct an amphibious exercise in Sardinia.

At 1:30 on the afternoon of 15 July 1958, BLT 2/2 stormed ashore in full battle regalia across a Lebanese beach filled with soft-drink peddlers and gawking sunbathers. At 7:30 the following morning, BLT 3/6 joined it and the two forces marched toward Beirut. Two days later, BLT 1/8 filed ashore and BLT 2/8 arrived by air. A British brigade landed in Jordan and the U.S. 24th Airborne Brigade from Germany joined Marine forces in Lebanon on 19 July. Despite predictions to the contrary, Lebanese elections were held without incident on 31 July. On 18 October the last of the Leathernecks departed; five days later, the president-elect took office.[2]

Widespread misgivings over Pate's managerial style of leadership notwithstanding, he was appointed to a second two-year term on 1 January 1958. Increasingly, however, Pate angered his civilian superiors. The Corps's two hundred thousand men and women absorbed one-fourth of the Navy Department's budget. Critical of the ballooning military-industrial complex, Eisenhower sought reductions. Citing congressional authority for three divisions and three wings, Pate opposed the lower manpower figures the administration favored. As Pate's second term of office approached its end in 1959, senior officials looked for a team player to replace him.

Lt. Gen. Merrill B. Twining, a brilliant planner and dedicated staff officer, appeared to be the odds-on favorite. But Eisenhower sought a dramatic shift in direction for the Marine Corps in the nomination of the next commandant. Twining's role in orchestrating the defeat of the Army's attempt to emasculate the Marine Corps during the defense unification squabble after World War II was legendary. The press release on 11 September 1959 stunned naval circles. The administration had bypassed Twining, four other lieutenant generals, and several senior major generals to select Maj. Gen. David M.

Shoup, who had earned the Medal of Honor at Tarawa, as the Corps's twenty-first commandant.

Shoup's highest priority was increasing the combat readiness of the Fleet Marine Force. While this was a goal with which all Marines could agree, the new commandant's often abrasive manner and impatience with what he considered outmoded traditions—swagger sticks, for one—raised many hackles, especially among the Corps's Old Guard. Col. Robert D. Heinl Jr. snarled that "Shoup was Eisenhower's way of getting even with the Marine Corps."[3] During the Shoup era the Navy reconfigured the escort carriers *Boxer* and *Princeton* as amphibious assault ships (LPHS), and construction began on a new class of LPH with the *Iwo Jima.* The trusty M1 rifle was replaced by the M14, firing the standard 7.62 NATO cartridges. Because one in four of the new M14 rifles contained a feature allowing fully automatic fire, the Browning automatic rifle went to the surplus pile. A new machine gun, the M60, replaced the .30 caliber of World War II and Korean War vintage. His critics notwithstanding, Shoup could thus take credit for overseeing the replacement of the Corps's entire arsenal of infantry weaponry; it would not happen again for another three decades.

In late 1962, intelligence reports revealing the construction of missile sites in Cuba brought the United States and the Soviet Union dangerously close to nuclear war. During the crisis, units from the 2nd Marine Division reinforced the naval base at Guantánamo Bay to near regimental strength. The remainder of the division sortied at sea between Florida and Cuba, the 2nd MAW deployed to Florida and Puerto Rico, and the 5th MEB steamed from Southern California to join the gigantic armada in the Caribbean. Army units moved to southern ports in anticipation of an invasion of Cuba. As tensions heightened, President John F. Kennedy's firm resolve forced the Soviet leadership to remove the offensive missiles from Cuba.

On 1 January 1964 Wallace M. Greene Jr., a graduate of the Naval Academy class of 1930, succeeded Shoup as commandant. Greene was known as a polished, proficient, hardworking officer whose extensive staff service made him well qualified to uphold the Corps's interests in the tumult of interservice rivalries. More of an internationalist than his predecessor, Greene did not share Shoup's misgivings over U.S. involvement in trouble spots worldwide.

In April 1965 disputing factions in the presidential elections in the Dominican Republic appeared to threaten U.S. lives and property. Learning that opponents of the elected government had taken control of Santo Domingo, President Lyndon B. Johnson ordered U.S. troops into the capital city. Clearly, Johnson feared that another Cuban-style Communist nation might be about to emerge in the Caribbean. In the waters nearby stood the 6th Marine Expeditionary Unit—composed of BLT 3/6 and HMM 264. U.S. ships began to evacuate American nationals at 1:00 P.M. on 27 April. That evening, the first Leathernecks filed ashore. The next day, all of 3/6 occupied Santo Domingo. The U.S. force increased rapidly; on 30 April a brigade of the 82nd Airborne arrived and the remaining elements of a Marine expeditionary brigade, BLT 1/6 and BLT 1/8, were flown in. BLT 1/2 was held offshore in reserve. As the government of the Dominican Republic regained control, a multinational peacekeeping force from several Latin American nations replaced the American military and naval contingents.

But just as the political turmoil in Latin America seemed to be settling down, a troubled area thousands of miles away had already begun to test the resolve of the U.S. government and its populace like no other conflict in its history. And for a decade the conflict engulfed the Marine Corps. The nations of Southeast Asia seemed to embody the "domino theory" of the 1950s and 1960s. Communist insurgencies inspired by China and the Soviet Union fed on the seedbeds of political and economic discontent. In the British colony and then commonwealth nation of Malaya, British and Malayan forces spent more than a decade suppressing a Communist terrorist movement that had taken root among the Chinese minority. The Kingdom of Thailand was confronted by no fewer than three insurgent groups, two of them Communist inspired. Across the border in Laos, Communist instigators from North Vietnam proselytized the native population to foment an insurgency—the Pathet Lao—against the royalist government. The governments of the United States and the Soviet Union became increasingly in-

volved in support of the factions in Laos, to the point of actually coming to loggerheads over the tiny, landlocked nation. A Marine helicopter squadron was sent to Thailand in 1961 because of the worrisome situation in Laos. Then, on 17 May 1962, an entire Marine expeditionary unit deployed to northeastern Thailand in a show of force meant to intimidate Pathet Lao forces and their North Vietnamese supporters. The deployment was brief. On 1 July the Leatherneck units began to withdraw, and by the end of the month all were out of Thailand. Both the United States and the Soviet Union agreed to disengage from the controversy in Laos, but the former merely began a series of covert operations in support of the royalist government while the latter funneled its support through Hanoi. Yet the real potential for trouble lay across the Annamite Mountains in the two Vietnams.

A former French colony, Vietnam had been split in two following an unsuccessful attempt by Ho Chi Minh, the charismatic leader of the Viet Minh—a Communist-controlled popular front fighting for liberation from French rule—to unify the three colonies encompassing Vietnam (Cochin China, Annam, and Tonkin) under the Communist banner. In the north, Ho held sway with the Lao Dong (Worker's Party) controlling a Marxist government. In the south, Ngo Dinh Diem led a presumably democratic government. In fact, the government of South Vietnam was riddled with corruption, and the Catholic Diem enjoyed little support from the primarily Buddhist population.

U.S. involvement in the troubled Vietnams began almost immediately after the Geneva Accords of 1954 divided the country to separate the warring factions. Convinced that Communist-inspired insurgencies would engulf the region, the United States organized the Southeast Asia Treaty Organization (SEATO), a defensive alliance composed of Great Britain, France, Australia, New Zealand, Pakistan, Thailand, and the Philippines, later that year. President Eisenhower ordered economic aid to the Diem government and the establishment of the Military Assistance and Advisory Group (MAAG), Vietnam, which in 1962 became the U.S. Military Assistance Command, Vietnam (MACV). From the beginning, Marines served in MAAG–Vietnam and MACV.

On 2 August 1954 Lt. Col. Victor J. Croizat became the first senior Marine Corps adviser, or *co-van* (trusted friend), to the Vietnamese Marine Corps. On 24 October of that year, President Eisenhower promised U.S. assistance to the Diem government in the face of aggression from the North Vietnamese. Soon, U.S. military advisers began training South Vietnamese forces, replacing French instructors. When the People's Republic of China signed an agreement providing economic aid to North Vietnam on 7 July 1955, the political and military situation in Vietnam became increasingly worrisome. By 1960 MAAG–Vietnam had grown from 327 advisers to 685; that same year, Hanoi announced the formation of the National Front for the Liberation of South Vietnam under its aegis. On 1–2 November 1963 Diem was overthrown and assassinated in a coup d'état. The leaders of the coup had the tacit approval of the United States, which, while deploring the murders, welcomed a change in leadership. Contrary to American expectations, South Vietnam drifted into anarchy as competing factions wrestled for power and a Communist-inspired infrastructure gained support among the rural populace.

In 1964 the United States instigated a series of covert activities—code-named Plan 34A—aimed at deterring North Vietnamese aggression. South Vietnamese commandos infiltrated into North Vietnam, and South Vietnamese Navy patrol boats launched raids against the coastline of the Communist north. Plan 34A put the United States and North Vietnam on a collision course.

On 2 August 1964 North Vietnamese torpedo boats launched an attack on the U.S. destroyer *Maddox* cruising in the Tonkin Gulf. Two days later, the *Maddox* and another U.S. destroyer, the *Turner Joy,* reported a similar attack. On 5 August President Johnson ordered a series of retaliatory air strikes from the carriers *Constellation* and *Ticonderoga.* BLT 2/3, which had just arrived in the Philippines from Okinawa for training, reembarked for a hurried transit to Vietnamese waters. Eventually, an entire Marine expeditionary brigade joined the amphibious force. Into the fall the force cruised up and down the Vietnamese coast, waiting for an expected order to land the landing force. At least twice Leathernecks drew ammunition and prepared to go ashore but were recalled. By the Marine Corps's birthday, all had returned to Okinawa.

Ashore in South Vietnam, however, the deadly struggle intensified. On 1 November Viet Cong (VC; literally, "Vietnamese Communist") units launched a mortar attack against the U.S. compound at Bien Hoa, inflicting heavy casualties on American personnel and destroying a number of aircraft. On 24 December a bomb exploded outside a billet housing U.S. advisers in Saigon, killing and wounding a number of Americans. By the beginning of 1965 more than twenty-three thousand U.S. military personnel were serving in Vietnam, yet the situation continued to worsen. On 7 February Viet Cong units attacked a U.S. barracks at Pleiku in the Central Highlands. President Johnson ordered another series of retaliatory air raids on the north. Three days later, VC sappers bombed an enlisted barracks at Qui Nhon and President Johnson ordered another air strike. By 2 March a bombing offensive aimed at North Vietnam—Operation Rolling Thunder—was under way. Meanwhile, in the south, the deteriorating military situation around Danang became increasingly alarming. Many believed that South Vietnam's second most populous city might fall into insurgent hands.

Danang was more than the commercial hub of an estimated quarter million Vietnamese. Its huge airfield supported a multitude of activities: Vietnamese Air Force, U.S. Air Force, and the South Vietnamese airline, Air Vietnam. The headquarters of Military Region I was located within the air base defensive perimeter. Intelligence estimates indicated the presence of at least six thousand Viet Cong in the immediate vicinity of Danang. MACV's commander, Gen. William C. Westmoreland, requested the dispatch of a Marine unit to secure the vital Danang airfield. U.S. ambassador Maxwell D. Taylor gave his reluctant approval, despite his conviction that American servicemen could not adapt to the fighting endemic to the jungles and rice paddies of Southeast Asia.

But CINCPAC, Adm. Ulysses S. Grant Sharp, disagreed: "The Marines," he snapped, "have a distinguished record in counter-guerrilla warfare."[4] Lt. Gen. Brute Krulak, the Corps's counterinsurgency expert, then commanding the Fleet Marine Force–Pacific, was generally believed to have provided the stimulus—if not the actual words—to Sharp's pithy response. Westmoreland's request passed from CINCPAC to the Pentagon, and then to the

I Corps Area, South Vietnam, 1965–1973

White House, where it received swift approval from President Johnson.

By 8 March 1965, Task Force 76 with the embarked troops of the 9th MEB was off the coast of South Vietnam; Brig. Gen. Frederick J. Karch, a dapper, mustached officer with a fondness for camouflage ascots and shoulder holsters, commanded. At 9:02 A.M., the first Leathernecks from 3/9 waded ashore at Red Beach just north of Danang. The heavily laden Marines, sweating in the tropical heat and humidity, were greeted not by armed and menacing Viet Cong but by a beaming mayor. Accompanying this gentleman were scores of beautiful Vietnamese girls wearing white *ao dais* over black silk trousers, each carrying a basket of flower garlands to present to the men who had come to protect them. Even before BLT 3/9 came ashore, approximately thirteen hundred Marines were already in Vietnam, either in a helicopter squadron or in the antiaircraft missile battalion poised to protect the Danang airstrip from air attack. In the two days following 3/9's landing, BLT 1/3 arrived by

The first A-4 Skyhawk landed at the newly completed airfield at Chu Lai, South Vietnam, on 1 June 1965. It was piloted by Lt. Col. J. D. Noble, the commander of MAG-12.

air from Okinawa. Karch ordered 1/3 to provide perimeter security for the airstrip and directed 3/9 to take up defensive positions on Hill 327, the terrain dominating the skyline to the west of Danang.

The buildup continued rapidly. On 10 April a squadron of Marine F-4s—VMFA-531—arrived and established its base alongside the Vietnamese Air Force and U.S. Air Force contingents on the Danang airstrip. A day later, BLT 2/3—diverted from a routine deployment from Thailand to the Philippines—came ashore. On 14 April another BLT (3/4) arrived by air from Hawaii and took up defensive positions around the ancient capital of Hue, which housed a critical U.S. Army signal intelligence facility.

Meanwhile, someone in Saigon with an ear for historical punctilio suggested that the term *expeditionary* might remind the Vietnamese of the hated French Corps d'Expéditionnaire; thus, the "9th Marine Expeditionary Brigade" became the "9th Marine Amphibious Brigade." The appellation stuck, and when III Marine Expeditionary Force replaced the 9th MEB (or 9th MAB) on 6 May, it became III Marine Amphibious Force, or III MAF. And so it remained for the remainder of the Vietnam War and well into the 1980s. On 11 May the 1st MAW established its headquarters alongside the busy airstrip at Danang. Four days earlier, the 3rd MAB had landed fifty-seven miles south of Danang and established a base near an un-

named beach called "Chu Lai," supposedly General Krulak's name rendered in Mandarin Chinese.

The buildup of free world forces accelerated as General Westmoreland predicted that the Army of the Republic of Vietnam (ARVN) was nearing collapse. By early June MACV included two U.S. Army, one Australian, and seven U.S. Marine Corps infantry battalions. On 22 June Westmoreland asked Washington to increase the number of U.S. battalions to thirty-three; instead, the JCS approved an increase to forty-four battalions of American infantry. MACV claimed that with these battalions in 1965, it could prevent South Vietnam from losing the war; with an additional twenty-four battalions in 1966, it could begin winning the war. Four days after his request, Westmoreland received authorization to commit U.S. troops to combat. On 12 July, 1st Lt. Frank S. Reasoner of Company A, 3rd Reconnaissance Battalion—a former enlisted Marine who won an appointment to the U.S. Military Academy—earned the first Leatherneck Medal of Honor in the Vietnam War. He was killed attempting to come to the aid of his wounded radio operator after being ambushed while on patrol deep in Viet Cong–controlled territory.

On 30 July 1965 General Westmoreland gave Maj. Gen. Lewis W. Walt, the commander of III MAF, operational control of all U.S. forces in I Corps. The corps's area embraced the five northernmost provinces of South

Vietnam, containing a civilian population of twenty-six million people. A Leatherneck battalion, 3/4, operated out of Phu Bai, near the ancient imperial capital of Hue; the 3rd Marines were west and north of Danang; the 9th Marines south of the city; and the 4th Marines at Chu Lai, far to the south. The 1st MAW counted four air groups in-country: MAG-12 with A-4s at Chu Lai, MAG-11 with F-4s at Danang, MAG-16 at Danang with helicopters, and MAG-36 at Chu Lai, also with rotary-wing aircraft.

Coincident with Walt's Marines taking to the field with the full panoply of traditional Leatherneck air support, his troops drew heavy fire not only from the illusive enemy but also from American journalists. On 3 August a company of the 9th Marines approached a village on the Cam Do River six miles southwest of Danang. On taking small arms fire, the Leathernecks responded with a fusillade of rifle, machine-gun, and mortar fire. Sweeping through the village, the company suffered casualties from surprise firing devices or booby-traps and deadly *punji* stakes—sharpened bamboo spikes dipped in excrement. As the Marines put the torch to the VC-controlled village, CBS reporter Morley Safer reported the attack, mournfully intoning that "if these people weren't VC-sympathizers before, they certainly are now!"[5] The *Chicago Daily News* chimed in: "[Marines] have killed or wounded a number of Vietnamese civilians and burned dozens of homes in the dirtiest war Americans ever had to fight."[6] From that time until the end of U.S. military involvement in Vietnam, members of the Fourth Estate appeared to relish reporting accounts of what it believed to be untoward conduct by allied forces—especially Americans—in the controversial war in Southeast Asia.

On 18 August the first large-scale Marine offensive of the war began. Intelligence reports indicated the presence of the two-thousand-strong 1st VC Regiment on the Van Tuong Peninsula, fifteen miles south of Chu Lai. Col. Oscar F. Peatross—a veteran of Carlson's Raiders of World War II fame—led his 7th Marines ashore on the peninsula in a combination amphibious and heliborne assault that decimated the enemy force. The Marines counted 964 VC dead while losing only 51 Marines killed and 203 wounded by the time Operation Starlite ended on 24 August. Unimpressed, Westmoreland criticized Walt and his senior commanders for their unwillingness

to leave coastal enclaves and move into the hinterland. Westmoreland and his staff thought III MAF preoccupied with the Corps's sacrosanct amphibious doctrine and its jealously guarded prerogatives with regard to fixed-wing close air support. From Hawaii, Krulak did indeed guard the Corps's amphibious fiefdom and the sanctity of its close air support. Senior Air Force officers longed to gain operational control of Leatherneck fixed-wing aviation. Westmoreland eventually accepted their argument, and in 1968 I MAW was subordinated to the "mission direction" of the Seventh Air Force. In practice, the consequences of the change proved slight. The Air Force had won a doctrinal victory, but the great majority of I MAW's missions continued to be flown in support of Marines on the ground.

By the end of 1965 General Westmoreland and the senior members of his staff stood poles apart from General Walt and his commanders. Their differences extended from doctrinal issues to overall strategy. Influenced perhaps by Krulak, Walt believed strongly that his Marines should provide a shield behind which the South Vietnamese government could gain strength and earn the confidence of the rural populace. Krulak—fond of quoting the ancient Chinese military sage Sun Tzu—knew all too well that the VC infrastructure would wither and die only when the rural populace accepted the Saigon regime. "Winning their hearts and minds" became an often-repeated phrase at senior levels of command; however, to the Marine in the bush it translated simply as "grab them by the balls, and their hearts and minds will follow!"[7] For his part, Westmoreland remained scornful of the Marines' penchant for endearing themselves to the peasantry and promoting "civic action." He continued to argue for a strategy of attrition to defeat the Communists: simply stated, friendly forces would kill more Viet Cong or NVA (North Vietnamese Army) troops than could be replaced; sadly, that concept proved flawed almost from the outset. In South Vietnam, Viet Cong cadres emptied the villages of healthy males aged seventeen to thirty-five in Communist-controlled areas; South Vietnamese authorities did the same in villages where they held political sway. In North Vietnam, draft-eligible young men were inducted into the NVA at age seventeen.

Despite the criticism from chair-bound detractors in

Members of Company H, 7th Marines, patrol along rice-paddy dikes in December 1965 to drive the Viet Cong away from populated areas.

Saigon and Washington, General Walt's Marines put their theories into practice. Near Phu Bai, 3/4 combined a squad of Marines with a platoon of locally recruited Vietnamese militia to operate at the village and hamlet levels. As the unit became woven into the life of the village, people began to trust first them and then the government of South Vietnam. The concept expanded quickly until Combined Action Platoons, or CAPS, operated throughout I Corps. The idea proved to be one of the most successful innovations of the Vietnam War.

Notwithstanding the increasing number of free world forces in Vietnam, and Marines in I Corps, enemy units continued to harass Leatherneck installations without hindrance. On 27 October VC sappers demonstrated their ability to infiltrate the heavily guarded lines of even rear-area cantonments. Crawling through the protective wire and minefields surrounding the Corps's helicopter base at Marble Mountain, just south of Danang, the VC destroyed twenty-four aircraft and damaged twenty-three others. That same night, VC sappers infiltrated the airstrip at Chu Lai, blowing up two and damaging six of MAG-12's A-4s.

The following month, ARVN units abandoned the town of Hiep Duc in Quang Tin Province, allowing easy entrance for enemy units to the two district capitals, Viet An and Que Son in the Que Son Valley. In Operation Harvest Moon, the first joint ARVN–USMC operation of the war, three ARVN battalions deployed into the area to find and fix major enemy units. When significant contact was made, Task Force Delta—the 7th Marines plus 2/1 (the Special Landing Force)—under Brig. Gen. Jonas M. Platt would enter the fray.

Operation Harvest Moon began on 8 December. Two of the ARVN battalions made contact almost immediately and were decimated by a sizable VC main force unit. Platt ordered in two of his battalions by helicopter, and before long the entire task force had joined the action. B-52 bombers, flying from Guam, dropped their first payloads in support of ground forces in Vietnam during Operation Harvest Moon. Platt's Leathernecks lost 45 men killed and 218 wounded before the Viet Cong melted into the jungle.

By the beginning of 1966 Westmoreland had his 44 battalions in the field, but his intelligence officers re-

Marines engaged in Operation Harvest Moon advance across a rice paddy toward a tree line that has just been blasted by a flight of A-4s. The operation began on 8 December 1965.

Maj. Gen. Lewis W. "Lew" Walt, the first commander of III MAF, discusses the progress of Operation Harvest Moon with the commander of Company E, 7th Marines.

ported 110 enemy battalions in South Vietnam; ominously, 27 of the Communist battalions were composed of North Vietnamese Army regulars. Faced with this escalation, MACV increased its requirements to win the war: by the end of 1966 it wanted 162 ARVN, 74 U.S., and 23 other battalions in-country. An alarmed Secretary of Defense Robert S. McNamara agreed, even though the new requirements meant a U.S. troop strength of four hundred thousand. As he requested approval for the new troop levels from President Johnson, McNamara predicted that an estimated one thousand American servicemen would be killed in action each month.

In February, General Walt traveled to Washington for a series of conferences. In a surprise move, President Johnson promoted Walt to lieutenant general. Senior military planners urged the immediate call-up of reserves to provide the manpower for the widening war. But the president and his advisers demurred because of domestic political considerations and urged other sources to provide forces. On 1 March the 5th Marine Division was reactivated; plans had already been made to increase the Corps's strength from 190,000 to more than 278,000.

General Walt returned to I Corps in time to face an up-

rising of militant Buddhists opposed to the Saigon regime. The upheaval brought the pacification effort in the northern provinces to a halt. Meanwhile, MACV grew increasingly fearful that North Vietnamese forces planned an offensive far to the north along the Demilitarized Zone (DMZ) near the border with Laos. Special Forces camps along the Laotian border in Thua Thien and Quang Tri (the two northernmost provinces) fell to enemy units in the early spring. At Westmoreland's insistence, 1/1 occupied the old Civilian Irregular Defense Group camp at Khe Sanh along Highway 9 leading from Dong Ha to the Laotian border just below the DMZ. Walt believed that the battalion would find nothing, and it returned to confirm his estimate.

Westmoreland continued to insist that the North Vietnamese would attack across the DMZ, and again urged Walt to position a battalion north of Dong Ha. The battalion again found nothing of significance on 30 May, and a second battalion sent into the area in June also came up empty-handed. This time, however, the 4th Marines established a patrol base at Dong Ha. Then, ARVN units in the area reported the capture of a North Vietnamese soldier claiming to be from the 324B Division.

Company G, 4th Marines, moves up a rugged slope in pursuit of North Vietnamese regulars during Operation Hastings (15 July–3 August 1966), two miles from the DMZ. A heavy artillery and mortar barrage preceded the assault, but the Marines encountered a well-fortified enemy armed with automatic weapons.

The prisoner told his interrogators that his division had crossed the DMZ into South Vietnam.

In response to this information, Task Force Delta was activated with three infantry battalions and an artillery battalion. Dong Ha grew quickly into a sizable logistical support area. Intelligence officers opined that the 324B Division was somewhere to the north of Dong Ha. Quickly making contact with the enemy force, the Leathernecks of Task Force Delta slammed into the NVA unit. Operation Hastings III lasted from 15 July until 3 August, ultimately involving eight thousand Marines and three thousand ARVN troops. More than eight hundred North Vietnamese regulars lost their lives in Hanoi's attempt to establish a foothold in the northernmost provinces of South Vietnam.

Walt and Westmoreland continued to disagree, the for-

Leathernecks of Company M, 7th Marines, move to board helicopters that will transport them to search an area for NVA troops spotted the evening before.

mer asserting that the NVA was only diverting attention from the pacification program, and the latter insisting that the two NVA divisions poised just above the Demilitarized Zone posed a real threat to I Corps. In August 1/4 moved west from Dong Ha to Cam Lo and almost immediately encountered the NVA on a ridge to the north. By then, ample intelligence reports indicated that the 341st NVA Division had crossed the DMZ to join forces with the 324B Division. In response, Operation Prairie was initiated. By the time its four phases concluded in May 1967, the threat to the northern provinces appeared to have subsided.

A month later, General Walt was called home to become assistant commandant of the Marine Corps. At that time, and for some years thereafter, he was convinced that the war could be won. Lt. Gen. Robert E. Cushman Jr. succeeded him in command of III MAF. That same spring, Marines in Quang Tri Province reluctantly began work on a gigantic project that Secretary McNamara had been ardently advocating since the preceding September—the construction of an anti-infiltration barrier just below the DMZ. The product of misguided technical wizardry, the barrier would consist of sophisticated sensors, mines, and a new defensive wire featuring razor-sharp edges. Senior officers from Vietnam to the Pentagon agreed that the concept was preposterous. General Greene flatly opposed the idea and made no secret of his misgivings. The secretary of defense ended all criticism

Marines check Viet Cong bodies during Operation Deckhouse VI in February 1967.

by simply forbidding public comment from the uniformed services.

As Marines installed the barrier, Westmoreland urged Cushman to reinforce the battalion of the 26th Marines that had been positioned at Khe Sanh since midsummer. But by late fall 1967 the monsoon rains had hit northern I Corps with a vengeance. The dirt roads in Quang Tri Province turned into impassible quagmires, and the heavy cloud cover made aerial supply for Khe Sanh increasingly difficult. On 13 December, III MAF alerted the 3rd Marine Division that intelligence sources indicated four NVA regiments in the vicinity of Khe Sanh. In response, the headquarters of the 26th Marines was added to the battalion already at Khe Sanh and reinforced with 3/26.

In the rice paddies and hamlets farther to the south, the pacification effort so assiduously emphasized by the Marines since 1965 experienced difficulty in balancing

reverses with successes. Idealistic American interlopers found it difficult to accept the Confucian maxim that "the writ of the emperor does not extend beyond the village gate." Soldiers and Leathernecks alike failed to comprehend the complicated political structure of Vietnam, with its twisting maze of nepotism. Western-oriented intelligence officers refused to believe that the half-starved Communist combatants, most suffering from malaria and other diseases, would be willing to fight on forever against seemingly hopeless odds.

General Cushman commanded all the free world military armed forces in I Corps—except, of course, the Vietnamese troops. To the south, the Americal Division held sway in Quang Ngai and Quang Tin Provinces. The veteran 1st Marine Division operated throughout Quang Nam Province, while the 3rd Marine Division maneuvered in Thua Thien and Quang Tri Provinces in the

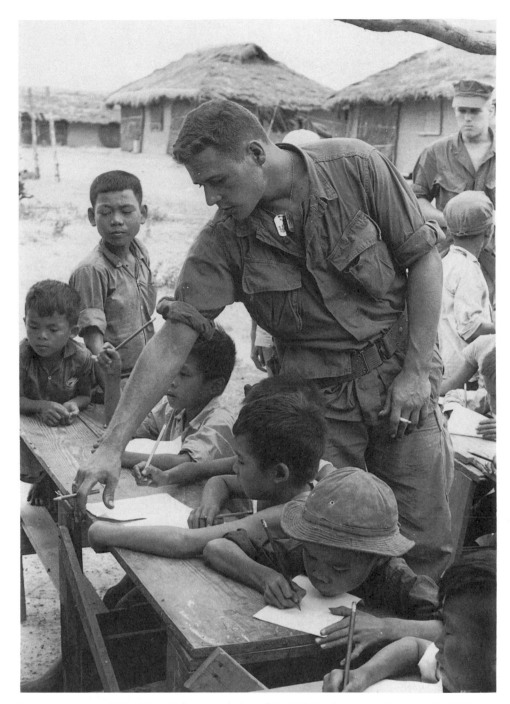

Twenty-two-year-old PFC M. J. Debets, a member of the 12th Marines, contributes to III MAF's "hearts and minds" program by giving English lessons to Vietnamese children at Camp Carroll in August 1967.

north. The latter had deployed to the two northernmost provinces in October. Approximately eighty thousand South Vietnamese troops also served in I Corps. Together, troop lists of free world forces included seventy-three allied infantry battalions in the five northernmost provinces of South Vietnam.

The 9th MAB maintained its headquarters on Okinawa as CINCPAC's strategic reserve. Components to form a nominal Marine Amphibious Unit rotated out of Vietnam, becoming part of the Seventh Fleet's Special Landing Force, and deployed by sea to the waters off South Vietnam. On 1 April 1967 CINCPACFLT ordered the acti-

The personal anguish of the Vietnam War is mirrored in this photograph of a Marine bowing his head in grief on learning that a close friend was killed during Operation Hickory near the DMZ in May 1967.

vation of a second amphibious ready group; thus, two special landing forces were available to support the operations of the Seventh Fleet. In reality, they were used to reinforce existing operations in the III MAF area of operations—although they were sent ashore infrequently to participate in combat operations in II, III, and IV Corps. Each Special Landing Force included a battalion landing team and a medium helicopter squadron.

At the end of 1967, 81,249 of the 298,498 Marines in uniform were serving in Vietnam: 21 of the Corps's 36 infantry battalions, 14 of its 33 fixed-wing squadrons, and 13 of its 24 helicopter squadrons. No other U.S. armed service contributed such a large percentage of its forces to the Vietnam War. Career Marines returned for second tours—later, some would begin third tours.

Meanwhile, the Johnson administration had been considering a replacement for General Greene, whose tenure as commandant was approaching its end. In the forefront of the contenders stood the generals most symbolic of Leatherneck participation in the war, Walt and Krulak. But although both of them called in every marker in their favor, the Oval Office and Pentagon chose an officer far removed from the conflagration in Southeast Asia. On 1 January 1968 Greene's chief of staff, Lt. Gen. Leonard F. Chapman Jr., became the twenty-fourth commandant of the Marine Corps. An artilleryman, Chapman had commanded a battalion in World War II and served with distinction in a variety of subsequent assignments. He would lead the Corps through some of the most trying times in its long history.

In the spring of 1967 Pentagon staffers concluded that a new rifle, the M16 firing the standard NATO 5.56 cartridge, offered advantages over the M14 because of its high volume of fire at short ranges. Never before had a military organization so dependent on the prowess of skirmishing infantry conducted such a wholesale change in its basic weaponry in the middle of a war. Veterans and rookies alike grumbled, and then swore vehemently as the M16 demonstrated a proclivity to jam. Journalists found grist for their mills in numerous reports taken from disgusted and confused soldiers and Marines. Only when troops learned to keep the chambers meticulously clean with the aid of wire-bristle bore brushes did the acrimony subside. But up and down the chain of command, the ill-timed adoption of the M16 was ridiculed as yet another of Secretary McNamara's innovations run amok.

More serious considerations than balky M16s plagued the MACV commanders, however, including a buildup of the NVA forces in Quang Tri Province. General Cushman had already responded by positioning all three of the 3rd Marine Division's infantry regiments in the northernmost provinces of I Corps. Enemy activity in the northwest corner of Quang Tri increased in intensity. NVA rockets, mortars, and artillery pounded ARVN and Marine installations at Gio Linh and Con Thien. Leatherneck patrols made heavy contact with the NVA units near Khe Sanh and Hill 861. The 3rd Marines joined an ARVN force to clear the area south of the Ben Hai River of enemy troops.

Westmoreland and his staff suspected an enemy offensive in the offing, but no one imagined the scope and intensity of Tet 1968. Since the Army's epic encounter in the Ia Drang Valley in late 1965, U.S. forces had proven themselves superior in every major encounter with Viet Cong and NVA units. The enemy appeared to be reeling under the weight of American firepower and logistical superiority. Confidence prevailed from MACV to CINCPAC to the White House. In response to the perceived threat in the north, Westmoreland ordered the 101st Airborne and 1st Air Cavalry divisions into the two northernmost provinces. Intelligence reports revealed the 325C and 304th NVA divisions massing outside Khe Sanh, and the 308th and 341st NVA divisions menacing Camp Carroll and the Rockpile closer to Dong Ha. The headquarters of the 3rd Marine Division moved to Dong Ha and sent 2/26 to Khe Sanh to give Col. David E. Lownds all three of his organic battalions.

On 2 January 1968 a patrol from Khe Sanh ambushed an NVA reconnaissance party, killing a regimental commander. Later in the month, a fusillade of rocket and mortar fire struck the base, setting off its ammunition dump and fuel farm. Cushman sent in 1/9 to reinforce the 26th Marines and, with a sense of diplomacy, asked for the loan of an ARVN ranger battalion. Two more batteries of 105-mm howitzers reinforced the artillery already at Khe Sanh. The base's defenders also gained solace from the knowledge that the Army's 175-mm gun battalion at Camp Carroll could fire in support of the outpost.

As expected, the Viet Cong announced a truce for the Tet holiday, 27 January–3 February, in celebration of the Lunar New Year. South Vietnam followed with its own cease-fire scheduled for thirty-six hours around 29 January. The enemy offensive probably began in earnest on the night of the government's cease-fire, when rockets and mortars hit military installations at Danang; the next night, Chu Lai received similar treatment. Communist forces throughout the country hoped to confine allied units to their cantonments, keeping them huddled behind sandbagged walls or in bunkers while they attacked provincial and district capitals to discredit and disrupt the South Vietnamese government and the pacification program. No less than six NVA divisions had entered the two northernmost provinces of I Corps. On 31 January two NVA regiments

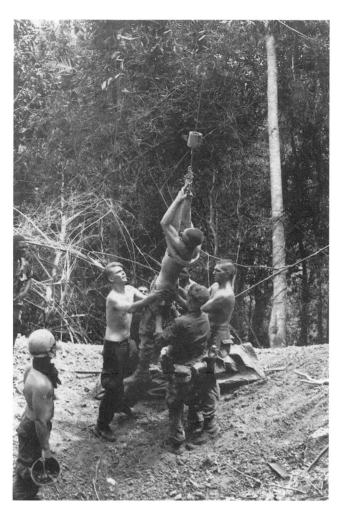

A wounded Marine from Company F, 4th Marines, is lifted out of heavy foliage during Operation Choctaw, conducted in the summer of 1967 just south of the DMZ. When the terrain prevented a landing by medevac helicopters, injured Leathernecks were often taken out of the field in this fashion.

joined Viet Cong units in Hue, Vietnam's third largest metropolitan center, and seized most of the city.

Just to the south of Hue stood the only friendly force available: Task Force X-Ray, with just three battalions of Leatherneck infantry to defend the base at Phu Bai and keep Highway 1 open between there and Danang. Regimental Landing Team 27 arrived from Camp Pendleton to take over the 5th Marines' sector south of Danang, and the veteran regiment moved north to recapture the ancient capital. The 1st Battalion, 1st Marines, marched from Phu Bai to attempt to breach the Citadel. On 4 February, 2/5 arrived from Quang Nam Province to join in the house-to-house fighting. But after

Company D, 5th Marines, moves through the streets of battle-scarred Hue during the Tet offensive of 1968. Desperate fighting to evict NVA forces destroyed much of the once-beautiful city.

a week of intense urban combat, both battalions were spent. On 12 February 1/5 moved on the Citadel with ARVN and South Vietnamese Marine units; it took another twelve days of bloody combat to rid the ancient fortress of the invaders.

U.S. Marine losses numbered 142 killed and 857 wounded. During their brief occupation of the city, NVA and VC death squads executed more than five thousand Vietnamese civilians considered a "threat" to the Communist revolution. Finally, on 2 March, the battle for Hue officially ended. Three Marine Corps and thirteen Vietnamese battalions had destroyed an estimated eight to eleven NVA battalions in one of the bitterest confrontations of the war. The beautiful ancient capital was in ruins, and many of its inhabitants lay dead in the rubble or in makeshift graves dug by their executioners.

Farther to the north, NVA forces laid siege to Khe Sanh. Colonel Lownds had more than six thousand men at his disposal, but fifteen to twenty thousand NVA troops were poised outside their position. Journalists, many of whom came no closer to the siege than the bars of their Saigon hotels, demonstrated a fondness for comparing the Leathernecks' situation with that of the beleaguered French at Dien Bien Phu in 1954. President Johnson, growing increasingly concerned, went so far as to require the Joint Chiefs of Staff to sign a memorandum "guaranteeing" that Khe Sanh would not fall. As they had done at Dien Bien Phu, the Communists practiced classic seventeenth-century siegecraft, pushing a complex network of trenches ever closer to the base's perimeter and shelling its interior. The difference was that at Khe Sanh they never succeeded in closing the defenders' airstrip or breaking into their positions.

On 6 February mortar and artillery shells signaled an NVA assault on the Civilian Irregular Defense Group camp at Lang Vei, between Khe Sanh and the Laotian border. The NVA took the camp, riding through its gates in Soviet-built PT-76 amphibious tanks. Only half of the estimated five hundred defenders escaped, most by fleeing with an assortment of refugees to Khe Sanh. Arriving from Saigon, General Westmoreland excoriated everyone in sight at III MAF headquarters: Marine fixed-wing aircraft should have provided more air support for the 1st Air Cavalry Division! Why was Lang Vei not reinforced? On the heels of his stormy visit, MACV announced the opening of a MACV forward command post (subsequently designated XXIV Corps) in the northernmost provinces of I Corps. Its operational control would include the 3rd Marine Division, 101st Airborne Division, and 1st Air Cavalry Division. However, the new headquarters was under the operational control of III MAF.

On 1 April Operation Pegasus began, an offensive by the 1st Air Cavalry Division, the 1st Marines, and four ARVN battalions aimed at reestablishing overland communications with Khe Sanh. Eleven days later, journalists, prodded by senior Army officers, gleefully reported the "relief" of Khe Sanh by units of the 1st Air Cavalry Division. At the remote outpost, however, no one registered particular joy, simply because they had never considered themselves in danger of being overrun. During the seventy-seven days the siege was calculated to have lasted, Khe Sanh's defenders had lost 205 men killed and 1,668 wounded. Enemy casualties were estimated at between ten thousand and fifteen thousand. At a White House ceremony, a greatly relieved President Johnson presented the Presidential Unit Citation to Colonel Lownds and his sergeant major, Agrippa W. Smith, to reward the 26th Marines for the gallant defense of Khe Sanh.

The Tet offensive shattered the VC infrastructure in the hamlets and villages—which had taken the Communists years to build—and decimated enemy forces. An estimated fifteen thousand VC and NVA soldiers were killed; Communists—in both the north and the south—experienced a number of surprises. To their bitter disappointment and chagrin, ARVN forces did not desert or defect; the people did not rally to the Communists, but instead looked on in horror at the senseless massacre of innocent civilians; and the people did not rise up against the Saigon regime.[8] Yet the military defeat of the Communist forces was lost in the wake of an obvious political disaster; millions of Americans watched their television screens in horror as Viet Cong stormed the U.S. embassy in Saigon and NVA units raised the flag of North Vietnam

A combat photographer captured a Leatherneck clambering through the rubble of Hue. For most Marines, pitched battles in an urban setting were an anomaly after months of fighting in the paddies of the lowlands.

over the Citadel of Hue. President Johnson announced that veteran politician Clark Clifford would replace McNamara as secretary of defense on 1 March. Gen. Creighton W. Abrams relieved Westmoreland, who was named chief of staff of the Army.

Then, on 31 March, President Johnson surprised the nation and the world with the announcement that he would not seek reelection. The president also announced a partial suspension of the bombing of North Vietnam. But his hope that these two concessions would bring the Communists to the peace table was disappointed. The enemy merely took comfort from his pronouncement and the subsequent American political turmoil. When the Communist Party of South Vietnam met for its Ninth Conference in July 1969, its leaders reaffirmed what they

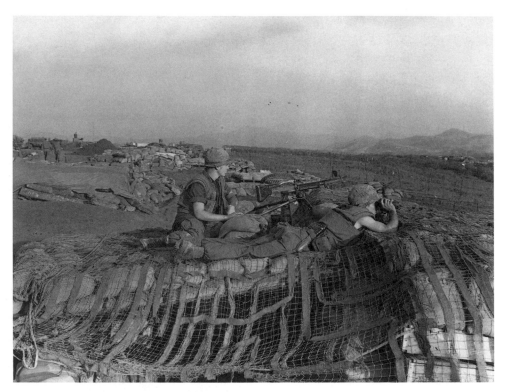

Marine machine gunners watch for enemy movement near sunset at Khe Sanh, 15 March 1968.

had learned the year before: that "the internal contradiction between the U.S. rulers and . . . the American people was the greatest weak point of the Americans at this time."

In the wake of the Tet Offensive, III MAF units pressed their counteroffensive along the DMZ. An enemy force attacked Dong Ha between Highway 1 and Route 9; then, on 29 April, an ARVN regiment locked horns with a sizable NVA unit. Lt. Col. William Weise's 2/4 entered the fray against the main body of the enemy force. Beginning on 1 May, the battalion attacked the fortified village of Dai Do. The commanding officer of Company G, Capt. M. Sando Vargas Jr., fought off several successive enemy counterattacks that night, despite being seriously wounded. Capt. James E. Livingston led Company E through intense fire to support Vargas. Although wounded as well, Livingston joined Vargas to lead the two companies in an assault through the village. By then Livingston had suffered another wound—as had the battalion commander. Both Livingston and Vargas earned Medals of Honor for their heroism at Dai Do.[9]

At a press conference in Washington on 10 June, General Westmoreland admitted that the war could not be won because of "our national policy of not extending the war." In other words, he blamed politicians' refusal to allow the military to exert the full fury of America's warmaking potential against North Vietnam. Thus began the argument that civilians in Washington had tied the hands of American fighting men in Southeast Asia. Many senior officers believed strongly that the only way to bring the conflict to a conclusion favoring South Vietnam and its supporters was to take the ground war to the north; but by then, antiwar sentiment in the United States precluded the adoption of such a strategy. The presidential election that fall made it clear that the American public wanted out of Vietnam. Republican candidate Richard M. Nixon promised a plan to end the war without surrendering, while Democrat Hubert H. Humphrey suggested that if he were elected, the United States would simply pull out of the conflict.

By the end of 1968 it was obvious that the Marine Corps had been in Vietnam too long. An aura of permanency prevailed in many of the cantonments. At Danang, the headquarters of III MAF, the 1st MAW, and the 1st Marine Division were air-conditioned and—except for

During Operation Lancaster II in July 1968, Company E, 3d Marines, climbed Mutters Ridge near the DMZ north of Dong Ha. Entrenched NVA defenders stalled the company's advance until Marines drove them out with well-aimed volleys of hand grenades.

the sandbags surrounding them and armed sentries in profusion—appeared not unlike similar installations outside Vietnam. Marines in rear areas ate in mess halls that provided meals just as tasty and varied as back home; even Leathernecks in the bush found the dismal diet of C rations varied with B rations, extra canned fruit and juices, and something new and tasty—the long-range patrol ration. Infantry companies were lifted by helicopter out of the paddies and jungles for a "breathing spell" at a mini–rest and recreation center at White Beach beside the sparkling Pacific waters near Danang. There, for a few brief hours, weary Marines could drink all the cold beer or soda they wanted and gorge themselves on steak and shrimp without worrying about being in someone's gun sight. Once each tour, a Marine might travel to Hawaii to meet his wife or to some exotic Pacific city in search of rest, relaxation, and "horizontal refreshment." From the time the first Marine marched ashore, senior officers demonstrated a determined effort to separate their men from the depravity that usually accompanies an

army in the field. Liberty in the populated areas was authorized only near the end of the Marine Corps's deployment in Vietnam. But troublesome trysts with local prostitutes occurred nonetheless, and substance abuse accompanied the dilemma for commanding officers. Young Marines in particular responded to the enticing and lurid refrains: "Hey, Marine, you want boom-boom?" or "Hey, Marine, you want smoke a joint?" without considering the consequences.[10]

The war had become a routine, and many Marines had grown indifferent to its persistent problems and challenges. ARVN units continued to perform inconsistently according to the whims of both commanders and weary Vietnamese troops who saw no end to the conflict. Returning Leathernecks found themselves attacking and seizing the same old terrain. The anticommunist motivation of 1965 was replaced by grave cynicism, as few believed that the South Vietnamese—with their corrupt political machinery and lackluster armed forces—could manage without the Americans. Ethnic slurs peppered

A CH-46 Sea Knight helicopter provides emergency resupply for Marines on Mutters Ridge.

the daily speech of Marines—officers as well as enlisted personnel—and the sad commentary heard in infantry units, "a dead Gook is a Viet Cong," rang true more often than not.[11]

Leatherneck commanders were forced to deal with increasingly frequent racial and drug-related incidents. Troops found a simple solution when faced with an unpopular officer or NCO: a fragmentation grenade tossed into a billet in the dark of night. "Fragging," as it was called, became yet another grim aspect of the Vietnam War that made the days long for Leatherneck commanders. But the endless war continued as friendly forces continued to win every battle, even though Washington and Saigon appeared to be working together to lose the war. Political opponents in the United States, growing more

militant and gaining support, became increasingly persuasive. On the battlefield, Marines found more and more that "Viet Cong" units consisted largely of NVA regulars. U.S. and allied victories had taken a deadly toll among the insurgents.

Late in 1968, intelligence sources reported NVA units hard at work to reopen infiltration routes from Laos into Quang Tri and Thua Thien Provinces. An estimated two NVA infantry regiments, supported by an artillery regiment and an engineer regiment, had moved along the border facing the A Shau and Da Krong Valleys southwest of Quang Tri and west of Hue. The commanding general of the 3rd Marine Division ordered Col. Robert H. Barrow's 9th Marines to interdict and destroy NVA units involved in the infiltration into I Corps's northernmost provinces. Thus began one of the most successful allied operations of the Vietnam War.

In early 1969 construction began on three fire-support bases (FSB) to support Operation Dewey Canyon: Shiloh, Razor, and Cunningham. Colonel Barrow positioned his headquarters and five batteries of artillery on FSB Cunningham, 1/9 heli-lifted into Shiloh, 3/9 occupied FSBs Henderson and Tun Tavern, and 2/9 operated out of FSB Vandegrift farther to the north. On 25 January 3/9 assaulted three landing zones on a ridge sixty-six hundred yards southwest of FSB Razor.[12]

On 10 February Barrow moved 1/9 from FSBs Vandegrift and Shiloh to a new fire-support base, Erskine, along with a 105-mm howitzer battery to support it. Increasing evidence pointed to a heavy enemy buildup of supplies and material just across the border in Laos in apparent anticipation of a major thrust into South Vietnam in the vicinity of Route 922. The usual truce for the Tet holiday went into effect on 16 February, followed by the usual number of expected violations. At 3:45 the following morning, NVA forces assaulted FSB Cunningham. Although the attackers penetrated the position's defensive perimeter, the Leathernecks succeeded in ejecting them.

Between 18 and 22 February the heaviest fighting of Operation Dewey Canyon took place. First Lt. Wesley L. Fox's Company A bore the brunt of the onslaught, and the veteran Marine—commissioned from the ranks after a sixteen-year career—earned the Medal of Honor. Al-

Elements of Company B, 4th Marines, ford a stream east of Vandegrift Combat Base during Operation Scotland II, which lasted from April 1968 to February 1969.

though wounded along with all of the other members of his headquarters group, Fox continued to command his company. He personally led an attack that captured a large bunker complex. Fox was "wounded again in the final assault . . . refused medical attention, established a defensive posture, and supervised the preparation of casualties for medical evacuation." His citation concluded that his "indomitable courage, inspiring initiative, and unwavering devotion to duty in the face of grave personal danger inspired his Marines to such aggressive action that they overcame all enemy resistance."[13]

During Operation Dewey Canyon, Marine aircraft flew 461 fixed-wing close air support missions, dropping more than two thousand tons of ordnance on enemy positions. MAG-36 and MAG-30 flew more than twelve hundred helicopter sorties in support of the 9th Marines and ARVN units. Colonel Barrow's supporting artillery fired more than 134,000 rounds. U.S. and South Viet-

namese forces suffered 130 dead and 920 wounded, while NVA units lost an estimated 1,617 dead. The amount of enemy ordnance seized stunned even the most optimistic planners.

Much farther to the south, intelligence officers at the headquarters of both the 1st Marine Division and III MAF took pains to sift every grain of evidence in the closing months of 1968 to determine if Communist forces planned another large offensive. While no major indications surfaced to suggest an offensive of the magnitude of Tet 1968, enemy troop movements and contact reports pointed toward a series of coordinated attacks in Quang Nam Province around the time of the lunar new year. On 17 January 1969 the 7th Marines captured a signal officer from the headquarters of Group 44—Communist headquarters in the region—who indicated that a winter-spring offensive was in the works.[14] Two weeks later the same regiment captured two NVA soldiers

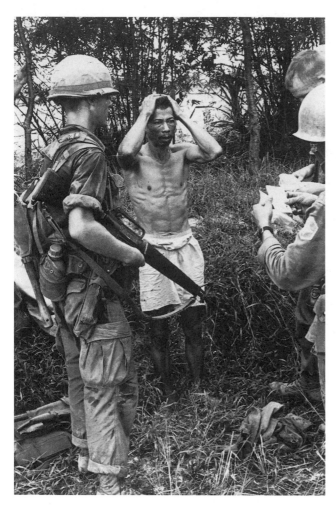

A Viet Cong captive awaits his fate as an ARVN interpreter studies documents found on him. As the number of Viet Cong combatants dropped through attrition, Marines increasingly encountered an enemy similar to this one: barefoot, attired only in shorts, and nearly emaciated as a result of operations denying him access to native foodstuffs.

On 23 February a squad-sized patrol from Capt. Paul K. Van Riper's Company M, 7th Marines, spotted an NVA force west of Danang. An hour later, another patrol observed an enemy unit through a Starlight scope. With an artillery fire mission in progress, two squads from the 3rd Platoon went out to ambush the force. A sweep of the area at first light revealed that M/3/7 had surprised an NVA mortar company. By daylight, Company M found itself engaged with a sizable enemy force. In a day punctuated by heavy hand-to-hand fighting—often in clouds of tear gas—the Leathernecks counted thirty NVA killed and took another three prisoners; the following day, another nine enemy died. Near Danang, a rocket ignited 240,000 gallons of JP4 aviation fuel at the 1st MAW fuel farm and another rocket struck the ARVN ammunition dump near III MAF headquarters.

By then the remainder of Lt. Col. Francis X. Quinn's 3/7 had entered the intense fighting that erupted with the onset of the long-awaited enemy offensive. Thick stands of bamboo and dense growths of elephant grass prevented observation and provided good cover for the enemy units. The intense heat and humidity taxed the Marines heavily. Individual heroism became commonplace in 3/7 during its fierce encounter with the NVA force. Lance Cpl. Lester W. Weber, a machine-gun squad leader in Company M, earned a posthumous Medal of Honor in some of the most savage combat recorded by Leathernecks in the Vietnam War. In the words of his citation, "Weber's platoon came under heavy attack from concealed hostile soldiers. He reacted by plunging into the tall grass, successfully attacking one enemy and forcing eleven others to break contact." Then, "upon encountering a second NVA soldier, [Weber] overwhelmed him in fierce hand-to-hand combat. Observing two other soldiers firing upon his comrades from behind a dike, Weber ignored the frenzied firing of the enemy and raced across the hazardous area and dived into their position." Wresting an AK-47 assault rifle from one, he beat them both to death with it. "Although by now the target for concentrated fire from hostile riflemen, Weber remained in a dangerously exposed position to shout words of encouragement to his emboldened companions. As he moved forward to attack a fifth enemy soldier, he was mortally wounded."[15]

claiming to be in the 21st Regiment, who also reported a major offensive in the making. ARVN forces also detected signs of an enemy offensive brewing. Then, just before the Tet holiday, an ARVN unit clashed with an enemy battalion south of Hill 55, killing forty-nine NVA troops. The two prisoners taken claimed to belong to the 36th NVA Regiment, which was apparently moving out of its rainy-season sanctuary in the southern end of the province. The 5th Marines in the An Hoa basin reported elements of at least two NVA regiments in their area, along with several Viet Cong units.

As Company M continued to attack, the remaining units of 3/7 joined in pursuit of the enemy. Early in the afternoon of 24 February, Capt. Fred T. Fagan led Company K across the highway leading from Danang and intercepted a sizable NVA force. In a sweep of the area the following morning, Company K discovered numerous enemy bodies and took several prisoners. One of the POWs turned out to be an NVA regimental commander.

Interrogation of the haughty captive revealed that the enemy hoped to hurt 3/7 badly enough to draw the remainder of the 1st Marine Division into the paddies west of Danang. There, at least two NVA regiments and an assortment of Viet Cong units would spring the trap.[16] The enemy's plan fell apart during the period 22–28 February, when 3/7 tore up the enemy task force and took its commander captive. Throughout I Corps, U.S. and allied units responded to the enemy offensive by repulsing every attempt to breach their positions.

In March, Lt. Gen. Herman Nickerson Jr. relieved General Cushman in command of III MAF. Three months thereafter, President Nixon's "Vietnamization" plan went into effect. This called for U.S. forces to conduct a phased withdrawal during which increased training and equipment turnovers would (supposedly) enable the South Vietnamese armed forces to shoulder the burden of defending their country by themselves. By 31 August the first increment of twenty-five thousand Americans—including several Leatherneck units—would depart Vietnam.

Even as the Oval Office announced the American retrenchment, the grim struggle in the paddies and jungles continued unabated. On 9 March the depleted ranks of the 141st NVA Regiment chanced a daylight crossing of Arizona Territory in hopes of slipping undetected across the Song Thu Bon to attack the headquarters of 1/7 on the north bank. Discovered by elements of both 1/5 and 1/7, the survivors of the abortive post-Tet offensive of 1969 were decimated by a rain of artillery shells fired by batteries from the 11th Marines and ordnance from 1st MAW aircraft. After the battle the Marines found 292 enemy bodies littering the rice paddies on the south side of the Song Thu Bon. Nevertheless, Communist headquarters merely inserted another regiment into the fray. In the early summer the 90th NVA Regiment began op-

Lance Cpl. Charles E. Soard, a scout with Company C, 5th Marines, carries an elderly Vietnamese woman to a helicopter for relocation to a refugee camp near the An Hoa Combat Base, 12 February 1970. While such operations removed villagers from the danger inherent in Viet Cong–controlled areas and denied the enemy access to native foodstuffs, the peasants were loathe to leave ancestral grave sites behind for a life in squalid camps.

erations in Arizona Territory west of the An Hoa Combat Base, but elements of the 5th Marines killed an estimated 320 troops from the new unit before the first rains of the fall monsoon fell.

In the early fall the White House announced another troop withdrawal that included two Marine regiments and a division headquarters. Almost as if Hanoi was working in concert with the American withdrawal, significant encounters with NVA forces fell markedly. By the fall of 1969 most enemy contact consisted of terrorist acts carried out by guerrillas.

On 9 March 1970 XXIV Corps and III MAF exchanged positions, with the latter displacing to a new headquarters beside Red Beach. III MAF's last commanders, Lt. Gens. Keith B. McCutcheon and Donn Robertson, controlled for the most part only U.S. forces in Quang Nam Province. The era of multibattalion operations had ended. The residual Leatherneck force concentrated on providing protection for populated areas. In September 1970 the 7th Marines stood down and prepared to return to Camp Pendleton; the 5th Marines followed in February 1971. This left Col. Paul X. Kelley's 1st Marines as the only Leatherneck ground combat force in-country. It would be up to the South Vietnamese to continue the struggle.

As the Americans prepared to depart, South Vietnamese forces prepared to launch their first independent large-scale operation. Lam Son 719, staged in early 1971, envisioned a spoiling operation across the border into the enemy sanctuaries in Laos from Quang Tri Province. U.S. advisers were pointedly excluded from the foray, as were American ground forces. Leathernecks from the 1st Marine Division provided security along Highway 9 for the ARVN units, and Marine Corps aviators flew some helicopter support missions. Otherwise, the operation was Vietnamese in its entirety—and it very quickly became a disaster. The South Vietnamese troops proved no match for the Communist forces, who both outnumbered and outmaneuvered them. The disaster of Lam Son 719 foreshadowed the military future of South Vietnam.

On 14 April 1971 the colors of III MAF, the 1st Marine Division, and 1st MAW were cased; 3rd MAB became the senior Marine Corps unit in Vietnam. But even this residual force was scheduled to depart by midsummer; all combat operations on the part of U.S. forces would cease on 7 May. The only Leathernecks remaining in-country would be the guards at the U.S. embassy in Saigon and the consulate in Danang, advisers to Vietnamese Marine units, and personnel assigned to the Air and Naval Gunfire Liaison Company (ANGLICO) that supported allied forces other than Marines.

Veterans of the lingering war wondered just how long it would take the North Vietnamese to attempt to overrun the south once the Americans had gone. In the spring of 1972 NVA forces in divisional strength struck across the DMZ and from Laos into the northernmost provinces. Farther to the south, another NVA force attacked from Cambodia into the Central Highlands. In Quang Tri Province, NVA forces quickly overran ARVN units next to the DMZ and occupied the old Leatherneck bases in the area; before long, the flag of North Vietnam flew over the provincial capital of Quang Tri City. As South Vietnamese forces rallied to repel the invaders, the United States responded with naval gunfire and close air support—but no ground troops other than advisers.

Closer to the intense combat along the DMZ, a lone Marine officer performed one of the most courageous acts of the war and succeeded in blunting the NVA attack. Capt. John W. Ripley, an adviser to a Vietnamese marine battalion, single-handedly emplaced more than five hundred pounds of explosives on the Dong Ha Bridge over the Cua Viet River. As he swung hand over hand across the beams supporting the bridge, Communist forces on the other side of the river took him under fire. An enemy column with an estimated two hundred tanks approached, hoping to cross the bridge and continue the assault into the northern provinces. Barely returning to safety on the south side of the bridge, Ripley detonated his charges and collapsed the center span of the bridge into the river. Timbers on both sides burned for a week.[17]

By fall, South Vietnamese units and their American advisers had beaten off the invasion. President Nixon's clear threat to resume hostilities was not lost on the leadership in Hanoi. When Communist negotiators walked out of the Paris peace talks, the United States resumed bombing the north and, for the first time, mined Haiphong harbor. However confident Hanoi appeared to be, its leaders knew they could expect a much tougher Nixon now that he had trounced Democratic hopeful George S. McGovern in the presidential election. On 27 January 1973 the Paris Peace Accords were signed, ending American participation in the Second Indochina War. Within the next month, 591 American POWS—including 26 Marines—returned home; earlier, 9 Leathernecks had escaped captivity, 3 were exchanged, and 8 died in captivity. Another 105 Marines remained on the MIA list, and 2 were listed as simply "unaccounted for." Capt. Donald G. Cook, captured in 1964, died in captivity; he earned a posthumous Medal of Honor for his unflagging courage in the face of hopeless odds and extreme peril.

The final chapter in the Marine Corps's involvement

in the Southeast Asian struggle occurred two years later. On 12 April 1975 CH-53 helicopters from HMH-462 and HMH-463 evacuated Americans, selected government officials, and foreign nationals from the Cambodian capital of Phnom Penh in Operation Eagle Pull five days before the Khmer Rouge entered the city in triumph. Later that month, South Vietnamese began to flee their country as North Vietnam launched an all-out conventional invasion. During 29–30 April, more than nine thousand people were evacuated from beleaguered Saigon by Marines flying helicopters from ships of the Seventh Fleet in Operation Frequent Wind. On 30 April, Saigon fell to the NVA. As President Nguyen Van Thieu fled, doubtless he carried with him President Nixon's letter of 14 November 1972, which stated: "You have my absolute assurance that if Hanoi fails to abide by the terms of the agreement it is my intention to take swift and retaliatory action."[18]

The longest war in the Corps's history ended on a sour note; 13,067 Leathernecks died in the divisive conflict. Another 88,633 were wounded, of whom 51,389 required hospitalization. Fifty-seven Marines—and a Navy chaplain and three hospital corpsmen serving with Leatherneck units—earned Medals of Honor, forty-six of them posthumously.[19]

14

The New Breed, 1976–2000

The Vietnam War took a heavy toll on the Marine Corps, sapping its strength and morale like no conflict before. Recruiters experienced difficulty filling enlistment quotas and often met their required numbers with young men and women who did not meet the Corps's usual standard. Many of the recruits of the early 1970s arrived at San Diego or Parris Island lacking the skills or desire requisite to be good Marines. Career Marines, both officers and NCOs, found their days long and dark. Civilian officials appeared to take an increasingly intrusive role in military and naval affairs. Conscientious commanding officers did their best, but at times it was difficult to carry on. Congressional critics convinced themselves that better living quarters for junior enlisted Marines would attract high-quality recruits. Instead, the "military motels" that replaced the traditional barracks only made it more difficult for commanders to control their troops. Civil libertarians in and out of uniform contributed to the growing malaise by providing seemingly insurmountable legal hurdles in the face of rising incidences of petty thievery, racially motivated assaults, and drug and alcohol abuse on an unparalleled scale. Many career Marines left the Corps rather than face a new generation of recruits who seemed unwilling or incapable of accepting the Leatherneck code of toughness and discipline.

When the Vietnam War ended, the strength of the Marine Corps dropped quickly to less than two hundred thousand. Yet historical commitments overseas, at home, and in support of the fleet remained. In traditional "can-do" fashion, senior Leathernecks ignored what was happening outside the gates and applied themselves to day-to-day problems. Shortages in the ranks resulted in many units reverting to cadre status. More than one grizzled Marine was heard to mutter: "We've done so much for so long with so little, we can now do everything with nothin'."

On 1 January 1972 Gen. Robert E. Cushman Jr. became the commandant, and thus inherited the social and political problems accompanying the postbellum standdown. Many observers—both in and out of forest green—concluded that the Corps was rapidly losing its élan. Just as had happened during the retrenchments following previous conflicts, critics declared that the Marine Corps had become an expensive anachronism unsuited to the defense needs of the United States. Defense Department officials, some members of the congressional armed services committees, and analysts at the prestigious Brookings Institute united in calling for a drastic restructuring of the Corps. Following the debacle in Southeast Asia, most pundits concluded that America's military orientation now lay in the direction of Western Europe and the armor-heavy defense of NATO. The Corps's expertise in amphibious warfare and light infantry structure appeared irrelevant.

General Cushman addressed the Corps's critics in much the same strident fashion as his predecessors had done: "We are pulling our heads out of the jungle and getting back into the amphibious business. . . . We are redirecting our attention seaward and reemphasizing our partnership with the Navy and our shared concern in the

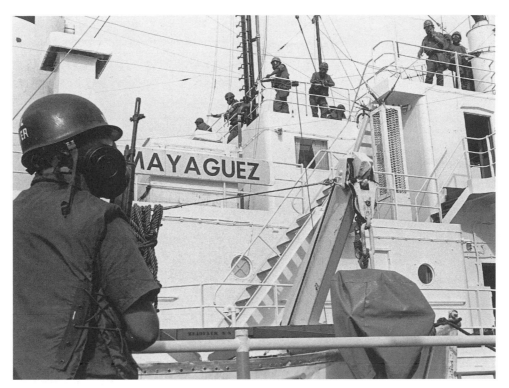

Marines from Company D, 9th Marines, board the SS *Mayaguez* from the destroyer escort *Harold E. Holt,* 15 May 1975.

maritime aspects of our national strategy."[1] The commandant and HQMC produced figures sure to delight congressional watchdogs: the Marine Corps provided 15 percent of the nation's ground divisions and 12 percent of the tactical Air Forces with only 3.6 percent of the defense budget. While the Navy supported the Corps initially by launching the first two multipurpose amphibious assault ships (LHAS), *Tarawa* and *Saipan,* and promised to build seven more, it cut the program to five; at the same time, the number of amphibious ships was reduced by half. In response to the extreme shortage of ships, naval planners proposed—and Congress approved—the deployment of a number of container ships holding the large quantities of heavy equipment and supplies necessary to sustain the operations of a forward-deployed Marine amphibious brigade. Strategically located throughout the world, the container ships supposedly would make up for the shortage of amphibious ships in the fleet.

Opponents of amphibious operations also found grist for their mills in an incident in Southeast Asia. On 12 May 1975 a Cambodian gunboat fired across the bow of the container ship SS *Mayaguez* as she crossed the Gulf of Siam en route from Hong Kong to Bangkok. A Khmer Rouge—Cambodian Communist—boarding party took over the defenseless vessel and directed it to an anchorage near Koh Tang, an island thirty-five miles from the Cambodian coast. Then, unknown to American officials, the captors moved the crew of the *Mayaguez* to the port of Sihanoukville. After meeting with his National Security Council, President Gerald R. Ford ordered a rescue mission.

The directive to "do something" passed through channels to the Seventh Air Force at Nakhon Phanom, Thailand. With no amphibious forces within easy steaming distance of Koh Tang, 2/9 (reinforced with D/1/4) boarded Air Force transports in Okinawa for a hurried flight to Utapao, Thailand. From this huge joint Thai-U.S. air base on the Gulf of Siam, Air Force CH-53 and HH-53 helicopters lifted off on 15 May to seize the *Mayaguez* and rescue her crew.

Sixty-nine Marines from D/1/4 boarded the *Mayaguez* after being off-loaded on the destroyer escort *Harold E. Holt.* When they scrambled aboard the container ship in a cloud of tear gas at 5:50 on the morning of 15 May, the men found her deserted. As America prepared to flex its military might, the government of Cambodia realized its tenuous position and began diplomatic overtures to release the crew of the merchant vessel. But at sea in the Gulf of Siam and in Thailand, U.S. forces began a complicated mission to rescue the captive crew of the *Mayaguez*.

A raid on Koh Tang began at 6:00 A.M. on the same day. Led by Lt. Col. Randall W. Austin, 2/9 assaulted the little island in the face of devastating ground fire from its defenders. The landing force had no way of knowing that the crew of the *Mayaguez* had already been released by Cambodian authorities and were aboard their ship, steaming south to Singapore. American casualties were heavy. Intense ground fire downed one of the first two helicopters to approach the eastern end of the island, killing seven Leathernecks, two Navy corpsmen, and the Air Force co-pilot. Three more Marines died as they attempted to swim from the wreckage. Another helicopter made it to the beach, but its tail rotor had been shot off. The survivors formed a defensive perimeter and fought off repeated Cambodian attacks throughout the day.

On the other side of Koh Tang, antiaircraft fire damaged one helicopter full of Marines; it limped back to Thailand. Five more helicopter loads of Marines landed, one carrying the battalion command group. Strikes from Air Force fighters and mortar fire from 2/9 drove the Cambodians into the jungle. Additional Leathernecks stormed ashore, and shortly after noon two of the three groups of Marines on the ground linked up. By then, 225 Americans were on the island. With news of the crew's release, evacuation of the force began. By 6:00 the small detachment on the eastern side of Koh Tang had departed for Thailand. Two hours later, a helicopter lifted out the last of the Leathernecks positioned on the western side of the island.[2]

The number of casualties disturbed some members of Congress. Of the fifteen Air Force helicopters involved, ground fire downed three and damaged ten. Forty-one American servicemen died in the brief engagement or in an associated helicopter crash in Thailand. Three Leathernecks were reported missing (verified killed in action but not removed from the island). Another forty-one Marines suffered wounds, as did two sailors and

seven airmen. Some commentators suggested that the flawed rescue attempt underscored the limitations of amphibious warfare.

Meanwhile, problems with recruit training plagued the Corps, whose claim to be able to mold a man and a Marine out of any boy, regardless of his education or background, came under scrutiny. On 6 December 1975 drill instructors allowed fellow recruits to beat Pvt. Lynn E. McClure unconscious with pugel sticks. When McClure died three months later from head injuries, the depot superiors chose to punish senior officers in the chain of command rather than the DIS themselves. Even before the outcry over the incident subsided, a Parris Island DI accidentally shot a recruit during marksmanship training. Reacting to these embarrassments was the responsibility of a new commandant, Gen. Lewis H. Wilson, a rugged Mississippian who succeeded General Cushman on 1 July 1975. The Corps's last World War II Medal of Honor recipient on active duty, Wilson seized the initiative by directing a talented subordinate, Lt. Gen. Robert H. Barrow, to recommend far-reaching corrective measures.

The result of the Barrow initiatives, approved by Wilson, saw a sharp increase in the number of officers involved in recruit training. Recruiters were challenged to increase the number of high school graduates among their recruits, and only after a recruit completed boot camp successfully did a recruiter receive credit for his or her accession. Old-timers decried these measures, charging that the Corps had taken a step backward by diluting traditional NCO prestige. Others applauded them, noting that brutality in basic training did little to improve the military potential of recruits. The widespread changes, coupled with a succession of enlightened senior officers at the two recruit depots, resulted in a rapid abatement of abuses. Equally important, commanders throughout the Corps noted a significant improvement in the quality of the Marines completing recruit training. The need for "a few good men [and women]" remained, for Leatherneck service obligations worldwide continued just as they had for Marines of earlier eras.

General Barrow took the helm of the Corps on 1 July 1979. Few expected bold innovations from him. Instead, most observers thought he would continue existing programs to increase the combat efficiency of the Corps. Like Wilson before him, Barrow enjoyed good relations with Congress and the Oval Office. A courtly, soft-spoken officer whose Louisiana drawl belied a tough and determined Marine, Barrow charmed bureaucrats in the Pentagon and members of Congress alike.

Although President Jimmy Carter chose not to respond with military means immediately following the seizure of the U.S. embassy in Teheran by Iranian revolutionaries in November 1979, or after the Soviet invasion of Afghanistan the following December, an unsuccessful attempt to rescue the American hostages in Iran—Operation Blue Light—took place in the spring of 1980. On 24 April Marine aviators piloted eight RH-53D helicopters from the *Nimitz* in an attempt to liberate the U.S. citizens held captive in the Iranian capital. When three of the helicopters experienced mechanical failure, the on-scene commander of the rescue mission ordered the operation aborted at the Desert One staging area two hundred miles south of Teheran. Unfortunately, on departing Desert One, a helicopter collided with one of the transports, killing five airmen and three Marines. Critics suggested that both crises underscored the limitations of military power—including amphibious force— in the complicated world of the 1980s. But during the subsequent presidencies of Ronald Reagan and George Bush, the Corps had ample opportunity to demonstrate the utility of amphibious forces.

On 25 May 1982 the 32nd MAU departed North Carolina in the ships of Amphibious Squadron Four. Like similar MAUs before it, the 32nd would cross the Atlantic and join the Sixth Fleet in the Mediterranean. During the six-month stint, the MAU expected to participate in an amphibious exercise in Portugal and otherwise enjoy the fine liberty of the region. The disintegrating political situation in Lebanon changed these plans. On 6 June 1982, the day the MAU arrived at Rota, Spain, Israeli forces invaded southern Lebanon to drive the troops of the Palestine Liberation Organization (PLO) away from their borders. As conditions in Lebanon deteriorated in the wake of the Israeli incursion and the lives of foreign nationals appeared threatened, the Lebanese government appealed to the international community for assistance in evacuating the innocent bystanders first, and then the fighters

of the PLO. The commandant underscored the seriousness of the deployment in a message to the MAU commander: "You will soon be engaged in carrying out an extremely important mission in Beirut. Clearly, it is also a most difficult and delicate one. Your soldierly virtues, especially discipline, will in all likelihood be severely tested."[3]

Lebanese military units brought several hundred civilian evacuees to Juniyah, a small port ten miles north of Beirut. From there, the 32nd MAU was to escort them to safety aboard merchant ships lying offshore. Expecting the worst, the Marines landed on 25 August only to find a pleasant seaside resort populated by sunbathers, waterskiers, and wind surfers. Approximately 6,436 refugees of all nationalities passed through the MAU checkpoint. On 30 August PLO leader Yasir Arafat himself was escorted through the processing station. By 1 September the last of the PLO forces had departed, and on 10 September the MAU left Lebanon to resume its normal deployment schedule. Once again its peaceful routine would be short-lived.

The assassination of Lebanon's president-elect on 4 September plunged the troubled nation deeper into turmoil. Eight days later, Lebanese Christian militiamen entered the PLO refugee camps of Sabra and Shatilla and massacred more than eight hundred Palestinians. Under these explosive circumstances Lebanese President Amin Gemayel requested the return of the multinational peacekeeping force, including U.S. Marines. On 22 September the 32nd MAU hurriedly left Naples to take up positions around Beirut International Airport.

Exactly one week later the MAU suffered its first casualty when a Marine was killed while removing an unexploded bomblet—one of thousands littering the airport grounds. That same day, the MAU took up semipermanent positions ashore, joining a greatly enlarged multinational force of twenty-two hundred Italian and French troops. Marines filled sandbags, dug bunkers, and fought tedium while performing a unique mission called "presence." There were some tense moments, but for the most part the Marines had to contend with nothing worse than boredom and minor discomfort brought on by unusually chilly weather in late fall. The 32nd MAU was relieved on 30 October by the 24th MAU. Marines patrolled the village of Hay-es-Salaam adjacent to the airstrip. In typical Marine fashion, the locale became "Hooterville,"

The Marine BLT building in August 1983, before it was destroyed by a terrorist bomb. U.S. Department of Defense Still Media Records Center

just as the tiny village hard against the airstrip at Danang had become "Dogpatch."

Tensions heightened considerably in April 1983 when terrorists bombed the U.S. embassy in Beirut. Marines from the 22nd (ex-32nd) MAU, which had rotated back to Beirut in February, supplemented the normal security guard. As a cordon of concrete and barbed wire grew increasingly tighter around the Marines' perimeter, Leathernecks received orders to allow no one to enter without specific authority. A determined corporal demonstrated that when a Marine receives an order, he carries it out to the letter. Stopping an approaching limousine at rifle point, the Marine waved away the driver's protests: "But this is the President of Lebanon." "I don't give a f——who he's the president of," the Marine responded. "My orders say nobody's coming through."[4]

On 23 May the 24th MAU once again replaced the 32nd. Throughout the long summer the Leathernecks patrolled the streets and alleys surrounding the airport. Presently, as the uneventful weeks passed, Marines could

be observed jogging around the airport perimeter. The cuisine improved substantially over the initial diet of field rations. Just as Vietnam came to be known to a generation of Marines as simply "Nam," Beirut became "the Root." The deployment in Lebanon was becoming routine. In early fall, however, the MAU issued warnings to its subordinate units to be wary of cars rigged with explosives attempting to breach the security line.

Sunday, 23 October, promised to be a fine day for the Marines and Navy men of the MAU. Their commanders ordered a delayed reveille at 6:30 with a modified holiday routine to follow. The MAU mess hall would serve brunch between 8:00 and 10:00, with an afternoon holiday picnic of hot dogs and hamburgers. As the sun rose over the hills dominating the skyline above Beirut, a sentry observed a yellow Mercedes truck circling the parking lot that separated the MAU compound from the airport. Then the vehicle sped away down the road to Beirut.

At approximately 6:22 A.M. the truck reappeared, crossed the parking lot, and crashed through the wire bar-

The BLT building after the blast. U.S. Department of Defense Still Media Records Center

ricade separating the parking lot from the building hous-ing three hundred sleeping servicemen. Detonating his lethal cargo in the lobby, the Arab suicide-driver set off an explosive charge equal to twelve thousand pounds of TNT that collapsed the building in one huge thunderclap. Two hundred and forty-one Americans died in the blast, including 220 Marines, the highest loss since D-day at Iwo Jima.

Once the shock wore off at home, the president and the Pentagon took several well-aimed salvos from critics of U.S. policy in Lebanon. Armchair tacticians de-manded disciplinary action against those in the chain of command whose apparent negligence had contributed to the tragedy. Their accusations were countered by the per-sonable and patrician Gen. Paul X. Kelley, who had be-come the Corps's twenty-eighth commandant on 1 July 1983. An eloquent speaker, Kelley had commanded both a battalion and a regiment in Vietnam and had served a tour with Britain's tough Royal Marines. He took imme-diate steps to diffuse criticism of his Leathernecks. In a widely reported interview he told of meeting Lance Cpl.

Jeffrey L. Nashton, a wounded Marine in the intensive care ward of the Air Force medical center in Wiesbaden, Germany:

> [He was in] critical condition with more tubes going in and out of his body than I have ever seen. When he heard me say who I was, he grabbed my camouflage coat, went up to the collar, and counted the stars. He squeezed my hand, and then attempted to outline words on his bed sheet. When what he was trying to write was not understood, he was given a piece of paper and pencil, and then he wrote "Semper Fi."[5]

Kelley requested the appointment of an independent commission to investigate the tragedy. Ultimately, a panel headed by Adm. Robert L. Long, USN (retired), ex-amined the ingredients culminating in the disaster. Its conclusions faulted senior military commanders and their civilian superiors for not providing an adequate expla-nation of the dubious mission of "presence." The Long Commission found that a specific set of rules for coun-tering terrorist attacks had not been prepared or promul-gated, despite numerous assaults by extremist Arab factions determined to achieve their political objectives through terrorism and intimidation. Finally, the commission blamed both the MAU and BLT commanders for failing to initiate proper precautions to protect their troops. But in his testimony on Capitol Hill, General Kelley argued that reasonable and prudent defensive measures had been taken; there was no way to predict the attack or adequately defend against it.

Yet the survivors carried the heaviest burden. Father George W. Pucciarelli, the 24th MAU's chaplain, provided a poignant recollection of 23 October 1983: "Three years have passed since that morning. Not a day goes by when I don't think of that moment and the long hours that followed. . . . When I think of the Marines who died in Beirut, I always think of one man, who for me has come to memorialize all the fine young men who died there." The chaplain, deeply moved by an experience that placed him closer to his God than he ever thought possible in this life, added that

> this Marine, trapped deep within the building, had survived the blast itself. . . . His left arm had been cut up badly and bled profusely. His legs were pinned in the fallen debris. Yet in his entrapment he found that he could still move his right arm. He took out a bandage in an effort to stop the bleeding. It was hopeless. He next reached into his wallet and withdrew photographs of his wife and children. He placed them on a ledge in front of him—and in this way, remembering his family, he died.[6]

As Americans mourned the loss of their servicemen in Beirut, events in the eastern Caribbean demanded yet another deployment of Marines. On 19 October the prime minister of Grenada was murdered in a military coup d'état, and the island nation, a minute member of the British Commonwealth, drifted rapidly into anarchy. President Reagan and his advisers had two concerns: first, the presence of seven hundred Americans on the island, mostly students at St. George's University Medical School; second, the Cuban-sponsored construction of a military-capable airfield at Point Salines, on the southern tip of the island, along with whatever else Cuba had in mind for the future of Grenada.

A request from the Joint Chiefs of Staff to the commander in chief, Atlantic (CINCLANT), Adm. Wesley McDonald, for an operations plan resulted in the formulation of a typical amphibious assault on the island. The 22nd MAU had sortied on 18 October from North Carolina for the Mediterranean. Additional amphibious forces from the 2nd Marine Division would join the MAU by air. These arrangements did not satisfy the Joint Chiefs, however; three of the group registered objections. The chairman, Gen. John Vesey, USA, and the chief of staff of the Army hoped to show the utility of the Army's new Ranger battalions. With the chief of staff of the Air Force siding with the two Army generals, a new and far more complicated joint-service venture evolved. An amphibious-airborne assault fraught with communications and coordination problems resulted.

The 22nd MAU consisted of BLT 2/8, HMM-261, and a service support group. At 10:00 P.M. on 22 October, the amphibious task force received instructions to turn toward Grenada. CINCLANT estimated that the Grenadian People's Revolutionary Army (GPRA) numbered approximately twelve hundred men, reinforced with a militia of two to five thousand men and an armed police force of three to four hundred. Six hundred armed Cubans were employed in the construction of the airfield at Point Salines.

Vice Adm. Joseph Metcalf III, the commander of the Second Fleet (COMSECFLT), was placed in tactical command of the operation. Metcalf notified the MAU's commander, Col. James P. Faulkner, that the main operation would be conducted by Army Paratroop and Ranger units in a daring airborne assault, with the Marines remaining in reserve. Nevertheless, the MAU continued to plan for an amphibious or heliborne landing on the island. During the hours of darkness on 23 October, liaison officers from CINCLANT arrived with a draft operations order for the assault. The amphibious task force, TF 124, received the mission of seizing the Pearls airport and the port of Grenville, both located on the windward, or Atlantic, midsection of the island. Army Rangers and units of the 82nd Airborne Division would land by parachute and secure the airfield at Point Salines.

D-day was set for 25 October; Admiral Metcalf directed that no landings take place before 4:00 A.M. A SEAL team dropped into the Pearls area to reconnoiter the beach reported conditions for an amphibious landing to be marginal at best. After the first two rifle companies had been heli-lifted ashore and had identified suitable

Leathernecks hit the ground at a run from a CH-53 Sea Stallion helicopter at Pearls airport during the intervention in Grenada, 25 October 1983. U.S. Department of Defense Still Media Records Center

beaches, perhaps the remainder of the MAU could deploy in landing craft. In a fitting and sentimental touch to the operation, Navy superiors changed the movie schedule for that evening aboard the *Guam* to show John Wayne in the epic *Sands of Iwo Jima*.

The first helicopters lifted off the *Guam* at 3:15 A.M. The CH-46s carrying the Marines and the AH-1 Cobra gunships escorting them made a total of twenty-one helicopters in the first wave. The Leathernecks landed without resistance or mishap just south of the airfield. A platoon from Company E seized a low hill near the landing zone, the few Grenadian troops occupying the anti-aircraft site fled, and scattered but ineffectual resistance marked the remainder of the movement ashore. Meanwhile, Company F was heli-lifted into the Grenville area. Again, little or no opposition was encountered and the Marines deployed to secure Grenville. To the surprise of the landing force, most Grenadians welcomed them as liberators from the harsh rule of the Military Council and pointed out members of the GPRA attempting to flee in the guise of civilians.

As the Leathernecks consolidated their position in the Pearls area, the Rangers at Point Salines encountered stiff resistance. At 2:05 P.M., two reinforced battalions of the 82nd Airborne landed at Salines to support a Ranger battalion locked in combat with Cuban troops. As the pockets of resistance diminished, the Rangers and paratroopers took control of the airfield and evacuated the American students from St. George's University Medical School.

The BLT commander, Lt. Col. Ray L. Smith, took up a position ashore in the Pearls/Grenville area with his two remaining rifle companies. Ordering Company G to move toward the governor-general's residence, he positioned tanks and LVTs at the race course to provide a base of fire. When the Marines burst into Government House, they found the governor-general, Sir Paul Scoon, his wife, and nine other civilians—all eager to accept evacuation to the *Guam*. Shortly thereafter, Admiral Metcalf alerted Colonel Faulkner that he had just learned of additional American medical students at a site on the southeastern side of the island. To support the rescue effort, the MAU provided nine CH-46s and four CH-53s to transport the Rangers in and the evacuees out.

As the tropical sun broke over the island on the morning of 28 October, most Grenadians found themselves under the control of the armed forces of the United States or nearby Caribbean nations. A total of 590 U.S. citizens were evacuated from Grenada, together with eighty foreign nationals who requested protection. Eighteen American servicemen died and 116 suffered wounds or injuries. Included in this number were three Marine dead and fifteen wounded. The U.S. force accounted for 707 Cubans, including 24 killed and 59 wounded. Forty-five Grenadian troops were killed. Captured documents revealed plans for a Cuban garrison of sixty-eight hundred. As additional elements of the 82nd Airborne arrived from Fort Bragg, Leatherneck units returned to the ships of the amphibious group. By the afternoon of 2 November, the Marines were ready to resume their journey to the Mediterranean.[7]

Three years later, Marines participated in the Reagan administration's aerial strike against terrorist facilities in Libya. Senior U.S. officials had long suspected that the sites harbored those responsible for recent attacks against Americans. Most damning was a signal intelligence intercept from Libya to the terrorist group in Germany responsible for the bombing of a Berlin discotheque crowded with off-duty U.S. servicemen. On 15 April 1986, F-111s flying from bases in Great Britain and aircraft catapulted from the carriers *America* and *Coral Sea* bombed targets in the North African nation. Included in the naval aviation forces participating in Operation Eldorado Canyon were Leatherneck aviators from VMFA-314 and VMFA-323.

The Marine Corps entered the last half of the 1980s burdened by a variety of troubles. Leathernecks assigned to the small embassy detachment in Moscow became embroiled in a scandal over allegations that two of their number allowed KGB agents to prowl sensitive areas of the embassy building in exchange for sexual favors from comely comrades. Another embassy Leatherneck faced charges of succumbing to blackmail after an affair with a Soviet woman. Although the Naval Investigative Service appeared to have bungled the investigations, the charges tarnished the Corps's image and its splendid record of providing security for U.S. embassies worldwide.

Whenever Leathernecks appear to be in disarray, civilian authorities find it easy to intervene in their affairs. In this case, the authority was an activist secretary of the Navy—James H. Webb Jr. A former Marine himself, Webb had graduated from the Naval Academy in 1968. As an infantry platoon leader in Vietnam, he earned the Navy Cross and suffered wounds that resulted in his medical discharge. Since then he had alternated between government service and a successful career as a novelist. Still passionately devoted to the Corps, he decided that it needed a commandant able to restore the warrior spirit and toughness he remembered from Vietnam, not a Washington manager.

The selection of Lt. Gen. Alfred M. Gray to be the twenty-ninth commandant in 1987 surprised most members of the Corps, not least Gray himself. Many applauded the change. An impression current in some quarters held that Kelley and his supporters at HQMC had become military bureaucrats, too remote from Marines in the field. Al Gray was expected to bridge the gap. More than thirty years a Marine, he had carried a rifle as a teenaged PFC in the Korean War. Tough, tobacco-chewing, plain-speaking Gray now found himself the champion of much of the Marine Corps. Perceiving an overall softness pervading the ranks, Gray promised more realistic training. He disparaged such hallowed traditions as jogging in tennis shoes—preferring forced marches—and spit and polish: "I don't give a shit how you look. I care how you are!" he once exclaimed to an audience of young Leathernecks.[8]

Yet Kelley, to his credit, left a modernized Marine Corps prepared to fight on the battlefields of the 1990s and beyond. Sophisticated personal equipment added to the lethality of the Leatherneck infantryman. The basic quality of the individual Marine improved markedly during Kelley's tenure, from an enlisted force composed almost totally of high school graduates to the better-educated officer corps. New aircraft replaced the aging warhorses of the Vietnam era. The light-armored vehicle entered the inventory, with an eight-wheel, thirteen-ton chassis that offered eight different configurations to provide ground commanders with new flexibility in maneuver warfare. By 1986 the last two of the thirteen promised maritime pre-position ships had been christened. Combat loads to support MAB-level operations were in

Members of Company D, 2nd Light Armored Infantry Battalion, stand guard outside the destroyed Panamanian Defense Force post at Arraijan on the opening day of Operation Just Cause.

U.S. Department of Defense Still Media Records Center

place in Diego Garcia and Guam, and shore-based equipment and supplies had been positioned in Norway.

The U.S. naval presence in the Persian Gulf grew markedly during the Iran-Iraq War of 1980–88. On 14 April 1988 the frigate *Samuel B. Roberts* struck an Iranian mine; only herculean efforts by the crew kept the ship afloat. A special force of Leathernecks, Marine Air-Ground Task Force 2-88, collaborated with Navy forces in Operation Praying Mantis to destroy the Iranian Sirri and Sassan offshore oil platforms, which were being used to support attacks on neutral shipping.

Even as the Soviet Union began to unravel, events in other parts of the world demanded the presence of Marines. The administration of President George Bush had been growing increasingly impatient with events in Panama—especially the arrogance of its president, Gen. Manuel Antonio Noriega. Mounting evidence revealed him to be at the center of a major drug-dealing operation. When the Panamanian strongman refused to allow his successor to take office, the United States reinforced its garrison in the Canal Zone with additional forces—including Marines.

On the steamy night of 16 December 1989, 1st Lt. Robert Paz and three other officers serving in Panama halted at a Panamanian roadblock. They were off duty, dressed in civilian clothing, and en route to a dinner party. When armed members of the Panamanian Defense Force attempted to drag the unarmed Americans from the car, the driver sped away. In the burst of small arms fire that followed, Paz was killed. At about the same time, an unarmed American Navy officer was beaten and his wife threatened with sexual assault. From the perspective of the Oval Office, Noriega and his band of thugs had overstepped even the limits of Yankee patience.

On Wednesday, 20 December, President Bush ordered an invasion of Panama to capture Noriega, destroy the forces loyal to him, and protect American lives and properties. By then, an additional seven thousand U.S. soldiers and Marines had joined the almost thirteen thousand troops already in the Canal Zone. Although the units that carried out Operation Just Cause came mainly from the Army, they included a token force of seven hundred Marines. Initially, Leathernecks were ordered to seize the Bridge of the Americas spanning the canal, two Panamanian military compounds, and the Arraijan Tank Farm,

Lt. Gen. Walter F. Boomer, the commander of I MEF, and President George Bush during the president's visit to the 1st Marine Division Combat Operations Center. President and Mrs. Bush spent the 1990 Thanksgiving holiday in Saudi Arabia with American troops deployed for Operation Desert Shield. U.S. Department of Defense Still Media Records Center

a strategic fuel storage area in the jungle approximately two miles from Howard Air Force Base, a U.S. cantonment on the outskirts of Panama City. The Marines assaulted positions held by Noriega's supporters, neutralized Panamanian Defense Force facilities, and provided roadblocks. Noriega was eventually apprehended, brought to the United States for trial, and subsequently imprisoned.

After the intervention in Panama, Leatherneck forces continued to remain on watch throughout the world. On 1 August 1990 the 13th MEU (Special Operations Capable [SOC])—unit designations having changed from "amphibious" back to "expeditionary"—was in Philippine waters. Ostensibly deployed for routine training ashore and a port visit, the force had been employed in assisting the Filipino people in earthquake relief. The 22nd MEU (SOC) stood off Liberia ready to evacuate American citizens should civil unrest topple the government of that West African nation. Elsewhere, the 24th and 26th MEUs continued predeployment workup training while the 11th MEU practiced special-operations skills. None of these and other peacetime training missions and deployments suggested that almost the entire operating forces of the Marine Corps would soon deploy to the Persian Gulf.

An hour after midnight on 1–2 August 1990, three Iraqi divisions crossed the border into the small, oil-rich sheikdom of Kuwait. A special-operations division landed by helicopter in Kuwait City and by the end of the next day had taken the capital hostage. Within twenty-four hours of the invasion, the Iraqis had positioned forces on the border of Saudi Arabia. By 7 August, even before the United Nations had granted approval or before a coalition of concerned nations had been formed, Secretary of Defense Richard B. Cheney directed JCS chairman Gen. Colin L. Powell to alert military, naval, and air units for possible deployment to the Persian Gulf. For the Marine Corps, this meant the 1st Marine Expeditionary Brigade in Hawaii, the 7th MEB on the West Coast, and the 4th MEB on the East Coast. On 10 August Gen. H. Norman Schwarzkopf, commander in chief, Central

Command (CENTCOM), requested the presence of the three MEBs in the Persian Gulf. Operation Desert Shield, the defense of Saudi Arabia, commenced. The 7th MEB deployed by air from Twentynine Palms, California, and arrived at Al Jubayl, Saudi Arabia, on 14 August. Meanwhile, the ships of Maritime Prepositioning Shipping Squadron 2 had steamed from their anchorage at Diego Garcia in the Indian Ocean. The squadron carried enough supplies and heavy equipment for thirty days of MEB operations. The 7th MEB was followed by the 1st MEB from Hawaii, and on 26 August Maritime Prepositioning Squadron 3 arrived from Guam to marry up with the 1st MEB. Meanwhile, the 4th MEB had sailed from North Carolina on 17 August with its own complement of supplies and heavy equipment.

On 2 September 1990, I MEF assumed command of all Marines in the theater of operations. The force was led by Lt. Gen. Walter E. Boomer, who had been decorated for heroism as an adviser to the Vietnamese Marines during the 1972 Easter offensive. By 6 September I MEF consisted of the 1st Marine Division, 3rd Marine Aircraft Wing, and 1st Force Service Support Group. The Joint Chiefs of Staff gave CENTCOM operational control of all Marine forces ashore. By November 1990 more than forty-two thousand Marines—nearly one-fourth of the Corps's active-duty strength—had deployed to the Persian Gulf. Of that total thirty-one thousand were ashore in I MEF; the 4th MEB and the 13th MEU sortied offshore to provide CENTCOM with a formidable amphibious capability.

On 8 November President Bush announced an anticipated increase of U.S. forces in the region by more than two hundred thousand men and women. For the Marine Corps, this meant the deployment of II MEF from the East Coast and the 5th MEB from California. In his characteristically outspoken manner, General Gray explained his personnel situation to a group of bemused journalists. "We now have four kinds of Marines: those in the Gulf; those going to the Gulf; those who want to go to the Gulf; and those who don't want to go to the Gulf, but are going anyway!"[9]

Five days after President Bush revealed the quantum increase of U.S. forces in the troubled region, a call-up of selected reservists began. As weekend warriors—

In a typical pose, gesturing wildly, Gen. Alfred M. Gray exhorts the Marines of 1/5 during Operation Desert Shield. Commissioned from the ranks, Gray claimed a special bond with enlisted personnel.   U.S. Department of Defense Still Media Records Center

many with skills honed in previous conflicts—answered the call to the colors, the first of a series of amphibious exercises in the region commenced with Operation Sea Soldier. Clearly, this seaborne posturing was intended to offer Iraqi strongman Saddam Hussein a snapshot of what might happen if he persisted in his aggression. On 1 December the 5th MEB steamed to the Persian Gulf from southern California to join the rapid buildup of military, air, and naval might in the region.

The next contingent of Leathernecks scheduled for the Persian Gulf was II MEF, consisting of the 2nd Marine Division, 2nd MAW (later absorbed by the 3rd MAW), and 2nd Force Service Support Group. The fly-in echelon began on 9 December with a lift rate of one thousand troops per day, and was not completed until 15 January

Marines move across the Saudi desert into position during Operation Desert Shield. U.S. Department of Defense Still Media Records Center

AV-8 Harrier II attack aircraft of VMA-513 on patrol in southwestern Asia. The squadron deployed to the Persian Gulf to support Leatherneck ground operations during Operations Desert Shield and Desert Storm. U.S. Department of Defense Still Media Records Center

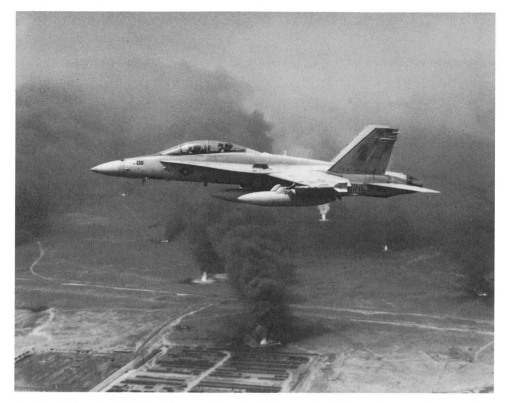

An F/A-18 Hornet of VMFA-121 over the burning Al Burqan oil field in southeastern Kuwait during Operation Desert Storm. Iraqi forces torched Kuwait's oil fields after the first day of the coalition's ground offensive. U.S. Department of Defense Still Media Records Center

1992. Maritime Prepositioning Squadron 1 steamed from the East Coast on 14 November and reached Al Jubayl on 12 December. By then, it had been determined that sufficient command elements existed in the theater, and II MEF remained in North Carolina. By 15 January 1991 approximately eighty-four thousand Marines—half the Corps's active-duty strength—had deployed to the Persian Gulf. Of this total, sixty-six thousand served ashore (including a thousand women) in I MEF units while the remaining eighteen thousand floated offshore with the 4th MEB, 5th MEB, and 13th MEU (SOC). This total approached the number of Marines in Vietnam during the peak year of 1968 and exceeded the total landed at Iwo Jima in 1945. But Operation Desert Shield was drawing rapidly to a close. Iraq indicated no willingness to abide by a United Nations resolution calling for its withdrawal from Kuwait; nor did Saddam Hussein demonstrate undue concern over the crippling oil embargo.

The Iraqi leadership appeared to be putting their faith in an illusionary anti-Western coalition of their Arab brothers. Libya and Iran blustered and Jordan's King Hussein eschewed joining the coalition against Iraq, but the remaining Arab nations in the region fell into line with nations worldwide willing to resort to arms to free Kuwait. The UN deadline for the evacuation of Kuwait came and went on 15 January with no lessening of the bellicose rhetoric from Iraq. Operation Desert Storm was about to commence with the air war phase.

On 17 January Air Force F-117 Stealth fighter-bombers, Navy Tomahawk cruise missiles, Army Apache helicopters, and Navy–Marine Corps fighter-attack aircraft eliminated the Iraqi armed force's command-and-control systems. During the first twenty-four hours of the air war, coalition aircraft flew two thousand sorties and dropped twenty-five hundred tons of ordnance. After the first day of intense air activity, CENTCOM reported the loss of only four aircraft. In response to the bombardment, Iraq fired lethal Scud missiles at targets in Israel and Saudi Arabia. The United States positioned Patriot ground-to-air missile units in the theater to counter the threat. Leaders in the Arab countries joined their counterparts throughout the world in condemning the Iraqi attacks; the coalition of nations intent on forcing Iraq to abandon Kuwait remained intact. The air war continued unabated for more than a month. Meanwhile, the first ground action took place.

After nightfall on 29 January, three Iraqi divisions rolled toward the Saudi border to deliver what was meant to be a major spoiling attack. Along the coast, the 5th Mechanized Division intended to break through the Arab contingents forming Joint Forces Command–East and seize the town of Ra's al Khafji. Inland, the 3rd Armored Division would penetrate the coalition front along the boundary between the Arabs and I MEF and wheel to the east and capture Al Mish'ab, a port twenty miles below Khafji. Farther inland, the 1st Mechanized Division would cover the Iraqis' western flank by attacking the U.S. Marine outposts in the vicinity of Umm Hujul.

Two of the Iraqi divisions soon came to grief. A Marine reconnaissance team discovered the advance of the 3rd Armored Division and called for air strikes that eliminated it from play. The 1st Mechanized Division achieved surprise but was beaten back by a combination of ground and air action at a cost of eleven Marine dead—tragically, all from friendly fire. The 5th Mechanized Division had better luck and was able to scatter the thin screen of coalition forces above Khafji and occupy the town.

I MEF could easily have responded to the incursion, but military etiquette dictated that the honor of liberating Khafji be reserved for the Saudis, supported by Leatherneck artillery and air power. Nevertheless, the Corps was represented on the ground. Two Marine recon teams were in Khafji when it was overrun. The senior NCO, Cpl. Charles Ingraham, reached a courageous decision quickly. Rather than join in the retreat, the Leathernecks climbed to a rooftop where they could call in fire for a counterattack. They remained undetected, and their fire directions proved instrumental in the town's recapture two days later. Concurrently, the 4th and 5th MEBs conducted Exercise Sea Soldier IV off Oman, and the 13th MEU(SOC) executed Operation Sting, an amphibious

The I MEF in Operation Desert Storm, 1991

raid on the Iraqi-occupied island of Maradim. Although enemy forces had abandoned the site, Marines seized large stocks of matériel.

By then CENTCOM had settled on its campaign plan—an end-run by the XVIII Airborne Corps and VII Corps around the desert flank of the Iraqi forces dug in above the Saudi frontier. The XVIII Airborne Corps would swing wide to reach the Euphrates and prevent the Iraqi Army in Kuwait from being withdrawn or reinforced; VII Corps's armor and mechanized infantry would destroy it. Initially, Army planners proposed to assign I MEF a secondary role in this operation. General Boomer did not take that news kindly, protesting that the Marines should be permitted to strike toward Kuwait City. General Schwarzkopf concurred, and later, when his staff suggested still another mission for I MEF, he exclaimed: "Stop screwing with the Marines."[10]

Boomer and his staff made plans to attack northeastward into Kuwait on both sides of Umm Hujul with I MEF's divisions in line—the 1st Marine Division (Maj. Gen. James M. Myatt) on the right and the 2nd Marine Division (Maj. Gen. William Keys) on the left. The 2nd Armored Division's Tiger Brigade, attached to I MEF for the campaign, would cover the Leathernecks' left flank. To support the advance, the Marine logistics command,

Marine gunners fire 155-mm shells from an M-198 howitzer at Iraqi positions inside Kuwait. U.S. Department of Defense Still Media Records Center

headed by Brig. Gen. Charles C. Krulak, a son of retired Lt. Gen. Brute Krulak, built an 11,280-acre, mostly underground supply base in the Saudi desert; Krulak christened it Al Khanjar, Arabic for "dagger." The idea of complementing the offensive with an amphibious assault was finally dropped in early February.

Encouraged by the Iraqis' poor showing in the January battles, Boomer counted on reaching Kuwait City in three days. CENTCOM planners, in contrast, believed that the Marines would merely absorb the Iraqis' attention while the Army's two corps enveloped them. Accordingly, I MEF and most of the XVIII Airborne Corps were scheduled to attack on the opening day of the ground war; VII Corps would not jump off until the next day.

On 14–15 February, I MEF opened its new command post near Al Khanjar. While the air war continued to pound Iraq, units of both Leatherneck divisions conducted screening operations and probed the Iraqi obstacle belts along the border. Four days later, both divisions began moving to

their final positions in preparation for the ground assault. Deception operations and tests of Iraqi defenses continued. Ground operations in Operation Desert Storm began at 4:00 A.M. on 24 February. Many analysts steeled themselves for reports of heavy casualties. Concerns over Iraq's chemical and biological weapons capability weighed heavily on the minds of commanders at all levels.

I MEF units spearheaded the attack toward Kuwait City, with the Arab joint forces' commands to their left and right following a day later. Leading elements of both Marine divisions breached the obstacle belts and penetrated into Kuwait at first light. Keys's Leathernecks moved forward to the inspiring strains of the "Marine Hymn," played at full volume from the loudspeakers of an Army psychological warfare unit attached to the Tiger Brigade. Combined-arms task forces from the 1st Marine Division captured the Al Jaber airfield, which had become an Iraqi fire base and command center, and reached the Al Burqan oil field. The invading Marines

Leatherneck tankers perform maintenance on their M-60A1 main battle tanks deep inside Kuwait on the afternoon of 27 February 1991. On the ground between the tanks are mine-clearing plows and rollers. U.S. Department of Defense Still Media Records Center

took twenty-one Iraqi tanks and more than four thousand POWs while suffering one Marine killed and nine wounded, and damage to three tanks and one light armored vehicle. In the 2nd Marine Division's zone, the 2nd Light Armored Infantry Battalion screened for the 6th and 8th Marines and the Tiger Brigade. Losing only one dead and eight wounded in the daring thrust, 2nd Marine Division units reported the capture intact of an entire Iraqi tank battalion—thirty-five T-55 tanks and five thousand prisoners, including a brigade commander. At the same time, the 3rd MAW flew 671 sorties in support of I MEF. Leatherneck aviators struck elements of six Iraqi divisions and reported the destruction of forty tanks, 121 vehicles, three antiaircraft artillery sites, and four missile sites. From Al Khanjar the 1st and 2nd Force Service Support Groups funneled supplies forward to support the tempo of combat operations. Offshore, the 5th MEB sent Regimental Landing Team-5 ashore to constitute a re-

serve force for I MEF. By nightfall, Boomer's troops were nearly halfway to Kuwait City.

The Marines' breathtaking breakthrough took CENT-COM planners by surprise. They had not expected I MEF to do more than fix the Iraqis in place until VII Corps slammed into their flank. Instead, the Marines were obviously well on the way to driving the Iraqis out of the theater of operations. At 1:00 P.M., Schwarzkopf ordered VII Corps to begin its attack that afternoon, a day ahead of schedule.

The next morning Leathernecks found the northern horizon shrouded by dense black smoke pouring from oil wells the enemy had set ablaze. Shortly after sunrise the Iraqis exploited the situation to launch their first and last counterattack. Two mechanized brigades, about 250 vehicles altogether, charged out of the smoke cloaking the Al Burqan oil field toward the 1st Marine Division. At one point, Iraqi armor approached to within four hundred

Marines roll into Kuwait International Airport in light armored vehicles on 27 February 1991, the final full day of Operation Desert Storm. A CH-53 Sea Stallion helicopter appears at right.

U.S. Department of Defense Still Media Records Center

yards of General Myatt's command post, but by midday the enemy thrusts had been repulsed. The division also cleared the remnants of the Iraqi defenders from the Al Jaber airfield. An estimated eighty enemy tanks and one hundred other vehicles dotted the desert, while more than two thousand prisoners added to the burgeoning bag of enemy soldiers opting to throw down their arms rather than face annihilation. The 2nd Marine Division enjoyed equal success, destroying 248 tanks and taking forty-five hundred prisoners. In support of these operations, the 3rd MAW flew 460 sorties. Offshore, the 4th MEB conducted a demonstration designed to convince the Iraqi leadership that a heliborne assault was imminent. Gunfire from the battleship *Missouri* added to the illusion. About 8:00 that evening, after approximately forty hours of ground combat, the Iraqi Army began to retreat from Kuwait.

On the third day of the ground war, 26 February, elements of the 1st Marine Division assaulted the Kuwait International Airport. By the time Iraqi forces in the area surrendered late that afternoon, 250 of their T-55 and T-62 tanks had been destroyed. Friendly personnel and equipment losses remained remarkably low. The next day the division consolidated positions around the airport and paved the way for Arab forces to enter Kuwait City. At the highest levels, it was deemed politically correct to allow units from Arab nations in the coalition to be the first to enter the Kuwaiti capital. Units of the 2nd Marine Division remained in blocking positions near Al Jahra. There they would join with Kuwaiti resistance forces to assist another contingent of Arab forces moving on Kuwait City.

At 8:00 on the morning of 28 February, just four days into the ground offensive, President Bush ordered a cease-fire. The costs to the opposing sides in Operation Desert Storm were ridiculously lopsided. The forces of I MEF destroyed or captured 1,040 tanks, 608 armored personnel carriers, 432 artillery pieces, five missile sites, and 22,308 POWs. Despite the somber predictions at home of heavy casualties, Marine commanders reported only five dead and forty-eight wounded in the four days of combat. An estimated 1,510 Iraqi troops had been killed by Leatherneck units. The 3rd MAW lost two aircraft during the ground offensive, and four fixed-wing keeping operations. An increasing emphasis on non-lethality pervades operational planning within traditional MEUs and MEBs operating with the fleets. Marines have deployed ashore to restore democracy in Haiti, to provide disaster relief in Bangladesh, and to protect the Kurdish minority in northern Iraq. And it was a rescue mission flown in a CH-53 from an offshore MEU that plucked Air Force Capt. Scott O'Grady from the clutches of Bosnian Serbs after the aircraft he was piloting was shot down. These and similar operations portend the pattern and tempo of Marine Corps operations now that the Soviet Union has collapsed and the specter of international communism no longer appears to threaten the free world.

Gen. Charles Krulak succeeded General Mundy to become the Corps's thirty-first commandant in 1995. While the Army and Navy gender-integrated their recruit training, the new commandant refused to budge on the sacrosanct exclusion of women from combat and the Marine Corps did not follow suit. Subsequent revelations of sexual harassment and improprieties at Army and Navy recruit training facilities served to justify Krulak's refusal to place men and women in the same units during entry-level training. At the same time, however, he embraced the wave of "jointness," or increased cooperation with the other services. In a move that startled naval and military circles, Krulak announced that he was moving the commandant's office and part of Headquarters Marine Corps to the Pentagon. His predecessors, since at least the World War I era, had demonstrated a dogged determination to distance their offices from both civilian superiors and Navy admirals. On 21 April 1999 President Bill Clinton announced the selection of Lt. Gen. James L. Jones to succeed Krulak as the thirty-second commandant when the latter's term of office expired in June.

In the more than two decades since the last Marine deployed to Southeast Asia, the Marine Corps has changed radically. From the early 1970s, senior Marines concluded that the Corps could not isolate itself from the political and socioeconomic turmoil outside the gate. A generation of Leathernecks may recall with little fondness the required attendance at human relations seminars ("hum-rel" in the vernacular of the day) designed to increase awareness of the needs and fears of women and minorities. "Hum-rel" has come and gone, but the number of minority Marines and women in the positions of authority has increased. On 27 April 1979 veteran aviator Frank E. Peterson became the first African American Marine selected for general officer rank. Women now serve in Marine security detachments at U.S. embassies worldwide and fill a variety of noncombatant positions throughout the Corps. Women deployed with both force service support groups during Operations Desert Shield and Desert Storm. No longer is it necessary to maintain separate organizations at posts and stations for "WMs." On 15 May 1985 Gail M. Reals became the first woman Marine to win a brigadier general's stars in competition with male Marines. Carol A. Mutter retired as a lieutenant general in 1998.

In short, a "new Corps" entered the twenty-first century. Veteran Marines would find that much remains of the "old Corps." Although it takes a more intelligent Marine to master the complexities of today's battlefield and the array of modern weaponry at his fingertips, many still believe that ultimately it is elemental guts that drives a man or woman to accept the challenge of being a Marine. Chesty Puller was known to growl: "Hell, the old Corps—the new Corps; there isn't a damned bit of difference."[11] But as a gunnery sergeant told one of the authors of this volume—then a flush-cheeked PFC with the sand of Marine Corps Recruit Depot, San Diego, still in his boondockers—"Son, the old Corps was yesterday!"[12]

Notes

For economy of space, only authors and short titles are given. Full publication details appear in the bibliography.

Chapter 1. Marines through the Ages

1. Field, *Britain's Sea-Soldiers,* 1:16.
2. Edye, *The Historical Records of the Royal Marines,* 1:6.
3. Smollett, *Roderick Random,* 188.
4. Fortescue, *A History of the British Army,* 2:71.
5. Field, *Britain's Sea-Soldiers,* 1:92.
6. Millett, *Semper Fidelis,* 4.
7. Spears, ed., *The Horizon History of the British Empire,* 57.
8. Field, *Britain's Sea-Soldiers,* 1:26.

Chapter 2. The Continental Marines, 1775–1783

1. Charles R. Smith, *Marines in the Revolution,* 250–51.
2. Ibid., 251.
3. Ibid.
4. Ibid.
5. Ibid.
6. Ibid., 7.
7. Ibid., 8.
8. Millett, *Semper Fidelis,* 7.
9. C. Smith, *Marines in the Revolution,* 53.
10. Ibid., 190.
11. Ibid., 331.
12. Ibid., 158.
13. Ibid., 142.
14. Morison, *John Paul Jones,* 153.
15. Simmons, *The United States Marines,* 15.
16. C. Smith, *Marines in the Revolution,* 378.

Chapter 3. The Early Years, 1798–1820

1. McClellan, "First Commandant of the Marine Corps William Ward Burrows," 135.
2. Moskin, *The U.S. Marine Corps Story,* 98.
3. "An Affair of Honor."
4. Allen, *Our Naval War with France,* 141.
5. Ibid., 184–85.
6. Ibid., 185.
7. Allen, *Our Navy and the Barbary Corsairs,* 173.
8. U.S. Navy Department, *Naval Documents Related to the United States Wars with the Barbary Powers,* 2:335.
9. Charles L. Lewis, *Famous American Marines,* 50.
10. Whipple, *To the Shores of Tripoli,* 228.
11. C. L. Lewis, *Famous American Marines,* 50.
12. Ibid.
13. Heinl, *Soldiers of the Sea,* 27.
14. McClellan, "Marine Corps History 1807 to 1812," 27.
15. Ibid., 36.
16. Ibid., 37.
17. Heinl, *Soldiers of the Sea,* 18.
18. Ibid.
19. Millett, *Semper Fidelis,* 47.
20. Porter, *Journal of a Cruise,* 203.
21. Heinl, *Soldiers of the Sea,* 20.
22. Ibid., 24.
23. Simmons, "Maj. Carmick at New Orleans," 8.
24. "Record of a court-martial, 18–26 September 1820," entry 20, Record Group (hereafter RG) 125, National Archives and Records Administration (hereafter NARA).

Chapter 4. The Era of Archibald Henderson, 1820–1859

1. Collum, *History of the United States Marine Corps,* 63–64.
2. Heinl, *Soldiers of the Sea,* 37.

3. Maclay, "An Early 'Globe-Circling' Cruise," 495.

4. Collum, *History of the U.S. Marine Corps,* 68.

5. Heinl, *Soldiers of the Sea,* 41.

6. Sprague, *The Origins, Progress, and Conclusion of the Florida War,* 176.

7. Moskin, *The U.S. Marine Corps Story,* 183.

8. Hoppin, *Life of Andrew Hull Foote,* 119.

9. Collum, *History of the U.S. Marine Corps,* 105.

10. Ibid., 105–6.

11. Moskin, *The U.S. Marine Corps Story,* 193.

12. Heinl, *Soldiers of the Sea,* 68.

13. Moskin, *The U.S. Marine Corps Story,* 194.

Chapter 5. Marines in Blue and Gray, 1859–1865

1. Metcalf, *A History of the United States Marine Corps,* 198.

2. Moskin, *The U.S. Marine Corps Story,* 218.

3. Donnelly, *The Confederate States Marine Corps,* 271.

4. U.S. Navy Department, *Official Records of the Union and Confederate Navies in the War of Rebellion* (hereafter, *ORN*), series 1, 7:47.

5. Ibid., 22.

6. Donnelly, *C.S. Marine Corps,* 42.

7. U.S. Senate, *Medal of Honor Recipients, 1863–1963,* 502.

8. Donnelly, *C.S. Marine Corps,* 174.

9. Thomas H. Stevens, "The Boat Attack on Fort Sumter," 4:49.

10. Scharf, *History of the Confederate States Navy,* 399.

11. *ORN,* ser. 1, 9:453–54.

12. Donnelly, *C.S. Marine Corps,* 51.

13. Heinl, *Soldiers of the Sea,* 75.

14. Welles, *The Diary of Gideon Welles,* 2:31.

15. Heinl, *Soldiers of the Sea,* 82.

16. *ORN,* ser. 1, 11:576.

17. Ibid.

18. Selfridge, "The Navy at Fort Fisher," 4:660.

19. *ORN,* ser. 1, 11:577.

20. Ibid., 447.

21. Selfridge, "The Navy at Fort Fisher," 4:660.

22. Dewey, *Autobiography,* 120.

23. *ORN,* ser. 1, 11:378.

24. Semmes, *Memoirs of Service Afloat,* 806.

25. Donnelly, *C.S. Marine Corps,* 61.

26. Ibid.

27. Parker, *Recollections,* 377.

Chapter 6. At Sea in the Gilded Age, 1865–1898

1. Heinl, *Soldiers of the Sea,* 87.

2. Shulimson, *The Marine Corps' Search for a Mission* (hereafter, *Search*), 138.

3. U.S. Navy Department, *Report of the Secretary of the Navy . . . December, 1867,* 55.

4. Shulimson, *Search,* 27.

5. U.S. Navy Department, *Annual Report of the Secretary of the Navy* (hereafter, *ARSN*), 1871, 304.

6. Ibid.

7. Ibid., 305.

8. Heinl, *Soldiers of the Sea,* 88.

9. *ARSN,* 1871, 306.

10. Ibid.

11. Moskin, *The U.S. Marine Corps Story,* 299.

12. *ARSN,* 1871, 284.

13. Shulimson, *Search,* 2, 17.

14. Millett, *Semper Fidelis,* 104.

15. Shulimson, *Search,* 18–19.

16. Ibid., 61.

17. Ibid., 147.

18. Young and Moore, *History of Our War with Spain,* 61.

Chapter 7. Colonial Infantry, 1898–1917

1. Shulimson, *Search,* 185.

2. Crane, *The War Dispatches of Stephen Crane,* 153–54.

3. Butler, *Old Gimlet Eye,* 36.

4. Ibid.

5. Wise, *A Marine Tells It to You,* 7.

6. Butler, *Old Gimlet Eye,* 193.

7. Ibid., 189.

8. Ibid., 148.

9. Venzon, ed., *General Smedley Darlington Butler: Letters of a Leatherneck,* 20.

10. C. L. Lewis, *Famous American Marines,* 162–63.

11. Heinl, *Soldiers of the Sea,* 140.

12. Schott, *The Ordeal of Samar,* 21.

13. Ibid., 105.

14. Ibid., 105.

15. Ibid., 145.

16. Heinl, *Soldiers of the Sea,* 126.

17. Butler, *Old Gimlet Eye,* 17.

18. Metcalf, *A History of the U.S. Marine Corps,* 312.

19. Heinl, *Soldiers of the Sea,* 149.

20. Abbot, ed., *The Letters of Archie Butt,* 134–35.

21. Abbot, ed., *Taft and Roosevelt,* 2:587.

22. Ibid., 587–88.

23. Wise, *A Marine Tells It to You,* 42.

24. Daniels, *The Wilson Era,* 2:322.

25. Heinl, *Soldiers of the Sea,* 159.

26. Butler, *Old Gimlet Eye,* 151.

27. Daniels, *The Wilson Era,* 2:322–23.

28. Millett, *Semper Fidelis,* 285.

29. Butler, *Old Gimlet Eye,* 179.

30. McCrocklin, *Garde d'Haiti,* 8.

31. Butler, *Old Gimlet Eye,* 194.

32. Ibid., 205.

33. Thrasher, "The Taking of Fort Rivière," 64.

Chapter 8. Over There, 1917–1918

1. Thomason, *Fix Bayonets!* x–xiii.

2. Pershing to the Adjutant General, War Department, 21 August 1917, no. 133, entry 6, RG 120, NARA.

3. Adjutant General, War Department, to Pershing, 17 September 1917, entry 6, RG 120, NARA.

4. Millett, *Semper Fidelis,* 291.

5. Catlin, *With the Help of God and a Few Marines,* 57.

6. Aquilina, "Over There," 22.

7. Clark, *Devil Dogs,* 94.

8. Catlin, *With the Help of God and a Few Marines,* 104.

9. Heinl, *Soldiers of the Sea,* 201.

10. Catlin, *With the Help of God and a Few Marines,* 119.

11. Wise, *A Marine Tells It to You,* 222.

12. McClellan, "A Brief History of the Fourth Brigade of Marines," 40–44.

13. Simmons, *The United States Marines,* 100.

14. On the interservice rivalry, see Bartlett, "Leathernecks, Doughboys, and the Press."

15. Frederick G. Wheeler to John A. Lejeune, 29 March 1919, reel 3, Lejeune MSS, Library of Congress.

16. Thomason, *Fix Bayonets!* 98–101.

17. Simmons, *The United States Marines,* 102.

18. Heinl, *Soldiers of the Sea,* 206.

19. U.S. Senate, *Medal of Honor Recipients, 1863–1963,* 780.

20. Lejeune's promotion to major general and command of the Second Division, AEF, are in Bartlett, *Lejeune,* 71–78.

21. Heinl, *Soldiers of the Sea,* 207.

22. Thomason, *Fix Bayonets!* ix.

23. Lejeune, *Reminiscences of a Marine,* 329.

24. Thomason, *Fix Bayonets!* 159.

25. McClellan, "The Battle of Blanc Mont Ridge," 287–88.

26. Lejeune, *Reminiscences of a Marine,* 402–3.

27. Simmons, *The United States Marines,* 106.

28. Smedley D. Butler to his wife, 20 May 1919, Butler MSS, Marine Corps Research Center.

29. Brigadier Paul D. Malone to Major General James G. Harbord, 13 June 1919, file 21676-A-592, RG 120, NARA.

30. Millett, *Semper Fidelis,* 318.

31. Mersky, *U.S. Marine Corps Aviation,* 12.

32. Hewett, *Women Marines in World War I,* 41.

33. Ibid.

Chapter 9. Between the Wars, 1919–1941

1. Wise, *A Marine Tells It to You,* 311.

2. Thomason, *—and a Few Marines,* 344.

3. Wise, *A Marine Tells It to You,* 311.

4. Thomason, *—and a Few Marines,* 339.

5. Wise, *A Marine Tells It to You,* 304.

6. Schmidt, *The United States Occupation of Haiti,* 106–7.

7. Seligman, "The Conquest of Haiti," 35.

8. Wise, *A Marine Tells It to You,* 334.

9. Charles F. Merkel file, reference section, Marine Corps Historical Center, Washington, D.C.; and file 26283-4352-2, RG 80, NARA.

10. Josephus Daniels to Franklin D. Roosevelt, 26 December 1934, container 95, reel 59, Daniels MSS, Manuscripts Division, Library of Congress.

11. CMC letter no. 1, 19 September 1922, Lejeune biographical file, Marine Corps Historical Center, Washington, D.C.

12. Ballendorf, "Earl Hancock Ellis," 78–87.

13. Lejeune, "The United States Marine Corps, 1926," 1969.

14. Edwin H. Denby to the Marine mail guards, 11 November 1921, container 2, Denby MSS, Burton Collection, Detroit Public Library; Robert H. Dunlap to CMC, 25 November 1921, Mail Guards file, reference section, Marine Corps Historical Center, Washington, D.C.

15. Schmidt, *Maverick Marine,* 174.

16. Heinl, *Soldiers of the Sea,* 292.

17. Schmidt, *Maverick Marine,* 179.

18. Gen. Lemuel C. Shepherd Jr. to Bartlett, 30 August 1979.

19. Metcalf, *A History of the United States Marine Corps,* 439.

20. Heinl, *Soldiers of the Sea,* 289.

21. Burke Davis, *Marine!* 48.

22. Candidates for Commandant file, container 36, Hoover MSS, Hoover Presidential Library.

23. George S. Simonds, "Amalgamation of the Marine Corps with the Army," 8 May 1931, folder M, Simonds MSS, Manuscripts Division, Library of Congress; Wilson, "Herbert Hoover and the Armed Forces," chaps. 2–3.

24. Millett, "Amphibious Warfare in the Interwar Era," in *Military Innovation in the Interwar Period; Records Relating to United States Fleet Problems I to XXII, 1923–1941,* ed. Murray and Millett, 50–95, microfilm, M964, NARA.

25. Clark, *Treading Softly,* 55–82.

26. *A Chronology of the United States Marine Corps, 1935–1946,* 101.

Chapter 10. World War Two: The South Pacific Campaign, 1942–1943

1. Urwin, *Facing Fearful Odds,* 514.

2. Ibid., 357.

3. General Devereux to Sweetman, Baltimore Roundtable of Military History.

4. Cates's oral history, Marine Corps Historical Center, Washington, D.C.

5. Heinl, *Soldiers of the Sea,* 356.

6. Vandegrift, *Once a Marine,* 142.

7. Griffith, *The Battle for Guadalcanal,* 119.

8. Ibid., 180.

9. Richard B. Frank, *Guadalcanal,* 333.

10. Toland, *The Rising Sun,* 393.

11. B. Davis, *Marine!* 155.

12. U.S. Senate, *Medal of Honor Recipients, 1863–1973,* 820–21.

13. Ibid., 194.

14. Vandegrift, *Once a Marine,* 204.

15. B. Davis, *Marine!* 194.

16. Toland, *The Rising Sun,* 347.

17. Ibid., 365.

Chapter 11. World War Two: The Central Pacific Drive, 1943–1945

1. Holland M. Smith, *Coral and Brass,* 23.

2. Toland, *The Rising Sun,* 469.

3. Alexander, *Utmost Savagery,* 174.

4. Heinl, *Soldiers of the Sea,* 413.

5. Simmons, *The United States Marines,* 148.

6. H. M. Smith, *Coral and Brass,* 111–12.

7. Cooper, *A Fighting General,* 105.

8. Toland, *The Rising Sun,* 488.

9. Ibid., 490.

10. Ibid., 495.

11. Ibid.

12. U.S. Senate, *Medal of Honor Recipients, 1863–1963,* 227.

13. Simmons, *The United States Marines,* 157, 161, 163.

14. Casualty figures for Peleliu, ibid., 166.

15. Toland, *The Rising Sun,* 644.

16. Heinl, *Soldiers of the Sea,* 484.

17. Toland, *The Rising Sun,* 650.

18. Alexander, *Closing In: Marines in the Seizure of Iwo Jima,* 11.

19. Sherrod, *On to the Westward,* 169, 651.

20. Ibid., 168.

21. Simmons, *The United States Marine Corps,* 173.

22. H. M. Smith, *Coral and Brass,* 261.

23. Simmons, *The United States Marine Corps,* 175.

24. H. M. Smith, *Coral and Brass,* 236.

25. Heinl, *Soldiers of the Sea,* 492.

26. Alexander et al., *A Fellowship of Valor,* 207.

27. Nichols and Shaw, *Okinawa,* 49.

28. U.S. Senate, *Medal of Honor Recipients, 1863–1973,* 119.

29. Simmons, *The United States Marines,* 504.

30. Toland, *The Rising Sun,* 723.

31. Simmons, *The United States Marines,* 183.

Chapter 12. The Unification Struggle and Korea, 1945–1953

1. *Chronology of the United States Marine Corps, 1947–64,* 3, 7, 9, 11.

2. Heinl, *Soldiers of the Sea,* 515.

3. Vandegrift, *Once a Marine,* 313–16.

4. Millett, *Semper Fidelis,* 463–64.

5. Heinl, *Soldiers of the Sea,* 512.

6. Mersky, *U.S. Marine Corps Aviation,* 120–28.

7. Vandegrift, *Once a Marine,* 327.

8. Shaw and Donnelly, *Blacks in the Marine Corps.*

9. Heinl, "Inchon, 1950," in Bartlett, ed., *Assault from the Sea,* 337.

10. Alexander and Bartlett, *Sea Soldiers in the Cold War,* 1.

11. Heinl, *Soldiers of the Sea,* 531.

12. Ibid., 539.

13. Ibid., 546.

14. Ibid., 547.

15. D. Clayton James, *The Years of MacArthur,* 3:470.

16. Cochran, "No Beaches to Land On," 49–50.

17. D. C. James, *The Years of MacArthur,* 3:476.

18. Heinl, *Victory at High Tide;* and *U.S. Marine Corps Operations in Korea,* vol. 2.

19. B. Davis, *Marine!* 277.

20. James, *The Years of MacArthur,* 3:490.

21. See Owen, *Colder than Hell;* and Russ, *Breakout.*

22. Moskin, *The U.S. Marine Corps Story,* 746.

23. B. Davis, *Marine!* 5–6.

24. Mersky, *U.S. Marine Corps Aviation,* 137.

25. Simmons, *The United States Marines,* 210.

26. *New York Times,* 28 June 1951.

Chapter 13. The Vietnam War, 1954–1975

1. Keith Fleming, *The U.S. Marine Corps in Crisis;* and John C. Stevens, *Court-martial at Parris Island.*

2. Steeves, "Crisis in Retrospect," 31–34.

3. Heinl, conversation with Bartlett, Annapolis, 24 April 1979.

4. Halberstam, *The Best and the Brightest,* 546.

5. Moskin, *The U.S. Marine Corps Story,* 6.

6. Ibid., 856n.

7. Bartlett's memory.

8. Oberdorfer, *Tet: The Turning Point of the War.*

9. Spector, *After Tet.*

10. Bartlett's memory.

11. Ibid.

12. For more on Dewey Canyon, see Gordon Davis, "Dewey Canyon," 32–40.

13. Shulimson, *U.S. Marines in Vietnam, 1969,* 372.

14. Bartlett's memory.

15. Weber's biographical file, Marine Corps Historical Center, Washington, D.C.

16. Interrogation of the NVA regimental commander, from Bartlett's memory.

17. Miller, *The Bridge at Dong Ha.*

18. Lewy, *America in Vietnam,* 202.

19. Simmons, *The United States Marines,* 246–47.

Chapter 14. The New Breed, 1976–2000

1. Simmons, *The United States Marines,* 299.

2. For more on the rescue of the *Mayaguez,* see J. M. Johnson et al., "Individual Heroism Overcame Awkward Command Relations," 24–34.

3. Benis M. Frank, *U.S. Marines in Lebanon,* 13.

4. Hammel, *The Root,* 79–80.

5. B. M. Frank, *U.S. Marines in Lebanon,* 101.

6. Pucciarelli, "After the Beruit Bombing," 65.

7. Spector, *U.S. Marines in Grenada, 1983.*

8. Sanza, "The Marines' 'Grunt' General," 17–18.

9. Alexander et al., *A Fellowship of Valor,* 372.

10. Michael R. Gordon and Bernard E. Trainor, *The Generals' War,* 161.

11. Andrew Geer, *The New Breed,* 375.

12. Bartlett's memory.

Selected Bibliography

Abbreviations

HMD–HQMC History and Museums Division, Headquarters Marine Corps, Washington, D.C.

USNIP U.S. Naval Institute Proceedings

Abbot, Laurence F., ed. *The Letters of Archie Butt.* Garden City, N.Y.: Doubleday, Page, 1924.

——. *Taft and Roosevelt: The Intimate Letters of Archie Butt.* 2 vols. Garden City, N.Y.: Doubleday, Doran, 1930.

"An Affair of Honor." *Marine Corps Gazette* 31 (September 1947): back cover.

Alexander, Joseph H. *Closing In: Marines in the Seizure of Iwo Jima.* Washington, D.C.: HMD–HQMC, 1994.

——. "Combat Leadership at Iwo Jima." *Marine Corps Gazette* 79 (February 1995): 66–71.

——. *Storm Landings: Epic Amphibious Battles in the Central Pacific.* Annapolis: Naval Institute Press, 1997.

——. "Swamp Ambush." *Military History* 14 (March 1998): 38–44.

——. *Utmost Savagery: The Three Days of Tarawa.* Annapolis: Naval Institute Press, 1995.

Alexander, Joseph H., and Merrill L. Bartlett. *Sea Soldiers in the Cold War.* Annapolis: Naval Institute Press, 1995.

Alexander, Joseph H., with Don Horan and Norman C. Stahl. *A Fellowship of Valor: The Battle History of the United States Marines.* New York: Harper, 1997.

Allen, Gardner W. *Our Naval War with France.* Boston: Houghton Mifflin, 1909.

——. *Our Navy and the Barbary Corsairs.* Boston: Houghton Mifflin, 1905.

Alvarez, Eugene. "Marines in the Movies." *Marine Corps Gazette* 69 (November 1985): 86–90, 92–95.

American Battle Monuments Commission. *American Armies and Battlefields in Europe.* Washington, D.C.: Government Printing Office, 1938.

Andrews, R. W. "Pass in Review" [history of the Basic School, initial officer training]. *Marine Corps Gazette* 51 (May 1967): 22–26.

Aquilina, Robert V. "Over There: The Marine Experience in World War I." *Fortitudine* 18 (fall 1982): 22–23.

Asprey, Robert B. "The Court Martial of Smedley Butler." *Marine Corps Gazette* 43 (December 1959): 28–34.

——. "Waller of Samar." *Marine Corps Gazette* 45 (May 1961): 36–41; (June 1961): 44–48.

Averill, G. P. "Final Objective" [operations in the Punchbowl, Korea, 1951]. *Marine Corps Gazette* 40 (August 1956): 10–16.

Ballendorf, Dirk Anthony. "Earl Hancock Ellis: A Final Assessment." *Marine Corps Gazette* 74 (November 1990): 78–87.

Ballendorf, Dirk Anthony, and Merrill Lewis Bartlett. *Pete Ellis: An Amphibious Warfare Prophet, 1880–1923.* Annapolis: Naval Institute Press, 1997.

Barnett, George. "Soldier and Sailor Too." Unpublished memoir. Barnett MSS, Marine Corps Research Center, Quantico, Va.

Bartlett, Merrill L. "Court-Martial of a Commandant" [Anthony Gale, 1820]. *USNIP* 111 (June 1985): 69–72.

——. "Leathernecks, Doughboys, and the Press." *Naval History* 7 (September–October 1993): 46–53.

——. *Lejeune: A Marine's Life, 1867–1942.* Columbia: University of South Carolina Press, 1991; reprint, Annapolis: Naval Institute Press, 1996.

——. "Old Gimlet Eye" [Smedley D. Butler]. *USNIP* 112 (November 1986): 65–72.

——. "Ouster of a Commandant" [removal of George Barnett, 1920]. *USNIP* 106 (November 1980): 60–65.

——. "The Road to Eighth and Eye" [selection of commandants]. *USNIP* 114 (November 1988): 73–80.

——, ed. *Assault from the Sea: Essays on the History of Amphibious Warfare.* Annapolis: Naval Institute Press, 1983.

Bauer, K. Jack. *The Mexican War, 1846–48.* New York: Macmillan, 1974.

——. *Surfboats and Horse Marines: U.S. Naval Operations in the Mexican War, 1846–1848.* Annapolis: U.S. Naval Institute Press, 1969.

Bellamy, David. "A Marine at the Front" [World War I]. *American History Illustrated* 5 (October 1971): 30–42.

Berry, Henry. *Hey Mac, Where Ya Been? Living Memories of U.S. Marines in the Korean War.* New York: St. Martin's, 1988.

Blair, Arthur H. *At War in the Gulf: A Chronology.* College Station: Texas A&M University Press, 1992.

Boyington, Gregory. *Baa Baa Black Sheep.* New York: Putnam's, 1958.

Buker, George E. *Swamp Sailors: Riverine Warfare in the Everglades, 1835–1842.* Gainesville: University Presses of Florida, 1975.

Butler, Smedley D., with Lowell Thomas. *Old Gimlet Eye: Adventures of Smedley D. Butler.* New York: Farrar and Rinehart, 1933.

Caporale, Louis G. "The Fleet Marine Force *circa* 1941." *Marine Corps Gazette* 75 (December 1991): 96–100.

———. "Marine Corps Historical Notes from the Gulf War." *Marine Corps Gazette* 75 (December 1991): 44–46.

Catlin, Albertus W. *With the Help of God and a Few Marines.* Garden City, N.Y.: Doubleday, Page, 1919.

Christmas, George R. "A Company Commander Reflects on Operation Hue City." *Marine Corps Gazette* 55 (January 1971): 34–39.

A Chronology of the United States Marine Corps, 1935–1946. Washington, D.C.: HQMC, 1965.

Clark, George B. *Devil Dogs: Fighting Marines of World War I.* Novato, Calif.: Presidio, 1999.

———. *Their Time in Hell: The 4th Marine Brigade at Belleau Wood.* Pike, N.H.: Brass Hat, 1996.

———. *Treading Softly: The U.S. Marines in China, from the 1840s to the 1940s.* Pike, N.H.: Brass Hat, 1996.

Clifford, Kenneth J. *Progress and Purpose: A Developmental History of the United States Marine Corps, 1900–1970.* Washington, D.C.: HMD–HQMC, 1973.

Cochran, Alexander S. Jr. "No Beaches to Land On." *Military History* 3 (December 1985): 47–52.

Coffman, Edward M. *The War to End All Wars: The American Military Experience in World War I.* New York and London: Oxford University Press, 1968.

Collum, Richard S. *History of the United States Marine Corps.* Philadelphia: Hamersly, 1890.

Condit, Kenneth W., and Edwin T. Turnbladh. *Hold High the Torch: A History of the 4th Marines.* Washington, D.C.: Government Printing Office, 1960.

Cooper, Norman V. *A Fighting General: The Biography of Gen. Holland M. "Howlin' Mad" Smith.* Quantico, Va.: Marine Corps Association, 1987.

Cosmas, Graham A., and Jack Shulimson. "The Culebra Maneuver and the Formation of the U.S. Marine Corps's Advance Base Force, 1913–14." In *Assault from the Sea: Essays on the History of Amphibious Warfare,* ed. Merrill L. Bartlett, 121–32. Annapolis: Naval Institute Press, 1983.

Craige, John. *Cannibal Cousins* [Marines in Haiti]. New York: Minton, Balch, 1934.

Crane, Stephen. *The War Dispatches of Stephen Crane.* Ed. R. W. Stallman and E. R. Hagemann. New York: New York University Press, 1964.

Cressman, Robert J. *A Magnificent Fight: The Battle for Wake Island.* Annapolis: Naval Institute Press, 1995.

D'Andrea, Thomas M. "Marines at Midway." *Marine Corps Gazette* 48 (November 1964): 27–31.

Daniels, Josephus. *The Wilson Era.* 2 vols. Chapel Hill: University of North Carolina Press, 1944–46.

Davis, Burke. *Marine! The Life of Lt. General Lewis B. "Chesty" Puller, USMC (Ret.).* Boston: Little, Brown, 1962.

Davis, Gordon M. "Dewey Canyon: All Weather Classic." *Marine Corps Gazette* 53 (July 1969): 32–40.

Dawson, Joseph G. III. "With Fidelity and Effectiveness: Archibald Henderson's Lasting Legacy to the U.S. Marine Corps." *Journal of Military History* 62 (October 1998): 727–53.

Devereux, James P. S. *The Story of Wake Island.* Philadelphia: Lippincott, 1947.

Dewey, George. *Autobiography of George Dewey: Admiral of the Navy.* New York: Scribner's, 1913; reprint, Annapolis: Naval Institute Press, 1987.

Dieckmann, Edward A. "All Business: The Saga of Sgt Maj John Quick." *Marine Corps Gazette* 47 (June 1963): 20–24.

———. "Manila John Basilone." *Marine Corps Gazette* 47 (October 1963): 28–32.

Dockery, Charles L. "Marine Air over Korea." *Marine Corps Gazette* 69 (December 1985): 38–50.

Dodge, R. A. "Massacre in Haiti" [1929]. *USNIP* 111 (November 1994): 60–64.

Donnelly, Ralph W. *The Confederate States Marine Corps: The Rebel Leathernecks.* Shippensburg, Pa.: White Mane, 1989.

———. "Officer Selection in the 'Old Corps.'" *Marine Corps Gazette* 66 (November 1982): 81–87.

Edye, L. *The Historical Records of the Royal Marines.* Vol. 1. London: Harrison, 1893.

Ellsworth, Harry Allanson. *One Hundred Eighty Landings of United States Marines, 1800 to 1934.* Washington, D.C.: Historical Section, Headquarters Marine Corps, 1934.

Esposito, Vincent J., chief ed. *The West Point Atlas of American Wars.* 2 vols. New York: Praeger, 1959.

Evans, M. H. H. *Amphibious Operations: The Projection of Sea Power Ashore.* London: Brassey's, 1990.

Ferguson, Gilbert W. "Guns at Da Nang" [1/12 in Vietnam, 1965]. *Marine Corps Gazette* 50 (February 1966): 27–31.

Field, Cyril. *Britain's Sea-Soldiers: A History of the Royal Marines.* 2 vols. Liverpool: Lyceum, 1924.

Fleming, Keith. *The U.S. Marine Corps in Crisis: Ribbon Creek and Recruit Training.* Columbia: University of South Carolina Press, 1990.

Fleming, Peter. *The Siege at Peking.* New York: Harper and Row, [1959].

Fortescue, J. W. *A History of the British Army.* Part 1: *To the Close of the Seven Years' War.* London: Macmillan, 1899.

Frank, Benis M., ed. *Marines in World War Two.* Commemorative Series. 25 vols. Washington, D.C.: HMD–HQMC, 1991–94.

———. *U.S. Marines in Lebanon, 1982–1984.* Washington, D.C.: HMD–HQMC, 1987.

Frank, Richard B. *Downfall: The End of the Imperial Japanese Empire.* New York: Random House, 1999.

———. *Guadalcanal: The Definitive Account.* New York: Random House, 1990.

Fuller, J. F. C. *Decisive Battles of the USA.* New York: Harper, 1942.

Fuller, Stephen M., and Graham A. Cosmas. *Marines in the Dominican Republic, 1916–1924.* Washington, D.C.: HMD–HQMC, 1974.

Gatchel, Theodore. *At the Water's Edge: Defending against the Modern Amphibious Assault.* Annapolis: Naval Institute Press, 1996.

Geer, Andrew. *The New Breed: The Story of the U.S. Marines in Korea.* New York: Harper, 1952; reprint, Nashville: Battery Press, 1989.

Gordon, George V. *Leathernecks and Doughboys.* Chicago: n.p., 1927; reprint, Pike, N.H.: Brass Hat, 1996.

Gordon, Michael R., and Bernard E. Trainor. *The Generals' War: The Inside Story of the Conflict in the Gulf.* Boston: Little, Brown, 1995.

Griffith, Samuel B. *The Battle for Guadalcanal.* New York: Ballantine Books, 1963; reprint, Annapolis: Nautical and Aviation Publishing Company of America, 1979.

Hagan, Kenneth J., ed. *In Peace and War: Interpretations of American Naval History, 1775 1984.* 2d ed. Westport, Conn.: Greenwood, 1984.

———. *This People's Navy: The Making of American Sea Power.* New York: Macmillan, Free Press, 1991.

Halberstam, David. *The Best and the Brightest.* New York: Random House, 1972.

Hammel, Eric M. "Guadalcanal: The Battle of the Matanikau." *Marine Corps Gazette* 66 (August 1982): 48–54.

———. *The Root: The Marines in Beirut, August 1982–February 1984.* New York: Harcourt, Brace, Jovanovich, 1985.

Harbord, James G. *Leaves from a War Diary.* Philadelphia: Dodd, Mead, 1925.

Harries, Meirion, and Susie Harries. *The Last Days of Innocence: America at War, 1917–1918.* New York: Random House, 1997.

Heinl, Robert D. Jr. *Soldiers of the Sea: The United States Marine Corps, 1775–1962.* Annapolis: U.S. Naval Institute Press, 1962.

———. *Victory at High Tide: The Inchon–Seoul Campaign.* Philadelphia and New York: Lippincott, 1968.

Heinl, Robert D. Jr., and Nancy Heinl. *Written in Blood: The Story of the Haitian People, 1492–1971.* Boston: Houghton Mifflin, 1978.

Hemingway, Al. *Our War Was Different: Marine Combined Action Platoons in Vietnam.* Annapolis: Naval Institute Press, 1994.

Hewett, Linda L. *Women Marines in World War I.* Washington, D.C.: HMD–HQMC, 1974.

Hillman, Rolf. "Crossing the Meuse." *Marine Corps Gazette* 72 (November 1988): 68–73.

———. "Fighters and Writers: World War I Marines Who Became Authors." *Marine Corps Gazette* 72 (November 1988): 90–98.

———. "Marines in the Rhineland Occupation, 1918–1919." *Naval History* 3 (summer 1989): 11–15.

History of U.S. Marine Corps Operations in World War II. 5 vols. Washington, D.C.: HMD–HQMC, 1958–64.

Hodgins, Michael C. *Reluctant Warrior* [Marine infantry officer, Vietnam, 1968–69]. New York: Fawcett Columbine, 1996.

Hoffman, Jon T. "The Legacy and Lessons of Operation Watchtower." *Marine Corps Gazette* 76 (August 1992): 68–73.

———. *Once a Legend: "Red Mike" Edson of the Marine Raiders.* Novato, Calif.: Presidio, 1994.

Holden-Rhodes, J. F. "The Adventures of Henry Clay Cochrane." *Marine Corps Gazette* 66 (November 1982): 69–70; (December 1982): 14–15; 67 (January 1983): 32–33; (February 1983): 46–47; (March 1983) 50–51; (April 1983): 54–55.

Hoppin, James Mason. *Life of Andrew Hull Foote, Rear-Admiral, United States Navy.* New York: Harper, 1874.

Hull, R. R. "Signal Encounter at Guantánamo." *Naval History* 12 (May 1998): 18–23.

Humanitarian Operations in Northern Iraq, 1991. Washington, D.C.: HMD–HQMC, 1993.

Hunt, George P. *The Story of the U.S. Marines.* New York: Random House, 1951.

Isely, Jeter A., and Philip A. Crowl. *The U.S. Marines and Amphibious War: Its Theory and Practice in the Pacific.* Princeton: Princeton University Press, 1951.

James, D. Clayton. *The Years of MacArthur.* 3 vols. Boston: Little, Brown, 1970–85.

James, William. *A Full and Correct Account of the Military Occurrences of the Late War between Great Britain and the United States of America.* 2 vols. London: William James, 1818.

Johnson, Douglas V. III, and Rolfe L. Hillman Jr. *Soissons, 1918.* College Station: Texas A&M University Press, 1999.

Johnson, Edward C. A. *Marine Corps Aviation: The Early Years, 1912–1940.* Ed. Graham Cosmas. Washington, D.C.: HMD–HQMC, 1977.

Johnson, J. M. Jr., R. W. Austin, and D. A. Quinlan. "Individual Heroism Overcame Awkward Command Relations" [rescue of the SS *Mayaguez*]. *Marine Corps Gazette* 61 (October 1977): 24–34.

Johnson, Robert Erwin. *Rear Admiral John Rodgers, 1812–1882.* Annapolis: U.S. Naval Institute Press, 1967.

Johnson, Robert Underwood, and Clarence Clough Buel, eds. *Battles and Leaders of the Civil War.* 4 vols. New York: Century, 1884, 1887–88.

Johnston, James W. *The Long Road of War: A Marine's Story of Pacific Combat.* Lincoln: University of Nebraska Press, 1998.

Jones, Wilbur D. Jr. *Gyrene: The World War Two United States Marine.* Shippensburg, Pa.: White Mane, 1998.

Keiser, Gordon W. "The Long March: Membership of the Commandant in the JCS." *Marine Corps Gazette* 73 (August 1989): 30–35.

Krulak, Victor H. *First to Fight.* Annapolis: Naval Institute Press, 1984.

———. "'This Precious Few . . .': The Evolution of Marine Recruit Training." *Marine Corps Gazette* 66 (April 1982): 48–55.

Langley, Lester D. *The Banana Wars: An Inner History of American Empire, 1900–1934.* Lexington: University Press of Kentucky, 1983.

Lee, Alex. *Force Recon Command: A Special Marine Unit in Vietnam, 1969–1970.* Annapolis: Naval Institute Press, 1995.

Lejeune, John A. "The Marine Corps, 1926." *USNIP* 52 (October 1926): 1961.

———. *Reminiscences of a Marine.* Philadelphia: Dorrance, 1930; reprint, Quantico, Va.: Marine Corps Association, 1979.

Levin, Dan. *From the Battlefield: Dispatches of a World War II Marine.* Annapolis: Naval Institute Press, 1995.

Lewis, Charles Lee. *Famous American Marines.* Boston: Page, 1950.

Lewis, Lloyd. *Captain Sam Grant.* Boston: Little, Brown, 1950.

Lewy, Guenter. *America in Vietnam.* New York and London: Oxford University Press, 1978.

Liddell Hart, B. H. "Marines and Strategy." *Marine Corps Gazette* 64 (January 1980): 22–31.

Linn, Brian McAllister. *Philippine War, 1899–1902.* Lawrence: University Press of Kansas, 1999.

Lord, Walter. *The Dawn's Early Light.* New York: Norton, [1972].

Macaulay, Neil. "Guerrilla Ambush." *Marine Corps Gazette* 47 (May 1963): 41–44.

———. *The Sandino Affair* [Nicaragua, 1930s]. Chicago: Quandrangle, 1967.

McClellan, Edwin N. "The Battle of Blanc Mont Ridge." *Marine Corps Gazette* 7 (March 1922): 1021.

———. "A Brief History of the Fourth Brigade of Marines." *Marine Corps Gazette* 4 (December 1919): 342–68.

———. "First Commandant of the Marine Corps William Ward Burrows." *Daughters of the American Revolution Magazine* 59 (March 1925): 155–58.

———. "Marine Corps History 1807 to 1812." *Marine Corps Gazette* 8 (March 1923): 24–43.

———. "Marine Corps History, 1817–1821." *Marine Corps Gazette* 9 (March 1924): 69–93.

———. "The Naval War with France." *Marine Corps Gazette* 7 (December 1922): 339–63.

———. *The United States Marine Corps in the World War.* Washington, D.C.: Headquarters Marine Corps, 1920.

McCormick, John. *The Right Kind of War* [Raiders in World War II]. Annapolis: Naval Institute Press, 1992.

McCrocklin, James H. *Garde d'Haiti, 1915–1934.* Annapolis: U.S. Naval Institute Press, 1956.

McKenzie, Scott W. "Tiger of the Mountains" [Augusto Sandino]. *Marine Corps Gazette* 55 (November 1955): 38–42.

Maclay, Edgar Stanton. "An Early 'Globe-Circling' Cruise." *USNIP* 44 (June 1918): 480–500.

Magruder, J. H. III. "The Brevet in the Marine Corps." *Marine Corps Gazette* 39 (November 1955): 54–57.

Mahon, John K. *History of the Second Seminole War, 1835–1847.* Gainesville: University of Florida Press, 1967.

———. *The War of 1812.* Gainesville: University of Florida Press, 1972.

Manchester, William. *Goodbye, Darkness* [memoir of a young Marine's Pacific War]. Boston: Little Brown, 1979.

Merillat, Herbert Christian. *Guadalcanal Remembered.* New York: Dodd, Mead, 1982.

Mersky, Peter. *U.S. Marine Corps Aviation: 1912 to the Present.* Annapolis: Nautical and Aviation Publishing Company of America, 1983.

Metcalf, Clyde H. *A History of the United States Marine Corps.* New York: Putnam's, 1939.

Miller, John G. *The Bridge at Dong Ha.* Annapolis: Naval Institute Press, 1989.

Millett, Allan R. "Assault from the Sea: The Development of Amphibious Warfare between the Wars—the American, British, and Japanese Experiences." In *Military Innovation in the Interwar Period,* ed. Williamson Murray and Allan R. Millett, 50–95. New York: Cambridge University Press, 1996.

———. *In Many a Strife: General Gerald C. Thomas and the U.S. Marine Corps, 1917–1956.* Annapolis: Naval Institute Press, 1993.

———. *Semper Fidelis: The History of the United States Marine Corps.* London and New York: Macmillan, 1980.

———, ed. *Commandants of the Marine Corps.* Annapolis: Naval Institute Press, forthcoming.

Millett, Allan R., and Peter Maslowski. *For the Common Defense: A Military History of the United States of America.* New York and London: Free Press, 1984.

Morison, Samuel Eliot. *History of United States Naval Operations in World War II.* 15 vols. Boston: Little, Brown, 1947–62.

———. *John Paul Jones: A Sailor's Biography.* Boston: Little, Brown, 1959; reprint, Annapolis: Naval Institute Press, 1989.

Moskin, J. Robert. *The U.S. Marine Corps Story.* New York: McGraw-Hill, 1977.

Murray, Williamson, and Allan R. Millett. *A War to Be Won: Fighting the Second World War.* Cambridge: Harvard University Press, 2000.

Neufeld, Gabrielle M., and James S. Santelli. "Smedley Butler's Air Corps: First Marine Aviators in China." *USNIP* 103 (April 1977): 48–59.

———. "1921–41: Squadrons of the Corps." *Marine Corps Gazette* 57 (November 1973): 48–55.

Nichols, Charles S. Jr., and Henry I. Shaw. *Okinawa: Victory in the Pacific.* Washington, D.C.: Historical Branch, HQMC, 1955.

Nolan, Keith W. "Battle at Hue City." *USNIP* 108 (April 1982): 50–58.

Oberdorfer, Don. *Tet: The Turning Point in the Vietnam War.* New York: Da Capo, 1984.

Owen, Joseph R. *Colder than Hell: A Marine Rifle Company at Chosin Reservoir.* New York: Ballantine Books, 1996.

Palmer, Michael A. *Stoddert's War: Naval Operations during the Quasi-War with France, 1798–1801.* Columbia: University of South Carolina Press, 1987.

Parker, William Harwar. *Recollections of a Naval Officer, 1841–1865.* New York: Scribner's, 1883; reprint, Annapolis: Naval Institute Press, 1985.

Peatross, Oscar F. "The Makin Raid." *Marine Corps Gazette* 63 (November 1979): 96–103.

Peckham, Howard H. *The Colonial Wars.* Chicago: University of Chicago Press, 1964.

Pershing, John J. *My Experiences in the World War.* 2 vols. New York: Stokes, 1931.

Pierce, Philip N., and Frank O. Hough. *The Compact History of the United States Marine Corps.* New York: Hawthorne, 1960.

Porter, David. *Journal of a Cruise Made to the Pacific Ocean by Captain David Porter in the United States Frigate* Essex *in the Years 1812, 1813, and 1814.* Ed. Robert D. Madison and Karen Hamon. Annapolis: Naval Institute Press, 1986.

Pucciarelli, George W. "After the Beirut Bombing." *Marine Corps Gazette* 113 (January 1987): 65.

Pvtyko, A. R. "An Epoch of Need" [Marine Corps aviation in the DMZ, Vietnam]. *Marine Corps Gazette* 57 (May 1973): 42–48.

Rawlins, Eugene W. *Marines and Helicopters, 1946–1962.* Washington, D.C.: HMD–HQMC, 1976.

Redicker, Jane. "The First Birthday Ball." *Marine Corps Gazette* 60 (November 1976): 24–27.

Ripley, R. S. *The War with Mexico.* 2 vols. New York: Harper, 1849.

Rodgers, William L. *Greek and Roman Naval Warfare.* Annapolis: U.S. Naval Institute Press, 1964.

———. *Naval Warfare under Oars: 4th to 16th Centuries.* Annapolis: U.S. Naval Institute Press, 1967.

Roosevelt, Theodore. *The Naval War of 1812.* New York: Putnam's, 1882; reprint, Annapolis: Naval Institute Press, 1987.

Russ, Martin. *Breakout: The Chosin Reservoir Campaign, Korea 1950.* New York: Fromm International, 1999.

Saburo, Hayashi, and Alvin D. Coox. *Kōgun: The Japanese Army in the Pacific War.* Tokyo: Taiheiyo Senso Rikusen, 1951; reprint, Quantico, Va.: Marine Corps Association, 1959.

Saburō, Ienaga. *The Pacific War: World War II and the Japanese, 1931–1945.* New York: Pantheon, 1978.

Santelli, James S., and Gabrielle M. Neufeld. "Regiments of the Corps." *Marine Corps Gazette* 55 (November 1972): 60–67.

Sanza, R. "The Marine 'Grunt General.'" *Newsweek,* 11 January 1988, 17–18.

Scharf, J. Thomas. *History of the Confederate Navy.* New York: Rogers and Sherwood, 1887.

Schmidt, Hans. *Maverick Marine: General Smedley D. Butler and the Contradictions of American Military History.* Lexington: University Press of Kentucky, 1987.

———. *The United States Occupation of Haiti, 1915–1934.* New Brunswick: Rutgers University Press, 1971.

Schott, Joseph L. *The Ordeal of Samar.* Indianapolis: Bobbs-Merrill, 1964.

Schuon, Karl. *Home of the Commandants.* Quantico, Va.: Marine Corps Association, 1974.

———. *U.S. Marine Corps Biographical Dictionary.* New York: Franklin Watts, 1963.

Selfridge, Thomas O. Jr. "The Navy at Fort Fisher." In *Battles and Leaders of the Civil War,* ed. Robert U. Johnson and Clarence C. Buel, 4:655–61. New York: Century, 1884, 1887–88.

Seligman, Herbert J. "The Conquest of Haiti." *Nation,* 10 July 1920, 35–36.

Sellers, James McBrayer. "Life aboard the *Henderson*" [aged troop transport used between the Spanish-American War and World War II]. *Marine Corps Gazette* 77 (June 1993): 72–74.

Semmes, Raphael. *Memoirs of Service Afloat during the War between the States.* Baltimore: Kelly, Piet, 1869.

Shaw, Henry I. Jr., and Ralph W. Donnelly. *Blacks in the Marine Corps.* Washington, D.C.: HMD–HQMC, 1973.

Sherrod, Robert. *On to Westward: The Battles of Saipan and Iwo Jima.* New York: Duell, Sloan, and Pierce, 1945.

———. *Tarawa: The Story of a Battle.* New York: Duell, Sloan, and Pearce, 1944; reprint, Fredericksburg, Tex.: Admiral Nimitz Foundation, 1973.

Shulimson, Jack. *The Marine Corps' Search for a Mission, 1880–1898.* Lawrence: University Press of Kansas, 1993.

———. "The Transitional Commandancy: Col. Charles G. McCaw-ley and Uneven Reform, 1876–1891." *Marine Corps Gazette* 72 (October 1988): 70–77.

———. "U.S. Marines in Panama, 1885." In *Assault from the Sea: Essays on the History of Amphibious Warfare,* ed. Merrill L. Bartlett, 107–20. Annapolis: Naval Institute Press, 1983.

———, ed. *The U.S. Marines in Vietnam.* 11 vols. Washington, D.C.: HMD–HQMC, 1977–1997.

Simmons, Edwin Howard. "Fort Fisher: Amphibious Finale to the Civil War." *Fortitudine* 16 (summer 1986): 3–8.

———. "Maj. Carmick at New Orleans." *Fortitudine* 24 (spring 1985): 3–8.

———. *The United States Marines: A History.* 3d ed. Annapolis: Naval Institute Press, 1998.

Smith, Charles R. *Marines in the Revolution: A History of the Continental Marines in the American Revolution, 1775–1783.* Washington, D.C.: HMD–HQMC, 1975.

Smith, Holland M., with Percy Finch. *Coral and Brass.* New York: Scribner's, 1949.

Smith, Justin M. *The War with Mexico.* 2 vols. New York: Macmillan, 1919.

Smollett, Tobias. *Roderick Random.* London: Dent, 1951.

Smythe, Donald. *Pershing: General of the Armies.* Bloomington: Indiana University Press, 1986.

Solis, Gary D. *Son Thang: An American War Crime.* Annapolis: Naval Institute Press, 1997.

Spears, Stephen, ed. *The Horizon History of the British Empire.* N.p.: American Heritage, 1973.

Spector, Ronald H. *After Tet: The Bloodiest Year in Vietnam.* New York: Macmillan, 1993.

———. *Grenada, 1983.* Washington, D.C.: HMD–HQMC, 1987.

Sprague, John T. *The Origins, Progress, and Conclusion of the Florida War.* New York: Appleton, 1848.

Steeves, W. D. Jr. "Crisis in Retrospect" [Lebanon, 1958]. *Marine Corps Gazette* 57 (February 1973): 31–34.

Stevens, John C. III. *Court-martial at Parris Island: The Ribbon Creek Incident.* Annapolis: Naval Institute Press, 1999.

Stevens, Thomas H. "The Boat Attack on Fort Sumter." In *Battles and Leaders of the Civil War,* ed. Robert U. Johnson and Clarence C. Buel, 4:47–51. New York: Century, 1884, 1887–88.

Suid, Lawrence. "Hollywood and the Marines." *Marine Corps Gazette* 62 (April 1978): 35–44.

Sweetman, Jack. *American Naval History: An Illustrated Chronology of the U.S. Navy and Marine Corps, 1775–Present.* 2d ed. Annapolis: Naval Institute Press, 1991.

———. *The Landing at Veracruz.* Annapolis: U.S. Naval Institute Press, 1968.

Talent, Robert W. "The Unlovable Latin" [Augustino Sandino]. *Marine Corps Gazette* 43 (November 1959): 88–92.

Thomason, John W. Jr. *—and a Few Marines.* New York: Scribner's, 1943.

———. *Fix Bayonets!* New York: Scribner's, 1926.

Thrasher, Thomas E. Jr. "The Taking of Fort Rivière." *Marine Corps Gazette* 15 (February 1931): 31–33, 64.

Toland, John. *No Man's Land: 1918—The Last Year of the Great War.* New York: Doubleday, 1980.

———. *The Rising Sun: The Decline and Fall of the Japanese Empire, 1936–1945.* New York: Random House, 1970.

Trask, David F. *The AEF and Coalition Warmaking, 1917–1918.* Manhattan: University Press of Kansas, 1993.

———. *The War with Spain in 1898.* New York and London: Macmillan, 1981.

Turner, Martha Anne. *The World of Col. John W. Thomason, USMC.* Austin, Tex.: Eahn Press, 1984.

Twining, Merrill B. *The Battle for Guadalcanal: No Bended Knee, The Memoir of Gen. Merrill B. Twining, USMC (Ret.).* Ed. Neil Carey. Novato, Calif.: Presidio, 1996.

Updegraph, Charles L. Jr. *U.S. Marine Corps Special Units of World War II.* Washington, D.C.: HMD–HQMC, 1972.

Urwin, Gregory J. W. *Facing Fearful Odds: The Siege of Wake Island.* Lincoln and London: University of Nebraska Press, 1997.

U.S. Marine Corps Operations in Korea, 1950–1953. 5 vols. Washington, D.C.: HMD–HQMC, 1954–1972.

U.S. Marines in the Persian Gulf, 1990–1991. 8 vols. Washington, D.C.: HMD–HQMC, 1991–98.

U.S. Navy Department. *Annual Report of the Secretary of the Navy . . . for the Year 1871.* Washington, D.C.: Government Printing Office, 1871.

———. *Naval Documents Related to the United States Wars with the Barbary Pirates.* 6 vols. Washington, D.C.: Government Printing Office, 1939–44.

———. *Official Records of the Union and Confederate Navies in the War of Rebellion.* 30 vols. Washington, D.C.: Government Printing Office, 1894–1927.

———. *Report of the Secretary of the Navy . . . 1867.* Washington, D.C.: Government Printing Office, 1867.

U.S. Senate. Subcommittee on Veterans' Affairs. *Medal of Honor Recipients, 1863–1973.* Washington, D.C.: Government Printing Office, 1975.

Utter, Leon N. "The Other Smedley Butler." *Marine Corps Gazette* 48 (November 1964): 36–42.

Vandegrift, Alexander A., with Robert B. Asprey. *Once a Marine.* New York: Norton, 1964.

Vandiver, Frank. *Black Jack: The Life and Times of John J. Pershing.* 2 vols. College Station: Texas A&M University Press, 1977.

Venzon, Anne Cipriano, ed. *General Smedley Darlington Butler: The Letters of a Leatherneck, 1898–1931.* New York: Praeger, 1992.

Warr, Nicholas. *Phase Line Green: The Battle for Hue, 1968.* Annapolis: Naval Institute Press, 1997.

Webb, James H. "Roles and Missions: Time for a Change." *Marine Corps Gazette* 55 (March 1972): 18–28.

Welles, Gideon. *The Diary of Gideon Welles.* 3 vols. Boston: Houghton Mifflin, 1911.

Whipple, A. B. C. *To the Shores of Tripoli: The Birth of the U.S. Navy and Marines.* New York: Morrow, 1991.

Wilcox, Cadmus M. *History of the Mexican War.* Washington, D.C.: Church News Publishing, 1892.

Williams, Robert H. *The Old Corps: A Portrait of the U.S. Marine Corps between the Wars.* Annapolis: Naval Institute Press, 1982.

Williams, Vernon L. "Littleton W. T. Waller: Politics of Command." In *New Interpretations in Naval History: Selected Papers from the Tenth Naval History Symposium,* ed. Jack Sweetman, Douglas C. Meister, Sharon Pfeiffer, and Brian VanDeMark, 169–80. Annapolis: Naval Institute Press, 1993.

Wilson, John Richard Meridith. "Herbert Hoover and the Armed Forces: A Study of Presidential Attitudes and Policy." Ph.D. diss., Northwestern University, 1971.

Wise, Frederick M., as told to Meigs O. Frost. *A Marine Tells It to You.* New York: Sears, 1929.

Young, James Rankin, and J. Hampton Moore. *History of Our War with Spain.* N.p.: J. R. Jones, 1898.

Index

Abrams, Creighton W., 261

Adams, Charles F., 168

Adams, John, 24–25

Addis Ababa, Ethiopia, 118

Admiral's Regiment. *See* Duke of York and Albany's Maritime Regiment of Foot

Advanced base mission, 109

"Advanced Base Operations in Micronesia, 1921" (Earl H. Ellis), 156

Advanced Base School, 118, 124

Aguinaldo, Emilio, 110, 114

Ahrens, Edward H., 176

AH-1 Cobra helicopter, 277

aircraft, fixed-wing: B-24, 198; B-52, 252; Curtis Jenny, 152; DeHavilland (DH)-4, 149, 152, 162; F4U Corsair, 191, 228, 237, 240; F-111, 278; F-117, 283; Grumman F4F-4 Wildcat, 173, 179; MiG-15, 243; Mitsubishi Zero, 172; PBY Catalina, 178; SBD 3 Dauntless, 179; Yak, 243

Al Burqan oil field, Kuwait, 285, 286–87

Al Jaber airfield, Kuwait, 285, 287

Al Khanjar, Saudi Arabia, 285, 286

Allison, Richard T., 71

Al Mish'ab, Saudi Arabia, 284

Almond, Edward M., 229

Alvarado, Mexico, 53, 54

Amelia Court House, Virginia, 86

Amelia Island, Florida, 39

Amory, William, 27

Anaconda Plan, 67

Andong, Korea, 24

An Hoa, Vietnam, 266, 267

Anthony, William, 104

Aogiri Ridge, New Britain, 192–93

Apache helicopter, 283

Apalachicola River, Florida, 39

Appomattox Court House, Virginia, 85

Arafat, Yasir, 273

Arias, Desiderio, 129

Arizona Territory, Vietnam, 267

Army of the Republic of Vietnam (ARVN): ARVNs in Operation Harvest Moon, 252–53; ARVN battalions in 1966, 253; ARVN ranger battalion at Khe Sanh, 259; ARVN Marines at Hue, 260; ARVNs in post-Tet Offensive, 1969, 266; response to NVA offensive, 1972, 268; Lam Son 719, 268

Arnold, Benedict, 17

Arnold, Henry H. "Hap," 185, 202

A Shau Valley, Vietnam, 264

Asiatic Squadron, 105

Aspin, Les, 289

Aspinall, Panama, 97

Austin, Randall, 272

Aviation Detachment, Advanced Base Force, 123

Bairiki Atoll, 198

Baker, Newton D., 133

Balangiga massacre, 114

Baldwin, Hanson, 244

Baltimore, Maryland, 38

Band, Marine Corps, 26, 42, 95–96

Barbary Wars, 28–31, 39

Barber, William E., 236

Barnett, George: selected as commandant, 124; offers a brigade for duty in France, 133; urges deployment of 5th Brigade to the AEF, 148; promises to meet all naval commitments during World War I, 151; Haitian scandal, 154; ousted by the secretary of the Navy, 155

Barney, Josiah, 37

Barrier Forts, China, 61

Barrow, Robert H., 233, 272

Basilone, "Manila" John, 187, 211

Batraville, Benoit, 152–53

Beall, Lloyd J., 71

Beals, Carleton, 162

Bearss, Hiram I. "Hiking Hiram," 116

Beirut, Lebanon, 273–75

Belén Gate, Mexico City, 57–58

Belknap, George E., 89

Bell, H. H., 89

Belleau Wood, Battle of, 137–40

Bended Knee Speech, 223

Benson, William S., 133

Benton, Thomas Hart, 48

Betio Island, 195–98

B-52, 252

Biddle, William P., 114, 120, 123

Bien Hoa, Vietnam, 248

Bill, David, 10

Bladensburg, Battle of, 36–38, 39, 41

Blanc Mont, France, 144–45

Bloody Ridge, Guadalcanal, 183

Bluefields, Nicaragua, 119, 121

Bolt, John F., 243

Boomer, Walter E., 281, 284, 286

Boutwell, E. B., 59

Boxer Rebellion, 112–14

Boyington, Gregory R. "Pappy," 191

Bradley, Omar N., 225

Branch, John, 43–44

Breese, K. R., 83

Brewster, David, 22–23

British military units: 2nd Battalion Scots Guards, 161; Devonshire Regiment, 97; Royal Air Force, 149; Royal Welch Fusiliers, 114

British naval ships: *Atalanta,* 22; *Cyane,* 35, 59; *Glasgow,* 15–16; *Levant,* 35; *Macedonian,* 34; *Penguin,* 35; *Rattler,* 61; *Reindeer,* 35; *Serapis,* 19; *Seringapatam,* 35; *Shannon,* 34; *Sybil,* 23; *Trepassey,* 22; *Yarmouth,* 18

British naval units: 41st Independent Commando, Royal Marines, 238; Duke of York and Albany's Maritime Regiment of Foot (Admiral's Regiment), 3, 4; Royal Marines, 9, 114, 238

Broad River Expedition, South Carolina, 81–82

Broke, Philip Vere, 34
Brooks, John, 36
Broome, James, 34
Broome, John L., 59, 75
Brown, Charles, 93
Brown, John, 65–66
Browne, Montfort, 14–15
B-24, 198
Buchanan, Franklin, 72, 80
Buchanan, James, 62, 63
Bucker, Simon Bolivar, 216, 218, 220
Buenos Aires, Argentina, 59
Bull Run, First Battle of, 67
Bunau-Varilla, Philippe, 118
Burden, George, 19
Burrows, William Ward, 25, 28
Buse, Henry W., Jr., 193
Bush, George Herbert Walker, 273, 279, 281, 287
Bush, William S., 34
"Butcher of Samar," 117
Butler, Benjamin F., 78–79, 83
Butler, Smedley D.: meets Waller, 112; impressions of Elliott, 117; deploys to Panama and Nicaragua, 121; Veracruz, 126–27; Haiti, 128; in World War I, 148; investigates charges of atrocities in Haiti, 154; uses father's influence, 156; at Quantico in the 1920s, 158; in China, 160; loses bid for commandancy, 168
Butler, Thomas S., 111, 156
Butler's Battalion, 119, 121
Butt, Archie, 120
Button, William R., 153

cacos, 127–28, 152
Cactus Air Force, 179, 185
Cadwalader, John, 17
Caldwell, Henry, 25
Cam Lo, Vietnam, 255
Camp Beall, Virginia, 74, 76, 78, 83
Camp Carroll, Vietnam, 259
Camp McCalla, Cuba, 105
Camp Pontanezen, France, 147, 148
Canton, China, 61
Cape Gloucester, New Britain, 191–93
Caperton, William B., 127
Carlson, Evans P., 188–89
Carmen, Mexico, 54
Carmick, Daniel, 24, 27, 32, 38–39
Carter, Jimmy, 273
Casey, Silas, 92
Castillo de San Marcos, Florida, 5, 32
Catalina (aircraft), 178
Cates, Clifton B.: in World War I, 141; at Guadalcanal, 176; at Iwo Jima, 209; appointed commandant, 224; under Truman budget restrictions, 225; Truman apologizes to, for insult to the Corps, 228
Catlin, Albertus W., 137–39

Central Pacific Fleet (Japanese), 203
Chaffee, Adna R., 114, 117
Chamorro, Emiliano, 161
Chapman, Leonard F., Jr., 258
Chapultepec, Mexico, 55–57
Charleston, South Carolina, 21–22, 80, 85
Cheney, Richard B., 280
CH-53 helicopter, 271, 277, 290
CH-46 helicopter, 271, 283
China: Barrier Forts, 61; Boxer Rebellion, 112–14; Canton, 61; Hong Kong, 61; Hsiku Arsenal, 113; Peking, 112–13, 114, 172; Shanghai, 61, 160–61, 171; Tientsin, 112–14, 160, 172; Ty-Ho Bay, 61
Chindong-ni, Korea, 228
Chinese forces, nationalist. See Kuomintang Army
Chinese MiG-15, 243
Chinese People's Liberation Army (CPLA): Ninth CPLA Group, 240; 59th CPLA Division, 236; 124th CPLA Division, 235; during Korean War, 235–36, 238, 240, 241, 244
Chinhung-ni, Korea, 236, 240
Chinju, Korea, 228
Choiseul Island, 190
Chorwon, Korea, 241
Chosin Reservoir Campaign, 235–40
Chu Lai, Vietnam, 230, 251, 252, 259
Civilian Irregular Defense Group camp, Lang Vei, Vietnam, 260–61
Clifford, Clark, 261
Clinch, Bartholomew, 26
Clinton, Bill, 190
Coatzacoalcos, Mexico, 54
Cochrane, Henry Clay: complains about slow promotions, 88; as a reformer, 94; deploys with force to halt seal slaughter, 101; in Spanish-American War, 105; promoted to colonel, 108; with Waller in Egypt, 111
Coco River patrols, Nicaragua, 167
Cole, Eli K., 148, 158–59
Colón, Panama, 118
Combined Action Platoons, Vietnam, 251
Confederate States Marine Corps: organized, 69; officer corps of, 69–71; operations in 1861–63, 71–74; operations in 1864–65, 77–79, 80, 81, 83, 85–86
Confederate States Marine Corps units: Company A, 71, 78; Company B, 71, 72, 73; Company C, 71, 72, 73, 77, 86; Company E, 75, 82, 85, 86; Company F, 75
Confederate States Navy ships: Alabama, 68; Chickamauga, 76; Chicora, 76; Jamestown, 72–73; Gaines, 81; Macon, 82; McRae, 75; North Carolina, 83; Patrick Henry, 72, 74; Raleigh, 83; Selma, 80–81; Tallahassee/Olustee, 76; Tennessee, 80–81; Virginia, 72–73
Confederate States Navy units: Charleston Squadron, 75, 85; James River Squadron,

72, 78, 86; Mobile Squadron, 75, 80–81; Tucker's Naval Brigade, 86
Conger, Edwin, 114
Con Thien, Vietnam, 258
Continental Marines: organized, 11–12; employment of, 16; in New Providence expedition, 12–16; with Washington's army, 17; second capture of Nassau by, 18–19; in Penobscot Expedition, 20–21; at defense of Charleston, 21–22
Cook, Donald, 268
Corinto, Nicaragua, 121
Corlett, Charles H., 201
Cornwallis, Charles, 22
Corsair, 191, 228, 237, 240
Coyotepe, Nicaragua, 121
Craig, Edward A., 225–26, 228
Crane, Stephen, 106, 108
Creek War, 45–46
Creswell, Lenard B., 180
Croyable (French privateer), 25, 26
Cukela, Louis, 141
Culebra, Puerto Rico, 123
Cullam, David, 19
Cunningham, Alfred A., 123, 149–50, 157
Cunningham, Winfield S., 174
Curtis Jenny, 152
Cushman, Robert E.: earns Navy Cross during invasion of Guam, 206; takes command of III MAF, 255–56; response to NVA build-up in northern I Corps, 258–59; becomes commandant, 270; reaffirms ties with Navy, 270–71; new amphibious shipping, 271
Cushman, Thomas H., 226
Cuzco Well, Cuba, 106–7

Dade, Francis L., 45
Dahlgren, John A., 76, 87
Dai Do, Vietnam, 262
Daigh, Harold, 243
Da Krong Valley, Vietnam, 264
Daly, Dan, 128, 138
Danang, Vietnam, 248–52, 259, 262–63, 266–68
Daniels, Josephus: description of William P. Biddle, 120; named secretary of the Navy, 123; accompanies the commandant to see the secretary of war, 133; pays tribute to women Marines, 151; response to Haitian scandal, 154; ousts Barnett as commandant, 155
Danville, Virginia, 85, 86
Darling, Willard, 172
Dauntless, 179
Davis, Henry C., 161
Davis, Jefferson, 71, 78
Davis, Raymond G., 208, 236–67
Dawson, Lucian L., 83–84
De Bellevue, F. B., 39
Decatur, Stephen, 29
DeHavilland (DH)-4, 149, 152, 162

DeLong, Phillip C., 243
Del Valle, Pedro A., 180, 217
Denby, Edwin H., 155
Derna, Tripoli, 30, 31
Devereux, James P. S., 173–74
Devonshire Regiment, 97
Dewey, George, 84, 105
Deyo, Morton L., 216
(DH)-4, 149, 152, 162
Díaz, Adolfo, 121, 161
Division of Operations and Training, Headquarters Marine Corps, 156
Dominican Republic, 129–31, 155, 247;
    Guardia Nacional, 155; Guayacanas, 131;
    Las Trencheras, 131; Macoris Province,
    155; Monte Cristi, 129; Navarette, 129, 130;
    1965 incursion, 247; Policia Nacional, 155;
    Puerto Plata, 129; San Francisco de Macoris, 131; Santiago de los Caballeros, 129,
    130; Santo Domingo, 129, 247; Seibo
    Province, 155
Dong Ha, Vietnam, 253–55, 262, 268
Donnelly, Ralph W., 69
Dougherty, James, 93
Doyen, Charles A., 136
Drewry, Augustus, 73
Drewry's Bluff, Virginia, 73–74, 78–79, 83, 85
Duke of York and Albany's Maritime Regiment
    of Foot, 3, 4
Dulany, William, 47, 48, 56
DuPont, Samuel F., 67, 87

Early, Jubal, 78
Eaton, William, 29–31
Edson, Alvin, 44, 53
Edson, Merritt A.: Coco River patrol, 167;
    Tulagi, 176; Bloody Ridge, 183, 188;
    Tarawa, 198; defense unification struggle,
    222
83rd Motorized Rifle Regiment (North Korean), 228
El Chipote, Nicaragua, 163
Elliott, George F., 106, 110–11, 117–18,
    119–20
Ellis, Earl H. "Pete," 156–67
Elrod, Henry T. "Hank," 174
Elwood, Thomas, 23
Employment of Helicopters (Tentative)-PHIB
    31, 223
Erskine, Graves B., 209, 214, 225
Ewell, Richard S., 85

Fagan, Fred T., 267
Farragut, David G., 75, 80–81
Feland, Logan, 161, 164
Fendall, James R. Y., 72
F4F-4 Wildcat, 173, 179
F4U Corsair, 191, 228, 237, 240
Fifth Fleet (World War II), 194, 201, 203,
    209, 217

Fighter One, Guadalcanal, 178, 179, 181
Fiji Islands, 59–60, 63
fire-support bases, Vietnam, 264
1st Force Service Support Group, 281, 286
Fists of Righteous Harmony (Boxers), 112
Fitzgerald, John, 105
Fitzpatrick, John, 16
Fleet Marine Force, creation of, 169
Fleming, Richard E., 175
Fletcher, Frank F., 125, 126
Fletcher, Frank Jack, 177
Florida Expedition for the Suppression of Indian Hostilities, 47–48
F-111, 278
F-117, 283
Ford, Gerald R., 271
Forêt de Retz, France, 141
Formosa, 89–90, 208
Forney, James, 89, 94
Forrestal, James, 210, 212
Fort Berthol, Haiti, 128
Fort Brooke, Florida, 46, 47
Fort Capois, Haiti, 128
Fort Dallas, Florida, 48
Fort Dipitié, Haiti, 128
Fort Fisher, North Carolina, 82–85
Fort Gaines, Alabama, 80–81
Fort George, Massachusetts, 21
Fort Jackson, Louisiana, 75
Fort McHenry, Maryland, 38
Fort Mercer, Pennsylvania, 17
Fort Mifflin, Pennsylvania, 17
Fort Mitchell, Alabama, 46
Fort Montagu, Bahamas, 14
Fort Morgan, Alabama, 80–81
Fort Nassau, Bahamas, 14, 15, 18
Fort Rivière, Haiti, 128
Fort St. Philip, Louisiana, 75
Fort Selon, Haiti, 128
Fort Sumter, South Carolina, 76–77
Forward (pirate steamer), 90
Foss, Joseph J., 187, 191
Fourth Army (French), 144
Fox, Wesley L., 264–65
"fragging," 264
France, World War I: Belleau Wood, 137–40;
    Blanc Mont, 144–45; Camp Pontanezen,
    147, 148; Forêt de Retz, 141; Meuse-Argonne, 145–46; Soissons, 140–41; St.-Mihiel
    salient, 143–44
Frémont, John C., 50
French military units: Fourth Army, 144; 17th
    Infantry, 144; XX Corps, 140; XXI Corps,
    144; Infanterie irlandaise, regiment de
    Welsh-Serrant, 19; regiment la Marine, 3
French naval ships: Bercceau, 26; Friendship,
    44; Insurgente, 26; Vengeance, 26
Frontera, Mexico, 53
Fullam, William F., 100–101, 123
Fuller, Ben H., 95, 155, 168–69

Fuller, Edward C., 139
Funchilin Pass, Korea, 239, 240

Gale, Anthony, 25, 39–40
Galvez, Bernardo D., 18
Gamble, John M., 35
Gendarmerie d'Haiti, 129, 161
Garland, Addison, 68
Geddis, Simon W., 26
Geiger, Roy A., 184, 206, 220, 223
General Board of the Navy, 109, 123
German High Seas Fleet, 145
Ghormley, Robert L., 175, 177
Gibbons, Floyd, 140
Gilbert Islands: Bairiki Atoll, 198; Makin Atoll,
    188–89; Tarawa Atoll, 195–98
Gillespie, Archibald H., 49–51, 58
Gillis, Alexander J., 243
Gio Linh, Vietnam, 258
Girty, George, 18
Gooch's Marines, 5–7
Gouraud, Henri, 144
Grande Riviére du Nord, Haiti, 152
Grant, Ulysses S., 58
Gray, Alfred M., 278, 289
Greene, Israel, 65, 70
Greene, Wallace M., Jr., 246, 255, 258
Greensboro, North Carolina, 86
Greer, James A., 100
Greer Board, 100
Grenada: invasion of, 276–78; Grenadian
    People's Revolutionary Army, 276
Gross, Samuel (Samuel Marguilies), 128
Group 44 (North Vietnamese), 265
Greytown, Nicaragua, 59
Grumman F4F-4 Wildcat, 173, 179
Guadalcanal Island: Bloody Ridge, 183; Fighter
    One, 178, 179, 181; Henderson Field, 178,
    179, 181; Medals of Honor at, 188; 6th
    Seabee Battalion, 184
Guadalupe Hidalgo, Treaty of, 58
Guam, 206
Guantánamo Bay, Cuba, 105–7
Guardia Nacional (Dominican Republic), 155
Guayacanas, Dominican Republic, 131
Guaymas, Mexico, 52
Gulick, Louis M., 163–64
"Gung ho," 189
Guss, William F., 243

Hagaru-ri, Korea, 236, 237, 238
Hagushi, Okinawa, 217
Haiti: atrocities, 154–55; Fort Berthol, 128;
    Fort Capois, 128; Fort Dipitié, 128; Fort Rivière, 128; Gendarmerie d'Haiti, 129, 161;
    Grande Riviére du Nord, 152; Marines in,
    27–28, 152–55, 161, 169–70; Mirebalais,
    152; Port-au-Prince, 127, 152, 153
Halsey, William F. "Bull," 187
Hamhung, Korea, 235

Hamilton, William (officer), 21
Hamilton, William (seaman), 19
Hampton Roads, Battle of, 86
Hanneken, Herman H., 153, 187, 207
Hanson, Robert M., 191
Harbord, James G., 136, 140
Harp, Will H., 158
Harpers Ferry, Virginia, 65–66
Harris, John, 47, 48, 68, 79
Hart, Franklin A., 201
Hatcheelustee, Florida, Battle of, 47, 64
Hawkins, William Deane, 195–97
Heinl, Robert D., Jr., 64, 167, 246
helicopters: AH-1 Cobra, 277; Apache, 283;
    CH-46, 271; CH-53, 271, 277, 290; HH-53,
    271; RH-53D, 273
Hellzapoppin Ridge, Bougainville, 190
Henderson, Archibald: in *Constitution,* 39;
    early years as commandant, 41–42; in Creek
    and Seminole wars, 45–47; opposes Plug-
    Uglies, 62–63; dies in office, 63–64
Henderson, Lofton R., 178
Henderson, Richard, 71–72, 86
Henderson Field, Guadalcanal, 178, 179, 181
Henley, John D., 29
Herbert, Hilary A., 88, 101
Heywood, Charles (father), 52
Heywood, Charles (son): in Civil War, 81; se-
    lected for commandant, 98; and Marine
    guards in ships, 100–101; during Spanish-
    American War, 105; urges Marine Corps ex-
    pansion, 108; retires, 117
HH-53 helicopter, 271
Hiep Duc, Vietnam, 252
Higgins, Andrew, 170
Higgins, Maggie, 239
High Seas Fleet (German), 145
Hittle, James C., 223
Hodge, John R., 216
Holcomb, Thomas, 170, 180, 199
Holmes, George, 78
Home Squadron, 52–54
Hong Kong, China, 61
Hopkins, Esek, 12, 14–15
Howard, Samuel L., 175
Howe, Tryingham, 15
Honshu, Japan, 221
Hsiku Arsenal, China, 113
Hue, Vietnam, 250, 259–60, 261, 264
Huerta, Victoriano, 124
Hull, Andrew, 61
Hull, Isaac, 27
Hungnam, Korea, 235, 240
Hunt, George P., 207
Hunt, Leroy P., 176
Huntington, Robert W., 105–7
Huntington's Battalion, 105, 108, 111
Hwachon Reservoir, Korea, 242
Hyakutake Haruyoshi, 179, 185, 193

Iams, Ross L., 128
Iceland, 171
Ichiki Kiyonao, 179
Inchon, Korea, 228–30
Indian Removal Act, 45
Infanterie irlandaise, regiment de Welsh-Ser-
    rant, 19
Infantry Tactics (Emory Upton), 94
Ingraham, Charles, 284
Iron Triangle, Korea, 241
Ito Seiichi, 218
Iwo Jima, 208–14; Suribachi, Mount, 210,
    212–13

Jackson, Andrew, 38
Jackson, Thomas J. "Stonewall," 67
Jaluit Atoll, 200
Japanese Zero, 172
Japanese army, armies: 17th Army, 179; 31st
    Army, 203; 32nd Army, 217
Japanese army brigades: 35th Brigade, 179;
    44th Independent Brigade, 217
Japanese army divisions: 2nd (Sendai) Divi-
    sion, 185, 186; 38th (Hiroshima) Division,
    187
Japanese army 2nd Infantry Regiment, 207
Japanese naval ships: *Haruna,* 186; *Hayate,*
    173; *Kisaragi,* 173; *Kongo,* 186; *Nisshin,*
    185; *Nitta Maru,* 174; *Yamato,* 218; *Yubari,*
    173
Japanese naval units: Central Pacific Fleet, 203;
    Sasebo 7th Special Naval Landing Force,
    195; Special Naval Landing Force, 176;
    Yokosuka Special Naval Landing Force, 203
Jefferson, Thomas, 28
Jenny (aircraft), 152
Jesup, Thomas S., 46–47
Jiménez, Juan Isidro, 129
Johnson, Louis A., 224–25
Johnson, Lyndon B.: Dominican Republic in-
    cursion, 247; response to Gulf of Tonkin in-
    cident, Viet Cong terrorism, 248; approves
    Westmoreland's request for more troops in
    Vietnam, 253; frets over security of Khe
    Sanh, 260; replaces McNamara with Clark
    Clifford, 261
Johnson, Opha M., 151
Jones, James L., 290
Jones, Louis R., 201
Jones, Thomas ap Catesby, 48
Joseph, Osiris, 153
Jouett, James E., 97

Kadena, Okinawa, 217
Karamanli, Hamet, 28–30
Karamanli, Yusef, 29–30
Karch, Frederick J., 249–50
Kawaguchi Kiyotake, 179
Kearny, Stephen W., 51

Keishi Ogata, 206
Kelley, Paul X., 268, 275–76, 278
Keys, William, 284–85
Khafji, Battle of, 284
Khe Sanh, Vietnam, 253, 256, 260–61
Kimberly, L. A., 90–92
Kimpo, Korea, 230, 233, 234, 243
King, Ernest J., 175, 193, 194, 202
Knapp, Harry S., 131
Knox, Frank, 183
Kocak, Matej, 141
Korean Expedition (1871), 90–94
Korean War, 235–44; Andong, 241; Chindong-
    ni, 228; Chinhung-ni, 236, 240; Chinju, 228;
    Chorwon, 241; Chosin Reservoir Campaign,
    235–40; Funchilin Pass, 239, 240; Hagaru-ri,
    236, 237, 238; Hamhung, 235; Hungnam,
    235, 240; Hwachon Reservoir, 242; Inchon,
    228–30; Iron Triangle, 241; Kimpo, 230,
    233, 234, 243; Kosong, 228; Koto-ri,
    236–40; Kumhwa, 241; Mupyong-ni, 236;
    Pohang, 241; Punchbowl, 242; Pusan,
    226–28, 230, 234; Pyonggang, 241; Pyong-
    taek, 241; Sachon, 228; Samchuk, 241;
    Seoul, 225, 228, 230–34, 241; Toktong Pass,
    236–37; Uijongbu, 234; Wonsan, 235, 237;
    Yanggu, 242; Yongdok, 241; Yongdungpo,
    233; Yudam-ni, 236
Kosong, Korea, 228
Koto-ri, Korea, 236–40
Krulak, Charles C., 285, 290
Krulak, Victor H.: commands 2nd Parachute
    Battalion at Choiseul, 190; defense unifica-
    tion struggle, 222–23; influences Ulysses S.
    Grant Sharp, 248; views on counterinsur-
    gency in Vietnam, 251; vies to succeed
    Greene as commandant, 258
Kumhwa, Korea, 241
Kuomintang Army, 160
Kuribayashi Tadamichi, 209, 210, 213–14
Kuwait, 280–87; Al Burqan oil field, 285,
    286–87; Al Jaber airfield, 285, 287
Kwajalein Atoll, 200
Kyushu, Japan, 221

LaKaye, Robert, 116
Lake Champlain, Battle of, 36
Lake Erie, Battle of, 36
Lamb, William, 85
La Mesa, California, Battle of, 51
Lam Son 719, 268
Landais, Pierre, 19
landing craft, mechanized (LCM), development
    of, 171
landing craft, vehicle and personnel (LCVP),
    development of, 170
landing vehicle, tracked (LVT), development
    of, 171
Lane, Enoch S., 28

Laos, 247
La Paz, Mexico, 52
Larkin, Thomas O., 49
Las Trencheras, Dominican Republic, action at, 131
Lawrence, James, 34
LCM. *See* landing craft, mechanized, development of
LCVP. *See* landing craft, vehicle and personnel, development of
Lear, Tobias, 31
Lee, Harry, 139
Lee, Robert E., 65, 78, 85, 86
Lejeune, John A.: graduates from the Naval Academy, 95; in Panama, 118; promoted to brigadier general, 132; promoted to major general, given command of 2nd Division, AEF, 142; investigates charges of atrocities in Haiti, 154; appointed commandant, 155; commandancy, 156–57; inspects Marines in Nicaragua, 164; retires, 168
Lejeune's Battalion, 118
León, Nicaragua, 122
Letcher, John, 65
Leyte Gulf, Battle of, 208–9
Liberia, 48, 280
Libya, 278
Lin Pao, 235
Litzenberg, Homer L., 234–36, 239
Liversedge, Harry B., 212
Livingston, James E., 262
Long, John G., 109
Long, Robert L., 275
López de Santa Ana, Antonio, 55
Loreto, Mexico, 52
Los Angeles, California, 50, 51
Louisbourg, Canada, 7, 8
Lovell, Solomon, 21
Low, Frederick F., 90
Lownds, David E., 259, 261
Lucas, Jacklyn H., 214
Lueddeke, Gustav F., 228
LVT. *See* landing vehicle, tracked, development of

MAAG, Vietnam. *See* Military Assistance Advisory Group, Vietnam
Maass, Gustavo, 125
MacArthur, Douglas: plan to absorb the Marine Corps into the Army, 169; departs Philippines, 175; 1st Marine Division comes under, 191; wants to keep Marines in his command, 193; argues to recapture New Guinea and the Philippines, 194; naval forces to support MacArthur's drive, 201–2; argues the moral obligation to liberate the Philippines, 208; Inchon landing, 228–30; calls for North Korean surrender, 234–35; orders advance into North Korea, 236

Macdonald, Wesley, 276
Macdonough, Thomas, 36
MacGruder, William, 62–63
Mackenzie, Alexander S., 89
Mackie, James, 73
Macoris Province, Dominican Republic, 155
MACV. *See* Military Assistance Command, Vietnam
Mahan, Alfred Thayer, 98
Mahomet, Rajah Po, 44
Makin Atoll, 188–89
Maleolap Atoll, 200
Mameluke sword, 94
Managua, Nicaragua, 121, 161, 162
Manila Bay, Battle of, 105, 120
Mangrum, Richard C., 179
Mannix, Daniel Pratt, 98, 100
Manzanillo, Mexico, 52
Marble Mountain, Vietnam, 252
Marguilies, Samuel (Samuel Gross), 128
Mariana Islands: Guam, 206; invasion of, 203–37; Saipan, 202–6; Tinian, 206–7
Marianas Turkey Shoot, 205
Marine Air Groups (MAG). *See* U.S. Marine Aircraft Groups
Marine Air Wings (MAW). *See* U.S. Marine Aircraft Wings
Marine Amphibious Forces (MAF). *See* U.S. Marine Corps amphibious and expeditionary forces
Marine Amphibious Units (MAU). *See* U.S. Marine Corps amphibious and expeditionary units
Marine Corps Association, 120–21
Marine Corps Band, 26, 42, 95–96
Marine Corps Equipment Board, 169
Marine Expeditionary Forces (MEF). *See* U.S. Marine Corps amphibious and expeditionary forces
Marine Expeditionary Units (MEU). *See* U.S. Marine Corps amphibious and expeditionary units
"Marine Hymn," origins of, 96
Maritime Prepositioning Squadrons, 281, 283
Marshall Islands: invasion of, 199–201; Jaluit Atoll, 200; Kwajalein Atoll, 200; Maleolap Atoll, 200; Parry Island, 201; Roi and Namur Islands, 201; Wotje Atoll, 200
Marston, Ward, 51
Martin, John "Keto," 16
Maruyama Masao, 185
Massachusetts State Prison Revolt, 43
Massaya, Nicaragua, 122
Mayaguez (merchant ship), 271–72
Mazatlán, Mexico, 52
McCain, Henry P., 134, 142
McCalla, Bowman H. "Billy Hell," 97, 105
McCawley, Charles G.: at Fort Sumter, 76–77; reforms, 95; as commandant, 97–98; School

of Application, 98; calls for assignment of Marines to secondary batteries in ships, 100
McClure, Lynn E., 272
McCutcheon, Keith B., 268
McDonough, Gordon L., 228
McDougal, William, 62
McGuffey, William Holmes, 43
McIlvain, William M., 123
McKee, Hugh W., 92
McKenzie, Allen, 25
McKeon, Matthew C., 245
McKnight, James, 26
McLaughlin, John T., 47–48
McLean, Francis, 20
McMullen, Robert A., 234
McNamara, Michael, 93
McNamara, Robert S., 253, 255, 258, 261
Meade, Robert L., 114
Medals of Honor: Boxer Rebellion, 114; Blanc Mont, 144; Guadalcanal, 188; Haiti, 128, 153; Korea (1871), 94; Korean War, 244; Philippine Insurrection, 116; Santo Domingo, 131; Spanish-American War, 107–8; Veracruz, 126–27; Vietnam, 269; World War I, 150; World War II, 207, 208, 214
Meiere, Julius E., 73, 75, 80–81
Mcna, Luis, 121
Meredith, Jonathan, 29
Merkel, Charles F., 155
Mervine, William, 50
Mess Night, origins of, 160–61
Metcalf, Joseph, III, 276–77
Metcalf, Victor H., 119
Meuse-Argonne Offensive, 145–46
Mexican War, 49–58
Mexico: Alvarado, 53, 54; Carmen, 54; Chapultepec, 55–57; Coatzacoalcos, 54; Frontera, 53; Guaymas, 52; La Paz, 52; Loreto, 52; Manzanillo, 52; Mazatlán, 52; Mexican War, 49–58; San Blas, 52; San José del Cabo, 52; San Lucas, 52; Seven Palms, 54; Tabasco, 53, 54; Tuxpan, 54; Veracruz, 53–54, 124–27
Mexico City, Mexico, 53, 55, 57–58; Belén Gate, 57–58; San Cosmé Gate, 57–58
Meyer, George von L., 120, 123
Midway, Battle of, 175
MiG-15, 243
Military Assistance Advisory Group (MAAG), Vietnam, 247
Military Assistance Command, Vietnam (MACV), 247
Miller, Samuel, 37–39, 41, 45–47, 48
Mirebalais, Haiti, 152
Mitscher, Marc A., 218
Mitsubishi Zero, 172
Mobile, Alabama, 72, 75, 80, 86
Mobile Bay, Battle of, 80–81
Molton, Michael, 18

Moncado, Juan M., 167
Monte Cristi, Dominican Republic, 129
Monterey, California, 48, 50
Moore, William B., 139
Morris Island, South Carolina, 76
Mortefontaine, Convention of, 28
Moses, Vivian M., 228
Mosquito Fleet, 47–48
Motobu Peninsula, Okinawa, 217, 218
Motoyama Plateau, Iwo Jima, 210, 214
M16 rifle, introduction of, 258
Mulcahy, Francis P., 216
Mullan, Robert, 12
Mundy, Carl, 289
Mupyong-ni, Korea, 236
Murray, Raymond L., 226, 229–30, 235–37
Muth, Lawrence, 153
Myatt, James M., 284
Myers, John T., 112

Nagumo Chuichi, 203
Naha, Okinawa, 218, 219
Nakagawa Kunio, 207
Namur Island. *See* Roi and Namur Islands
Nashton, Jeffrey L., 275
Nassau, Bahamas, 14–15, 18, 19
Naval Acts: 27 March 1794, 24; 27 March
     1798, 24; 2 March 1799, 25; 5 August 1882,
     95; 1910, Butler rider to, 120
Navarette, Dominican Republic, 129, 130
Navy Board of Organization, Tactics, and Drill
     (Greer Board), 100
Negro Rebellion, 132
Neville, Wendell C., 95, 141, 142, 168
New Bern, North Carolina, 77
New Britain Island: Aogiri Ridge, 192–93;
     Cape Gloucester, 191–93; Suicide Creek,
     192; Walt's Ridge, 192
New Georgia Island, 190
New Orleans, Louisiana, 32, 75
New Providence expedition, Bahamas, 14–16
New Zealand forces, 8th Brigade Group, 190
Nicaragua: Coco River patrols, 167; Corinto,
     121; Coyotepe, 121; El Chipote, 163; Grey-
     town, 59; León, 122; Managua, 121, 161,
     162; Marines in, 119, 121–22, 161–67; Mas-
     saya, 122; Nueva Segovia Province, 162–63,
     167; Ocotal, 162; Poteca, 167; Quilali, 164;
     Sandino, Augusto C., 162–64, 167; San Juan
     del Sur, 129, 247; Telepaneca, 162
Nicholas, Samuel, 12, 14–16, 17
Nicholson, A. S., 58
Nickerson, Herman R., Jr., 242, 267
Nimitz, Chester R.: proposes sending 1st
     Raiders to Tulagi, 175; argues for Central Pa-
     cific drive, 194; selects Holland M. Smith to
     command Marines in Central Pacific Drive,
     195; settles dispute between Smith and
     Turner, 200; convinced that Fifth Fleet
     should continue amphibious advance, 201;

directed to bypass Truk and the Carolines,
     202; ordered to assault Iwo Jima and Oki-
     nawa, 208; in awe of seizure of Iwo Jima,
     214; snubs Holland M. Smith, 221
Norfolk, Virginia, 72, 73
Noriega, Manuel Antonio, 279
North Atlantic Squadron, 105
Northern Bombing Group, 1st Aviation Com-
     pany, Squadron 9, 148
North Korean divisions: 6th Division, 228; 18th
     Division, 233
North Korean 83rd Motorized Rifle Regiment,
     228
North Korean 25th Brigade, 234
North Korean Yak (aircraft), 243
North Vietnamese divisions: 308th Division,
     259; 324B Division, 254, 255; 341st Divi-
     sion, 255, 259. *See also* Viet Cong
North Vietnamese Group 44, 265
North Vietnamese regiments: 21st Regiment,
     266; 36th Regiment, 266; 141st Regiment,
     267. *See also* Viet Cong
Novaleta, Philippines, Battle of, 110–11
Nueva Segovia Province, Nicaragua, 162–63,
     167

O'Bannon, Presley, 30–31
Obregon, Eugene A., 234
Ocotal, Nicaragua, 162
officer selection boards, 156, 170
Oglethorpe, James, 5
O'Grady, Scott, 290
Okinawa, invasion of, 214–21; Hagushi, 217;
     Kadena, 217; Motobu Peninsula, 217, 218;
     Naha, 218, 219; Oroku Peninsula, 219, 220;
     Shuri Castle, 219; Shuri Ridge, 219; Sugar
     Loaf, 219; Yontan, 217
Operations involving U.S. Marines: Blue
     Light, 273; Chromite, 228–29; Coronet, 221;
     Desert Shield, 280–83; Desert Storm,
     283–89; Detachment, 208–14; Dewey
     Canyon, 264; Eagle Pull, 269; Flintlock,
     200; Forager, 202; Frequent Wind, 269; Har-
     vest Moon, 252; Hastings III, 254; Iceberg,
     214; Lam Son 719, 268; Olympic, 221;
     Prairie, 255; Praying Mantis, 279; Rolling
     Thunder, 248; Starlite, 251; Watchtower,
     175–88
Orange Plans, 194
Oroku Peninsula, Okinawa, 219, 220
Osborne, William S., 29
Ota Minoru, 217
outposts, U.S. Marine, in Korea, 243

Pacific Fleet (World War II), 194
Paige, Mitchell, 187
Palestine Liberation Organization, 273
Panama, 97–98, 118, 279–80
Panama City, Panama, 59, 97, 280
Parris Island, establishment of, 134

Parry, Francis F. "Fox," 238
Parry Island, 201
Patch, Alexander M., 188
Patriot's War, 32
PBY Catalina, 178
Pearl Harbor, Hawaii, 172–73
Peatross, Oscar F., 251
Peking, China, 112–13, 114, 172
Peleliu Island, 207–8
Pendleton, Joseph H., 121–22, 129–31, 132
Penobscot Expedition, 20–21
Penrose, Boise, 120
Pensacola, Florida, 71
Péralte, Charlemagne Masséna, 152–53
Perdicaris, Ion, 119
Perkins, Constantine M., 110
Perkins, J. L. "Si," 154
Perry, Matthew C., 53–55, 59
Perry, Oliver Hazard, 36
Pershing, John J., 134, 142, 145, 146
Philippine Insurrection, 110, 114–17
Philippines: Novaleta, Battle of, 110–11;
     Manila Bay, Battle of, 105, 120; Philippine
     Insurrection, 110, 114–17; Philippine Sea,
     Battle of the, 205; Sohoton Cliffs, 115–6
Philippine Sea, Battle of the, 205
Phnom Penh, Cambodia, 269
Phu Bai, Vietnam, 251, 259
Pillow, Gideon J., 55–56
Pillsbury, John E., 119
piracy, suppression of, 42–43
Plan 34A, 248
Platt, Jonas M., 252
Pleiku, Vietnam, 248
Plug Uglies, 62–63
Pohang, Korea, 241
Policia Nacional (Dominican Republic), 155
Pollock, Lenard A., 180
Pollock, Oliver, 18
Port-au-Prince, Haiti, 127, 152, 153
Porter, David, 35–36
Porter, David Dixon, 83, 87
Port Royal Expedition, 67
Post–Tet Offensive, Vietnam (1969), 265–67
Poteca, Nicaragua, 167
Potsdam Declaration, 221
Powell, Colin L., 280
Pratt, William Veazie, 169
Preble, Edward, 28
Princeton, Battle of, 17
Pritchard, Samuel, 22
Proceedings, U.S. Naval Institute, 100–101
provinces, Vietnam: Quang Nam, 256, 259,
     265, 268; Quang Ngai, 256; Quang Tin, 252,
     256; Quang Tri, 253, 256, 258, 264, 268;
     Thua Thien, 253, 256, 264
Pucciarelli, George W., 276
Puerto Plata, Santo Domingo, 26, 129
Puller, Lewis B. "Chesty": in Haiti and
     Nicaragua, 167–68; in China, 171; com-

mands 1/7 at Guadalcanal, 184, 187; at Peleliu, 207; at Inchon, 230; at Seoul, 233; in North Korea, 235; at Koto-ri, 238; and Maggie Higgins, 239; bravado during the breakout from North Korea, 239–40; rotates home from Korea, promoted to lieutenant general, 242; quoted, 290

Punchbowl (Korea), 242

Purvis, Hugh, 93

Pusan Perimeter, 226–28, 230, 234

Putnam, Paul A., 173

Pyonggang, Korea, 241

Pyongtaek, Korea, 241

Quallah Battoo, Sumatra, 44

Quasi-War with France, 24–25

Que Son, Vietnam, 252

Quick, John H., 106–7, 116, 139

Quilali, Nicaragua, 164

Quinn, Francis X., 266

Quinn, Luke, 65

Quitman, John A., 55–56

Raisouli, 119

Ra's al Khafji, Saudi Arabia, 284

Rathbun, John Peck, 18–19

Reagan, Ronald, 273, 276, 278

regiment la Marine, 3

Republic of Korea (ROK) 1st Marine Regiment, 242

Republic of Korea forces. See South Korean corps; South Korean divisions

Reynolds, John G., 55, 66–67, 76, 79

RH-53D helicopter, 273

Richmond, Virginia, 69, 73, 74, 78–79, 85

Ridgeway, Matthew B., 241

Ripley, John W., 268

Ripley, Roswell S., 58

Robertson, Donn, 268

Robinson, Robert G., 149–50

Rochambeau, Jean Baptiste, 23

Rockey, Keller E., 209, 216

Rodgers, John, 90, 94

Roi and Namur Islands, 201

Roise, Harold S., 237

Roosevelt, Franklin D., 143, 183

Roosevelt, James, 189

Roosevelt, Theodore, 114, 118, 119–20

Rosecrans, Harold E., 176

Rosenthal, Joe, 212–13

Ross, Robert, 36, 38

Rowell, Ross E., 161–62

Royal Air Force, 149

Royal Marines, 9, 114, 238; 41st Independent Commando, 238

Royal Welch Fusiliers, 114

Rupertus, William H., 176, 181, 191, 207

Ruppert, Matthew, 65

Russell, John H.: graduates from the Naval Academy, 95; commands 1st Brigade in Haiti, 152; orders courts-martial for atrocities in Haiti, 154; appointed high commissioner in Haiti, 161; commandant, 169–70

Russell, William W., 65, 79

Russell Islands, 190

Sacasa, Juan B., 167

Sachon, Korea, 228

Safer, Morley, 251

Saigon, Vietnam, 250–51, 261, 268–69

Saint-Mihiel salient, 143–44

Saipan Island, 202–6

Saito Yoshitsugu, 203

Saltonstall, Dudley, 21

Saltonstall, Gilbert, 10–11

Samar Island, 114–17

Samchuk, Korea, 241

Samoan Uprising, 110

Sampson, William T., 105, 107, 109

San Blas, Mexico, 52

San Cosmé Gate, Mexico City, 57–58

San Diego, California, 50, 51

San Francisco, California, 50, 51

San Francisco de Macoris, Dominican Republic, 131

San Gabriel, California, Battle of, 51

San Juan del Sur, Nicaragua, 129, 247

San José del Cabo, Mexico, 52

San Lucas, Mexico, 52

San Pedro, California, 50

Santa Ana, Antonio López de, 55

Santa Barbara, California, 50, 51

Sandino, Augusto C., 162–64, 167

Sandwich (French privateer), 26

Santiago, Cuba, Battle of, 107, 111

Santiago de los Caballeros, Dominican Republic, 129, 130

Santo Domingo, Dominican Republic, 129, 247

Sasebo 7th Special Naval Landing Force, 195

Saudi Arabia: Al Khanjar, 285, 286; Al Mish'ab, 284; Ra's al Khafji, 284

Savannah, Georgia, 71, 75, 80, 81–82

Saylor's Creek, Virginia, Battle of, 86

SBD 3 Dauntless, 179

Scala, Francis Marie, 42, 95

Schilt, Christian F., 163–64

Schley, Winfield Scott, 92–93

Schmidt, Harry, 201, 209

Schmuck, Donald M., 240

Schwarzkopf, H. Norman, 280, 284, 286

Scoon, Sir Paul, 277

Scots Guards, 2nd Battalion, 161

Scott, Winfield, 53, 55, 57

Scout-Sniper Platoon, 2nd Marines, 195–96

Seattle, Washington, 59

2nd Force Service Support Group, 281, 286

Seibo Province, Dominican Republic, 155

Selden, John T., 243

Selkirk, Earl of, 19

Seminole War, 45–48

Semmes, Raphael, 68, 85

"Semper Fidelis," 96–97

Senate Bill 2044, 222–23

Seoul, Korea, 225, 228, 230–34, 241

Seven Palms, Mexico, 54

Seventh Air Force (U.S. Air Force), 251, 271–72

Sevier, Alexander, 33

Seymour, Sir Edward, 112–13

Shafter, William R., 107, 109

Shanghai, China, 61, 160–61, 171

Shapley, Allan, 172

Sharp, Ulysses S. Grant, 248

Shaw, Samuel, 17, 18

Shearer, Maurice, 139

Shepherd, Lemuel C., Jr.: mess night in China, 160–61; Marianas, 203; Okinawa, 218; and atomic bomb, 223; candidate for commandancy, 224; Inchon, 229; in North Korea, 239; retires, 245

Sheredine, Nathan, 26

Sherman, Forrest P., 225

Sherman, Willam T., 81–82

Sherrod, Robert, 197, 210, 211

Shibasaki Keijo, 195–98

Shirley, William, 7

Shoup, David M., 196–97, 246–47

Shubrick, Irvine, 44

Shuri Castle, Okinawa, 219

Shuri Ridge, Okinawa, 219

Sigsbee, Charles B., 104

Simms, John D., 61, 70, 73, 86

6th Machine Gun Battalion, 136

6th Seabee Battalion, 184

Sloan, Thomas T., 47

Sloat, John D., 50

Smith, Agrippa W., 261

Smith, Alvin E., 229

Smith, Bernard L., 123

Smith, H. J. "Hog Jaw," 230

Smith, Holland M. "Howlin' Mad": background, 194–95; at Tarawa, 197; condemns the invasion of Tarawa, 198; invasion of the Marianas, 203–36; invasion of Iwo Jima, 210; comments on casualties at Iwo Jima, 214

Smith, Jabez, Jr., 10

Smith, Jacob H. "Hell-Roaring Jake," 115, 117

Smith, John L., 179

Smith, Julian, 195, 197, 198

Smith, Oliver P., 229–30, 235, 237–40

Smith, Ralph C., 195, 205–6

Smith, Ray L., 277

Smith, Robert, 26

Sohoton Cliffs, Philippines, 115–6

Soissons, France, 140–41

Solomon Islands: Choiseul, 190; New Georgia, 190; Tulagi, 176–77. *See also* Guadalcanal Island

Somoza, Anastasio, 167
Sousa, John Philip, 95–96
South Atlantic Blockading Squadron, 76, 81
South Korean corps: ROK I Corps, 235; ROK II Corps, 235. *See also* Republic of Korea 1st Marine Regiment
South Korean divisions: ROK Capital Division, 235; ROK 3rd Division, 235. *See also* Republic of Korea 1st Marine Regiment
South Vietnamese air force, 248
South Vietnamese army. *See* Army of the Republic of Vietnam
Spanish-American War, 105–8
Special Landing Forces (Vietnam), 257–58
Special Naval Landing Force (Japanese), 176
Spicer, W. F., 106
Spruance, Raymond: commands Fifth Fleet, 194; invasion of the Marshalls, 200; invasion of the Marianas, 203, 205–56; invasion of Okinawa, 214
Stallings, Lawrence, 151
Starr, David, 10
St. Augustine, Florida, 32, 33, 67
Stevens, Thomas H., 76
Stilwell, Joseph H. "Vinegar Joe," 220
Stimson, Henry L., 161, 167
Stockton, Robert F., 50
Stoddard, George C., 81–82
Stuart, J. E. B., 65
Sugar Intervention, Cuba, 132
Sugar Loaf, Okinawa, 219
Suicide Creek, Cape Gloucester, 192
Suribachi, Mount, Iwo Jima, 210, 212–13

Tabasco, Mexico, 53, 54
Talbot, Ralph, 149–50
Talbot, Silas, 26
Tansill, Robert, 70
Taplett, Robert D., 229
Tarawa Atoll, 195–98
Task Force 54 (Okinawa), 216, 218
Task Force 58 (Iwo Jima), 210
Task Force 76 (Vietnam), 249
Task Force 124 (Grenada), 276
Task Force Kean, 228
Task Force X-Ray, 259
Tatnall, John R. F., 70, 75, 82, 85
Taylor, Algernon A., 70
Taylor, Maxwell D., 248
Taylor, Zachary, 52
Telepaneca, Nicaragua, 162
Tentative Landing Operations Manual, 169
Terrett, George: at Quallah Battoo, 44; in Seminole War, 47; in Mexican War, 56–57; joins Confederate Marine Corps, 70; forms a three-company battalion, 74; at Drewry's Bluff, 79; captured at Amelia Court House, 86
Terry, Alfred H., 83
Tet Offensive, Vietnam (1968), 259–61

"Teufelhunden," 139
Thom, Reuben T., 71–77
Thomas, Gerald C., 183, 222, 242
Thomason, John W., Jr.: description of new Marines in World War I, 133–34; describes Forêt de Retz, 141; recalls bombardment at Blanc Mont, 144; *Fix Bayonets!,* 151; description of Herman H. Hanneken, 153
Thompson, Smith, 40
Thomson, Ruffin, 74
Thorpe, George C., 118
Thua Thien Province, Vietnam, 253, 257, 264
Tientsin, China, 112–14, 160, 172
Tiger Brigade, 2nd Armored Division, 284
"Tiger of Seibo" (Charles F. Merkel), 155
Tilton, McLane, 90–93
Tinian Island, 206–7
Tingey, Thomas, 38
Tipitapa, Peace of, 161
Tojo Hideki, 206
Toktong Pass, Korea, 236–37
Tokyo Rose, 204
Tracy, Benjamin F., 98, 100
Trenton, New Jersey, Battle of, 17
Trevett, John, 10, 18–19
Tripoli (Barbary ship), 28
Trippe, John, 29
Truxtun, Thomas, 26
Tucker, John R., 85
Tulagi Island, 176–77
Tun Tavern, 12
Turnage, Allen H., 203
Turner, Richmond Kelly: commands amphibious force at Guadalcanal, 176–77, 184; commands amphibious forces, Fifth Fleet, 194; relationship with Holland M. Smith, 195; at Tarawa, 198; assault on the Marshalls, 200–201; assault on the Marianas, 203; relief of Ralph Smith, 205–6; declares Saipan secure, 206; assault on Okinawa, 214–16
Tuxpan, Mexico, 54
25th Brigade (North Korean), 234
Twiggs, David E., 55, 56
Twiggs, Levi, 55
Twining, Merrill B., 222, 223, 246
Ty-Ho Bay, China, 61
Tyler, Henry B., 62, 70

Uijongbu, Korea, 234
Upton, Emory, and *Infantry Tactics,* 94
U.S. Air Force. *See* Seventh Air Force
U.S. Army armies: First Army, AEF, 143, 145; Sixth Army, 191; Eighth Army, 226, 235, 241, 242, 244; Tenth Army, 216; Army of Cuban Pacification, 118; Army of the South, 46–47; Army of the West, 51
U.S. Army corps: V Corps, 107, 145; VII Corps, 284, 285, 286; IX Corps, 241; XVIII Airborne Corps, 284, 285; XXIV Corps, 216, 217, 218, 284, 285

U.S. Army battalions: 3rd Battalion, 164th Infantry, 187; California Battalion, 50, 51
U.S. Army brigades: 3rd Brigade, 144, 145; Tiger Brigade, 2nd Armored Division, 284
U.S. Army divisions: 24th Airborne, 246; 82nd Airborne, 276; 101st Airborne, 259; 1st Air Cavalry, 259, 261; 3rd Armored, 284; 1st Cavalry, 234, 235; 1st Infantry, 55, 134, 140; 2nd Infantry, 55, 134, 140, 141, 142, 143, 144, 145; 3rd Infantry, 55, 140; 4th Infantry, 55; 7th Infantry, 201, 216, 220, 229, 230, 237; 24th Infantry, 228, 242; 25th Infantry, 188, 228; 27th Infantry, 195, 203, 216; 36th Infantry, 144; 37th Infantry, 190; 40th Infantry, 193; 77th Infantry, 203, 216; 96th Infantry, 216; 1st Mechanized, 284; 5th Mechanized, 284
U.S. Army regiments: 6th Infantry, 58; 9th Infantry, 113, 114, 145; 23rd Infantry, 145; 81st Infantry, 207; 105th Infantry, 206; 164th Infantry, 185; 165th Infantry, 206; Pennsylvania Volunteers, 55, 56
U.S. Army task forces: Task Force Kean, 228; Task Force X-Ray, 259
Ushijima Mitsuru, 217, 221
U.S. Marine Corps Aircraft Groups (MAG): MAG-11, 172, 280; MAG-12, 235, 251, 252; MAG-13, 201; MAG-14, 219, 221; MAG-16, 251; MAG-21, 172; MAG-22, 201, 221; MAG-23, 191; MAG-30, 265; MAG-31, 201, 221; MAG-36, 251, 265
U.S. Marine Corps Aircraft Wings (MAW): 1st MAW, 229, 262, 266, 267, 268; 2nd MAW, 246, 283; 3rd MAW, 281, 286; 4th MAW, 219–20; 4th Marine Base Defense Wing, 201
U.S. Marine Corps amphibious and expeditionary forces: III Marine Amphibious Force (MAF), 250, 256, 261, 262, 265, 267, 276; I Marine Expeditionary Force (MEF), 281, 283, 284, 285, 287; II MEF, 281, 283; Northern Troops and Landing Force, 203; Southern Troops and Landing Force, 203
U.S. Marine Corps amphibious and expeditionary units: 22nd Marine Amphibious Unit (MAU), 273–74, 274–75; 32nd MAU, 273; 6th Marine Expeditionary Unit (MEU), 247; 11th MEU, 280; 22nd MEU, 276–77; 24th MEU, 280; 26th MEU, 280; 13th MEU (Special Operations Capable [SOC]), 280, 281, 283, 284
U.S. Marine Corps Amphibious Corps: I Marine Amphibious Corps, 189; III Marine Amphibious Corps, 216, 217; V Marine Amphibious Corps, 194, 201, 209, 210
U.S. Marine Corps aviation companies. *See* U.S. Marine Corps aviation units, companies, and detachments
U.S. Marine Corps aviation detachments. *See* U.S. Marine Corps aviation units, companies, and detachments

U.S. Marine Corps aviation squadrons. *See* U.S. Marine Corps squadrons, fighter; U.S. Marine Corps squadrons, helicopter; U.S. Marine Corps squadrons, observation; U.S. Marine Corps squadrons, scout-bombing

U.S. Marine Corps aviation units, companies, and detachments: 1st Aeronautical Company, Squadron 9, Northern Bombing Group, 148; 1st Aviation Company, Advanced Base Force, 148; Aviation Detachment, Advanced Base Force, 123. *See also* U.S. Marine Corps squadrons, fighter; U.S. Marine Corps squadrons, helicopter; U.S. Marine Corps squadrons, observation; U.S. Marine Corps squadrons, scout-bombing

U.S. Marine Corps battalions: 1/1, 180, 192, 208, 239, 253, 259; 2/1, 180, 252; 3/1, 192, 238; 2/2, 196, 198; 3/2, 198, 198; 1/3, 250; 2/3, 246, 248, 250; 3/4, 250, 252; 1/5, 260, 267; 2/5, 175, 181, 183, 237, 259; 3/5, 139, 192; 1/6, 198, 247; 3/6, 198, 246, 247; 1/7, 184, 187, 236–37, 267; 2/7, 189, 192; 3/7, 192, 266, 267; 1/8, 246, 247; 2/8, 196; ; 3/8, 196, 197, 198; 1/9, 259, 264; 2/9, 264; 3/9, 249, 264; 1/10, 160, 228–29, 236; 1/11, 228; 1/26, 214; 3/26, 256; 6th Machine Gun Battalion, 136; Butler's Battalion, 119, 121; Huntington's Battalion, 105, 108, 111; Lejeune's Battalion, 118; Waller's Battalion, 113, 115. *See also* U.S. Marine Corps battalions, defense; U.S. Marine Corps battalions, parachute; U.S. Marine Corps battalions, raider

U.S. Marine Corps battalions, defense: 1st Defense Battalion, 172, 173, 201; 3rd Defense Battalion, 191; 9th Defense Battalion, 203; 14th Defense Battalion, 203; 15th Defense Battalion, 201. *See also* U.S. Marine Corps battalions; U.S. Marine Corps battalions, parachute; U.S. Marine Corps battalions, raider

U.S. Marine Corps battalions, parachute: 1st Parachute Battalion, 176, 181, 183; 2nd Parachute Battalion, 190. *See also* U.S. Marine Corp battalions; U.S. Marine Corps battalions, defense; U.S. Marine Corps battalions, raider

U.S. Marine Corps battalions, raider: 1st Raider Battalion, 175, 176, 183; 2nd Raider Battalion, 188–89. *See also* U.S. Marine Corps battalions; U.S. Marine Corps battalions, defense; U.S. Marine Corps battalions, parachute

U.S. Marine Corps combat service support units: 1st Force Service Support Group, 281, 286; 2nd Force Service Support Group, 281, 286

U.S. Marine Corps companies: A/1/1, 233; A/1/9, 264; Company A, 3rd Reconnaissance Battalion, 250; D/1/4, 271; E/2/4, 262; F/2/4, 262; F/2/7, 236–37; F/2/9, 206; G/3/5, 229; I/3/5 234; K/3/1, 207; L/3/7, 267; M/3/7, 266; Scout-Sniper Platoon, 2nd Marines, 195–96

U.S. Marine Corps divisions, 1st: 1942–1943, 175, 178, 188, 191, 193; 1943–1945, 194, 199, 207–8; 1945–1953, 229, 235, 239, 240; 1954–1975, 256, 262, 265, 267, 268; 1976–2000, 284, 285, 286–87

U.S. Marine Corps divisions, 2nd: 1943–1945, 194, 195, 199, 203, 204, 206, 216, 217, 218, 220; 1954–1975, 246; 1976–2000, 284, 286, 287

U.S. Marine Corps divisions, 3rd: 1942–1943, 190; 1943–45, 194, 199, 203, 209, 210, 211, 219; 1954–1975, 256–57, 258, 259

U.S. Marine Corps divisions, 4th, 1943–1945: 194, 199, 201, 203, 204, 206, 207, 210, 219

U.S. Marine Corps divisions, 5th: 1943–1945, 199, 209, 210; 1954–1975, 253

U.S. Marine Corps divisions, 6th, 1943–1945: 216, 218, 219, 220

U.S. Marine Corps regiments, 1st: 1942–1943, 176; 1943–1945, 207, 229; 1954–1975, 230, 235

U.S. Marine Corps regiments, 2nd, 196, 197, 204

U.S. Marine Corps regiments, 3rd: 1942–1943, 190, 211; 1954–1975, 259

U.S. Marine Corps regiments, 4th: 1898–1917, 129; 1919 1941, 160, 171; 1954–1975, 251, 253

U.S. Marine Corps regiments, 5th: 1917–1918, 133, 134, 136, 141, 145, 148; 1942–1943, 176, 181, 184, 193; 1943–1945, 207; 1945–1953, 226, 229, 230, 235–36, 237, 238, 242, 243; 1954–1975, 259, 266

U.S. Marine Corps regiments, 6th: 1917–1918, 133, 134, 136, 137, 144, 148; 1919–1941, 160, 170–71

U.S. Marine Corps regiments, 7th: 1942–1943, 176, 181, 183, 192, 193; 1943–1945, 207; 1945–1953, 229, 235–36, 237, 238, 242; 1954–1975, 251, 252

U.S. Marine Corps regiments, 8th, 1943–1945, 204, 220

U.S. Marine Corps regiments, 9th: 1942–1943, 190; 1954–1975, 251, 261, 264

U.S. Marine Corps regiments, 11th: 1917–1918, 148; 1954–1975, 267

U.S. Marine Corps regiments, 13th, 1917–1918, 148

U.S. Marine Corps regiments, 15th, 1919–1941, 155

U.S. Marine Corps regiments, 21st, 1942–1943, 190

U.S. Marine Corps regiments, 22nd, 1943–1945, 201, 210

U.S. Marine Corps regiments, 23rd, 1943–1945, 201, 204, 210, 213

U.S. Marine Corps regiments, 24th, 1943–1945, 202, 204

U.S. Marine Corps regiments, 25th, 1943–1945, 210, 213

U.S. Marine Corps regiments, 26th, 1954–1975, 252, 259, 261

U.S. Marine Corps regiments, 27th: 1943–1945, 210; 1954–1975, 259

U.S. Marine Corps regiments, 28th, 1943–1945, 210, 212, 213

U.S. Marine Corps squadrons, fighter: VMF-211, 191; VMF-214, 214, 228, 237, 238; VMF-215, 191; VMF-312, 235, 243; VMF-323, 228, 237; VMF-452, 214, VMFA-314, 259; VMFA-323, 278; VMF-513, 235; VMFA-531, 250. *See also* U.S. Marine Corps squadrons, helicopter; U.S. Marine Corps squadrons, observation; U.S. Marine Corps squadrons, scout-bombing

U.S. Marine Corps squadrons, helicopter: HMX-1, 223; HMH-261, 269; HMH-463, 269; HMM-261, 276; HMR-161, 242. *See also* U.S. Marine Corps squadrons, fighter; U.S. Marine Corps squadrons, observation; U.S. Marine Corps squadrons, scout-bombing

U.S. Marine Corps squadrons, observation: VMO-4, 210; VMO-5, 210; VMO-6, 237. *See also* U.S. Marine Corps squadrons, fighter; U.S. Marine Corps squadrons, helicopter; U.S. Marine Corps squadrons, scout-bombing

U.S. Marine Corps squadrons, scout-bombing: VMSB-144, 191; VMSB-234, 191. *See also* U.S. Marine Corps squadrons, fighter; U.S. Marine Corps squadrons, helicopter; U.S. Marine Corps squadrons, observation

U.S. Navy fleet exercises: 1922, 158; 1923–24, 158–59; 1925, 159; 1935, 170

U.S. Navy flects: Fifth Fleet (World War II), 194, 201, 203, 209, 217; Pacific Fleet (World War II), 194

U.S. Navy forces. *See* Florida Expedition for the Suppression of Indian Hostilities; 6th Seabee Battalion; U.S. Navy fleets; U.S. Navy ships; U.S. Navy squadrons; U.S. Navy task forces

U.S. Navy ships: *Alaska,* 90; *Alfred,* 12, 16, 18; *Alliance,* 18, 20, 22; *Andrew Doria,* 12, 17; *Annapolis,* 121; *Argonaut,* 189; *Badoeng Strait,* 226; *Bataan,* 243; *Benicia,* 90; *Bennington,* 214, 216; *Bonhomme Richard,* 19–20; *Boston,* 17, 18, 21; *Boxer,* 246; *Bunker Hill,* 214, 216; *Cabot,* 12, 16, 17; *Cleveland,* 161; *Colorado,* 90; *Columbus,* 16, 18; *Confederacy,* 18, 22; *Congress,* 72; *Constellation,* 26, 28, 31, 248; *Constitution,* 26, 29, 34–35; *Coral Sea,* 278; *Cumberland,* 72, 81; *Deane (Hague),* 18, 22, 23; *Diligent,* 20; *Dixie,* 118; *Dolphin,* 106–7; *Enterprise,* 28, 172, 173; *Experiment,* 26, 28; *Florida,* 125; *Fly,* 12; *Franklin,* 214; *Galena,* 73–74; *General Gates,* 18; *Guam,* 277; *Hancock,* 17; *Harold E. Holt,* 271; *Hartford,* 89; *Hornet* (sloop), 12; *Hornet* (later sloop), 35; *Hunter Liggett,* 188; *Insurgent,* 26, 28; *Iwo Jima,*

U.S. Navy ships: *(continued)*
246; *John Adams,* 59; *Kearsarge,* 68; *Levant,* 61; *Lexington* (aircraft carrier), 172–73; *Lexington* (frigate), 16–17; *Long Island,* 179; *Maddox,* 248; *Maine,* 104; *Merrimack,* 72; *Minnesota,* 72; *Mohican,* 90; *Monitor,* 72–73; *Monocacy,* 90–92; *Morgan,* 79–80, 85; *Mount McKinley,* 229; *Nashville,* 85; *Nautilus,* 189; *Nimitz,* 273; *Palos,* 90; *Patapsco,* 27; *Philadelphia,* 28–29; *Plymouth,* 61, 89; *Potomac,* 44; *Powhatan,* 61; *Princeton,* 246; *Providence,* 12, 18–21; *Queen of France,* 18, 21–22; *Raleigh* (frigate), 17–18; *Ranger,* 18–19, 21; *Reprisal,* 16–17, 19; *Retaliation,* 28; *Richard,* 20; *Rover,* 89; *Saipan,* 271; *Sally,* 26; *Samuel B. Roberts,* 279; *San Jacinto,* 61 *Saratoga* (carrier), 172, 173; *Saratoga* (frigate), 22; *Tarawa,* 271; *Tecumseh,* 80–81; *Ticonderoga,* 248; *Trumbull,* 10–11, 18, 22; *Turner Joy,* 248; *United States,* 4; *Utah,* 125; *Vengeance,* 26, 28; *Virginia* (frigate), 18; *Warren,* 18, 20; *Wasp* (aircraft carrier), 214, 216; *Wasp* (schooner), 11; *Wasp* (sloop), 35; *Watt,* 10, 11; *Wyoming,* 89
U.S. Navy squadrons: Asiatic Squadron, 105; Home Squadron, 52, 54; Maritime Prepositioning Squadron 1, 283; Maritime Prepositioning Squadron 2, 281; Maritime Prepositioning Squadron 3, 281; North Atlantic Squadron, 105; South Atlantic Blockading Squadron, 76, 81
U.S. Navy task forces: Special Landing Force, Seventh Fleet (Vietnam), 257–58; Task Force 54 (Okinawa), 216, 218; Task Force 58 (Iwo Jima), 210; Task Force 76 (Vietnam), 249; Task Force 124 (Grenada), 276

Valcour Island, Battle of, 17
Van Benthuysen, Alfred C., 71, 73, 83, 85
Vandegrift, Alexander A.: preparations for landing in the Solomons, 175–76; on Guadalcanal, 176–88; commands I Marine Amphibious Corps, 190; MacArthur argues to keep Vandegrift's Marines, 193; becomes commandant, 199; receives letter from Holland M. Smith reflecting uneasiness over assault of Iwo Jima, 210; defense unification struggle, 222–23
Van Fleet, James A., 242
Van Riper, Paul K., 266
Van Tuong Peninsula, Vietnam, 251
Vargas, M. Sando, Jr., 262
Veracruz, Mexico, 53–54, 124–27
Vernon, Edward, 6
Vessey, John, 276
Viet An, Vietnam, 252
Viet Cong (Vietnamese communist), 248, 264;

1st Viet Cong Regiment, 251. *See also* North Vietnamese Group 44; North Vietnamese divisions; North Vietnamese regiments
Vietnam War: A Shau Valley, 264; An Hoa, 266, 267; Arizona Territory, 267; Bien Hoa, 248; Cam Lo, 255; Camp Carroll, 259; Chu Lai, 230, 251, 252, 259; Con Thien, 258; Dai Do, 262; Da Krong Valley, 264; Danang, 248–52, 259, 262–63, 266–68; Dong Ha, 253–55, 262, 268; Gio Linh, 258; Hiep Duc, 252; Hue, 250, 259–60, 261, 264; Khe Sanh, 253, 256, 260–61; Marble Mountain, 252; Phu Bai, 251, 259; Pleiku, 248; Post-Tet Offensive (1969), 265–67; Que Son, 252; Saigon, 250–51, 261, 268–69; Tet Offensive, 259–61; Van Tuong Peninsula, 251; Viet An, 252. *See also* Civilian Irregular Defense Group camp, Lang Vei, Vietnam; fire-support bases, Vietnam; provinces, Vietnam
Vietnamization, 267
Vita Levu, Fiji, 61
Viti, Tui, 61
Vizcaya (Spanish ship), 104
Vladivostok, Russia, 151
Vouza, Jacob C., 179

Waddell, James I., 76
Wainwright, Jonathon M. , 175
Wainwright, Robert D., 43
Walker, Walton H., 226, 241
Waller, Littleton W. T.: in Boxer Rebellion, 112, 113–14; fails to be made commandant, 123–24; in Haiti, 128; promoted to brigadier general, 131; in World War I, 148
Waller's Battalion, 113, 115
Wallingford, Samuel, 19
Walt, Lewis H.: Tulagi, 177; Cape Gloucester, 192; Walt's Ridge, New Britain, 192; Korea, 243; commands Marines in Vietnam, 250; disagrees with Westmoreland over importance of civic action, 251; promoted to lieutenant general, 253; disagrees with Westmoreland over NVA threat in I Corps, 253–55; becomes assistant commandant, 255; vies for commandant, 258
Warren, James, Jr., 22
Washington, George, 7, 11, 14, 17
Washington, Lawrence, 7
Washington, Lewis, 65
Watson, Samuel E., 54
Watson, Thomas E., 201
Waya, 63
Weber, Lester W., 266
Weise, William, 262
Welles, Gideon, 67, 79–80
Welsh, John, 21
Westmoreland, William C.: requests Marine

force to secure Danang airfield, 248; predicts ARVN near collapse, asks for more U.S. troops, 250; gives Walt operational control of I Corps, 250; scorns civic action programs of Marines, 251; asks for more troops because of NVA threat, 252–53; urges Cushman to reinforce Khe Sanh, 256; Tet Offensive 1968, 258–59; relieved by Creighton W. Abrams, 261; admits war cannot be won, 262
Wharton, Franklin, 31–32
Whiting, W. H. C., 85
Wilcox, Cadmus M., 58
Wildcat (aircraft), 173, 179
Willemstad, Curaçao, 27
Williams, Alexander S., 117, 160
Williams, Dion, 158–59
Williams, Ernest C., 131
Williams, John, 32–33
Williams, Lloyd W., 137–38
Willing, James, 18
Wilmington, North Carolina, 80, 82
Wilson, Louis H., Jr., 206, 272
Wilson, Thomas S., 77
Winder, William H., 37
Wise, Frederick M. "Fritz," 152, 154–55
Wolmi-do Island, Inchon, 228–29
Women Marine Corps Reserve, 199
Womens Armed Forces Integration Act, 224
Wonsan, Korea, 235, 237
Wood, John Taylor, 77–78
Woodbury, Levi, 44
Woods, Louis E., 184, 219
Worth, William J., 55
Wotje Atoll, 200
Wren, Solomon, 29
Wynkoop, Dyre S., 28

Yak (N. Korean aircraft), 243
Yanggu, Korea, 242
Yokosuka Special Naval Landing Force, 203
Yongdok, Korea, 241
Yongdungpo, Korea, 233
Yontan, Okinawa, 217
Ypiranga (German steamer), 125
Yudam-ni, Korea, 236

Zeilin, Jacob: with Perry in Japan, 59; at Bull Run, 66–67; becomes commandant, 80; keeps rank of brigadier general, 87; and reformist effort, 94; adoption of Marine Corps' motto, 96–97
Zelaya, José Santos, 119
Zeledón, Benjamin, 121
Zembsch, Lawrence, 157
Zero (aircraft), 172

About the Authors

Merrill L. Bartlett retired from the Corps in 1983, after serving as a Marine for twenty-four years. While teaching history at the U.S. Naval Academy, he earned the William P. Clements Award as the outstanding military instructor (1979). He has written, edited, and collaborated on seven volumes of naval history. Two of his essays, "Ouster of a Commandant" (U.S. Naval Institute *Proceedings,* 1980) and "Old Gimlet Eye" (U.S. Naval Institute *Proceedings,* 1987), won the Robert D. Heinl, Jr. Award. Col. Bartlett lives on Vashon Island, near Seattle, Washington.

Jack Sweetman taught history at the U.S. Naval Academy for twenty years. A graduate of Stetson University he served as a company commander in the U.S. Army and was later a Ford Fellow at Emory University, where he earned a Ph.D. in 1973. He is the author, editor, or translator of numerous Naval Institute Press books, and he is currently the series editor for the press's Classics of Naval Literature collection. A recipient of the U.S. Navy League's Alfred Thayer Mahan Award for Literary Achievement, the *Naval History* Author of the Year Award, and the North American Society for Oceanic History's John Lyman Book Award, Dr. Sweetman was recently elected a Fellow of the Royal Historical Society. He lives in Orlando, Florida.